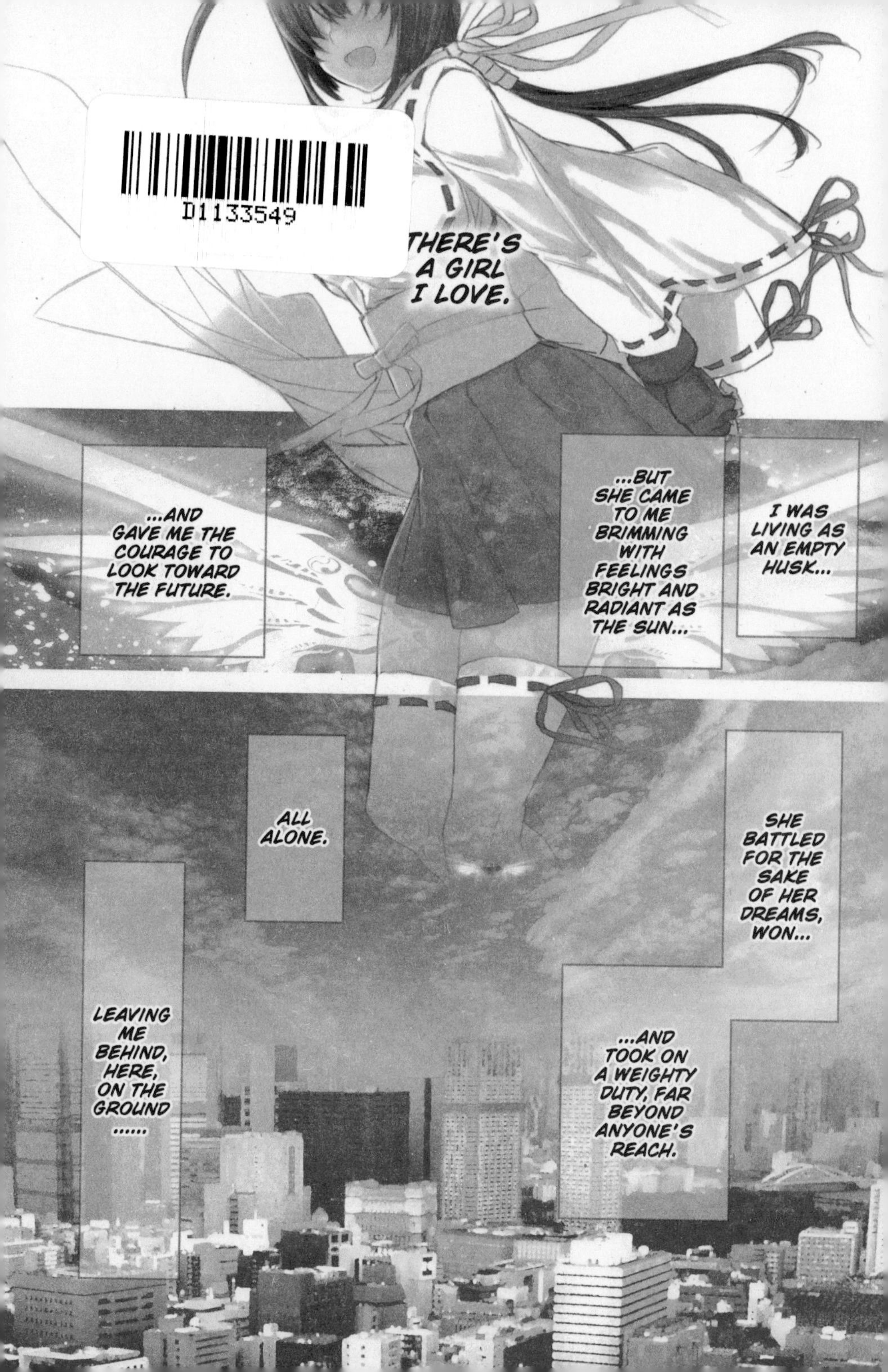
THERE'S A GIRL I LOVE.
I WAS LIVING AS AN EMPTY HUSK...
...BUT SHE CAME TO ME BRIMMING WITH FEELINGS BRIGHT AND RADIANT AS THE SUN...
...AND GAVE ME THE COURAGE TO LOOK TOWARD THE FUTURE.
SHE BATTLED FOR THE SAKE OF HER DREAMS, WON...
...AND TOOK ON A WEIGHTY DUTY, FAR BEYOND ANYONE'S REACH.
ALL ALONE.
LEAVING ME BEHIND, HERE, ON THE GROUND ......

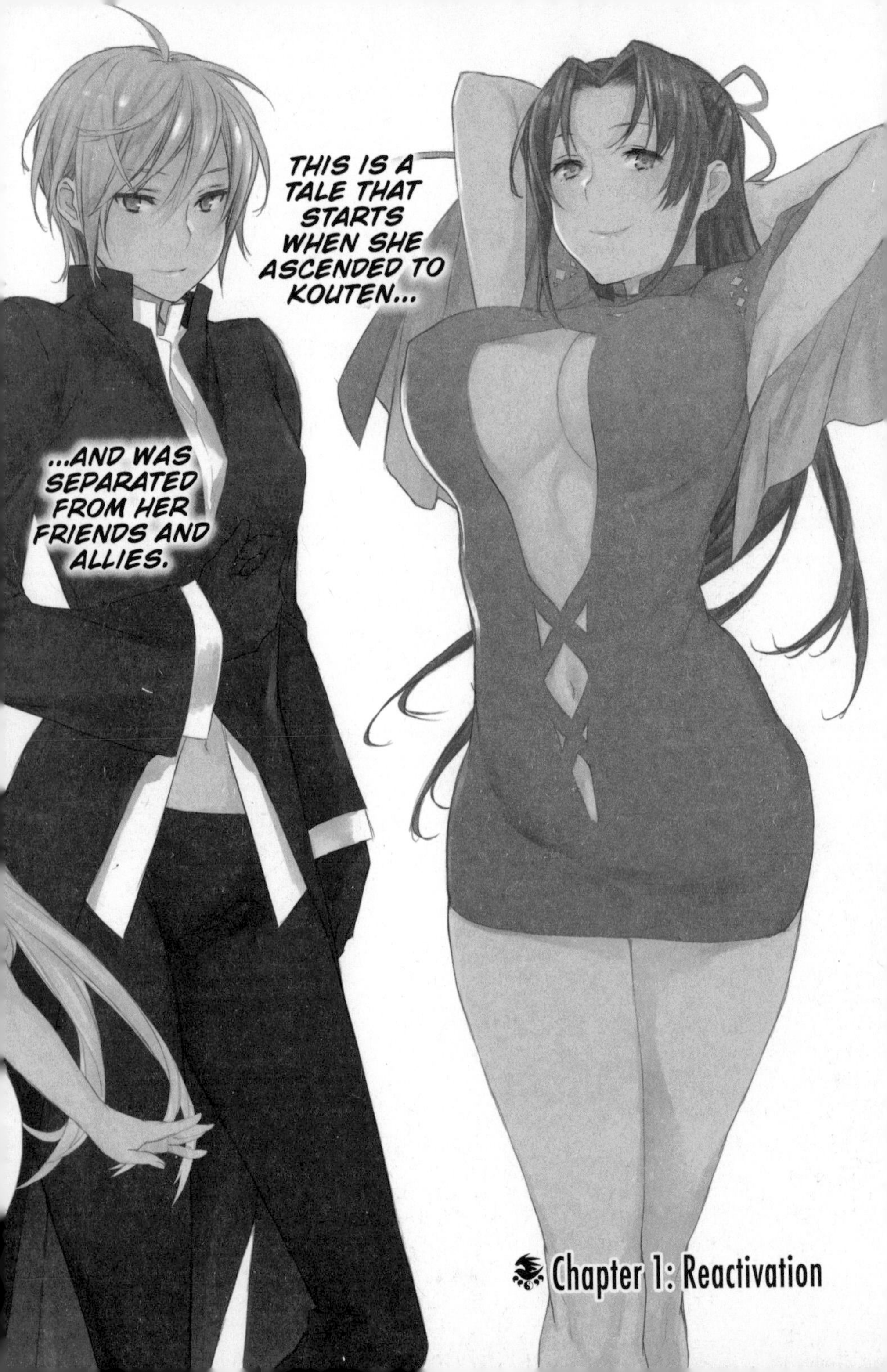
THIS IS A TALE THAT STARTS WHEN SHE ASCENDED TO KOUTEN...
...AND WAS SEPARATED FROM HER FRIENDS AND ALLIES.

Chapter 1: Reactivation

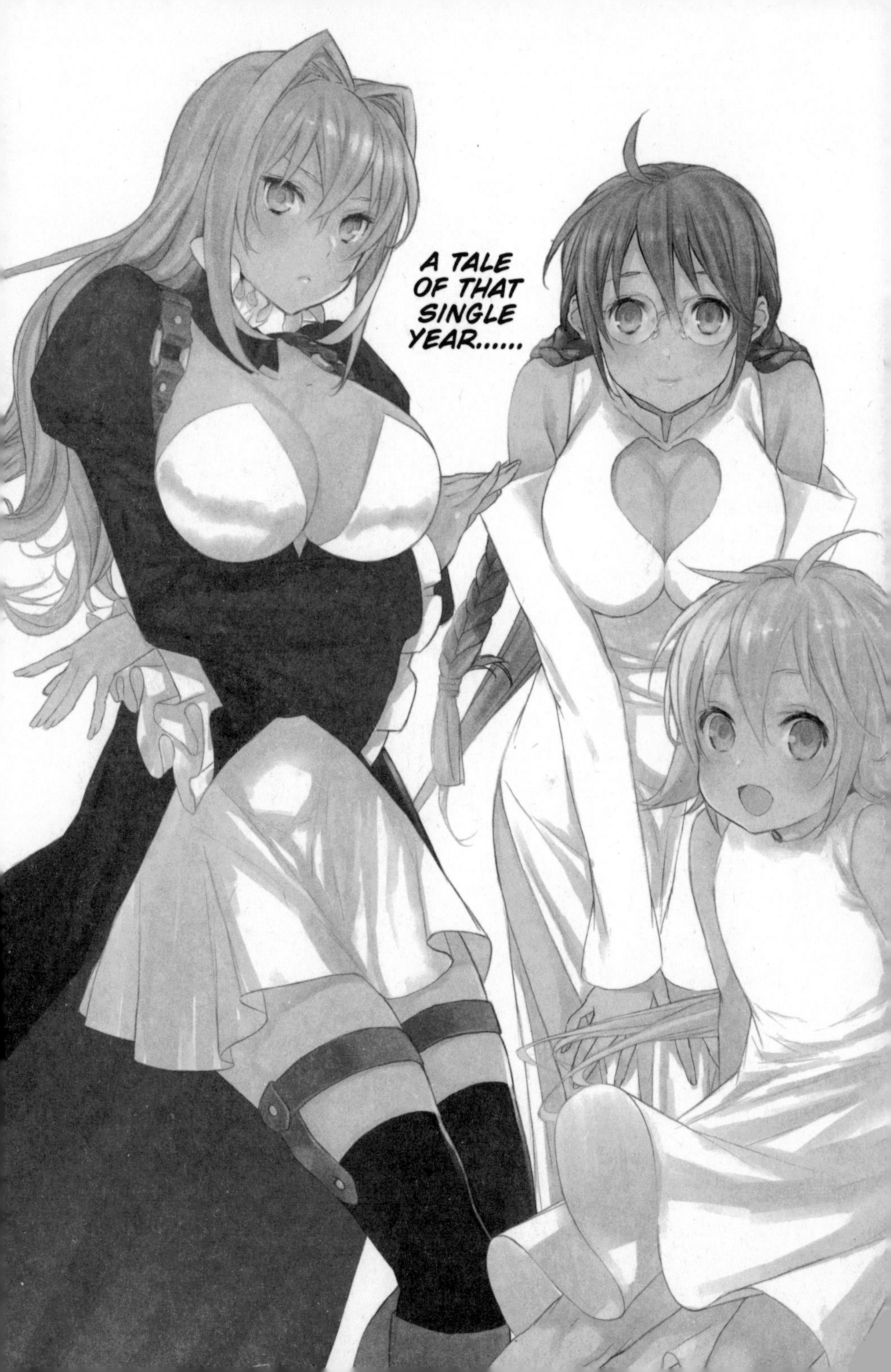
A TALE OF THAT SINGLE YEAR......

ROAR
AT FIRST, THE PLAN WAS TO HAVE THE BEAR POWER UP LOOK LIKE THIS, BUT IT'S PRETTY SIMILAR TO THE UNDER-THE-COVER CHARACTERS, SO I SCRAPPED THAT IDEA.
BEAR GOD
BULGE
BULGE
KOUTEN

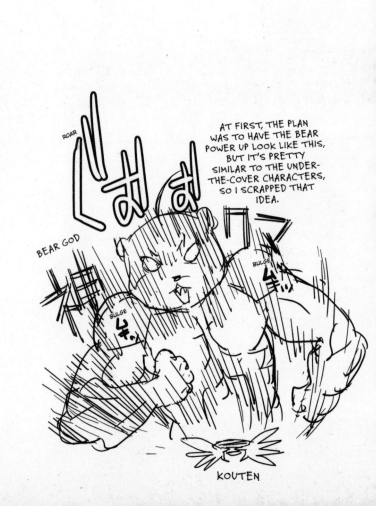

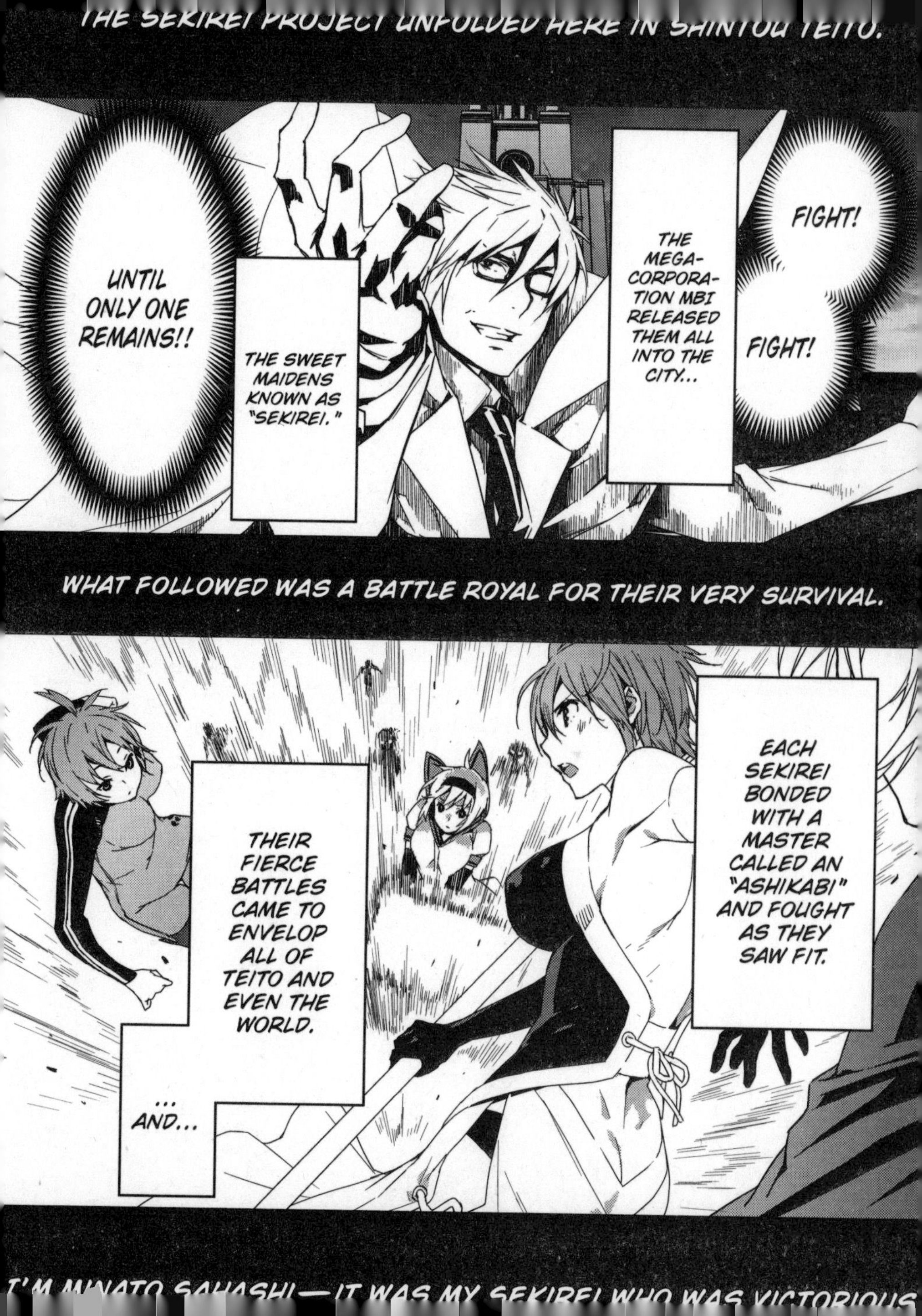
THE SEKIREI PROJECT UNFOLDED HERE IN SHINTOU TEITO.
FIGHT!
FIGHT!
THE MEGA-CORPORATION MBI RELEASED THEM ALL INTO THE CITY...
THE SWEET MAIDENS KNOWN AS "SEKIREI."
UNTIL ONLY ONE REMAINS!!
WHAT FOLLOWED WAS A BATTLE ROYAL FOR THEIR VERY SURVIVAL.
EACH SEKIREI BONDED WITH A MASTER CALLED AN "ASHIKABI" AND FOUGHT AS THEY SAW FIT.
THEIR FIERCE BATTLES CAME TO ENVELOP ALL OF TEITO AND EVEN THE WORLD.
...AND...
I'M MINATO SAHASHI—IT WAS MY SEKIREI WHO WAS VICTORIOUS

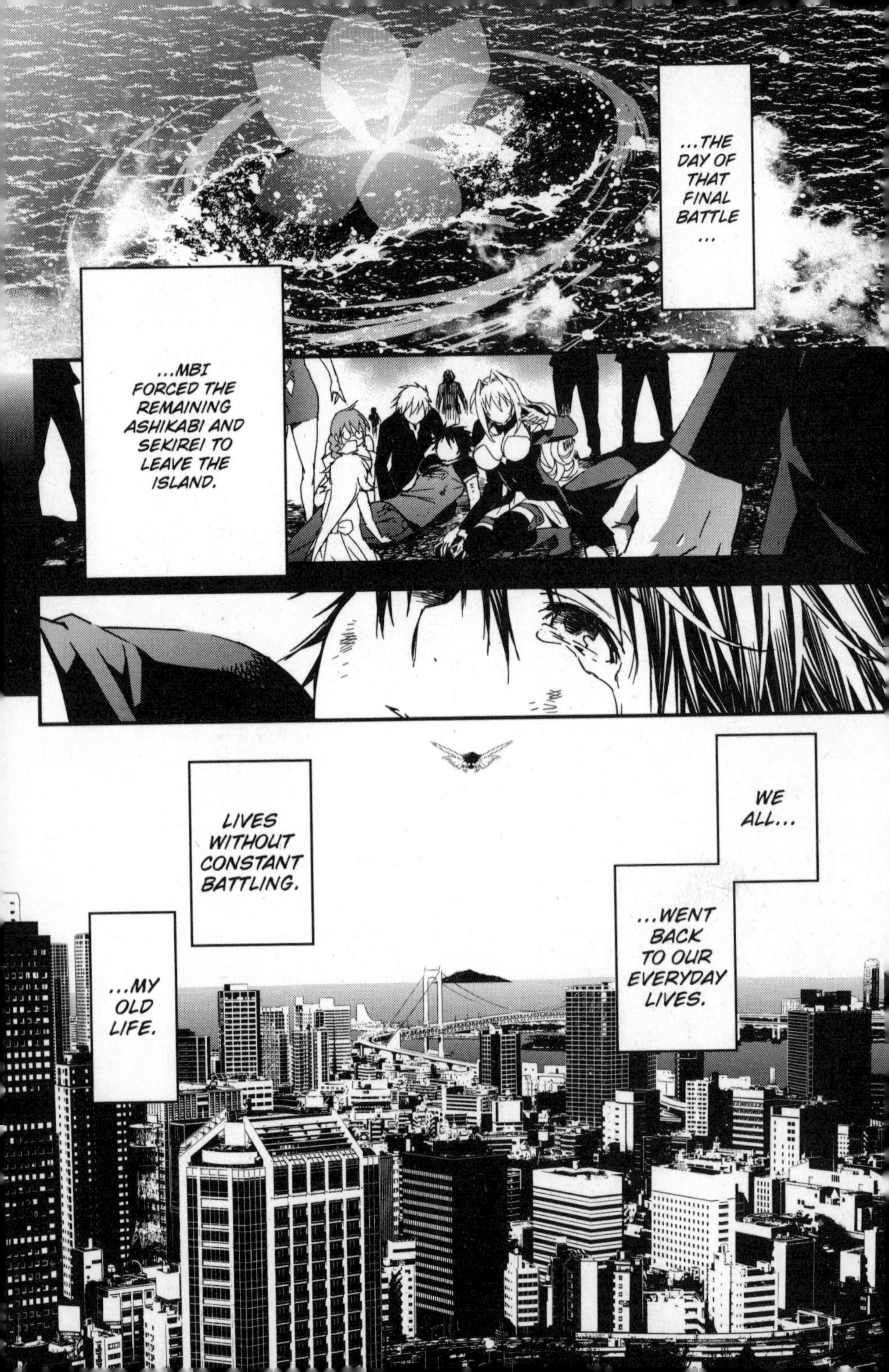
...THE DAY OF THAT FINAL BATTLE...
...MBI FORCED THE REMAINING ASHIKABI AND SEKIREI TO LEAVE THE ISLAND.
WE ALL...
...WENT BACK TO OUR EVERYDAY LIVES.
LIVES WITHOUT CONSTANT BATTLING.
...MY OLD LIFE.

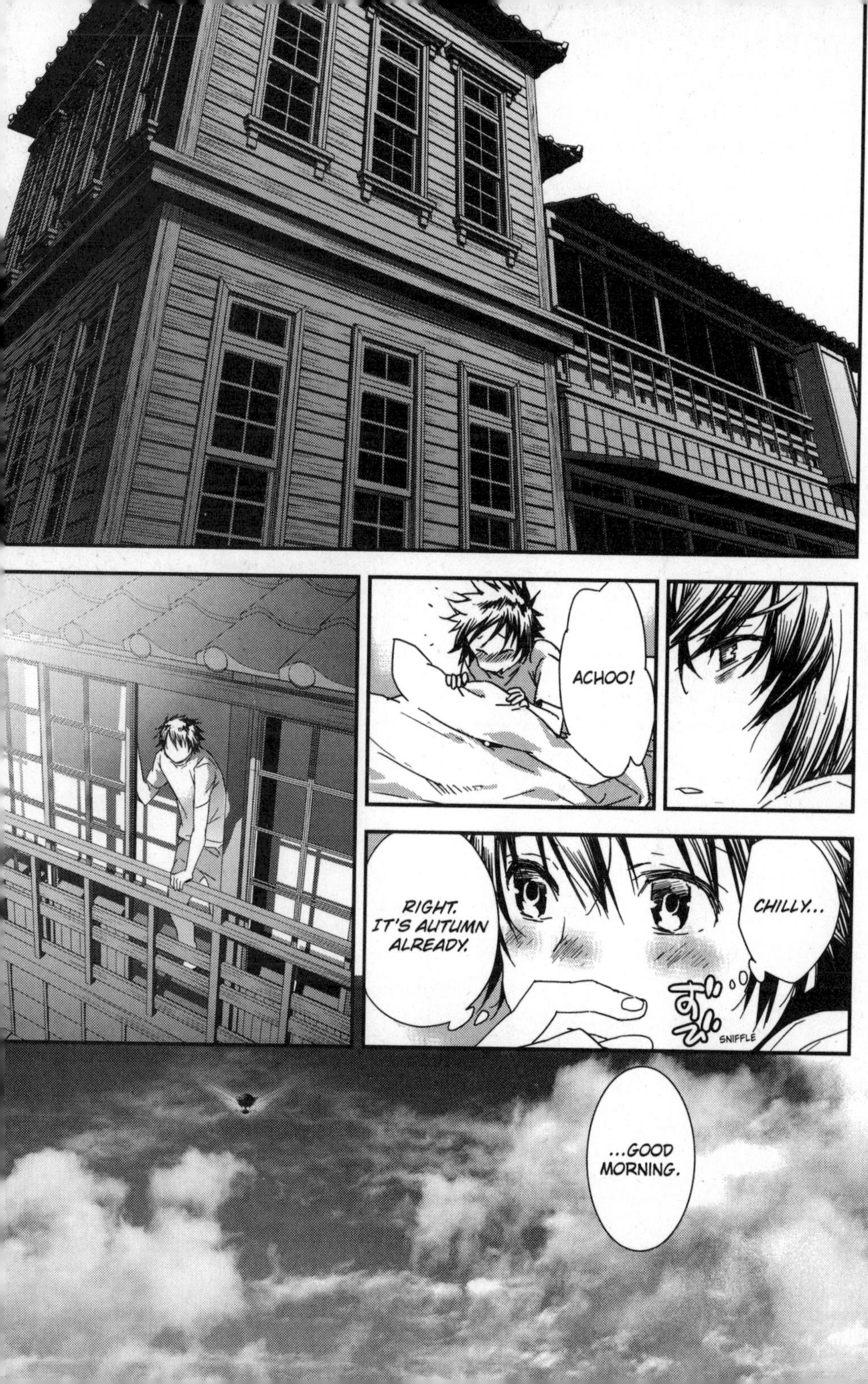
ACHOO!
CHILLY...
ずび
SNIFFLE
RIGHT. IT'S AUTUMN ALREADY.
...GOOD MORNING.

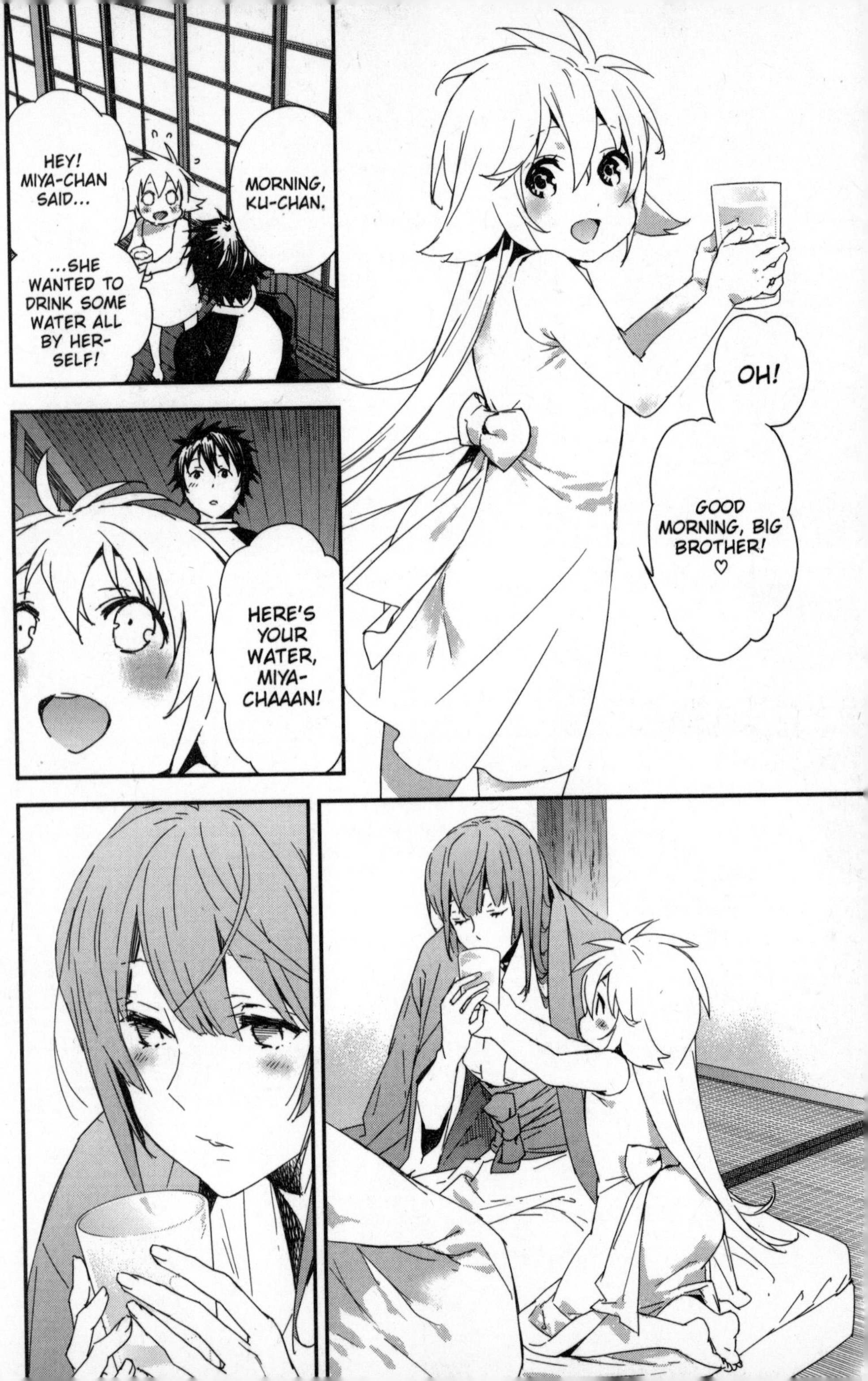
OH!
GOOD MORNING, BIG BROTHER! ♡
MORNING, KU-CHAN.
HEY! MIYA-CHAN SAID...
...SHE WANTED TO DRINK SOME WATER ALL BY HER-SELF!
HERE'S YOUR WATER, MIYA-CHAAAN!

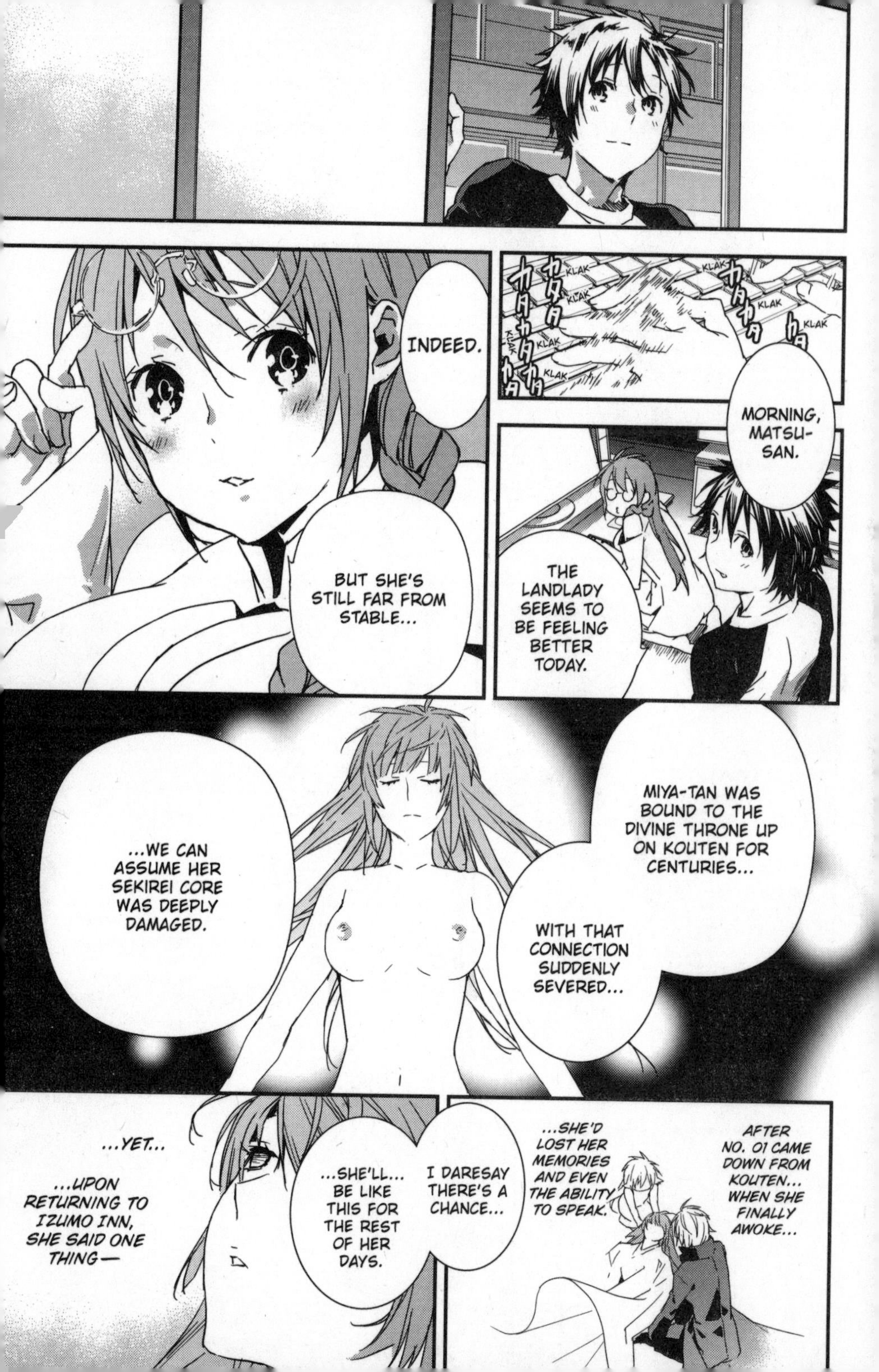
KLAK KLAK KLAK KLAK KLAK KLAK KLAK KLAK
MORNING, MATSU-SAN.
THE LANDLADY SEEMS TO BE FEELING BETTER TODAY.
INDEED.
BUT SHE'S STILL FAR FROM STABLE...
MIYA-TAN WAS BOUND TO THE DIVINE THRONE UP ON KOUTEN FOR CENTURIES...
WITH THAT CONNECTION SUDDENLY SEVERED...
...WE CAN ASSUME HER SEKIREI CORE WAS DEEPLY DAMAGED.
AFTER NO. 01 CAME DOWN FROM KOUTEN... WHEN SHE FINALLY AWOKE...
...SHE'D LOST HER MEMORIES AND EVEN THE ABILITY TO SPEAK.
I DARESAY THERE'S A CHANCE...
...SHE'LL... BE LIKE THIS FOR THE REST OF HER DAYS.
...YET...
...UPON RETURNING TO IZUMO INN, SHE SAID ONE THING—

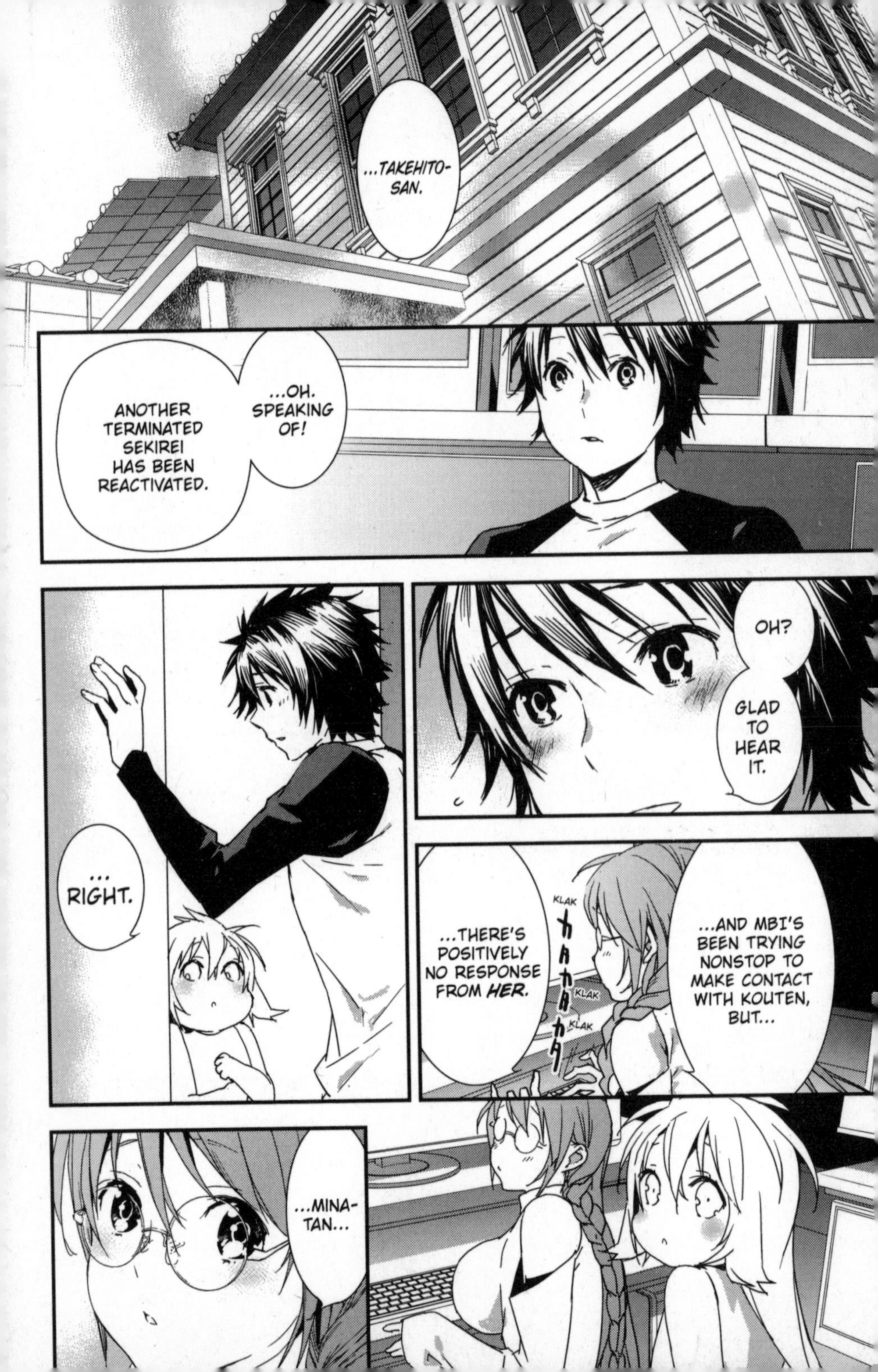
...TAKEHITO-SAN.
...OH. SPEAKING OF!
ANOTHER TERMINATED SEKIREI HAS BEEN REACTIVATED.
OH?
GLAD TO HEAR IT.
...AND MBI'S BEEN TRYING NONSTOP TO MAKE CONTACT WITH KOUTEN, BUT...
KLAK
KLAK
KLAK
...THERE'S POSITIVELY NO RESPONSE FROM *HER*.
... RIGHT.
...MINA-TAN...

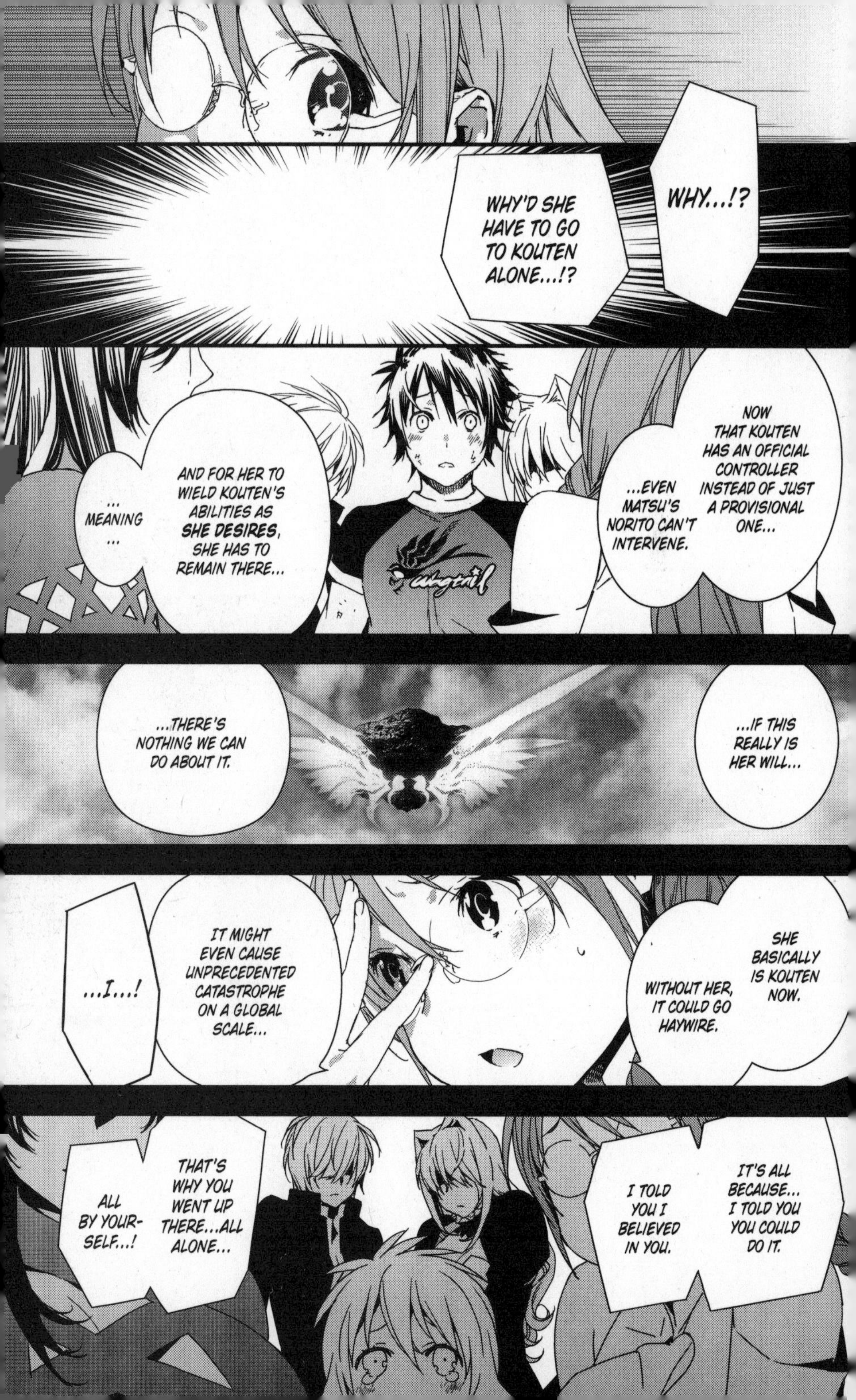
WHY...!?
WHY'D SHE HAVE TO GO TO KOUTEN ALONE...!?
NOW THAT KOUTEN HAS AN OFFICIAL CONTROLLER INSTEAD OF JUST A PROVISIONAL ONE...
...EVEN MATSU'S NORITO CAN'T INTERVENE.
AND FOR HER TO WIELD KOUTEN'S ABILITIES AS **SHE DESIRES**, SHE HAS TO REMAIN THERE...
... MEANING ...
...IF THIS REALLY IS HER WILL...
...THERE'S NOTHING WE CAN DO ABOUT IT.
SHE BASICALLY IS KOUTEN NOW.
WITHOUT HER, IT COULD GO HAYWIRE.
IT MIGHT EVEN CAUSE UNPRECEDENTED CATASTROPHE ON A GLOBAL SCALE...
...I...!
IT'S ALL BECAUSE... I TOLD YOU YOU COULD DO IT.
I TOLD YOU I BELIEVED IN YOU.
THAT'S WHY YOU WENT UP THERE...ALL ALONE...
ALL BY YOUR-SELF...!

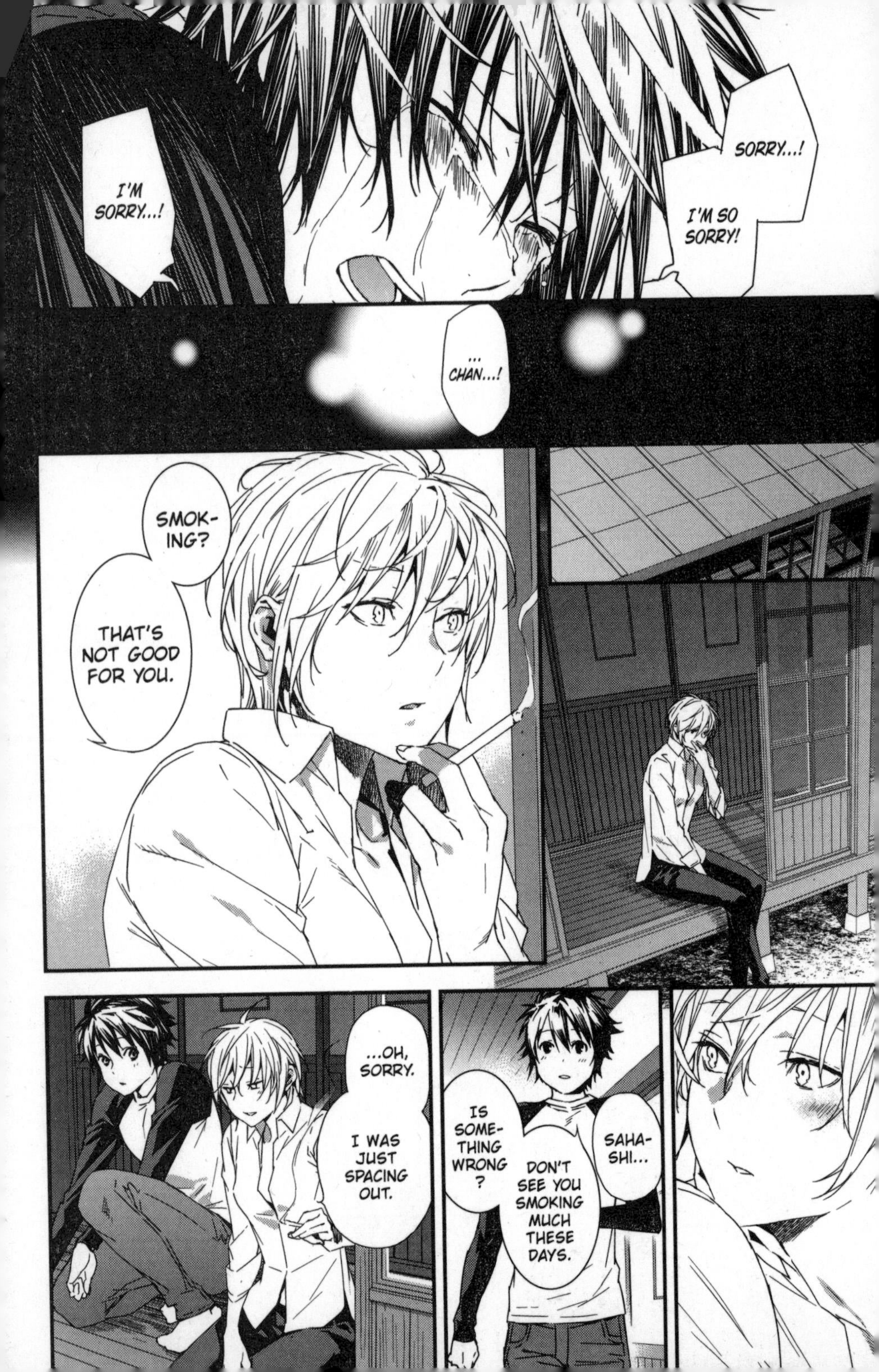
SORRY...!
I'M SO SORRY!
I'M SORRY...!
... CHAN...!
SMOK-ING?
THAT'S NOT GOOD FOR YOU.
SAHA-SHI...
DON'T SEE YOU SMOKING MUCH THESE DAYS.
IS SOME-THING WRONG?
...OH, SORRY.
I WAS JUST SPACING OUT.

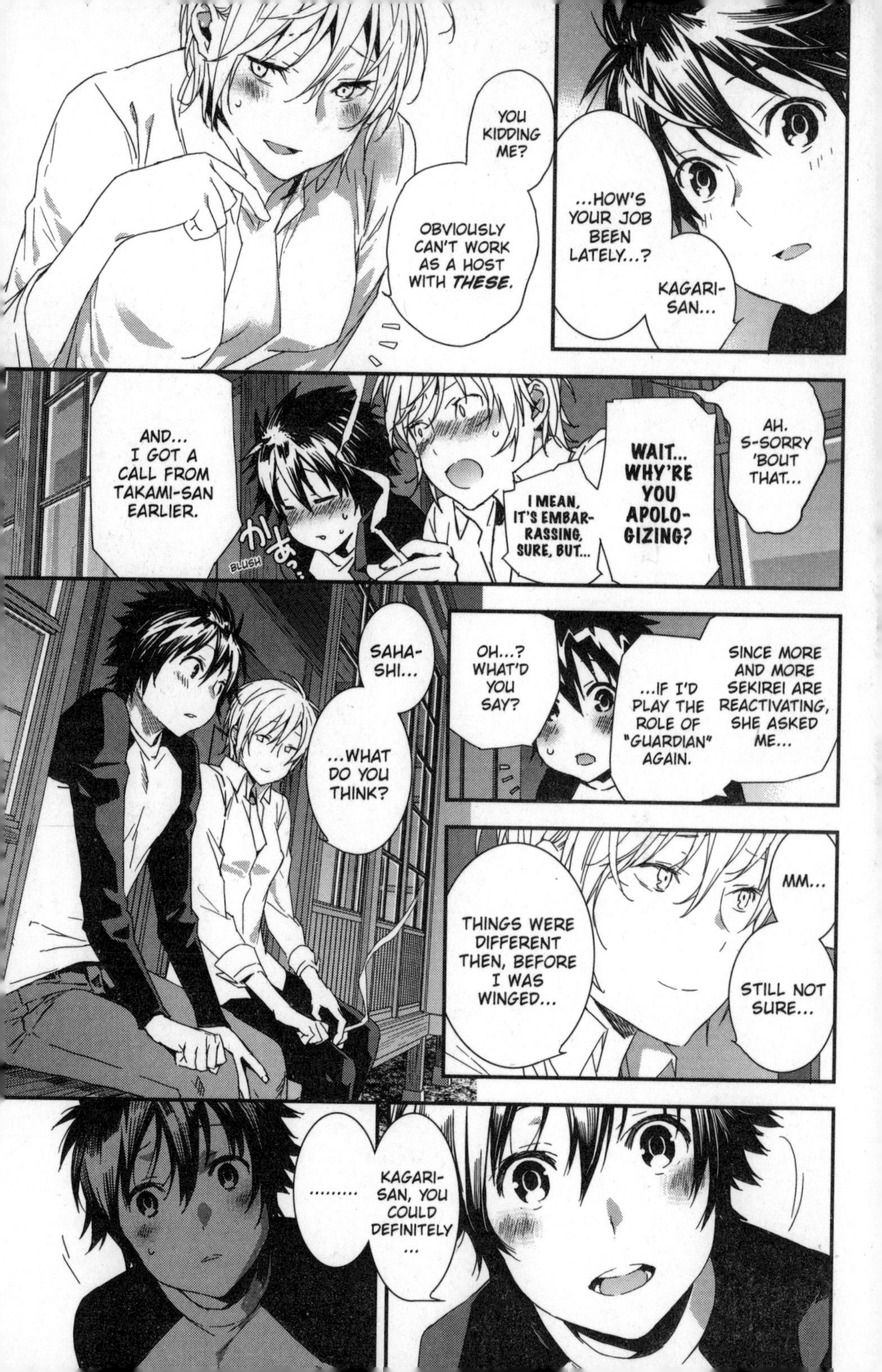
KAGARI-SAN...
...HOW'S YOUR JOB BEEN LATELY...?
YOU KIDDING ME?
OBVIOUSLY CAN'T WORK AS A HOST WITH *THESE.*
AH. S-SORRY 'BOUT THAT...
WAIT... WHY'RE YOU APOLOGIZING?
I MEAN, IT'S EMBARRASSING, SURE, BUT...
AND... I GOT A CALL FROM TAKAMI-SAN EARLIER.
BLUSH
SINCE MORE AND MORE SEKIREI ARE REACTIVATING, SHE ASKED ME...
...IF I'D PLAY THE ROLE OF "GUARDIAN" AGAIN.
OH...? WHAT'D YOU SAY?
MM...
STILL NOT SURE...
THINGS WERE DIFFERENT THEN, BEFORE I WAS WINGED...
SAHA-SHI...
...WHAT DO YOU THINK?
KAGARI-SAN, YOU COULD DEFINITELY ...
....

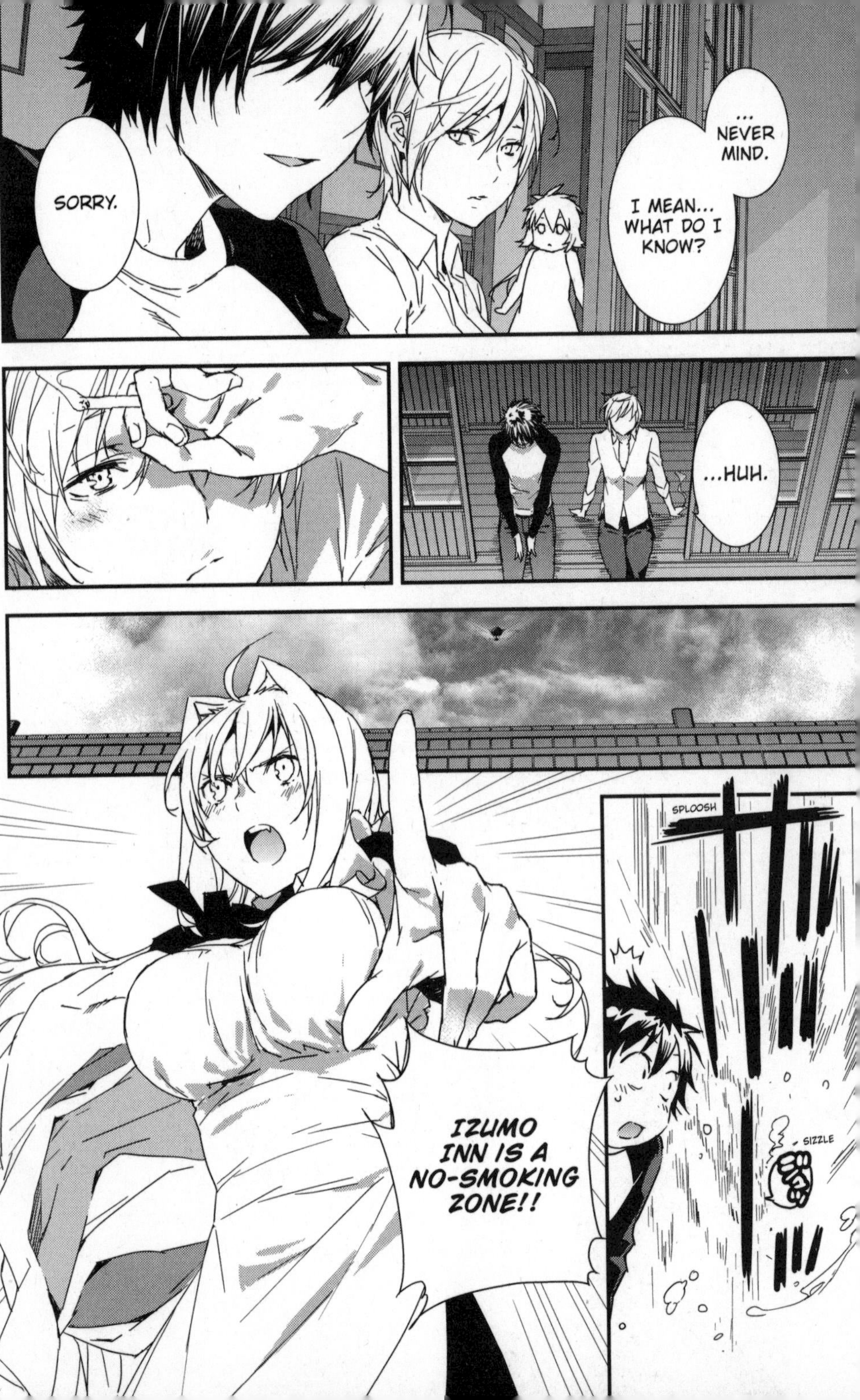
...NEVER MIND.
I MEAN... WHAT DO I KNOW?
SORRY.
...HUH.
SPLOOSH
SIZZLE
IZUMO INN IS A NO-SMOKING ZONE!!

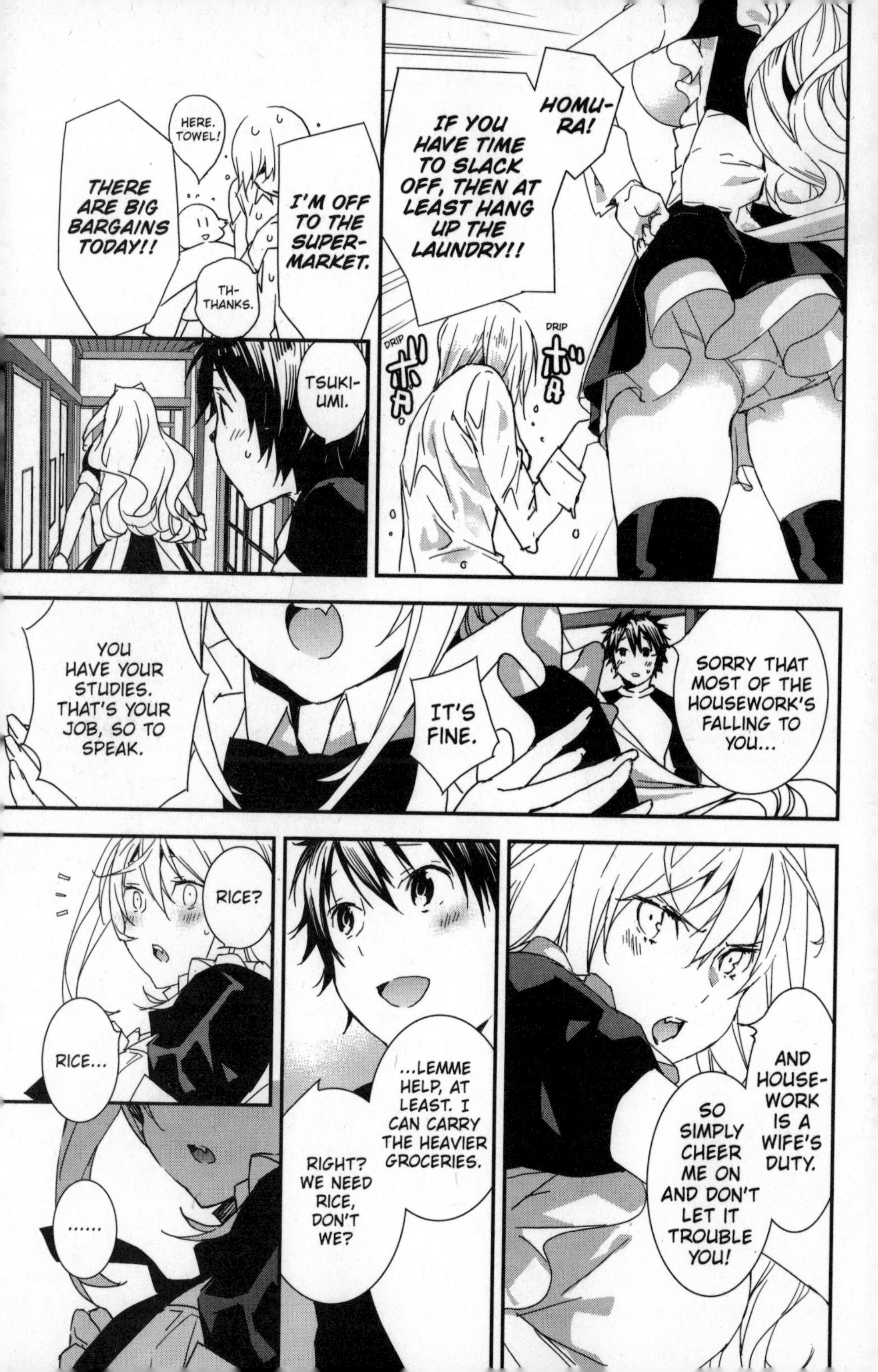
HOMU-RA!
IF YOU HAVE TIME TO SLACK OFF, THEN AT LEAST HANG UP THE LAUNDRY!!
DRIP
DRIP
I'M OFF TO THE SUPER-MARKET.
HERE. TOWEL!
THERE ARE BIG BARGAINS TODAY!!
TH-THANKS.
TSUKI-UMI.
SORRY THAT MOST OF THE HOUSEWORK'S FALLING TO YOU...
IT'S FINE.
YOU HAVE YOUR STUDIES. THAT'S YOUR JOB, SO TO SPEAK.
AND HOUSE-WORK IS A WIFE'S DUTY.
SO SIMPLY CHEER ME ON AND DON'T LET IT TROUBLE YOU!
...LEMME HELP, AT LEAST. I CAN CARRY THE HEAVIER GROCERIES.
RIGHT? WE NEED RICE, DON'T WE?
RICE?
RICE...
......

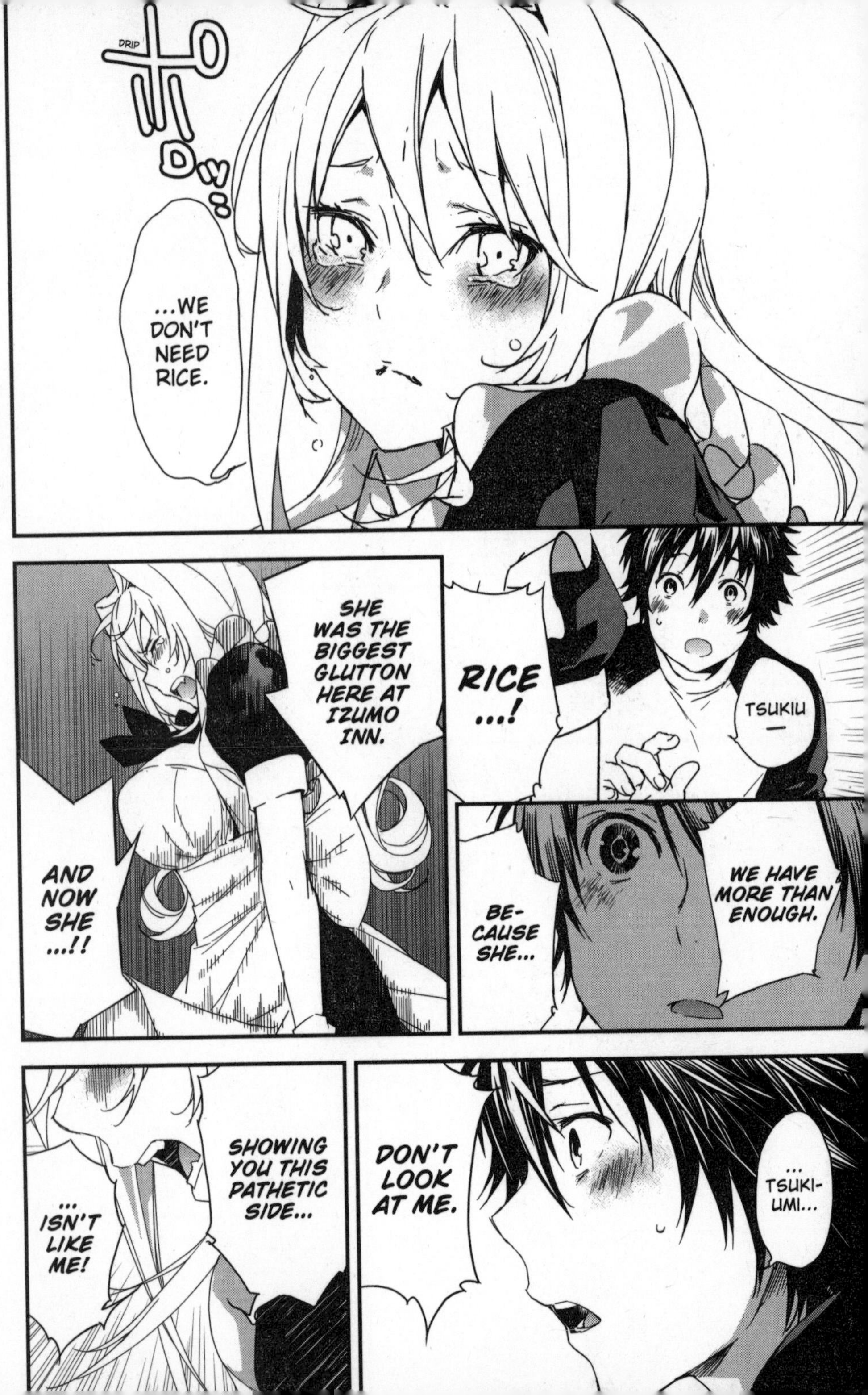
DRIP
...WE DON'T NEED RICE.
TSUKIU—
RICE ...!
WE HAVE MORE THAN ENOUGH.
BE-CAUSE SHE...
SHE WAS THE BIGGEST GLUTTON HERE AT IZUMO INN.
AND NOW SHE ...!!
... TSUKI-UMI...
DON'T LOOK AT ME.
SHOWING YOU THIS PATHETIC SIDE...
... ISN'T LIKE ME!

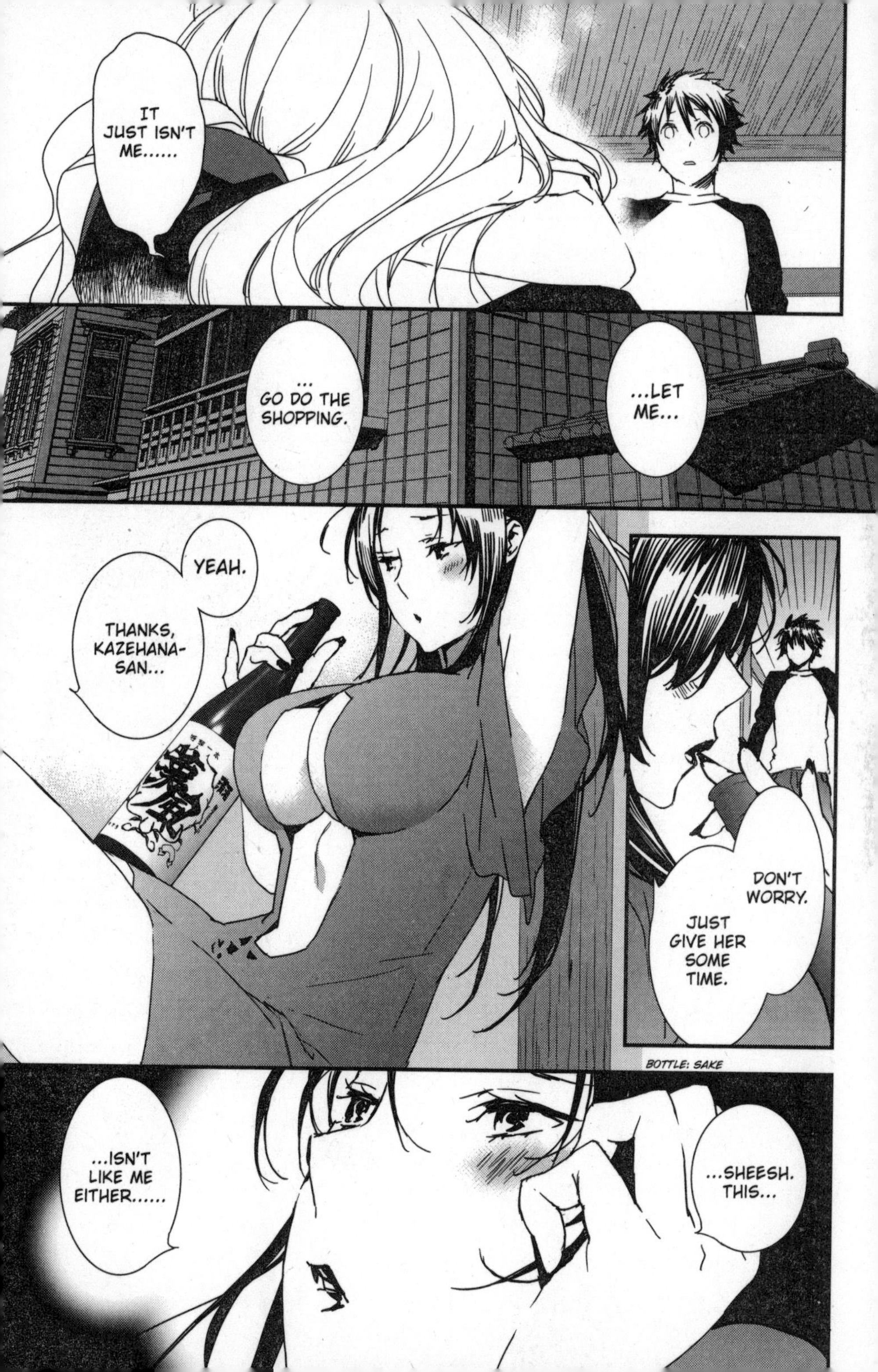
IT JUST ISN'T ME......
...LET ME...
... GO DO THE SHOPPING.
DON'T WORRY.
JUST GIVE HER SOME TIME.
YEAH.
THANKS, KAZEHANA-SAN...
BOTTLE: SAKE
...SHEESH. THIS...
...ISN'T LIKE ME EITHER......

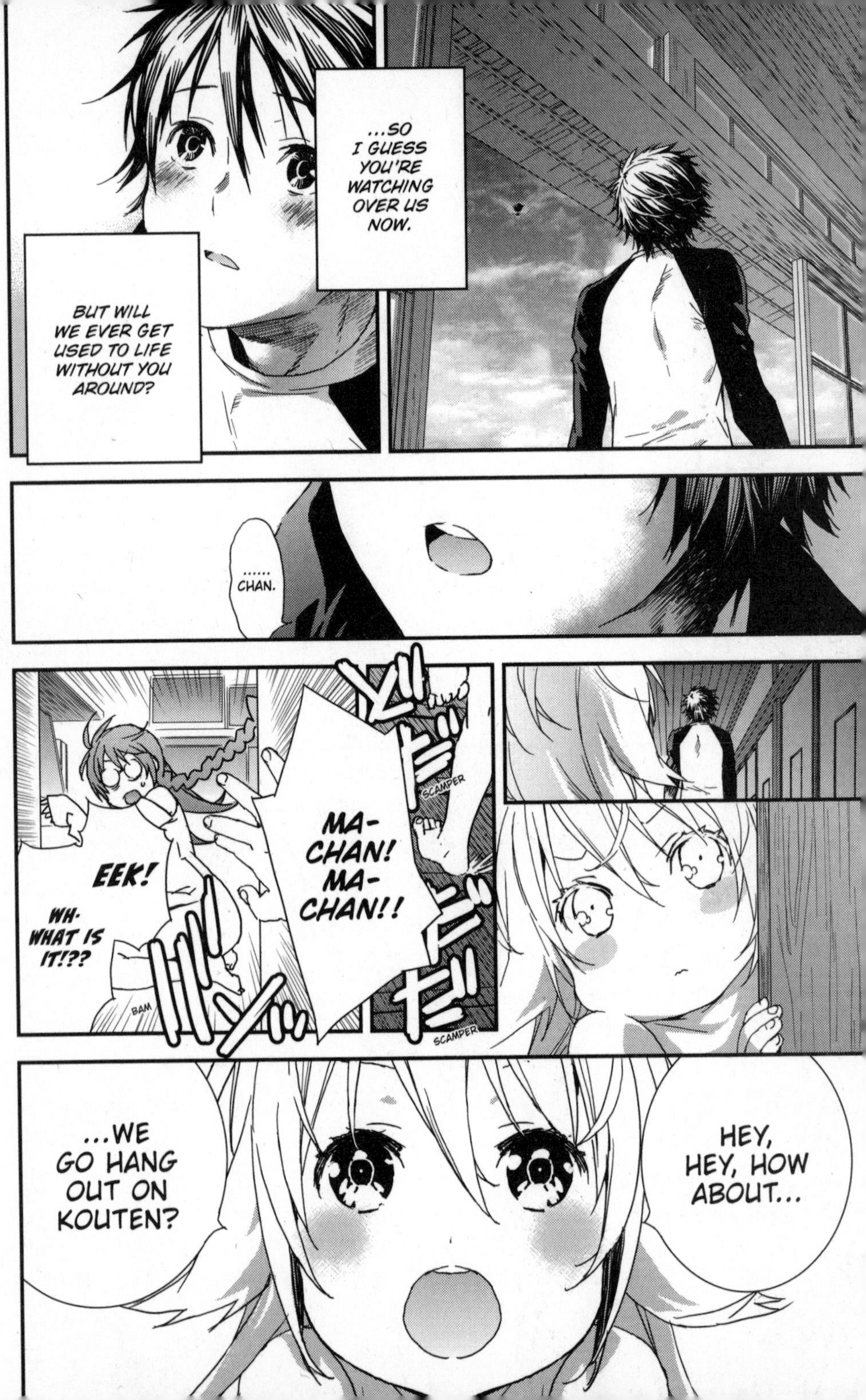
...SO I GUESS YOU'RE WATCHING OVER US NOW.
BUT WILL WE EVER GET USED TO LIFE WITHOUT YOU AROUND?
......CHAN.
SCAMPER
MA-CHAN! MA-CHAN!!
SCAMPER
EEK!
WH-WHAT IS IT!??
BAM
HEY, HEY, HOW ABOUT...
...WE GO HANG OUT ON KOUTEN?

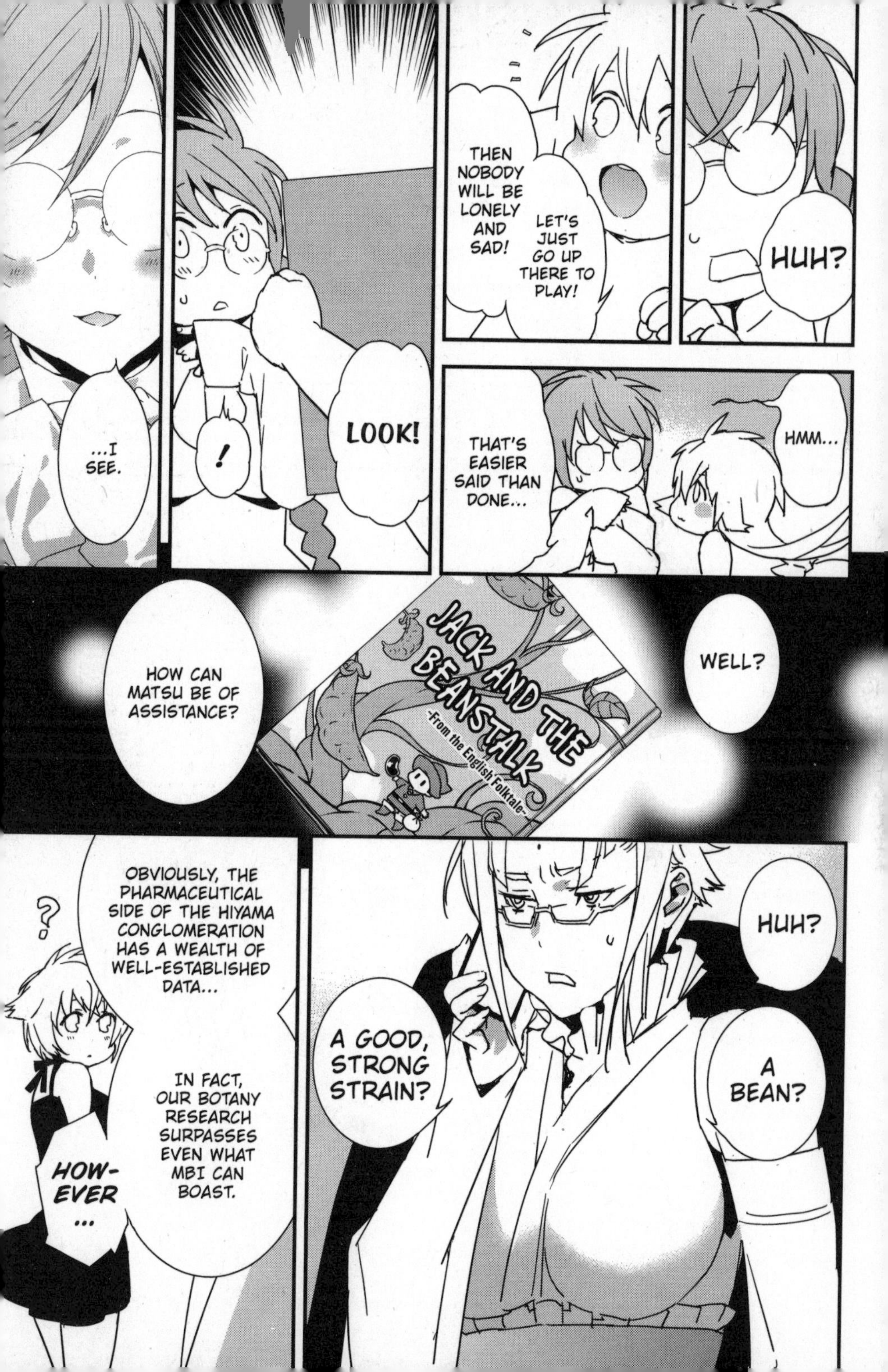
HUH?
LET'S JUST GO UP THERE TO PLAY!
THEN NOBODY WILL BE LONELY AND SAD!
HMM...
THAT'S EASIER SAID THAN DONE...
LOOK!
!
...I SEE.
WELL?
JACK AND THE BEANSTALK
-From the English Folktale-
HOW CAN MATSU BE OF ASSISTANCE?
HUH?
A BEAN?
A GOOD, STRONG STRAIN?
OBVIOUSLY, THE PHARMACEUTICAL SIDE OF THE HIYAMA CONGLOMERATION HAS A WEALTH OF WELL-ESTABLISHED DATA...
IN FACT, OUR BOTANY RESEARCH SURPASSES EVEN WHAT MBI CAN BOAST.
HOW-EVER...
?

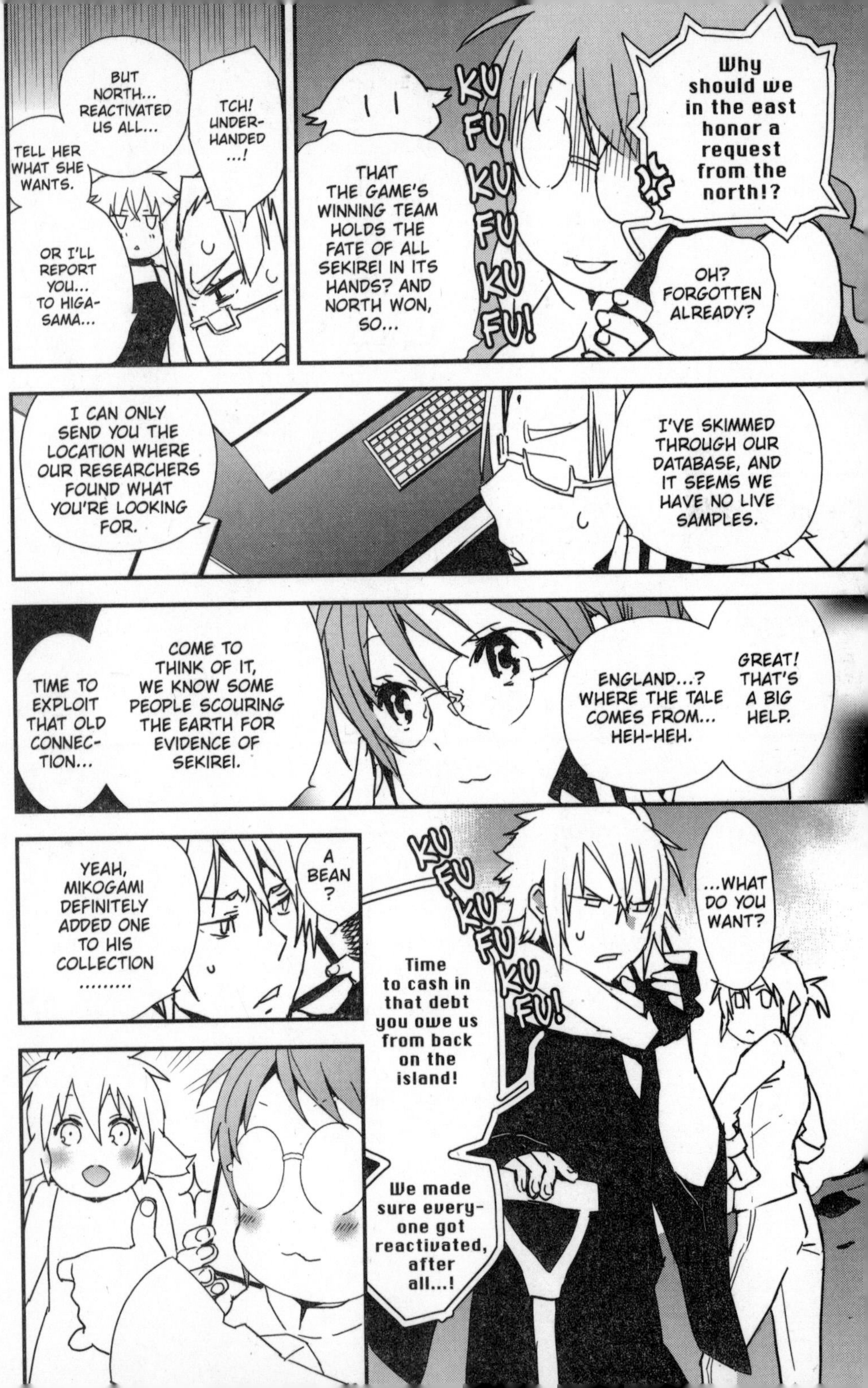
Why should we in the east honor a request from the north!?
KU FU KU FU KU FU!
OH? FORGOTTEN ALREADY?
THAT THE GAME'S WINNING TEAM HOLDS THE FATE OF ALL SEKIREI IN ITS HANDS? AND NORTH WON, SO...
TCH! UNDER-HANDED ...!
BUT NORTH... REACTIVATED US ALL...
TELL HER WHAT SHE WANTS.
OR I'LL REPORT YOU... TO HIGA-SAMA...
I'VE SKIMMED THROUGH OUR DATABASE, AND IT SEEMS WE HAVE NO LIVE SAMPLES.
I CAN ONLY SEND YOU THE LOCATION WHERE OUR RESEARCHERS FOUND WHAT YOU'RE LOOKING FOR.
GREAT! THAT'S A BIG HELP.
ENGLAND...? WHERE THE TALE COMES FROM... HEH-HEH.
COME TO THINK OF IT, WE KNOW SOME PEOPLE SCOURING THE EARTH FOR EVIDENCE OF SEKIREI.
TIME TO EXPLOIT THAT OLD CONNEC-TION...
...WHAT DO YOU WANT?
KU FU KU FU KU FU!
Time to cash in that debt you owe us from back on the island!
We made sure every-one got reactivated, after all...!
A BEAN?
YEAH, MIKOGAMI DEFINITELY ADDED ONE TO HIS COLLECTION ....

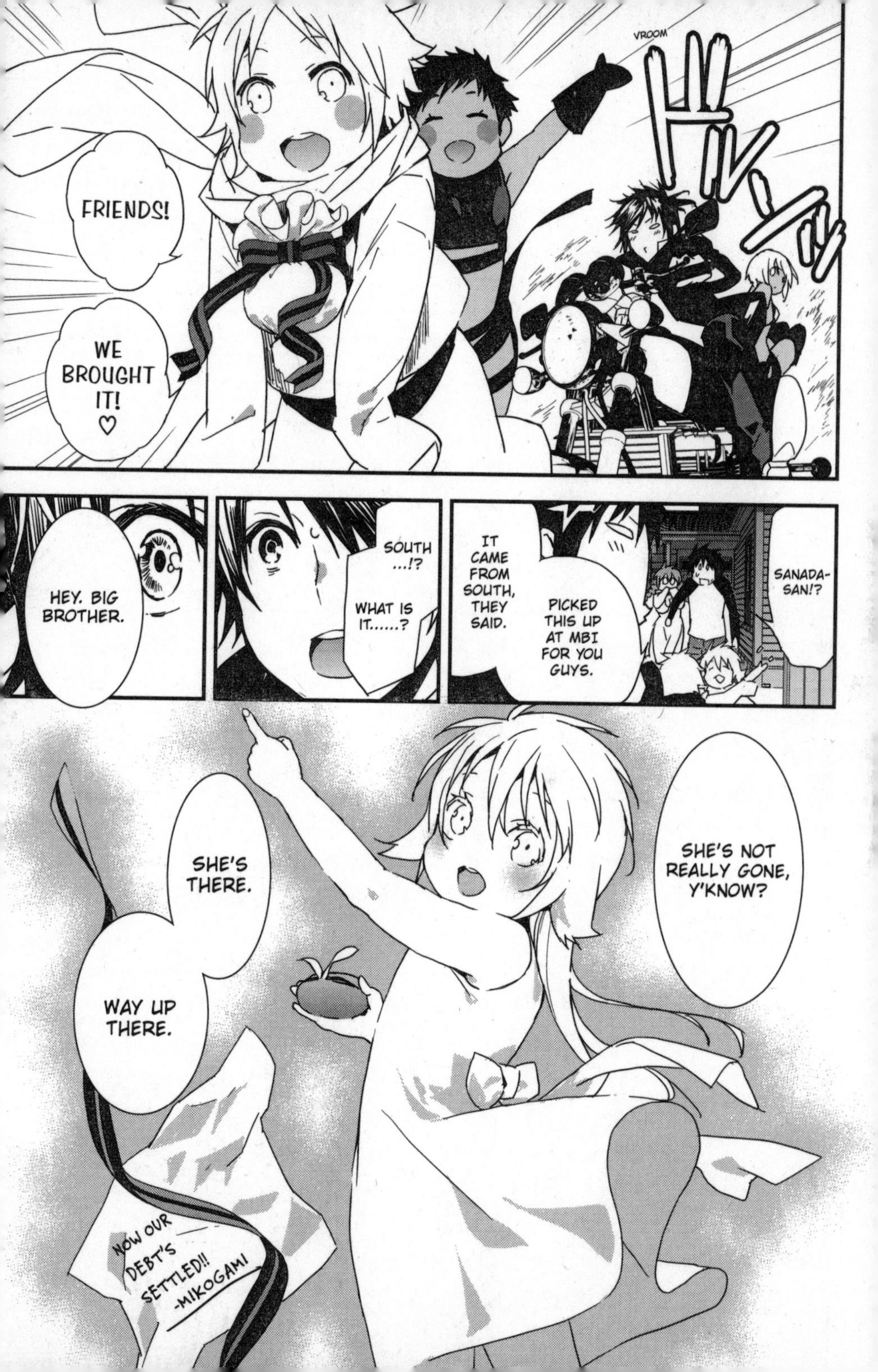
VROOM
FRIENDS!
WE BROUGHT IT! ♡
SANADA-SAN!?
PICKED THIS UP AT MBI FOR YOU GUYS.
IT CAME FROM SOUTH, THEY SAID.
SOUTH ...!?
WHAT IS IT......?
HEY. BIG BROTHER.
SHE'S NOT REALLY GONE, Y'KNOW?
SHE'S THERE.
WAY UP THERE.
NOW OUR DEBT'S SETTLED!! -MIKOGAMI

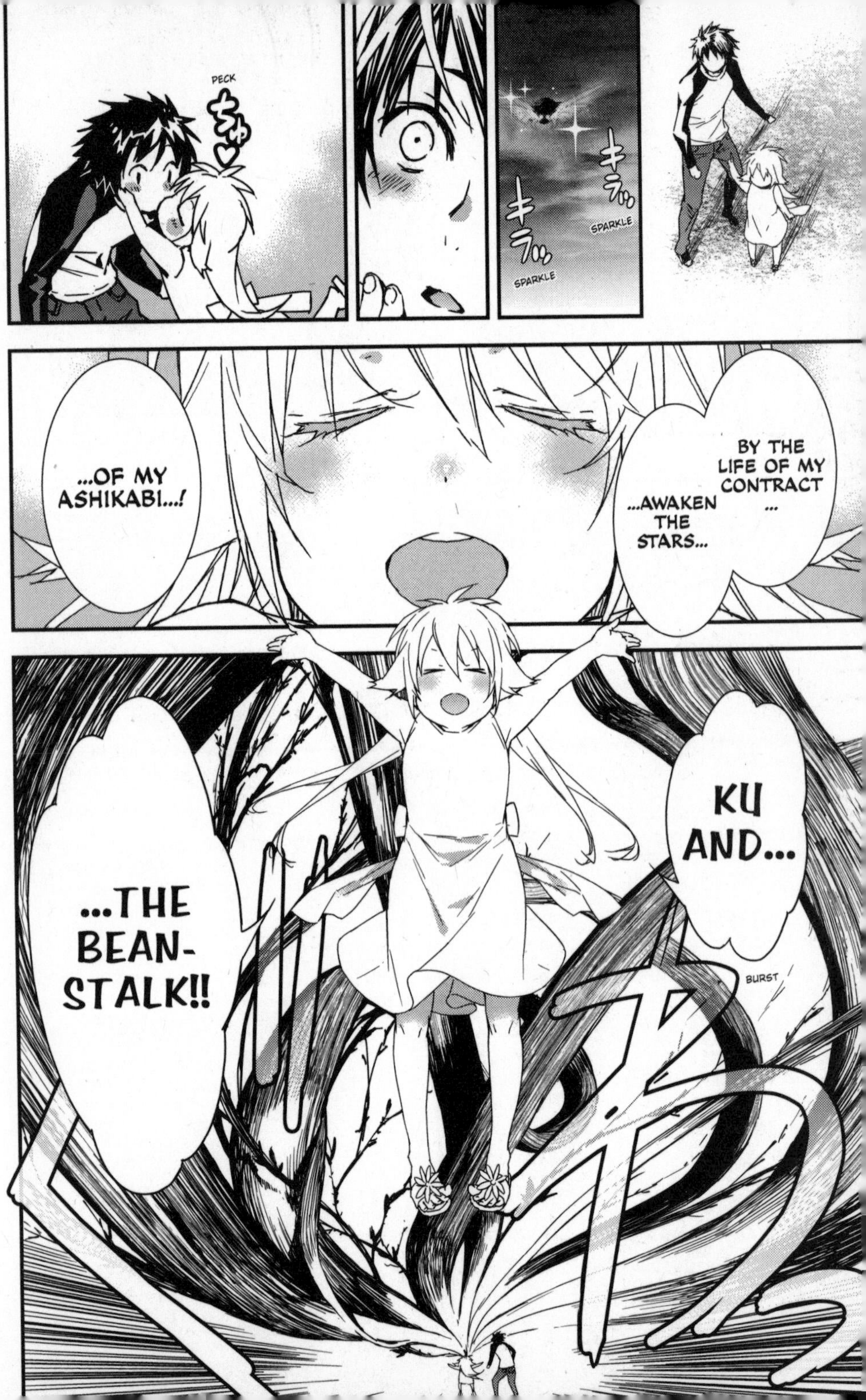
キラッ
SPARKLE
キラッ
SPARKLE
PECK
ちゅ♡
BY THE LIFE OF MY CONTRACT ...
...AWAKEN THE STARS...
...OF MY ASHIKABI...!
KU AND...
BURST
...THE BEAN-STALK!!

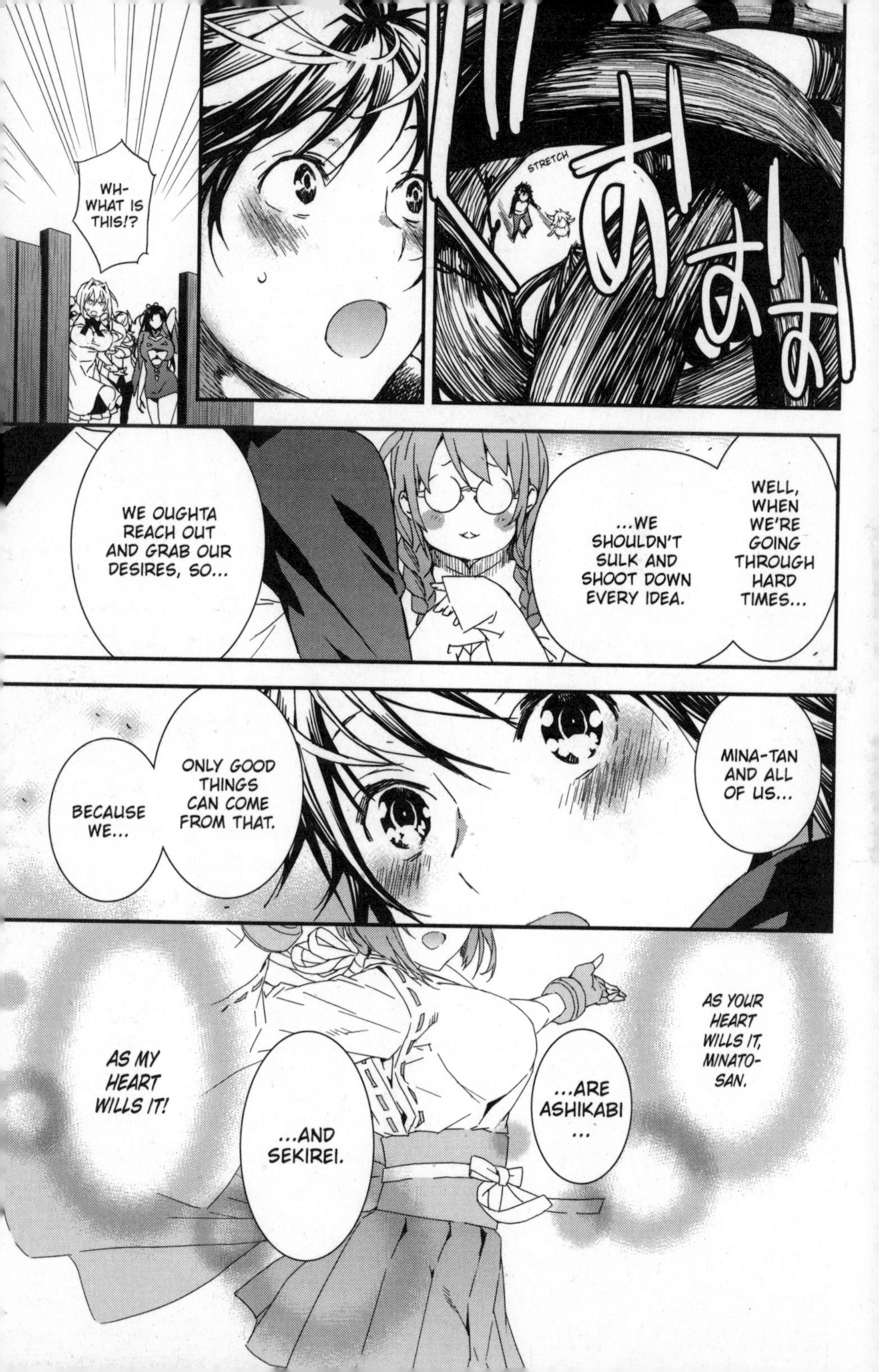
STRETCH
WH- WHAT IS THIS!?
WELL, WHEN WE'RE GOING THROUGH HARD TIMES...
...WE SHOULDN'T SULK AND SHOOT DOWN EVERY IDEA.
WE OUGHTA REACH OUT AND GRAB OUR DESIRES, SO...
MINA-TAN AND ALL OF US...
ONLY GOOD THINGS CAN COME FROM THAT.
BECAUSE WE...
AS YOUR HEART WILLS IT, MINATO-SAN.
...ARE ASHIKABI...
...AND SEKIREI.
AS MY HEART WILLS IT!

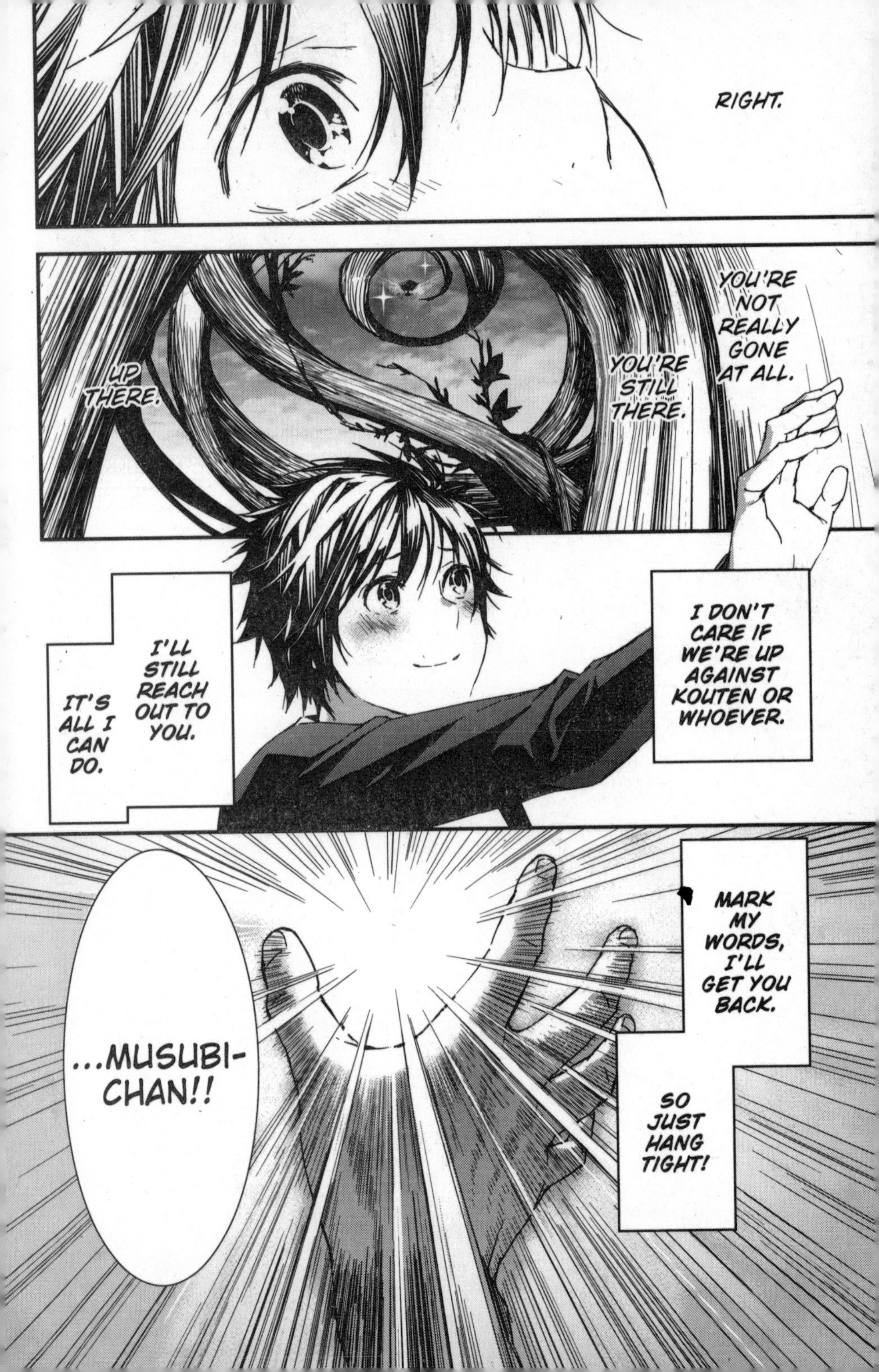
RIGHT.
YOU'RE NOT REALLY GONE AT ALL.
YOU'RE STILL THERE.
UP THERE.
I DON'T CARE IF WE'RE UP AGAINST KOUTEN OR WHOEVER.
I'LL STILL REACH OUT TO YOU.
IT'S ALL I CAN DO.
MARK MY WORDS, I'LL GET YOU BACK.
SO JUST HANG TIGHT!
...MUSUBI-CHAN!!

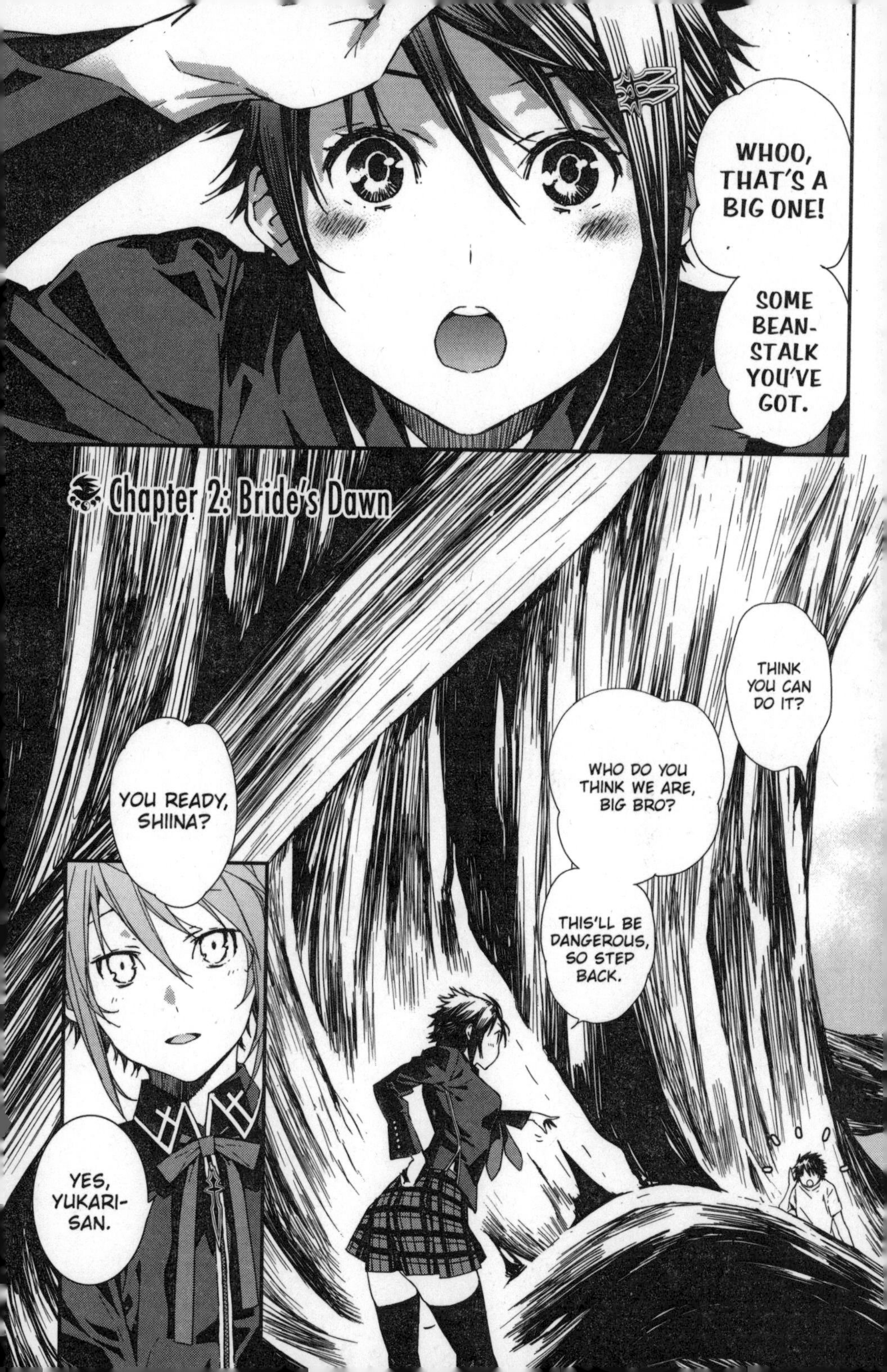
WHOO, THAT'S A BIG ONE!
SOME BEAN-STALK YOU'VE GOT.
Chapter 2: Bride's Dawn
THINK YOU CAN DO IT?
WHO DO YOU THINK WE ARE, BIG BRO?
THIS'LL BE DANGEROUS, SO STEP BACK.
YOU READY, SHIINA?
YES, YUKARI-SAN.

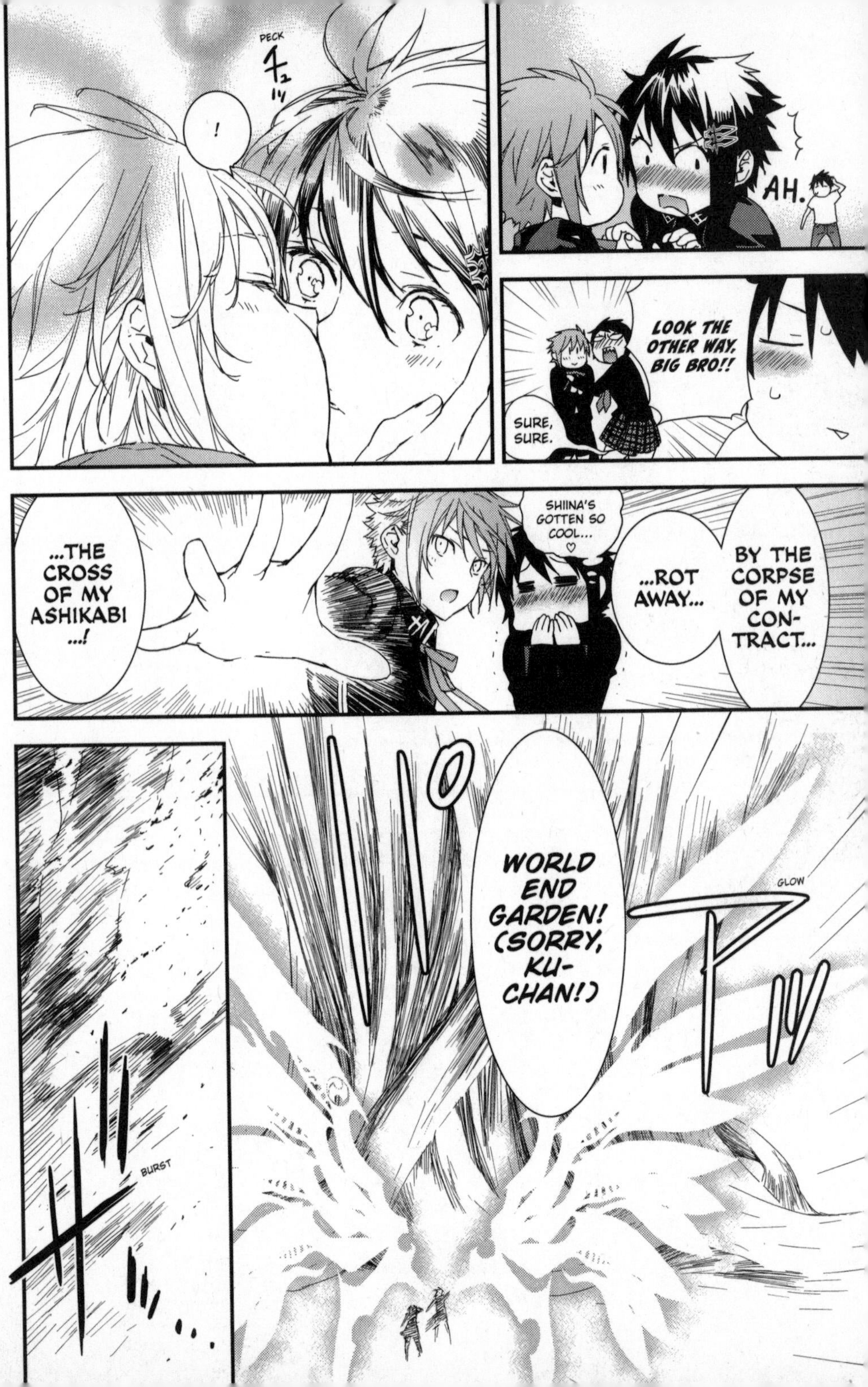
AH.
LOOK THE OTHER WAY, BIG BRO!!
SURE, SURE.
PECK
!
BY THE CORPSE OF MY CON-TRACT...
...ROT AWAY...
SHIINA'S GOTTEN SO COOL... ♡
...THE CROSS OF MY ASHIKABI ...!
GLOW
WORLD END GARDEN! (SORRY, KU-CHAN!)
BURST

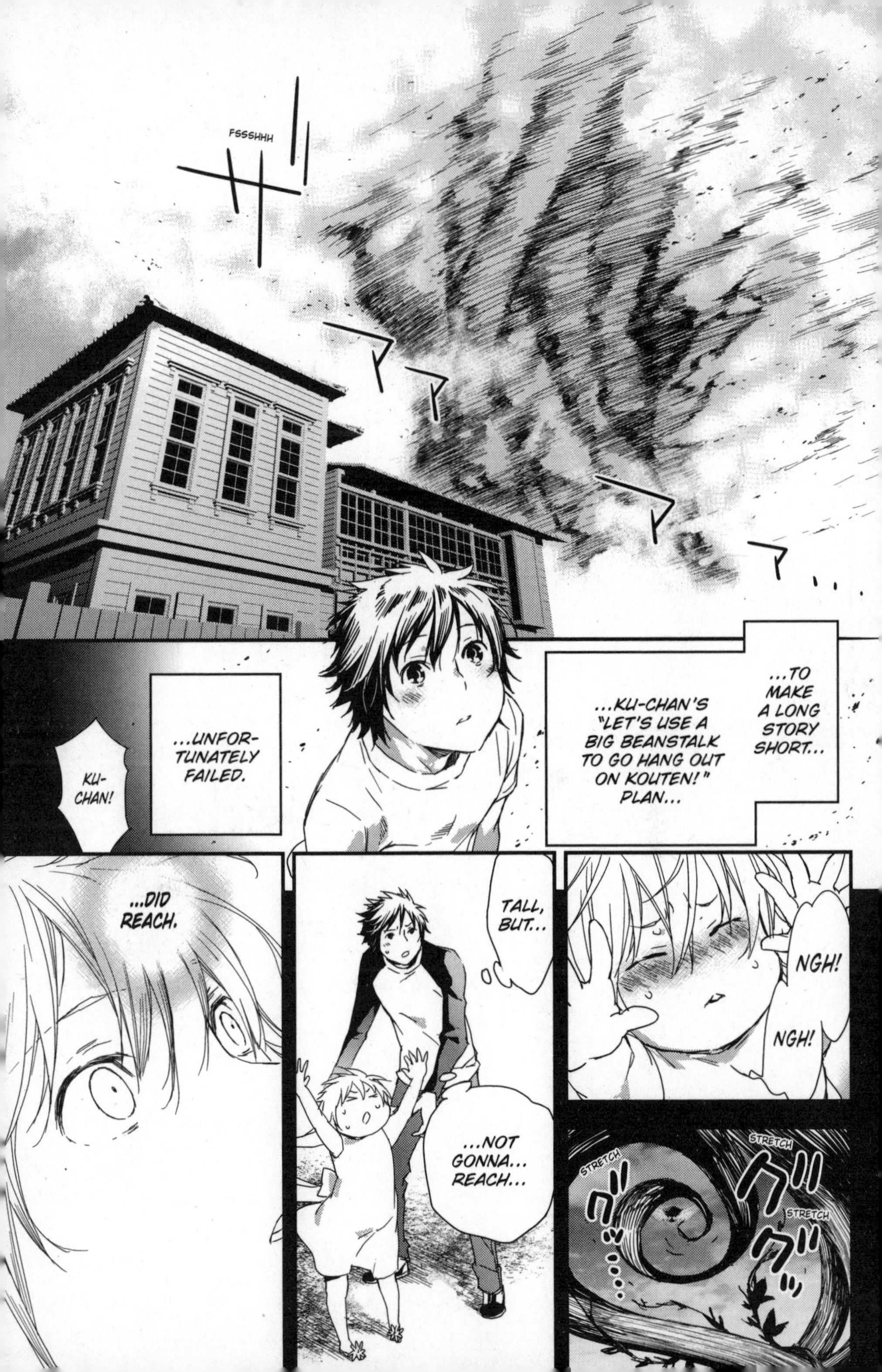
FSSSHH
...TO MAKE A LONG STORY SHORT...
...KU-CHAN'S "LET'S USE A BIG BEANSTALK TO GO HANG OUT ON KOUTEN!" PLAN...
...UNFORTUNATELY FAILED.
KU-CHAN!
NGH!
NGH!
STRETCH
STRETCH
STRETCH
TALL, BUT...
...NOT GONNA... REACH...
...DID REACH.

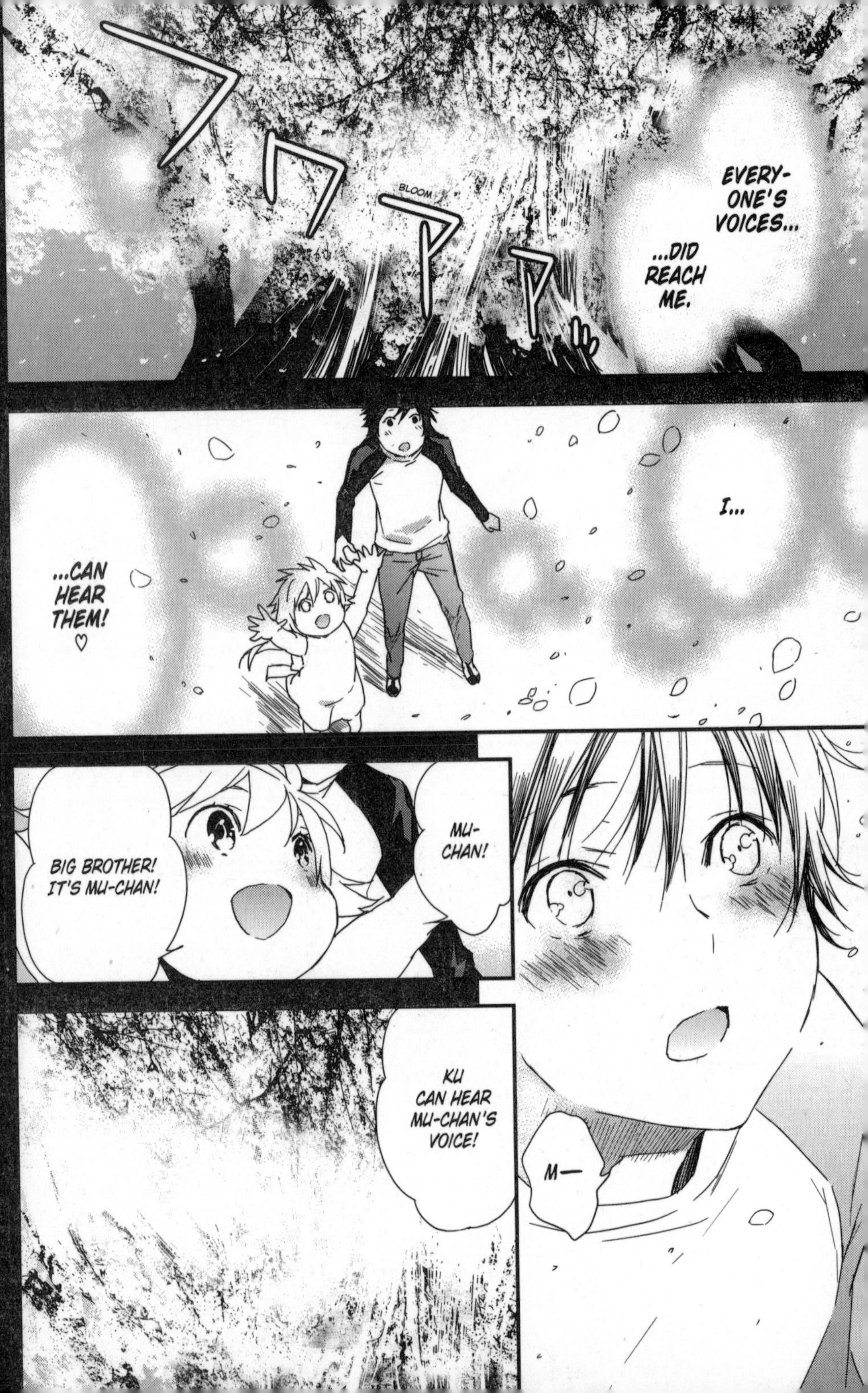
BLOOM
EVERY-ONE'S VOICES...
...DID REACH ME.
I...
...CAN HEAR THEM! ♡
M—
MU-CHAN!
BIG BROTHER! IT'S MU-CHAN!
KU CAN HEAR MU-CHAN'S VOICE!

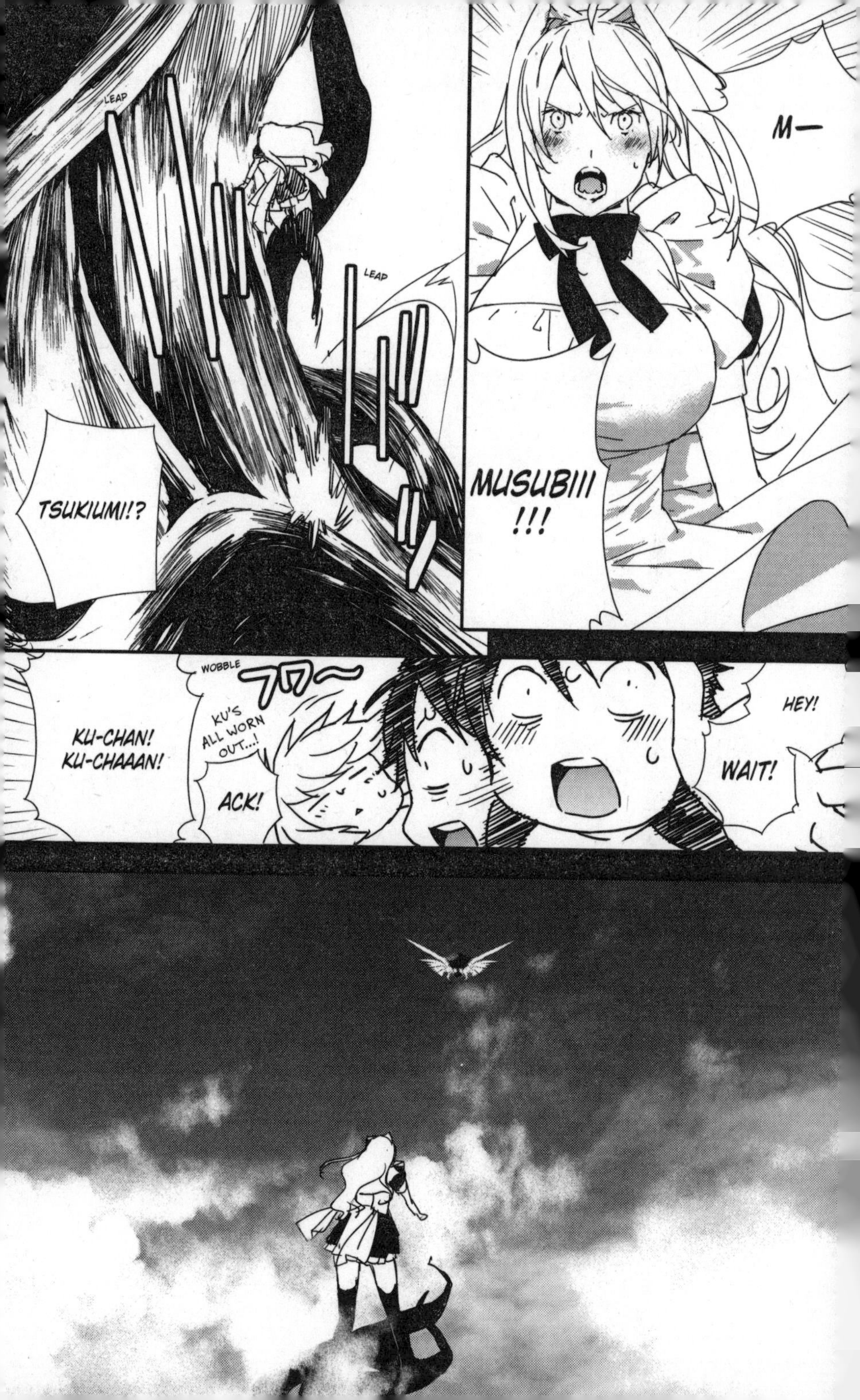
M—
MUSUBIIII
!!!
LEAP
LEAP
TSUKIUMI!?
HEY!
WAIT!
WOBBLE
フワ〜
KU'S ALL WORN OUT...!
ACK!
KU-CHAN! KU-CHAAAN!

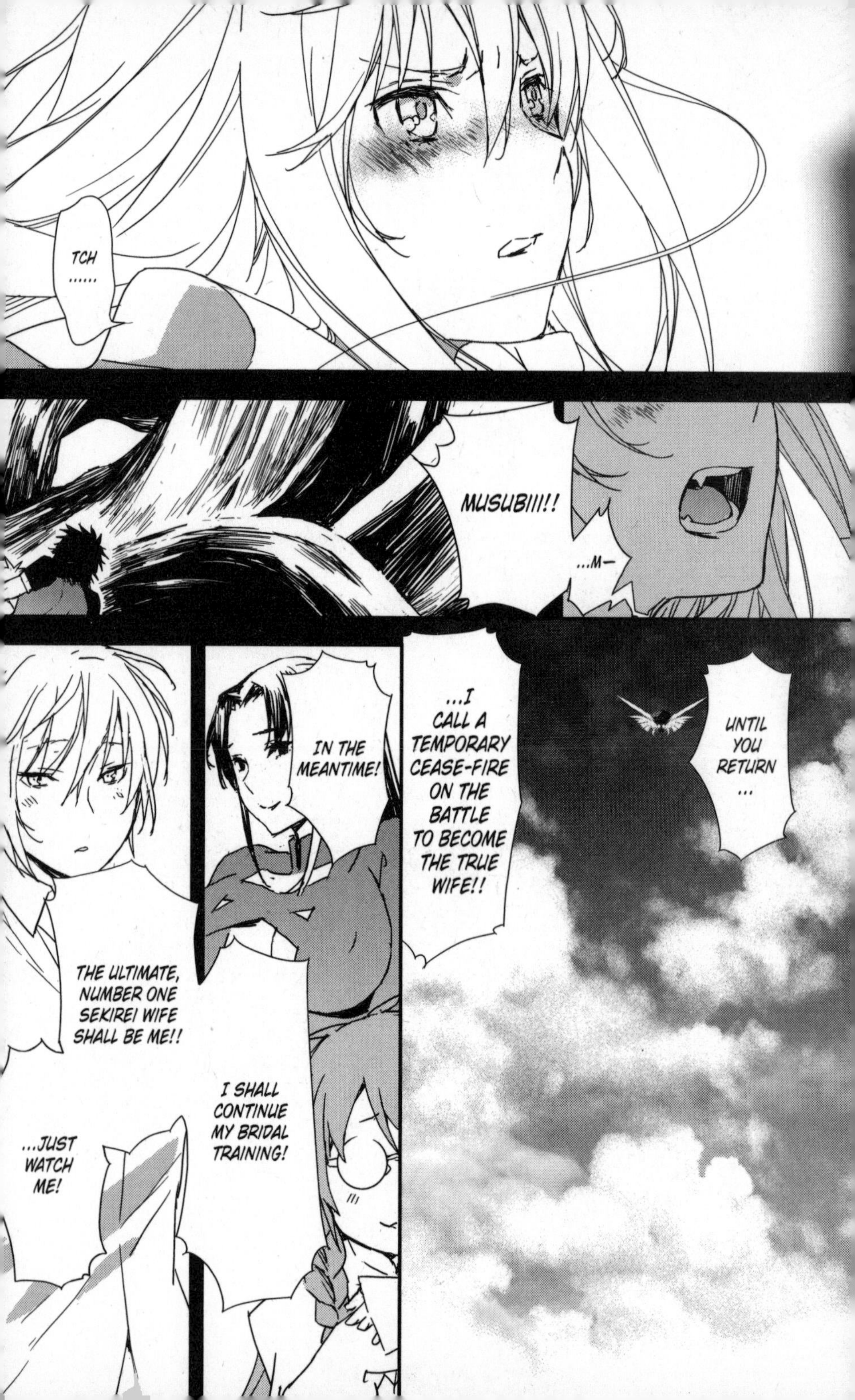
TCH ......
...M—
MUSUBIIII!!
UNTIL YOU RETURN ...
...I CALL A TEMPORARY CEASE-FIRE ON THE BATTLE TO BECOME THE TRUE WIFE!!
IN THE MEANTIME!
I SHALL CONTINUE MY BRIDAL TRAINING!
THE ULTIMATE, NUMBER ONE SEKIREI WIFE SHALL BE ME!!
...JUST WATCH ME!

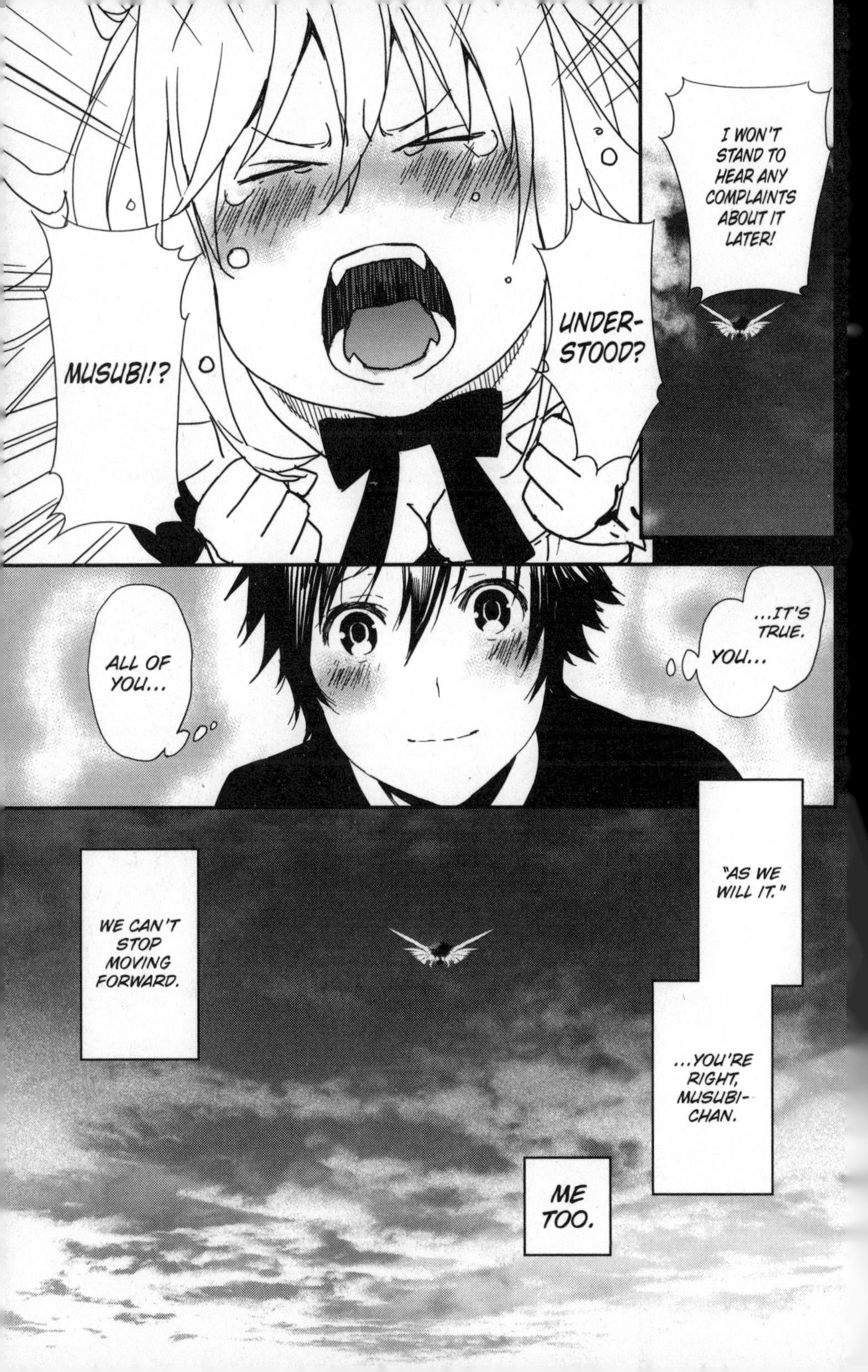
I WON'T STAND TO HEAR ANY COMPLAINTS ABOUT IT LATER!
UNDER-STOOD?
MUSUBI!?
...IT'S TRUE. YOU...
ALL OF YOU...
"AS WE WILL IT."
WE CAN'T STOP MOVING FORWARD.
...YOU'RE RIGHT, MUSUBI-CHAN.
ME TOO.

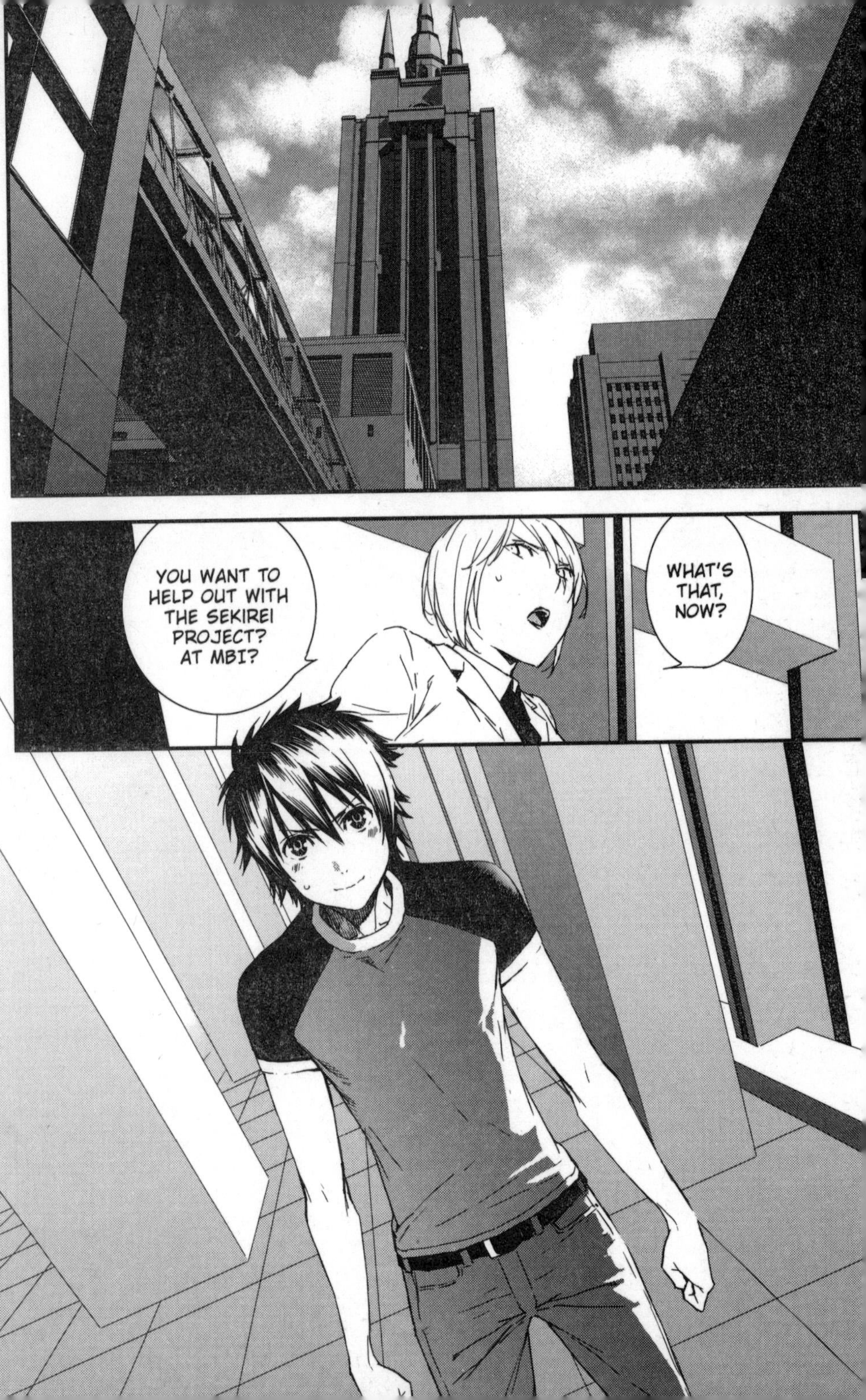
WHAT'S THAT, NOW?
YOU WANT TO HELP OUT WITH THE SEKIREI PROJECT? AT MBI?

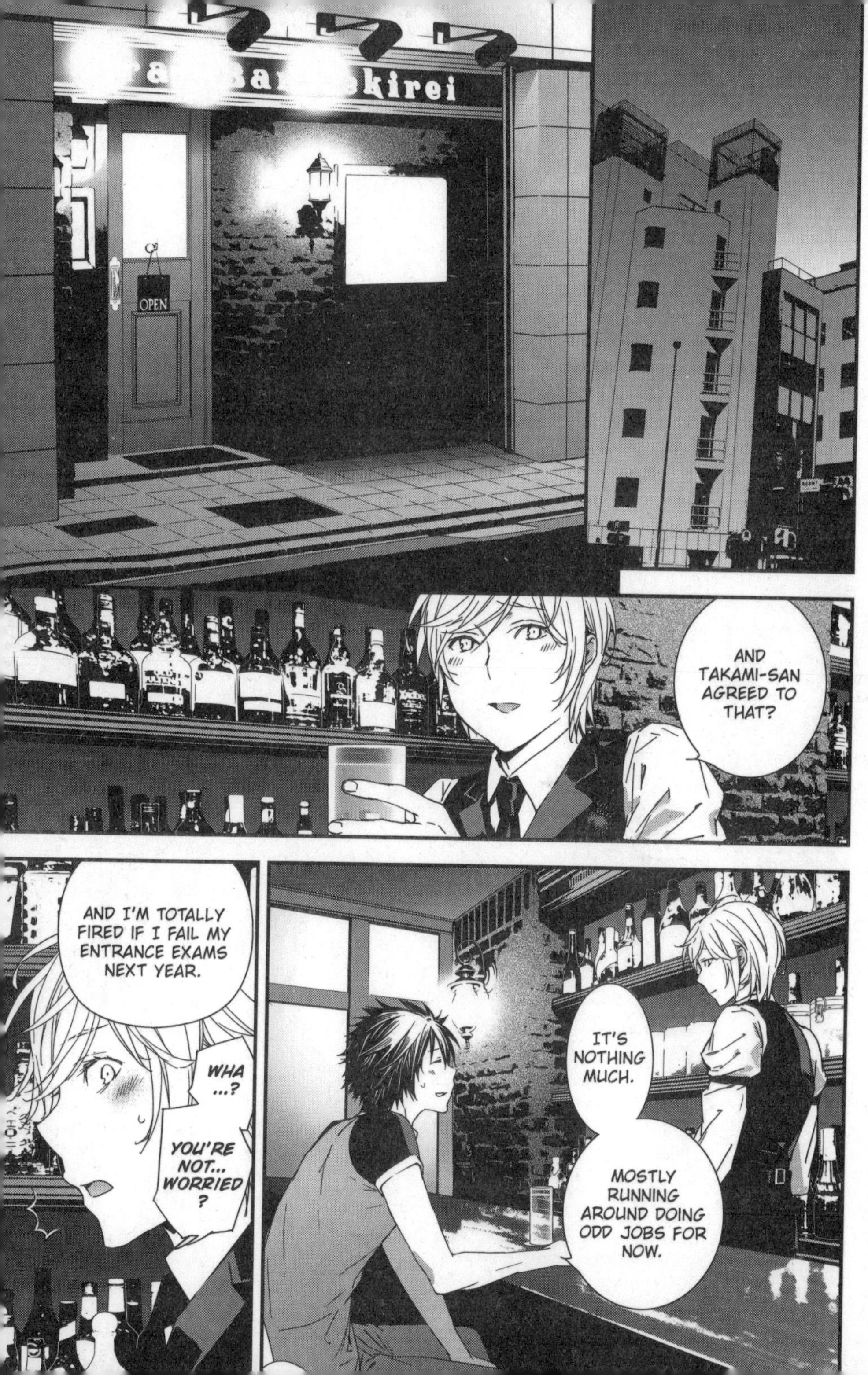
OPEN
AND TAKAMI-SAN AGREED TO THAT?
IT'S NOTHING MUCH.
MOSTLY RUNNING AROUND DOING ODD JOBS FOR NOW.
AND I'M TOTALLY FIRED IF I FAIL MY ENTRANCE EXAMS NEXT YEAR.
WHA...?
YOU'RE NOT... WORRIED?

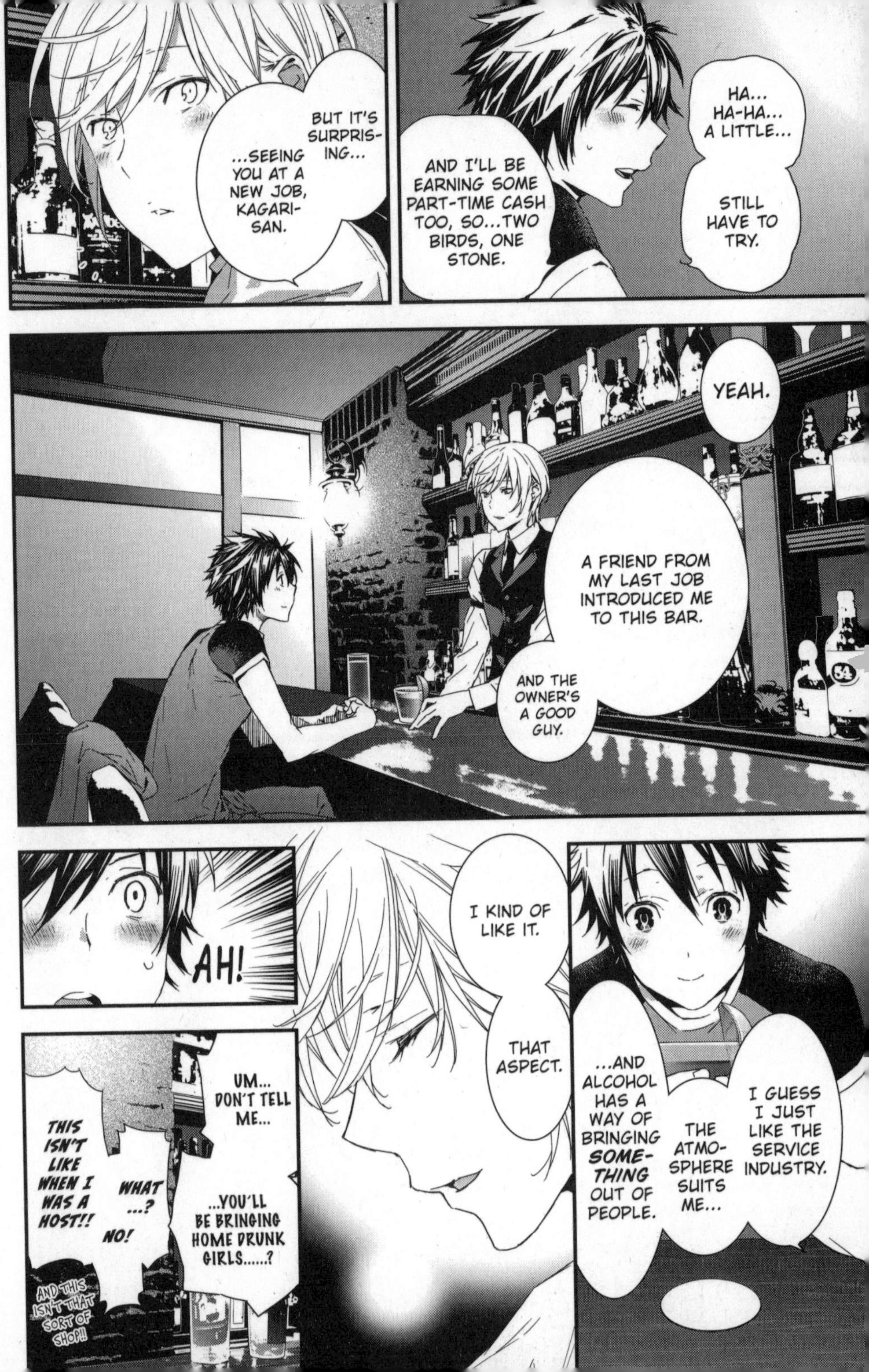
HA... HA-HA... A LITTLE...
STILL HAVE TO TRY.
AND I'LL BE EARNING SOME PART-TIME CASH TOO, SO...TWO BIRDS, ONE STONE.
BUT IT'S SURPRISING...
...SEEING YOU AT A NEW JOB, KAGARI-SAN.
YEAH.
A FRIEND FROM MY LAST JOB INTRODUCED ME TO THIS BAR.
AND THE OWNER'S A GOOD GUY.
I GUESS I JUST LIKE THE SERVICE INDUSTRY.
THE ATMOSPHERE SUITS ME...
...AND ALCOHOL HAS A WAY OF BRINGING SOMETHING OUT OF PEOPLE.
I KIND OF LIKE IT.
THAT ASPECT.
AH!
UM... DON'T TELL ME...
...YOU'LL BE BRINGING HOME DRUNK GIRLS......?
WHAT ...?
NO!
THIS ISN'T LIKE WHEN I WAS A HOST!!
AND THIS ISN'T THAT SORT OF SHOP!!

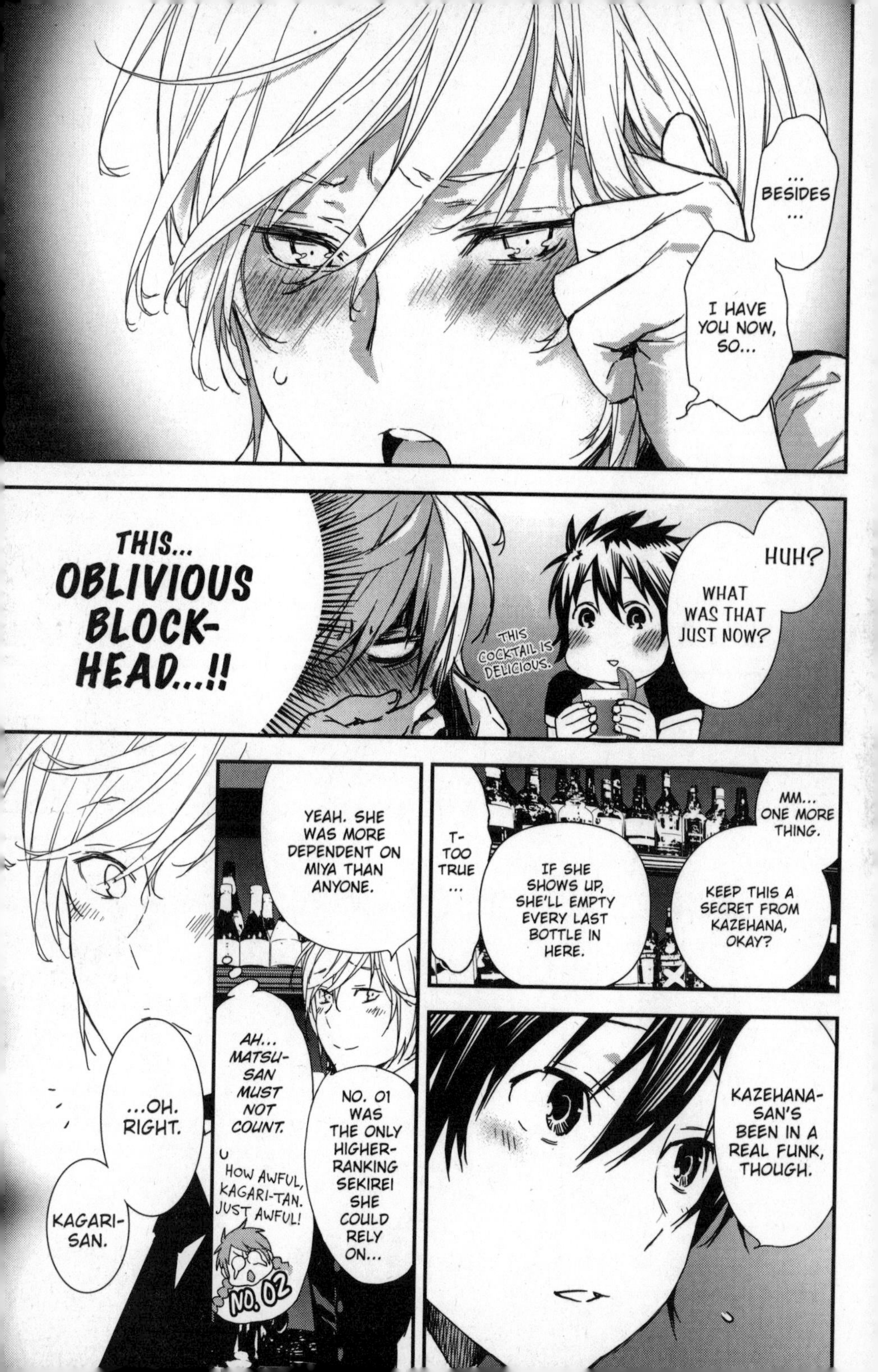
...BESIDES...
I HAVE YOU NOW, SO...
HUH?
WHAT WAS THAT JUST NOW?
THIS COCKTAIL IS DELICIOUS.
THIS... OBLIVIOUS BLOCK-HEAD...!!
MM... ONE MORE THING.
KEEP THIS A SECRET FROM KAZEHANA, OKAY?
IF SHE SHOWS UP, SHE'LL EMPTY EVERY LAST BOTTLE IN HERE.
T-TOO TRUE...
KAZEHANA-SAN'S BEEN IN A REAL FUNK, THOUGH.
YEAH. SHE WAS MORE DEPENDENT ON MIYA THAN ANYONE.
NO. 01 WAS THE ONLY HIGHER-RANKING SEKIREI SHE COULD RELY ON...
AH... MATSU-SAN MUST NOT COUNT.
HOW AWFUL, KAGARI-TAN. JUST AWFUL!
NO. 02
...OH. RIGHT.
KAGARI-SAN.

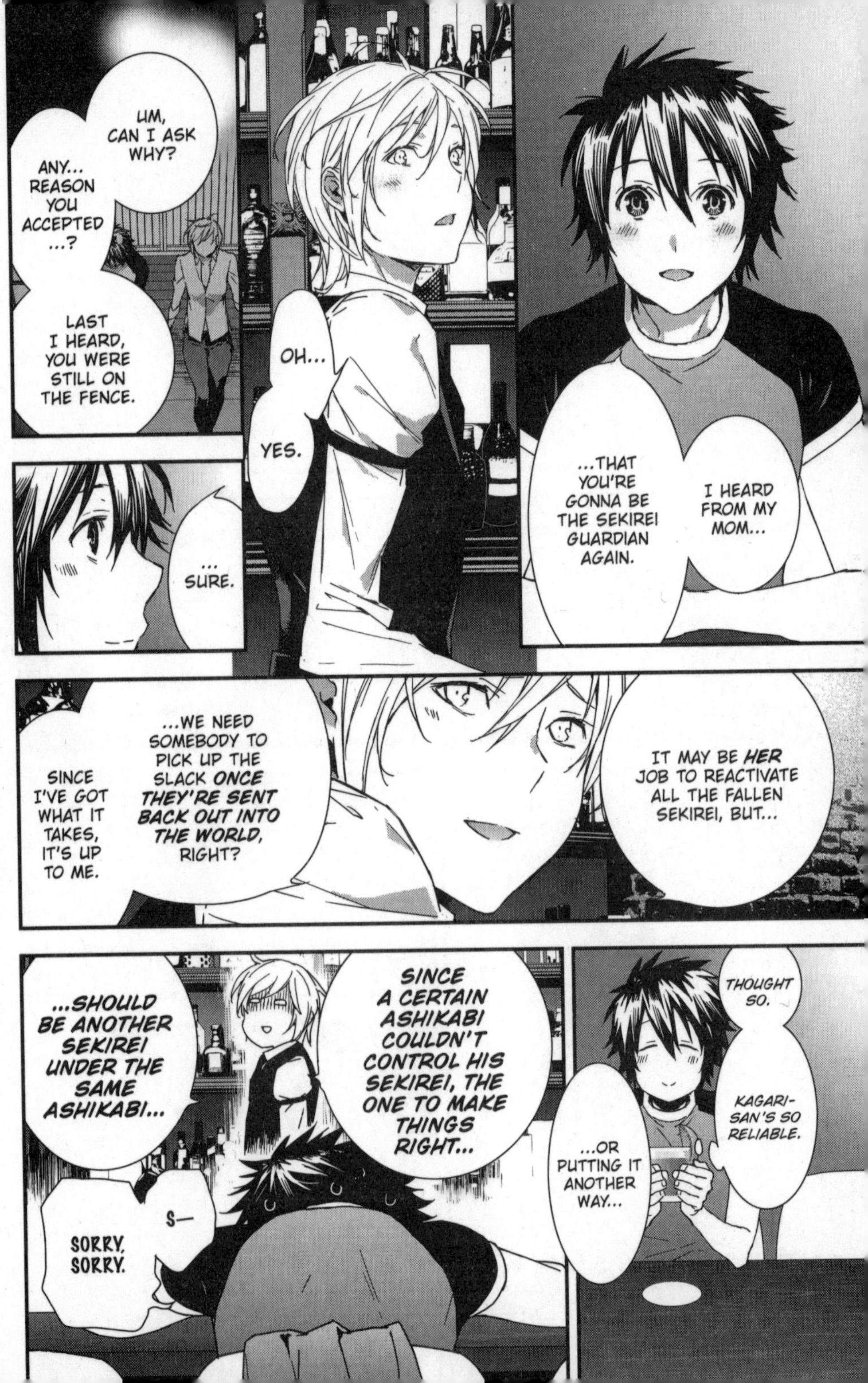
I HEARD FROM MY MOM...
...THAT YOU'RE GONNA BE THE SEKIREI GUARDIAN AGAIN.
OH...
YES.
UM, CAN I ASK WHY?
ANY... REASON YOU ACCEPTED ...?
LAST I HEARD, YOU WERE STILL ON THE FENCE.
... SURE.
IT MAY BE *HER* JOB TO REACTIVATE ALL THE FALLEN SEKIREI, BUT...
...WE NEED SOMEBODY TO PICK UP THE SLACK *ONCE THEY'RE SENT BACK OUT INTO THE WORLD*, RIGHT?
SINCE I'VE GOT WHAT IT TAKES, IT'S UP TO ME.
THOUGHT SO.
KAGARI-SAN'S SO RELIABLE.
...OR PUTTING IT ANOTHER WAY...
SINCE A CERTAIN ASHIKABI COULDN'T CONTROL HIS SEKIREI, THE ONE TO MAKE THINGS RIGHT...
...SHOULD BE ANOTHER SEKIREI UNDER THE SAME ASHIKABI...
S—
SORRY, SORRY.

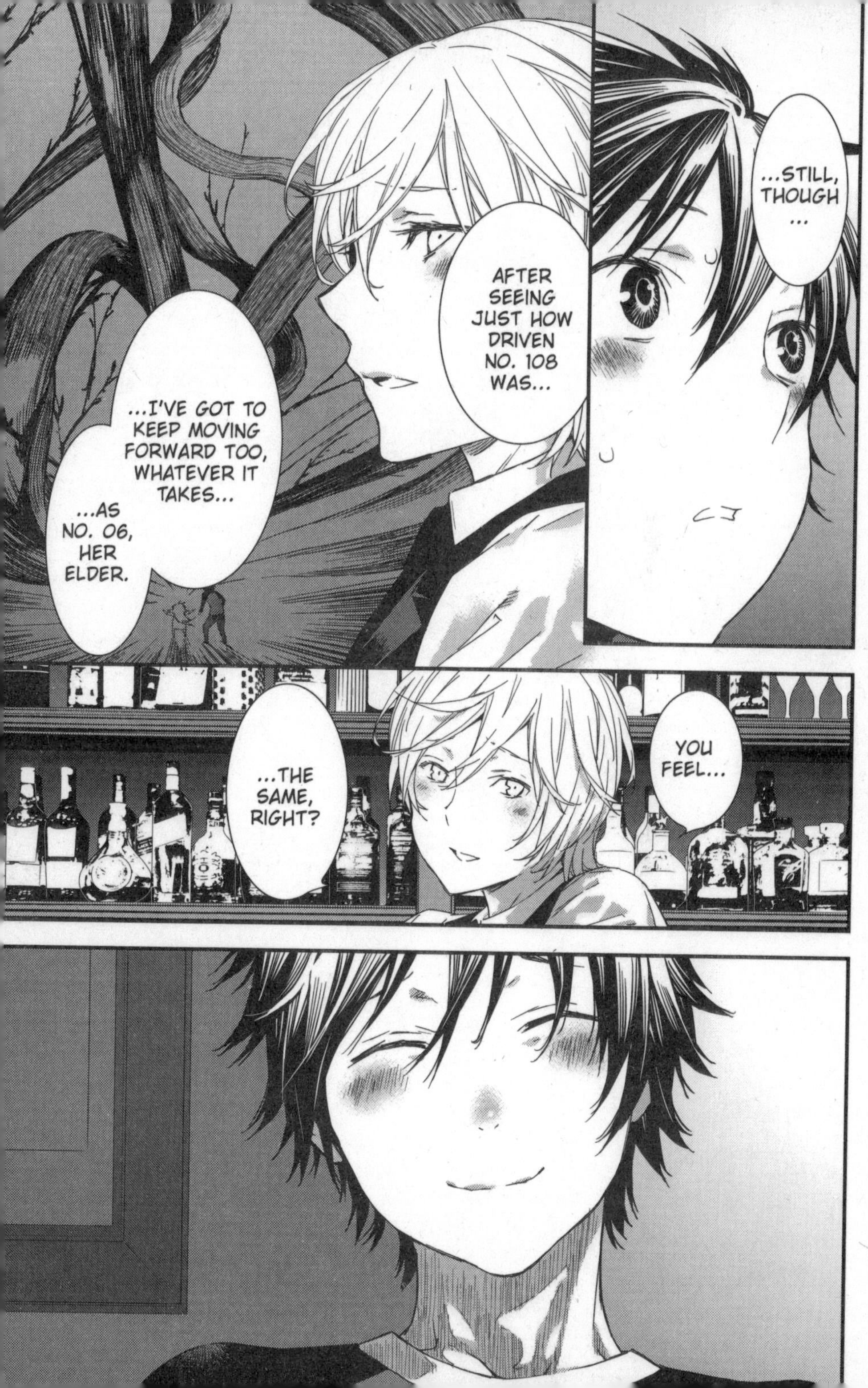
...STILL, THOUGH...
AFTER SEEING JUST HOW DRIVEN NO. 108 WAS...
...I'VE GOT TO KEEP MOVING FORWARD TOO, WHATEVER IT TAKES...
...AS NO. 06, HER ELDER.
YOU FEEL...
...THE SAME, RIGHT?

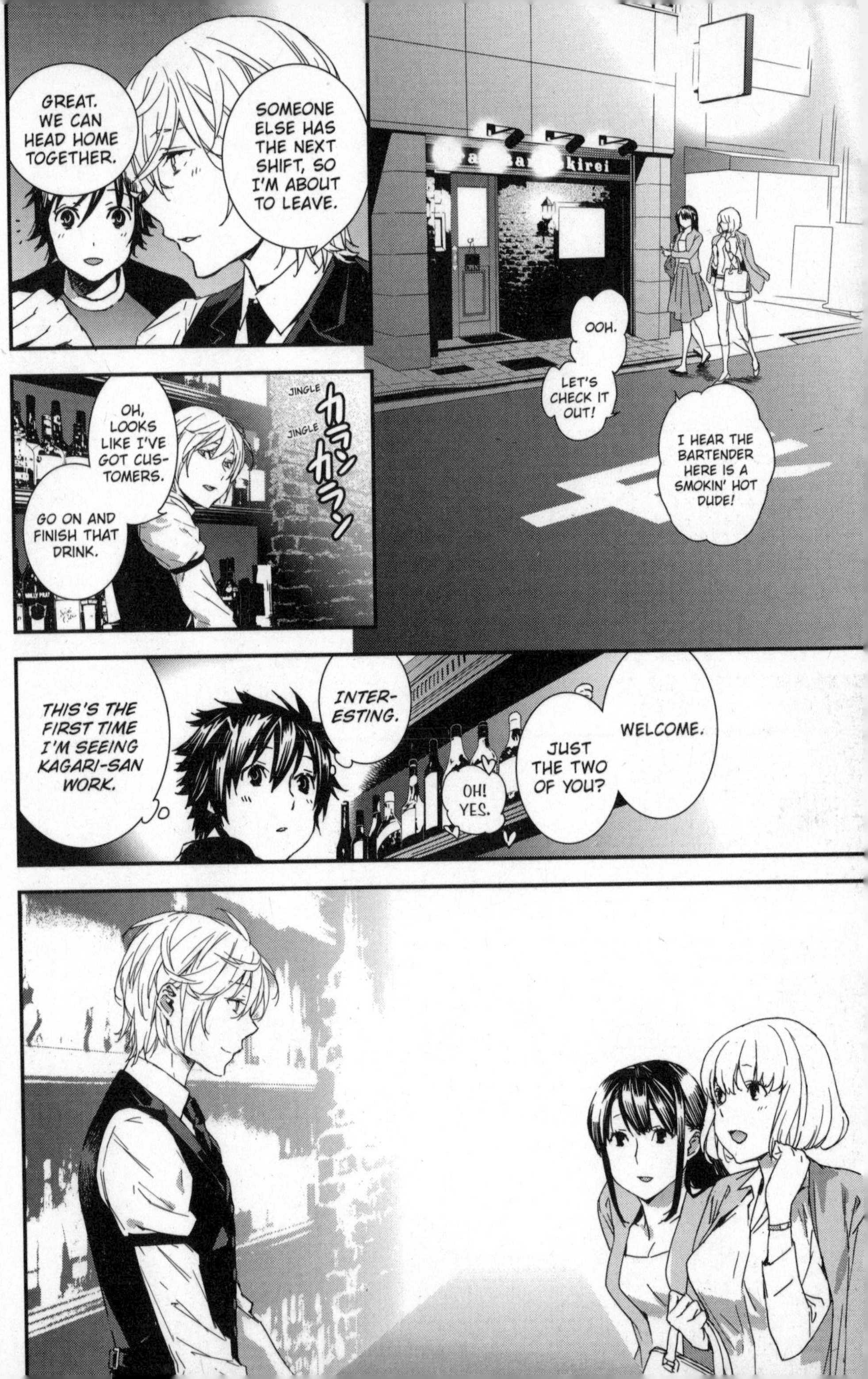
kirei
I HEAR THE BARTENDER HERE IS A SMOKIN' HOT DUDE!
OOH.
LET'S CHECK IT OUT!
SOMEONE ELSE HAS THE NEXT SHIFT, SO I'M ABOUT TO LEAVE.
GREAT. WE CAN HEAD HOME TOGETHER.
カランカラン
JINGLE JINGLE
OH, LOOKS LIKE I'VE GOT CUS-TOMERS.
GO ON AND FINISH THAT DRINK.
WELCOME.
JUST THE TWO OF YOU?
OH! YES.
INTER-ESTING.
THIS'S THE FIRST TIME I'M SEEING KAGARI-SAN WORK.

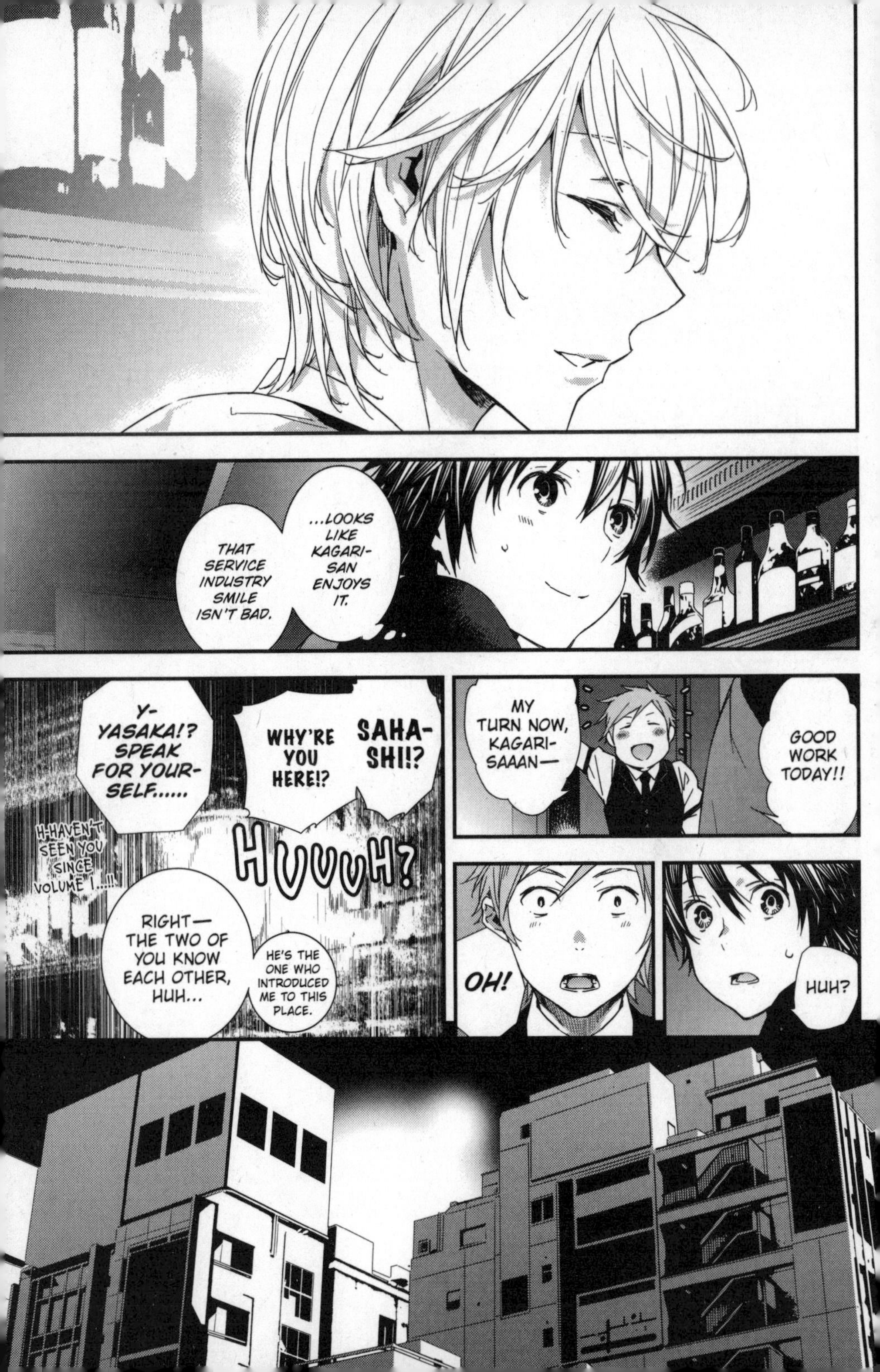
...LOOKS LIKE KAGARI-SAN ENJOYS IT.
THAT SERVICE INDUSTRY SMILE ISN'T BAD.
GOOD WORK TODAY!!
MY TURN NOW, KAGARI-SAAAN—
HUH?
OH!
SAHA-SHI!?
WHY'RE YOU HERE!?
Y-YASAKA!? SPEAK FOR YOURSELF......
HUUUH?
H-HAVEN'T SEEN YOU SINCE VOLUME 1...!!
RIGHT—THE TWO OF YOU KNOW EACH OTHER, HUH...
HE'S THE ONE WHO INTRODUCED ME TO THIS PLACE.

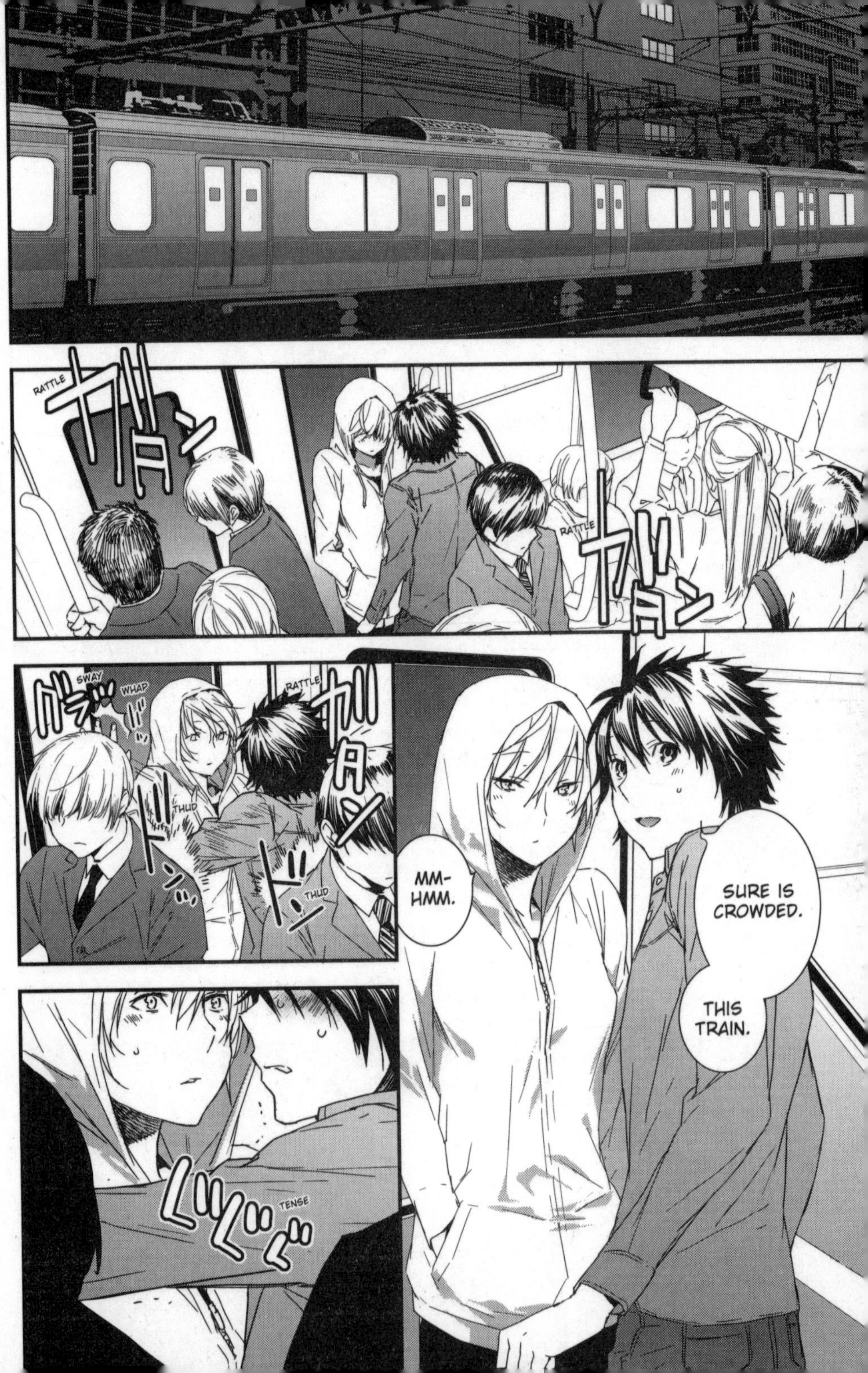
RATTLE
RATTLE
SURE IS CROWDED.
THIS TRAIN.
MM-HMM.
RATTLE
SWAY
WHAP
THUD
THUD
TENSE

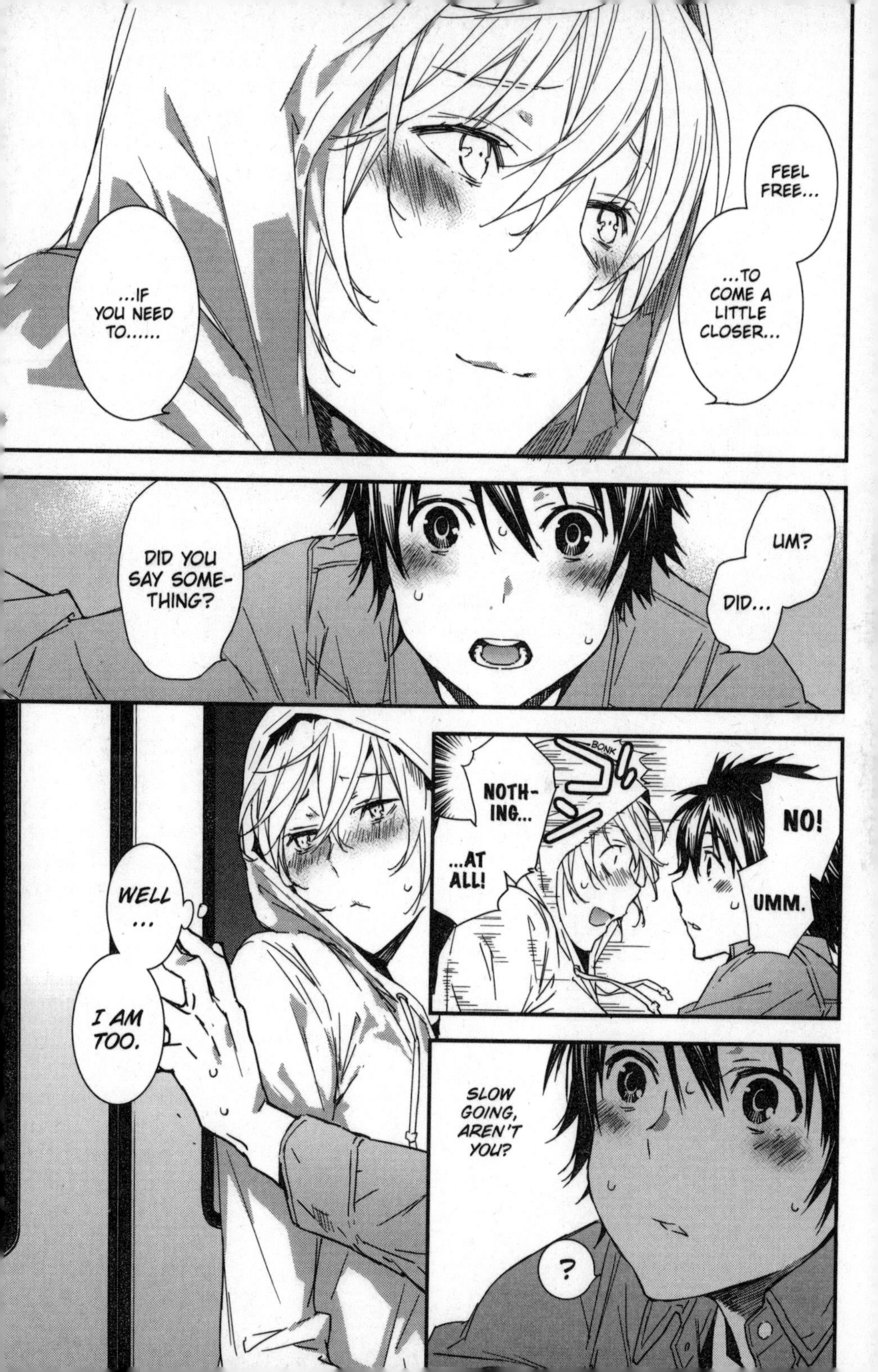
FEEL FREE...
...TO COME A LITTLE CLOSER...
...IF YOU NEED TO......
UM?
DID...
DID YOU SAY SOME-THING?
BONK
NO!
NOTH-ING...
UMM.
...AT ALL!
SLOW GOING, AREN'T YOU?
?
WELL ...
I AM TOO.

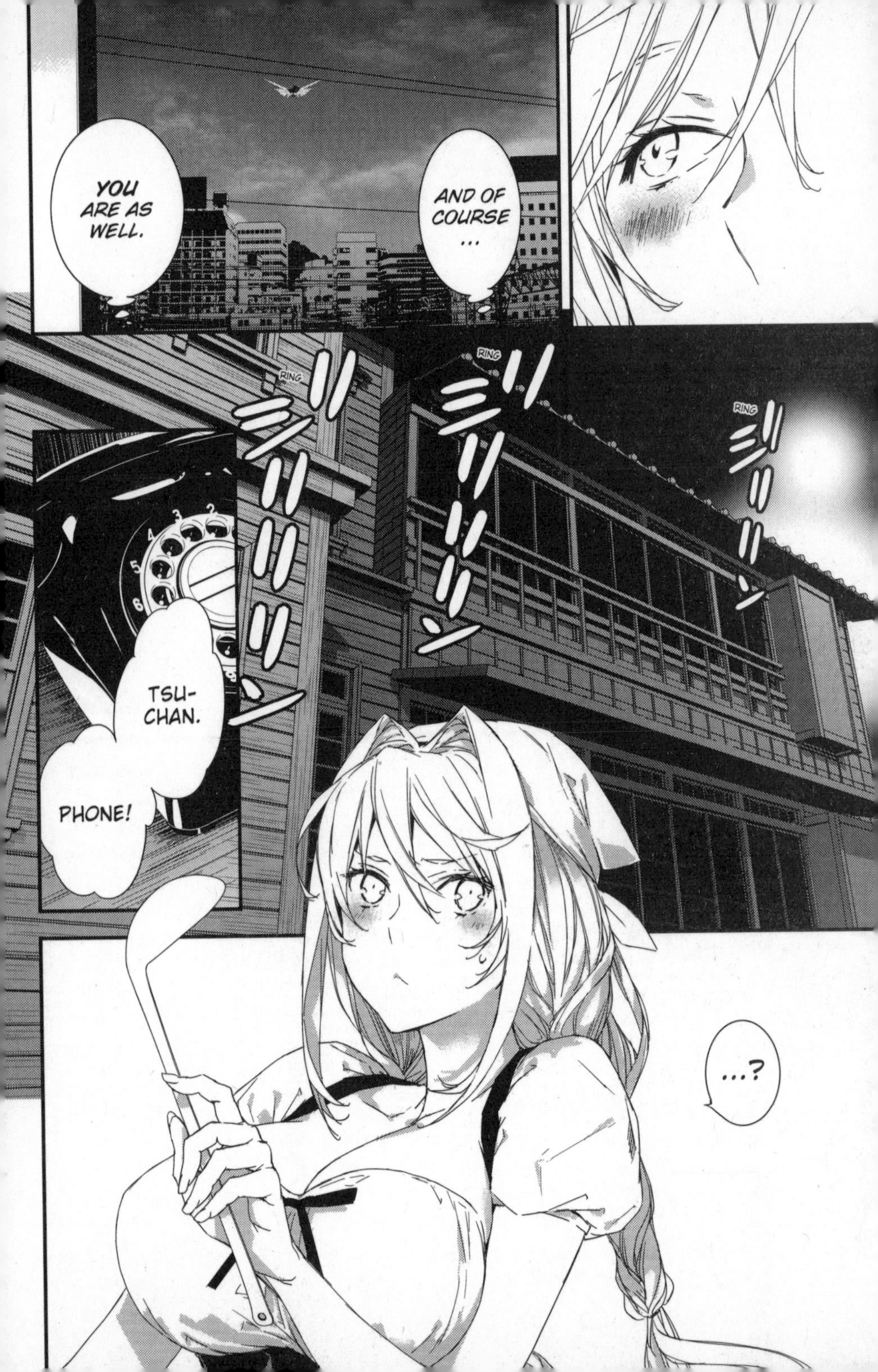
AND OF COURSE ...
YOU ARE AS WELL.
RING
RING
RING
TSU-CHAN.
PHONE!
...?

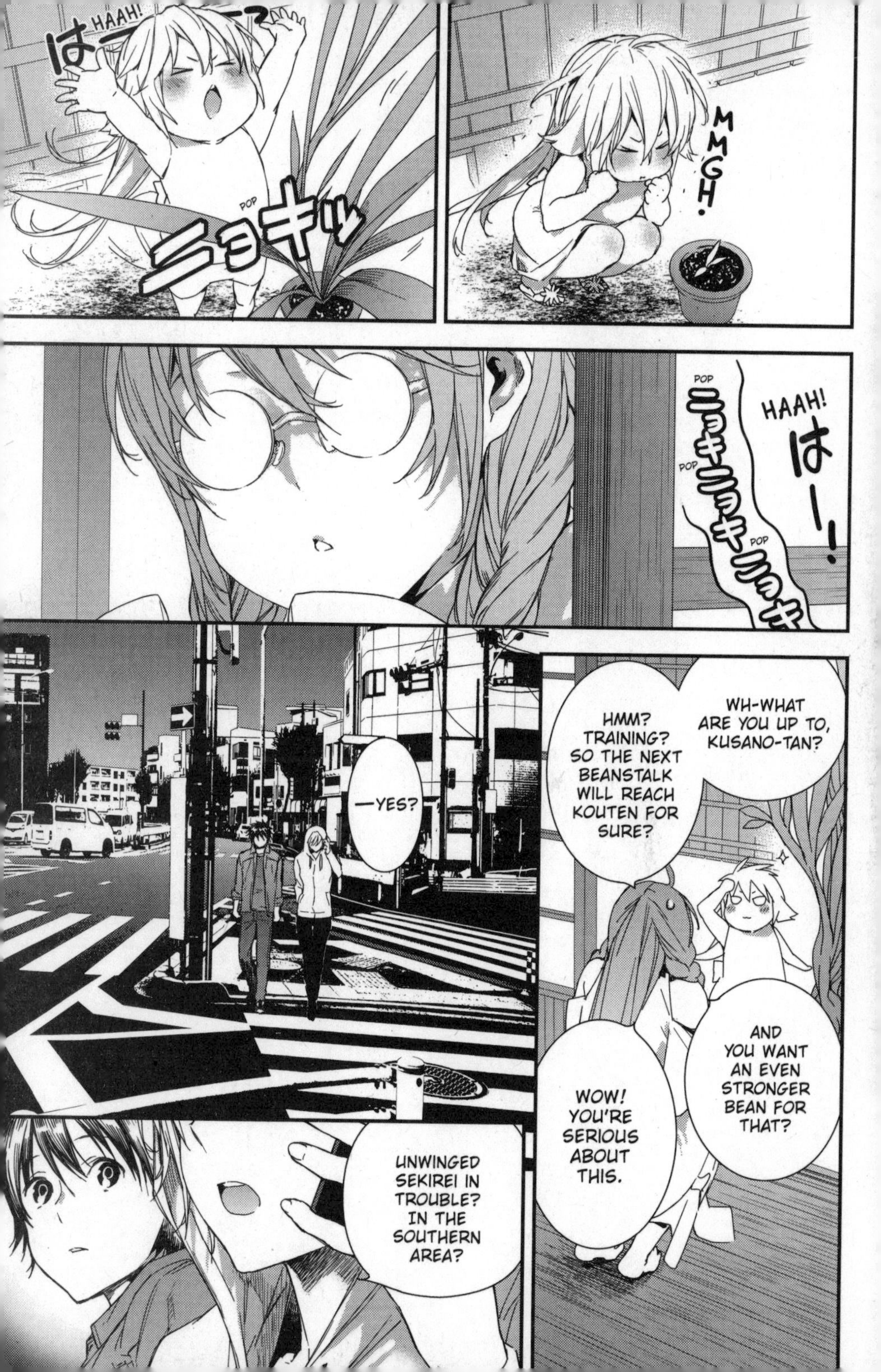
MMGH!
HAAH!
は
POP
ニョキッ
HAAH!
はー!
POP
POP
POP
ニョキニョキニョキ
WH-WHAT ARE YOU UP TO, KUSANO-TAN?
HMM? TRAINING? SO THE NEXT BEANSTALK WILL REACH KOUTEN FOR SURE?
AND YOU WANT AN EVEN STRONGER BEAN FOR THAT?
WOW! YOU'RE SERIOUS ABOUT THIS.
—YES?
UNWINGED SEKIREI IN TROUBLE? IN THE SOUTHERN AREA?

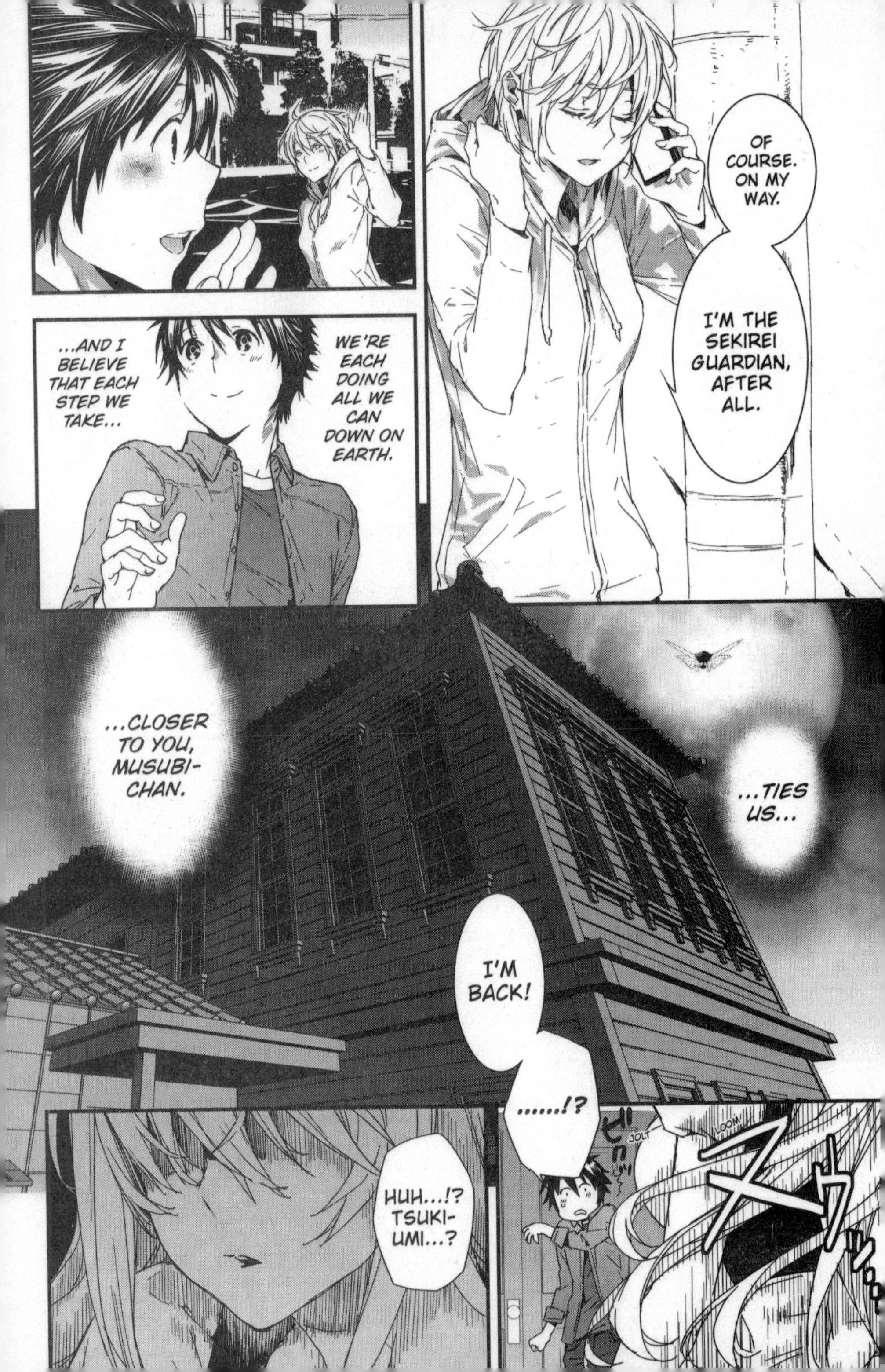
OF COURSE. ON MY WAY.
I'M THE SEKIREI GUARDIAN, AFTER ALL.
WE'RE EACH DOING ALL WE CAN DOWN ON EARTH.
...AND I BELIEVE THAT EACH STEP WE TAKE...
...TIES US...
...CLOSER TO YOU, MUSUBI-CHAN.
I'M BACK!
......!?
JOLT
LOOM
HUH...!? TSUKI-UMI...?

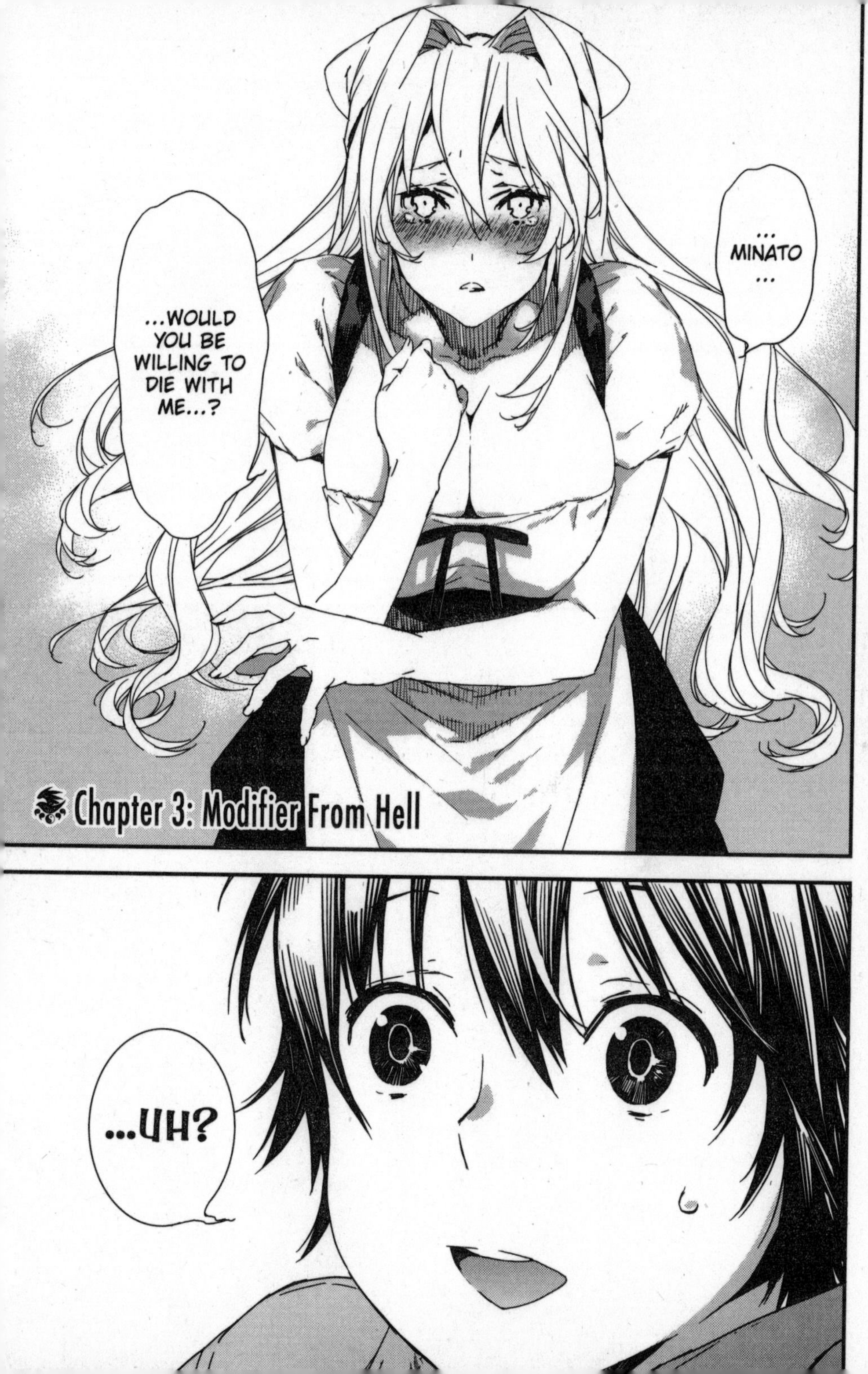
...MINATO...
...WOULD YOU BE WILLING TO DIE WITH ME...?
Chapter 3: Modifier From Hell
...UH?

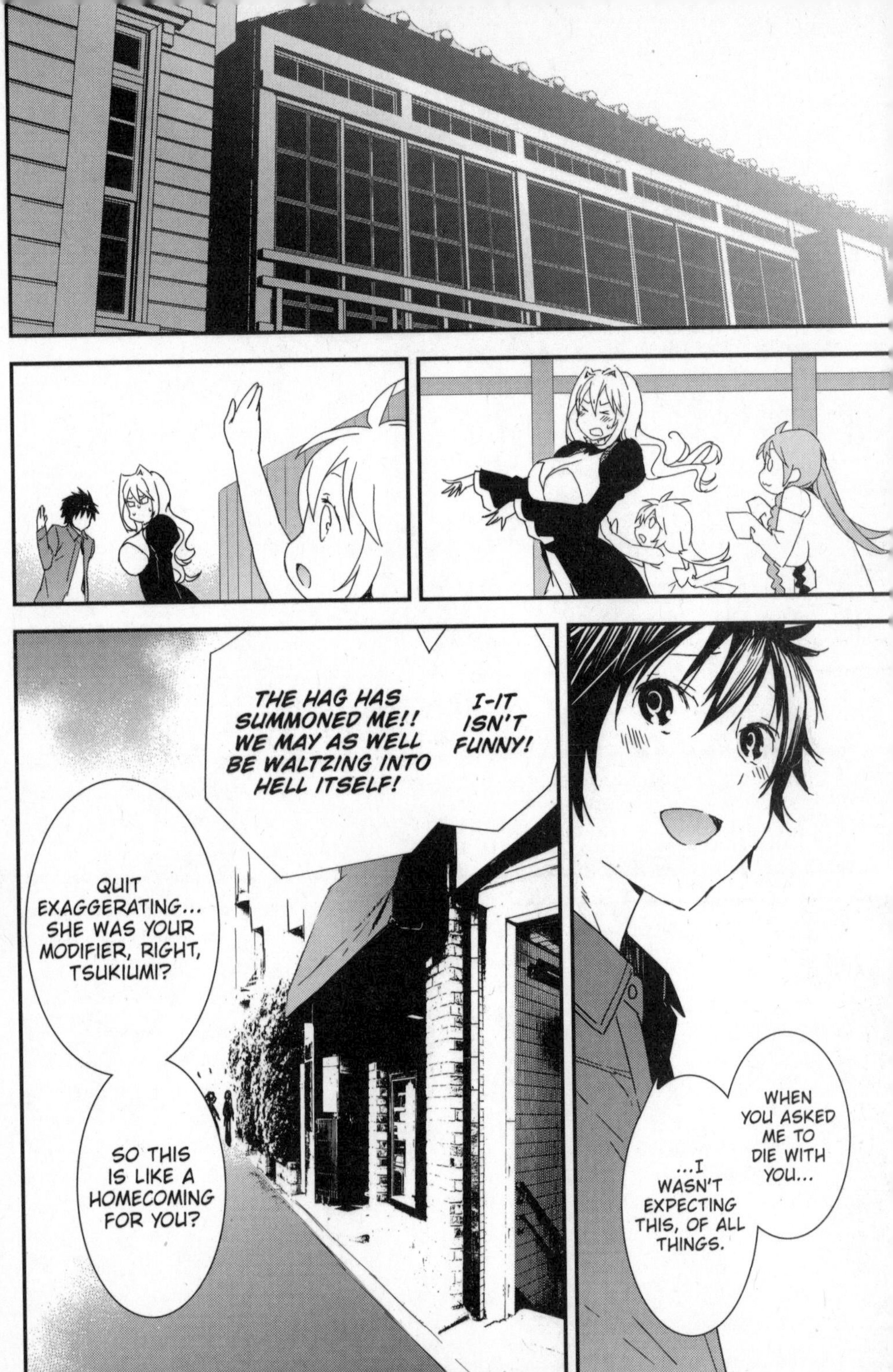
WHEN YOU ASKED ME TO DIE WITH YOU...
...I WASN'T EXPECTING THIS, OF ALL THINGS.
I-IT ISN'T FUNNY!
THE HAG HAS SUMMONED ME!! WE MAY AS WELL BE WALTZING INTO HELL ITSELF!
QUIT EXAGGERATING... SHE WAS YOUR MODIFIER, RIGHT, TSUKIUMI?
SO THIS IS LIKE A HOMECOMING FOR YOU?

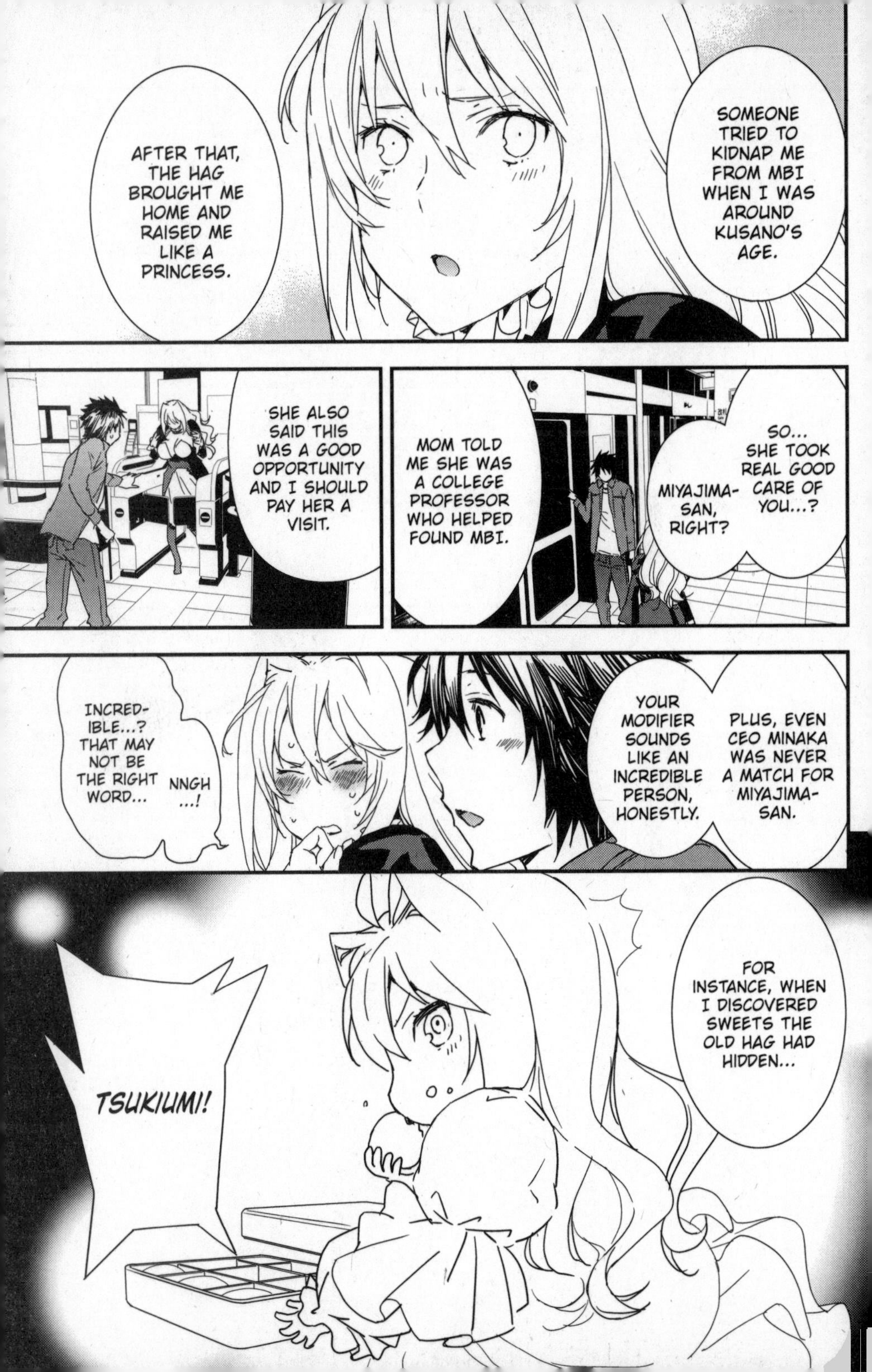
SOMEONE TRIED TO KIDNAP ME FROM MBI WHEN I WAS AROUND KUSANO'S AGE.
AFTER THAT, THE HAG BROUGHT ME HOME AND RAISED ME LIKE A PRINCESS.
SO... SHE TOOK REAL GOOD CARE OF YOU...?
MIYAJIMA-SAN, RIGHT?
MOM TOLD ME SHE WAS A COLLEGE PROFESSOR WHO HELPED FOUND MBI.
SHE ALSO SAID THIS WAS A GOOD OPPORTUNITY AND I SHOULD PAY HER A VISIT.
PLUS, EVEN CEO MINAKA WAS NEVER A MATCH FOR MIYAJIMA-SAN.
YOUR MODIFIER SOUNDS LIKE AN INCREDIBLE PERSON, HONESTLY.
NNGH ...!
INCRED-IBLE...? THAT MAY NOT BE THE RIGHT WORD...
FOR INSTANCE, WHEN I DISCOVERED SWEETS THE OLD HAG HAD HIDDEN...
TSUKIUMI!

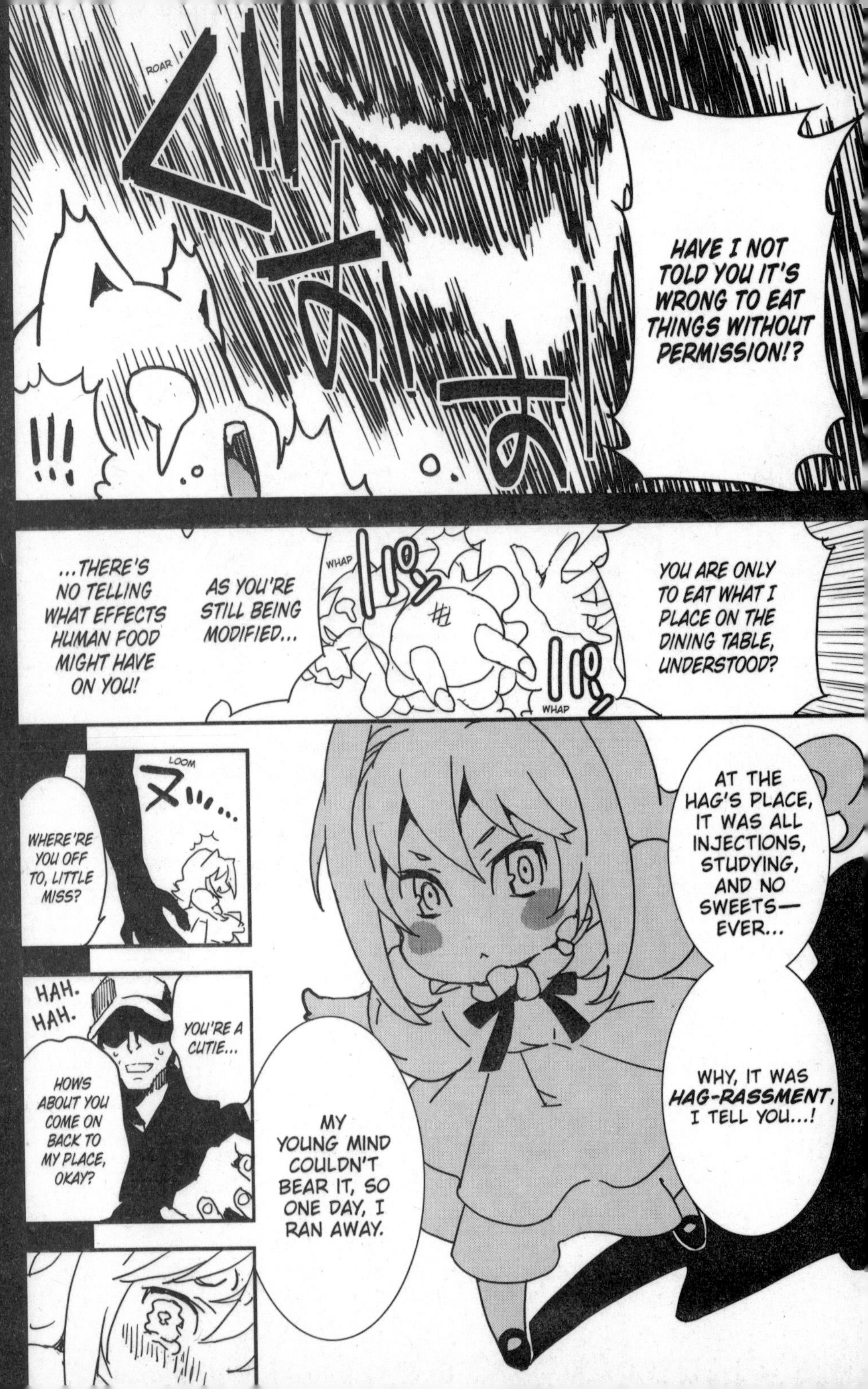
HAVE I NOT TOLD YOU IT'S WRONG TO EAT THINGS WITHOUT PERMISSION!?
ROAR
!!!
YOU ARE ONLY TO EAT WHAT I PLACE ON THE DINING TABLE, UNDERSTOOD?
WHAP
WHAP
AS YOU'RE STILL BEING MODIFIED...
...THERE'S NO TELLING WHAT EFFECTS HUMAN FOOD MIGHT HAVE ON YOU!
AT THE HAG'S PLACE, IT WAS ALL INJECTIONS, STUDYING, AND NO SWEETS—EVER...
WHY, IT WAS HAG-RASSMENT, I TELL YOU...!
MY YOUNG MIND COULDN'T BEAR IT, SO ONE DAY, I RAN AWAY.
LOOM
WHERE'RE YOU OFF TO, LITTLE MISS?
HAH. HAH.
YOU'RE A CUTIE...
HOWS ABOUT YOU COME ON BACK TO MY PLACE, OKAY?

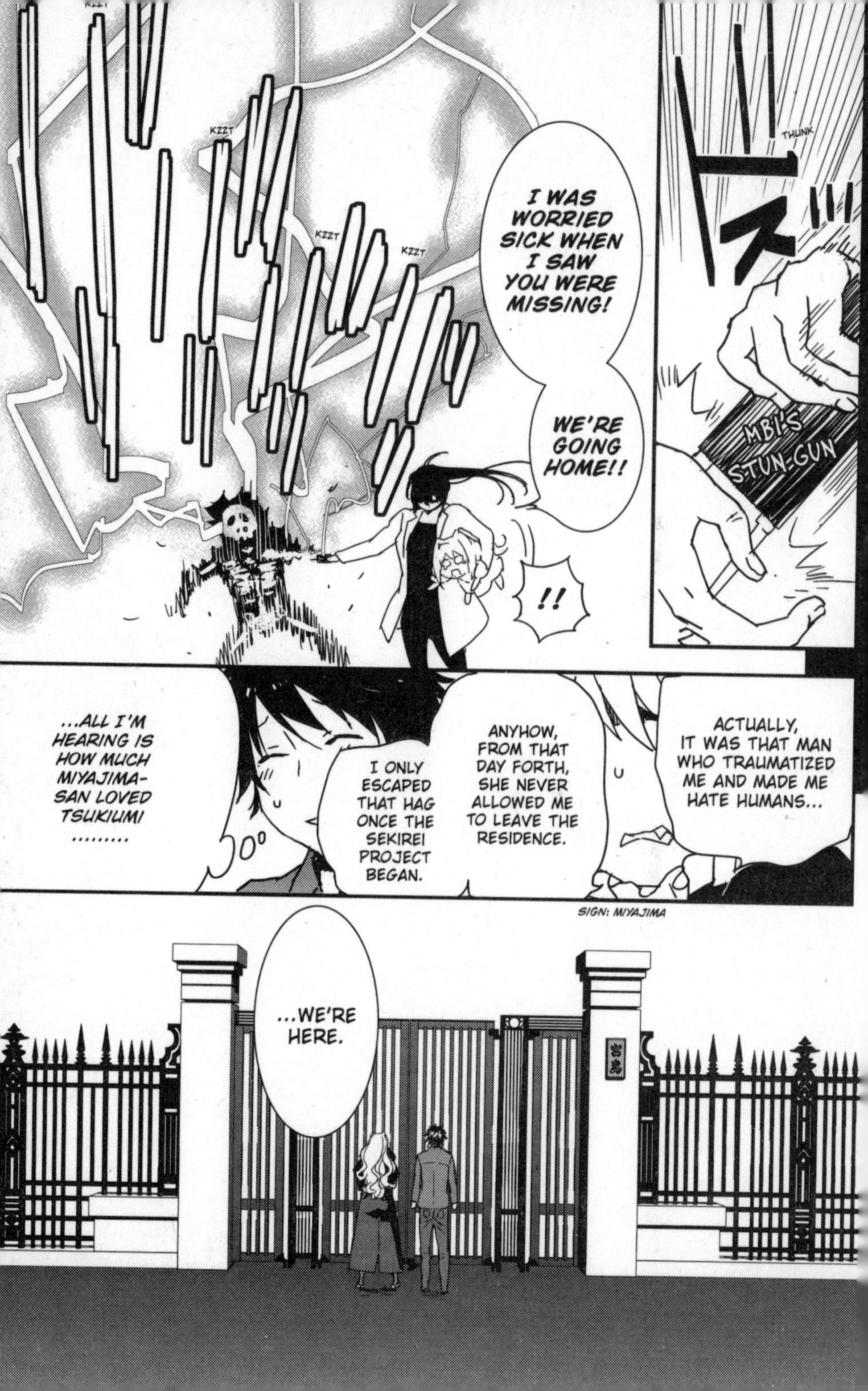
THUNK
MBI'S STUN-GUN
KZZT
KZZT
KZZT
I WAS WORRIED SICK WHEN I SAW YOU WERE MISSING!
WE'RE GOING HOME!!
!!
ACTUALLY, IT WAS THAT MAN WHO TRAUMATIZED ME AND MADE ME HATE HUMANS...
ANYHOW, FROM THAT DAY FORTH, SHE NEVER ALLOWED ME TO LEAVE THE RESIDENCE.
I ONLY ESCAPED THAT HAG ONCE THE SEKIREI PROJECT BEGAN.
...ALL I'M HEARING IS HOW MUCH MIYAJIMA-SAN LOVED TSUKIUMI ....
SIGN: MIYAJIMA
...WE'RE HERE.

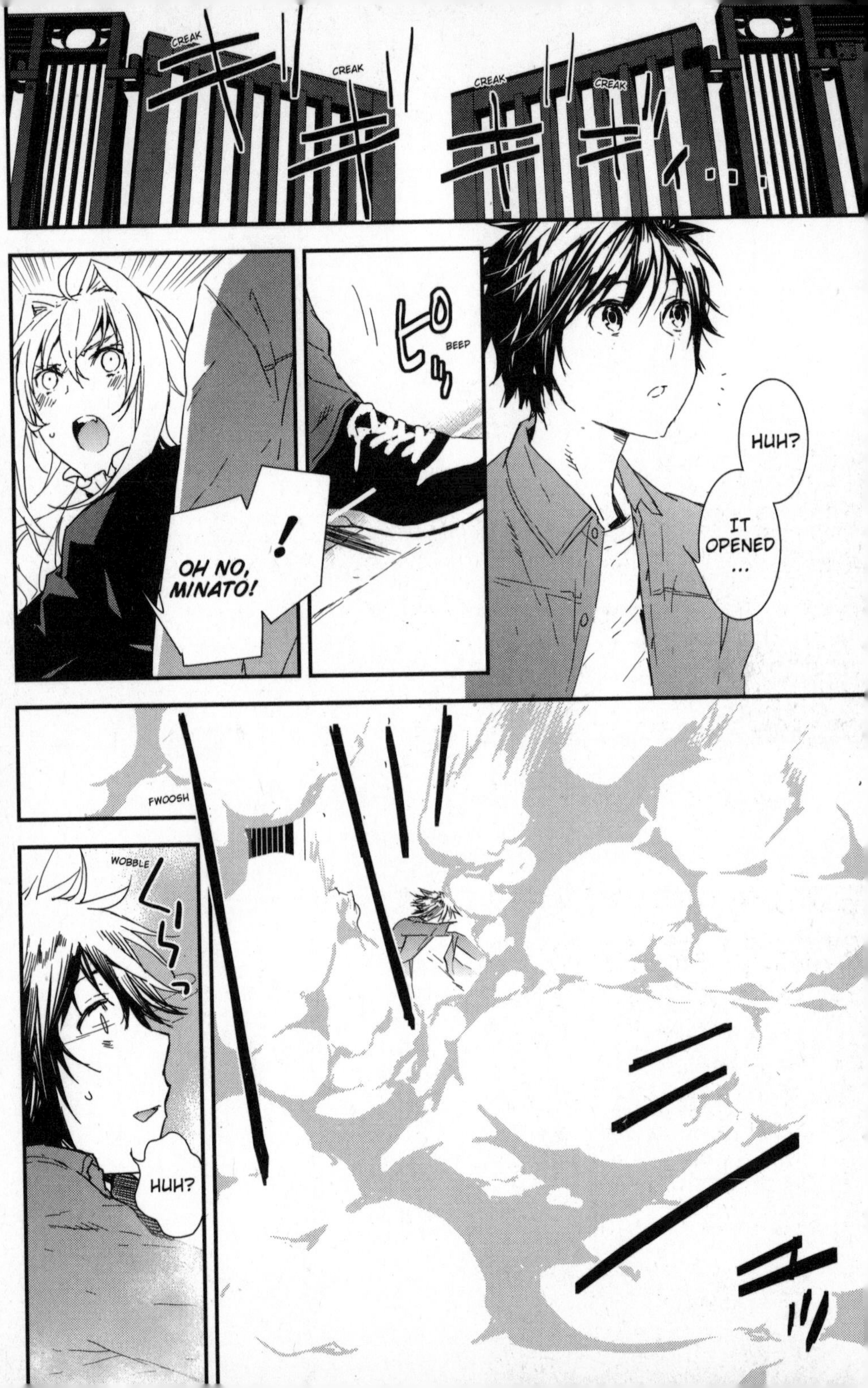
CREAK
CREAK
CREAK
CREAK
HUH?
IT OPENED ...
BEEP
!
OH NO, MINATO!
FWOOSH
WOBBLE
HUH?

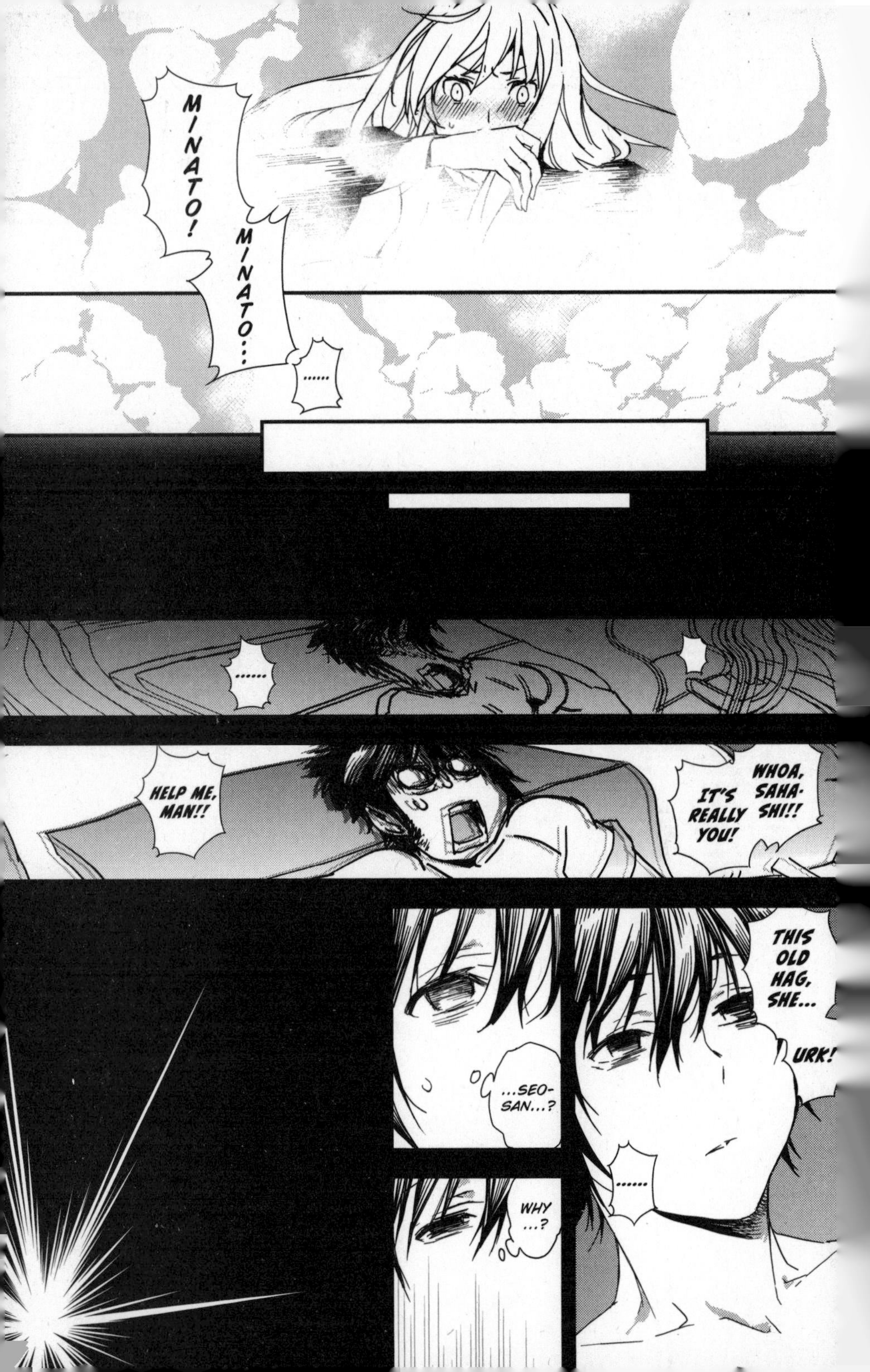
MINATO!
MINATO...
......
......
WHOA, SAHASHI!!
IT'S REALLY YOU!
HELP ME, MAN!!
THIS OLD HAG, SHE...
URK!
......
...SEO-SAN...?
WHY...?

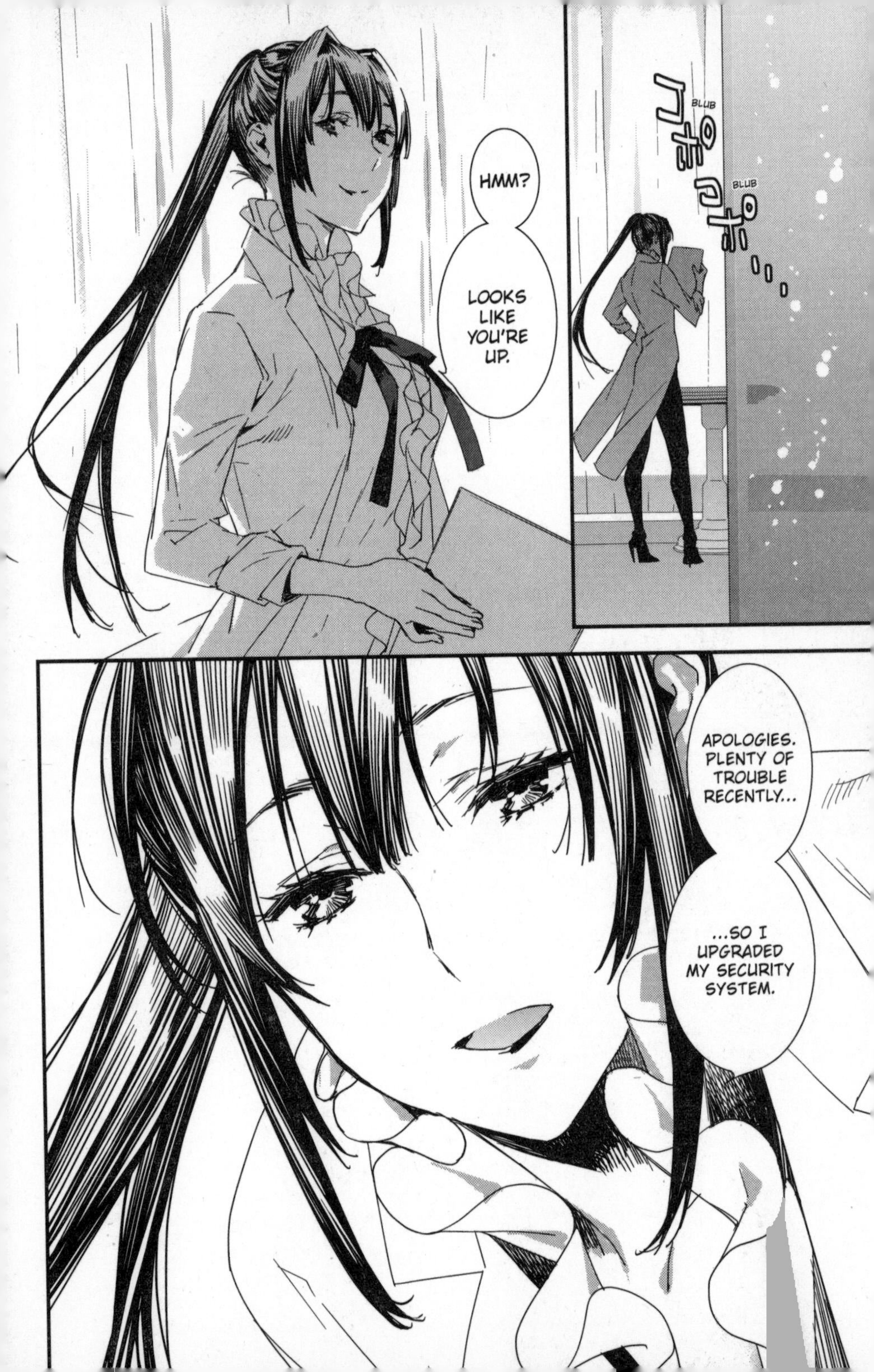
BLUB
BLUB
HMM?
LOOKS LIKE YOU'RE UP.
APOLOGIES. PLENTY OF TROUBLE RECENTLY...
...SO I UPGRADED MY SECURITY SYSTEM.

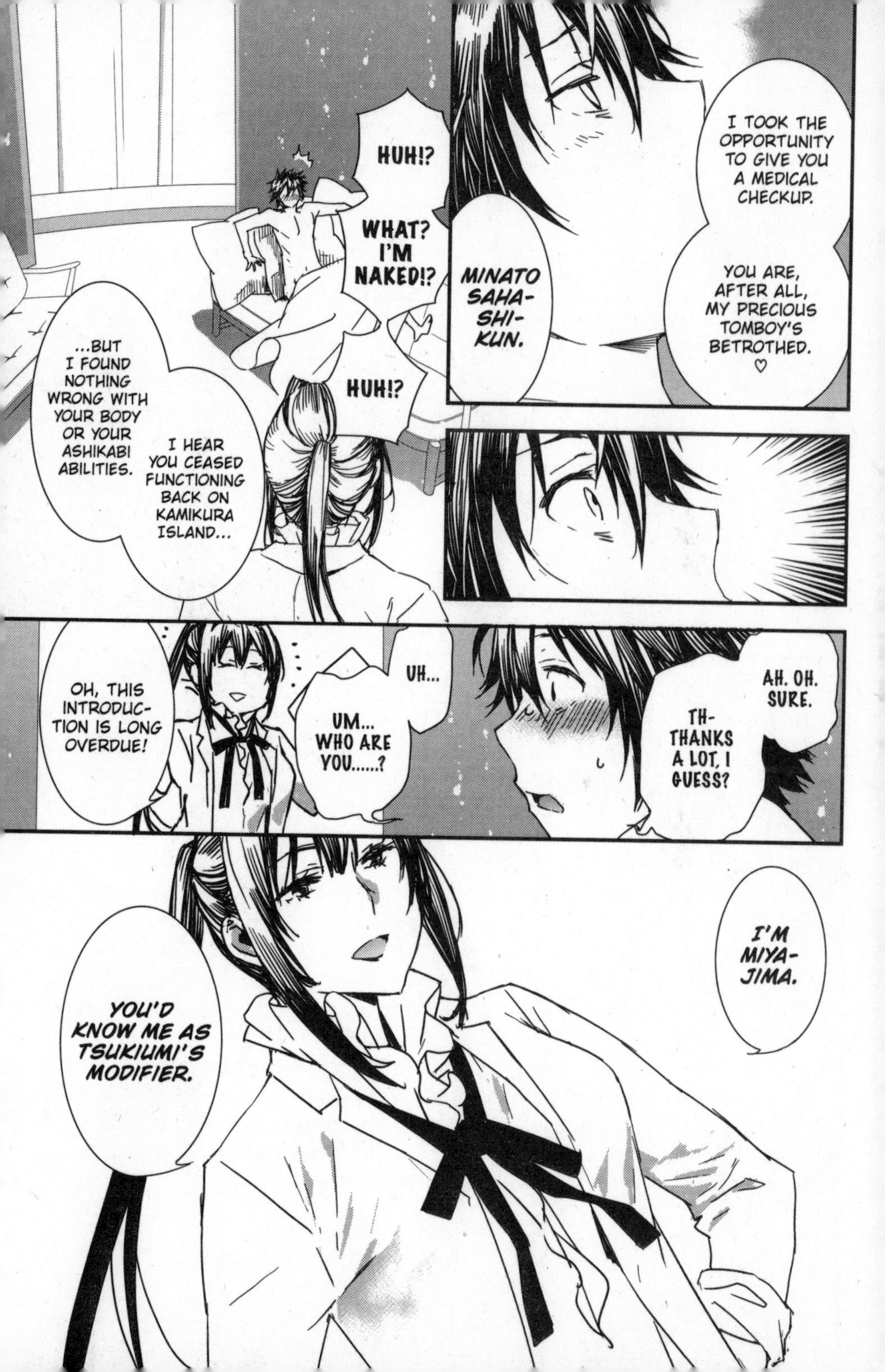

I TOOK THE OPPORTUNITY TO GIVE YOU A MEDICAL CHECKUP.
YOU ARE, AFTER ALL, MY PRECIOUS TOMBOY'S BETROTHED. ♡
MINATO SAHA-SHI-KUN.
HUH!?
WHAT? I'M NAKED!?
HUH!?
I HEAR YOU CEASED FUNCTIONING BACK ON KAMIKURA ISLAND...
...BUT I FOUND NOTHING WRONG WITH YOUR BODY OR YOUR ASHIKABI ABILITIES.
AH. OH. SURE.
TH-THANKS A LOT, I GUESS?
UH...
UM... WHO ARE YOU......?
OH, THIS INTRODUCTION IS LONG OVERDUE!
I'M MIYA-JIMA.
YOU'D KNOW ME AS TSUKIUMI'S MODIFIER.

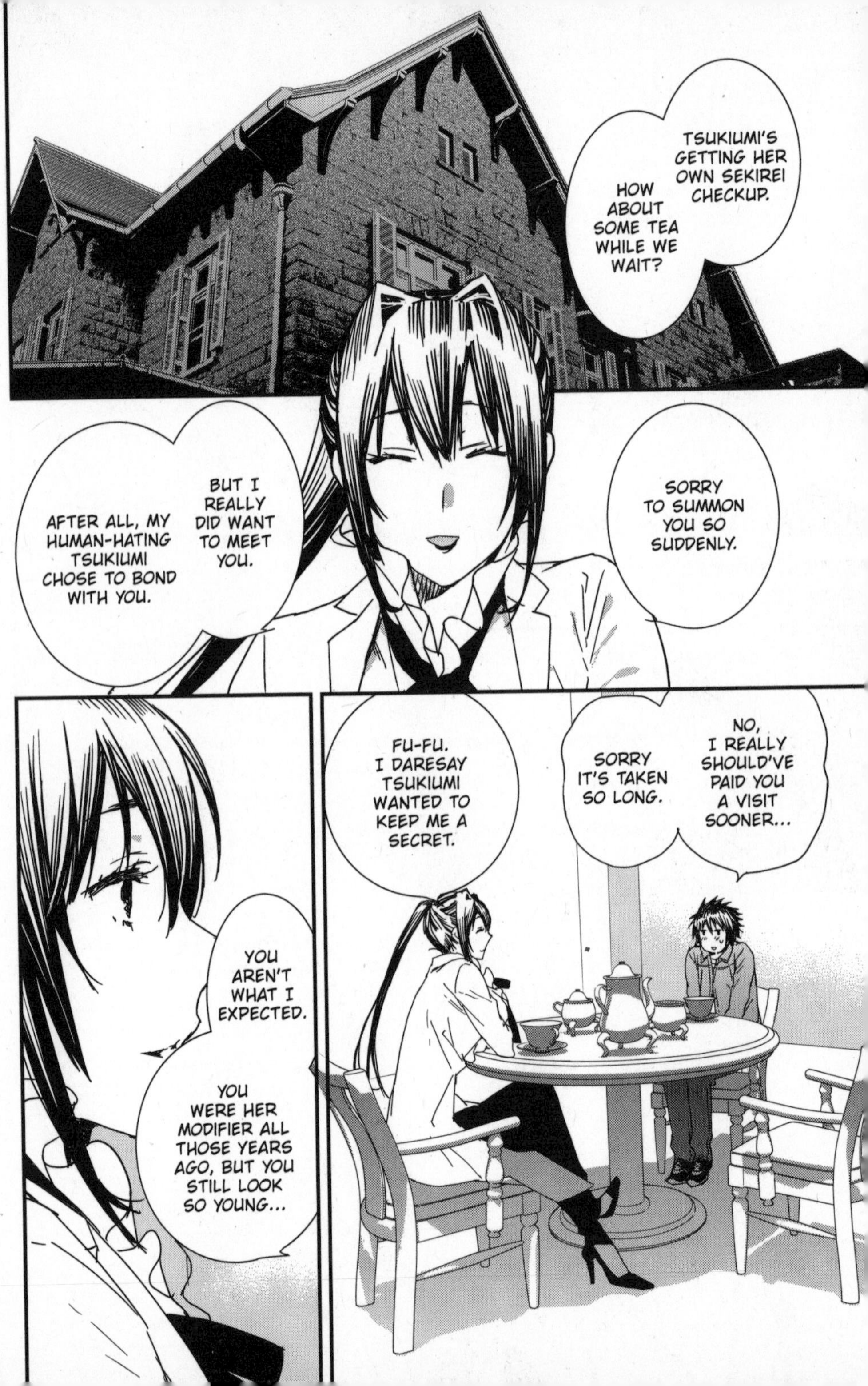
TSUKIUMI'S GETTING HER OWN SEKIREI CHECKUP.
HOW ABOUT SOME TEA WHILE WE WAIT?
SORRY TO SUMMON YOU SO SUDDENLY.
BUT I REALLY DID WANT TO MEET YOU.
AFTER ALL, MY HUMAN-HATING TSUKIUMI CHOSE TO BOND WITH YOU.
NO, I REALLY SHOULD'VE PAID YOU A VISIT SOONER...
SORRY IT'S TAKEN SO LONG.
FU-FU. I DARESAY TSUKIUMI WANTED TO KEEP ME A SECRET.
YOU AREN'T WHAT I EXPECTED.
YOU WERE HER MODIFIER ALL THOSE YEARS AGO, BUT YOU STILL LOOK SO YOUNG...

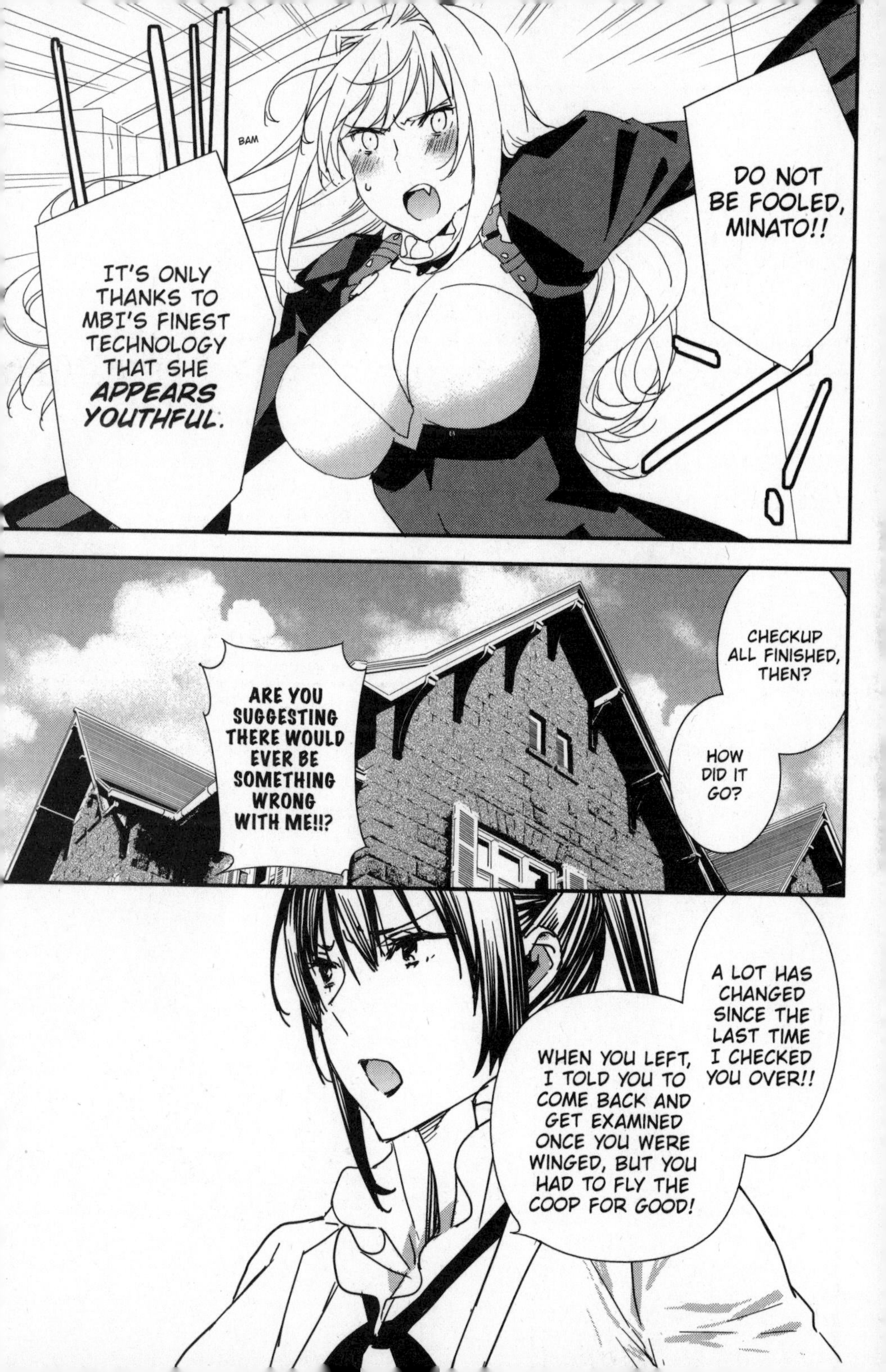
DO NOT BE FOOLED, MINATO!!
BAM
IT'S ONLY THANKS TO MBI'S FINEST TECHNOLOGY THAT SHE APPEARS YOUTHFUL.
CHECKUP ALL FINISHED, THEN?
HOW DID IT GO?
ARE YOU SUGGESTING THERE WOULD EVER BE SOMETHING WRONG WITH ME!!?
A LOT HAS CHANGED SINCE THE LAST TIME I CHECKED YOU OVER!!
WHEN YOU LEFT, I TOLD YOU TO COME BACK AND GET EXAMINED ONCE YOU WERE WINGED, BUT YOU HAD TO FLY THE COOP FOR GOOD!

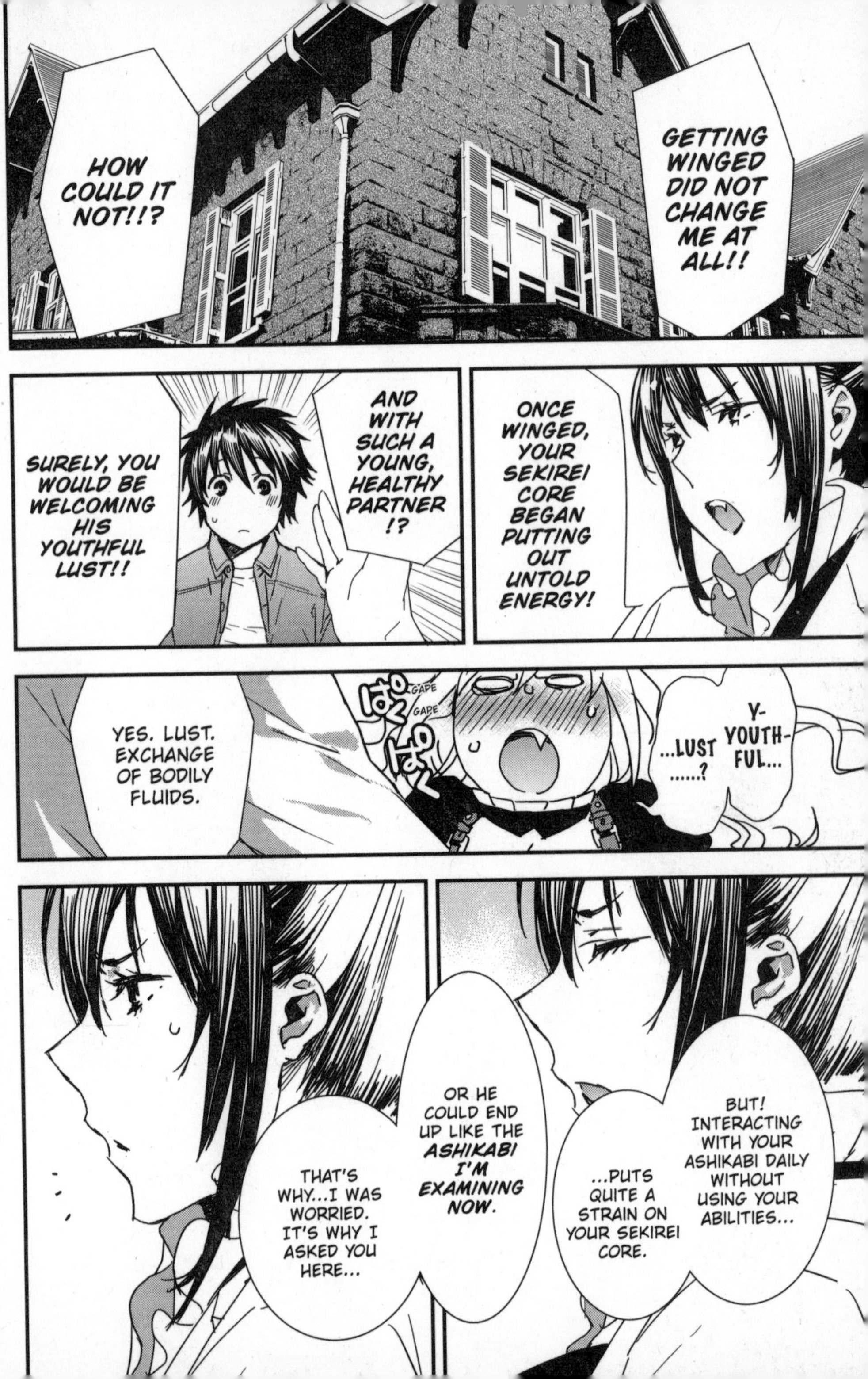
GETTING WINGED DID NOT CHANGE ME AT ALL!!
HOW COULD IT NOT!!?
ONCE WINGED, YOUR SEKIREI CORE BEGAN PUTTING OUT UNTOLD ENERGY!
AND WITH SUCH A YOUNG, HEALTHY PARTNER!?
SURELY, YOU WOULD BE WELCOMING HIS YOUTHFUL LUST!!
Y-YOUTH-FUL...
...LUST ......?
ぱくぱく
GAPE GAPE
YES. LUST. EXCHANGE OF BODILY FLUIDS.
BUT! INTERACTING WITH YOUR ASHIKABI DAILY WITHOUT USING YOUR ABILITIES...
...PUTS QUITE A STRAIN ON YOUR SEKIREI CORE.
OR HE COULD END UP LIKE THE *ASHIKABI I'M EXAMINING NOW*.
THAT'S WHY...I WAS WORRIED. IT'S WHY I ASKED YOU HERE...

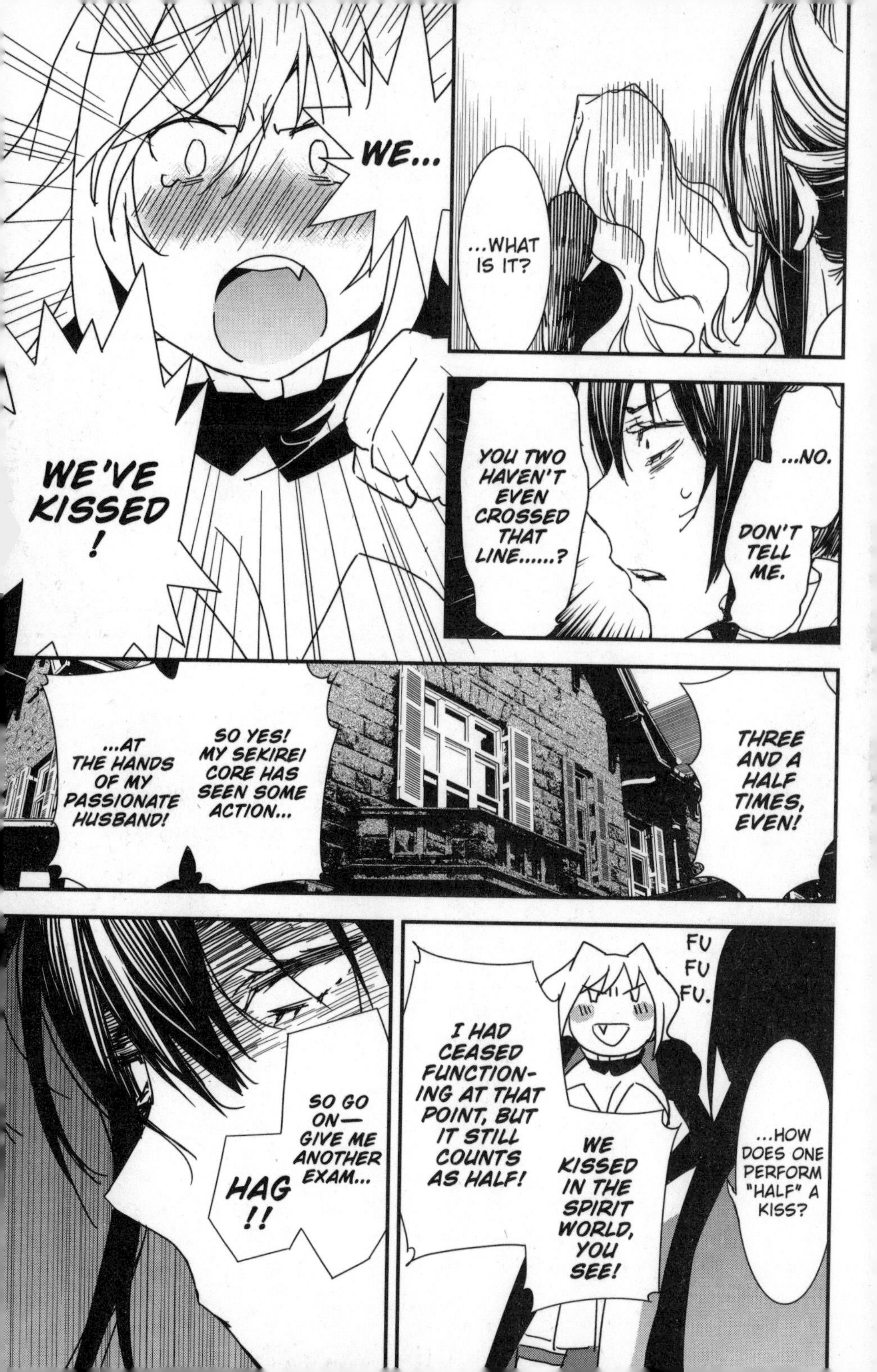
...WHAT IS IT?
...NO.
DON'T TELL ME.
YOU TWO HAVEN'T EVEN CROSSED THAT LINE......?
WE...
WE'VE KISSED!
THREE AND A HALF TIMES, EVEN!
SO YES! MY SEKIREI CORE HAS SEEN SOME ACTION...
...AT THE HANDS OF MY PASSIONATE HUSBAND!
FU FU FU.
...HOW DOES ONE PERFORM "HALF" A KISS?
WE KISSED IN THE SPIRIT WORLD, YOU SEE!
I HAD CEASED FUNCTION-ING AT THAT POINT, BUT IT STILL COUNTS AS HALF!
SO GO ON— GIVE ME ANOTHER EXAM...
HAG!!

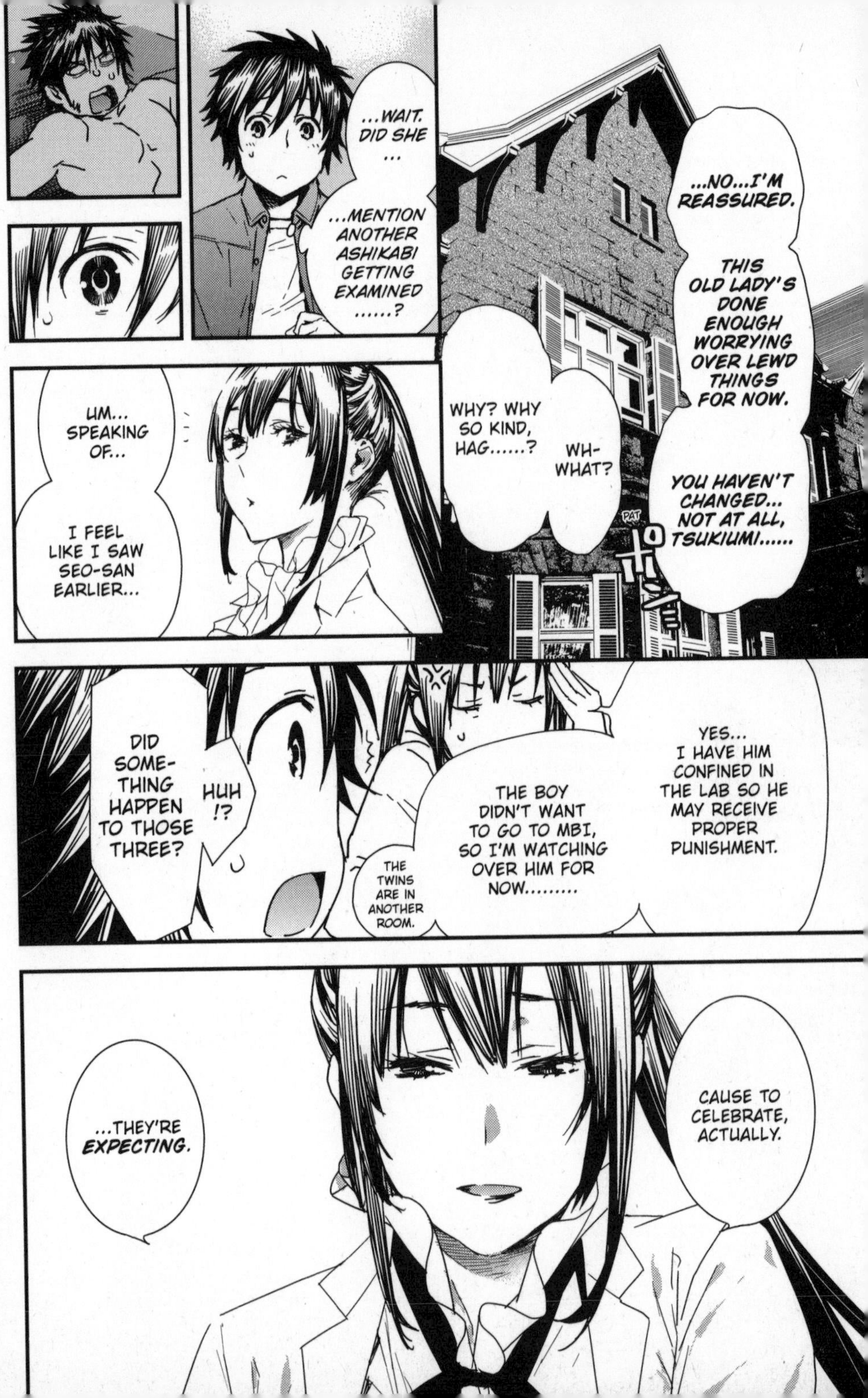

...NO...I'M REASSURED.
THIS OLD LADY'S DONE ENOUGH WORRYING OVER LEWD THINGS FOR NOW.
YOU HAVEN'T CHANGED... NOT AT ALL, TSUKIUMI......
PAT
WH-WHAT?
WHY? WHY SO KIND, HAG......?
...WAIT. DID SHE ...
...MENTION ANOTHER ASHIKABI GETTING EXAMINED......?
UM... SPEAKING OF...
I FEEL LIKE I SAW SEO-SAN EARLIER...
YES... I HAVE HIM CONFINED IN THE LAB SO HE MAY RECEIVE PROPER PUNISHMENT.
THE BOY DIDN'T WANT TO GO TO MBI, SO I'M WATCHING OVER HIM FOR NOW.........
THE TWINS ARE IN ANOTHER ROOM.
HUH !?
DID SOME-THING HAPPEN TO THOSE THREE?
CAUSE TO CELEBRATE, ACTUALLY.
...THEY'RE *EXPECTING*.

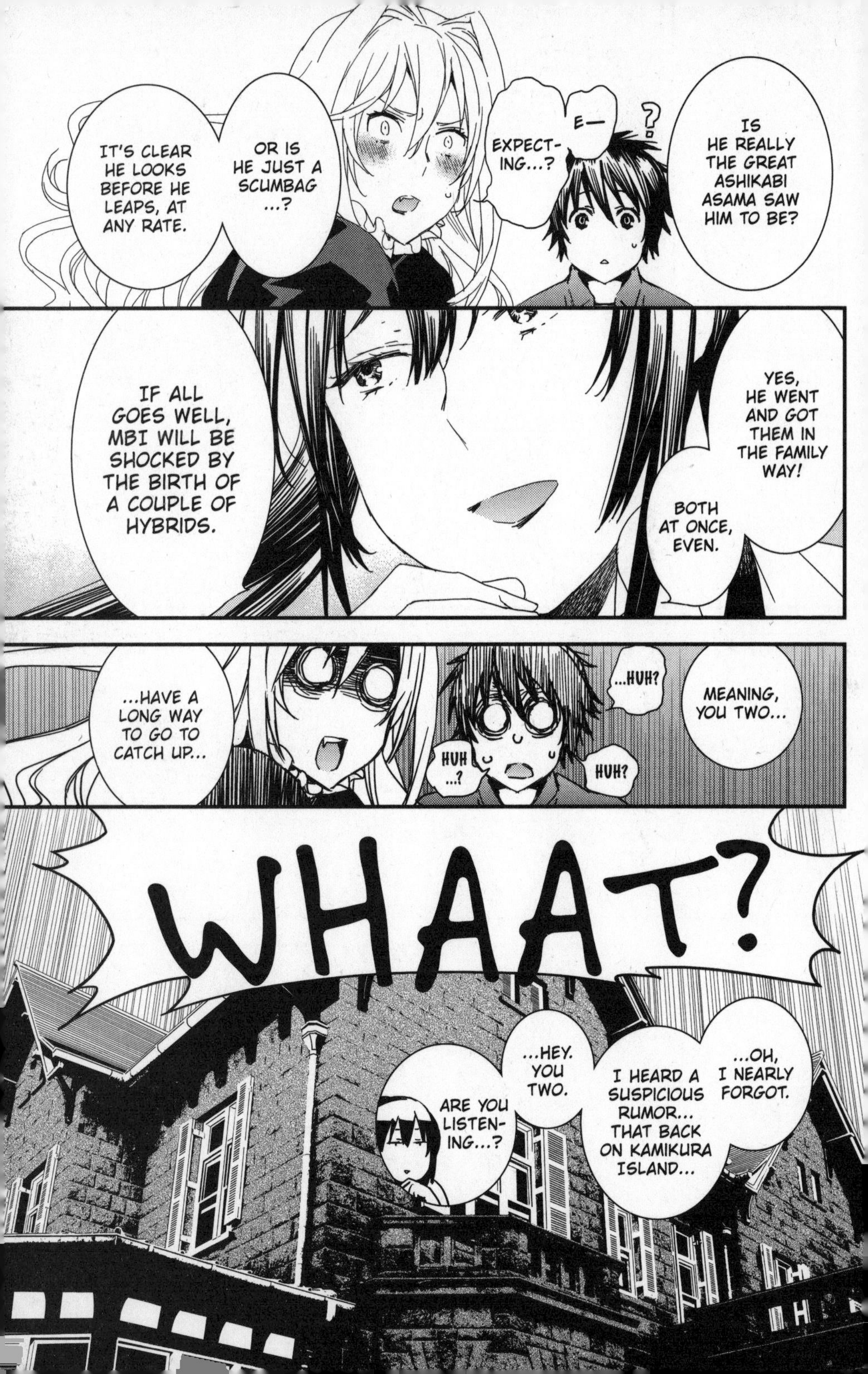
IS HE REALLY THE GREAT ASHIKABI ASAMA SAW HIM TO BE?
E—
EXPECTING...?
OR IS HE JUST A SCUMBAG ...?
IT'S CLEAR HE LOOKS BEFORE HE LEAPS, AT ANY RATE.
YES, HE WENT AND GOT THEM IN THE FAMILY WAY!
BOTH AT ONCE, EVEN.
IF ALL GOES WELL, MBI WILL BE SHOCKED BY THE BIRTH OF A COUPLE OF HYBRIDS.
MEANING, YOU TWO...
...HUH?
HUH?
HUH ...?
...HAVE A LONG WAY TO GO TO CATCH UP...
WHAAT?
...OH, I NEARLY FORGOT.
I HEARD A SUSPICIOUS RUMOR... THAT BACK ON KAMIKURA ISLAND...
...HEY. YOU TWO.
ARE YOU LISTENING...?

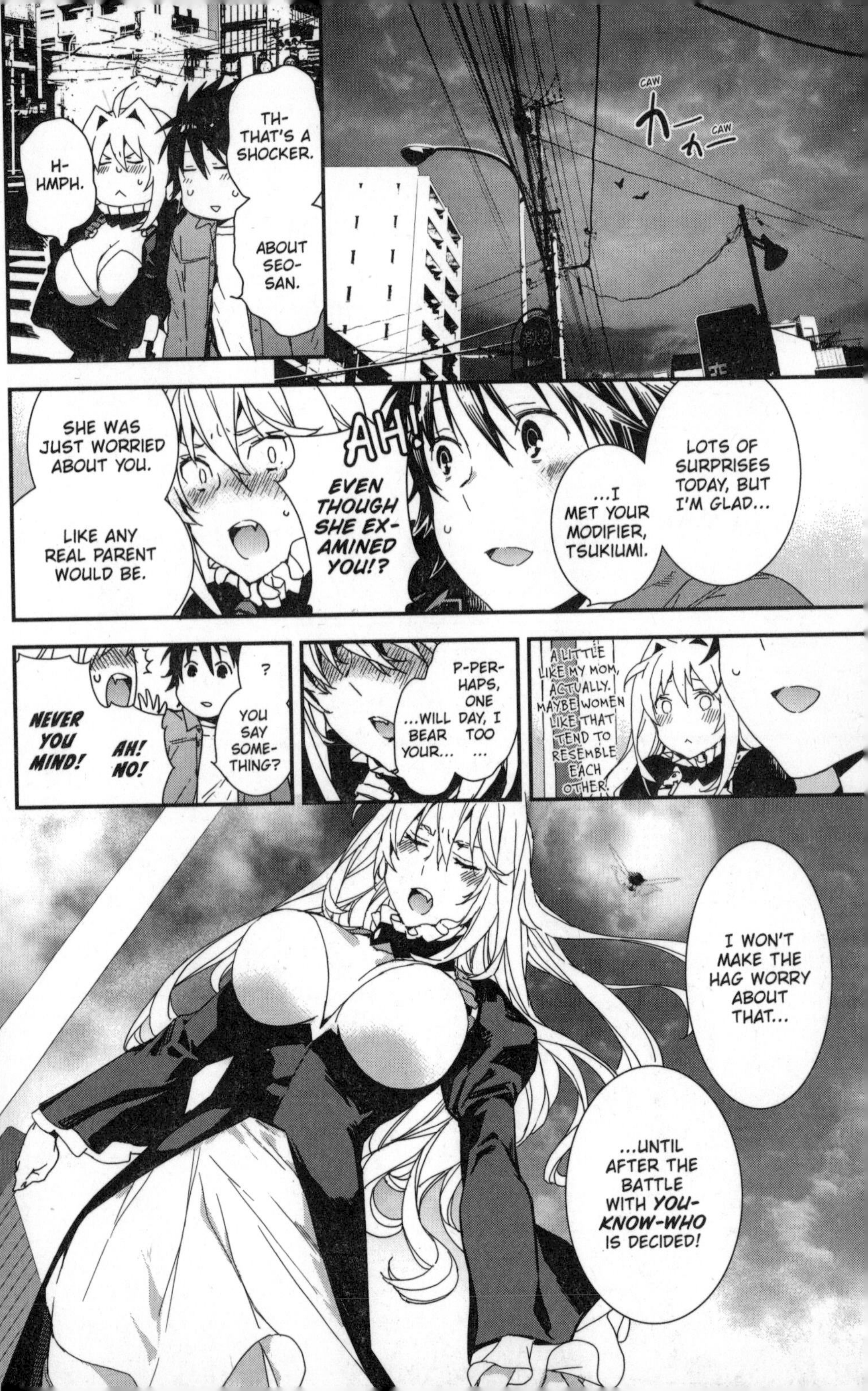
CAW
CAW
TH- THAT'S A SHOCKER.
ABOUT SEO-SAN.
H- HMPH.
LOTS OF SURPRISES TODAY, BUT I'M GLAD...
...I MET YOUR MODIFIER, TSUKIUMI.
AH!
EVEN THOUGH SHE EXAMINED YOU!?
SHE WAS JUST WORRIED ABOUT YOU.
LIKE ANY REAL PARENT WOULD BE.
A LITTLE LIKE MY MOM, ACTUALLY. MAYBE WOMEN LIKE THAT TEND TO RESEMBLE EACH OTHER.
P-PERHAPS, ONE DAY, I TOO ...
...WILL BEAR YOUR...
?
YOU SAY SOMETHING?
AH! NO!
NEVER YOU MIND!
I WON'T MAKE THE HAG WORRY ABOUT THAT...
...UNTIL AFTER THE BATTLE WITH YOU-KNOW-WHO IS DECIDED!

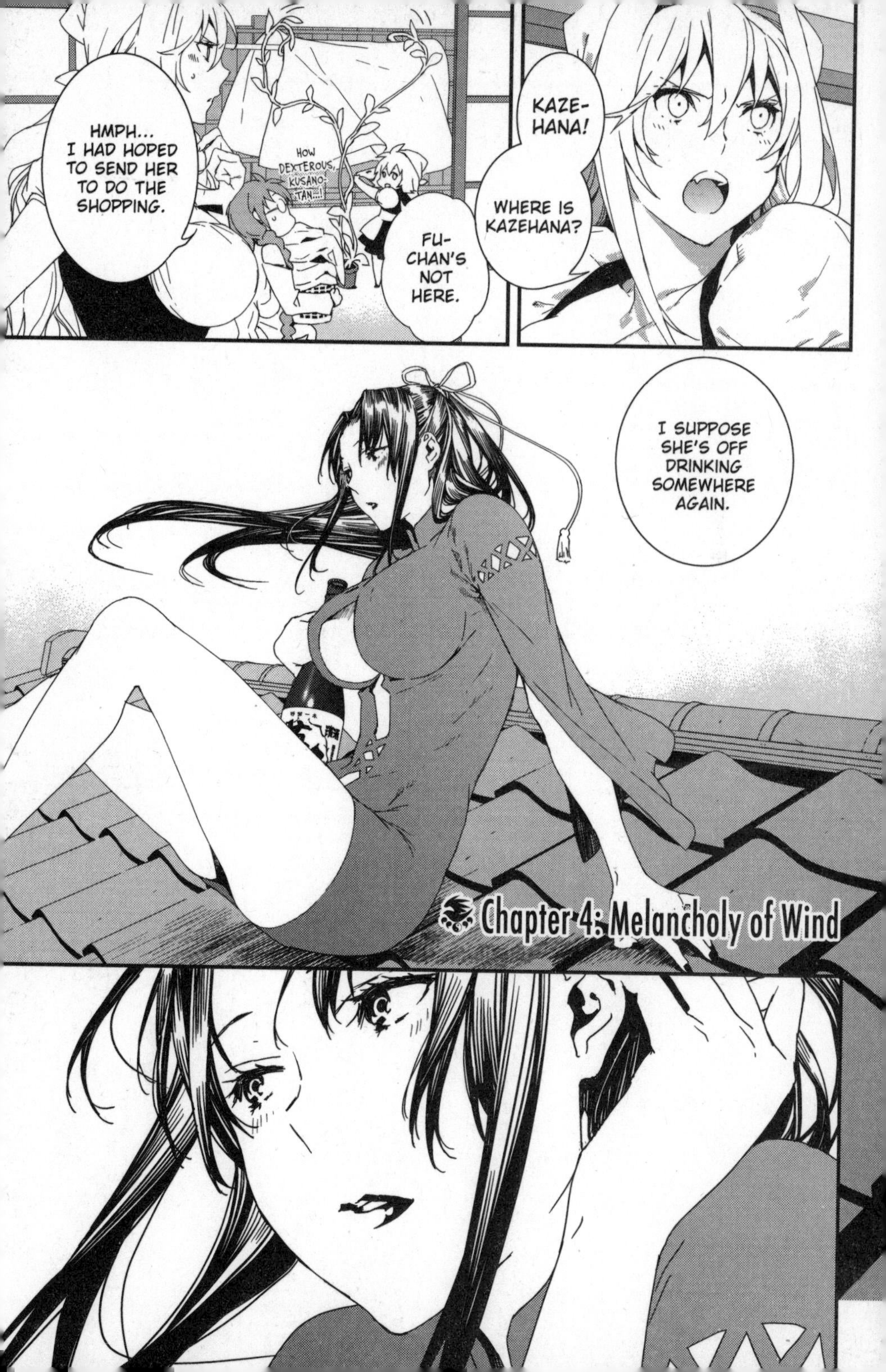
KAZE-HANA!
WHERE IS KAZEHANA?
FU-CHAN'S NOT HERE.
HOW DEXTEROUS, KUSANO-TAN...!
HMPH... I HAD HOPED TO SEND HER TO DO THE SHOPPING.
I SUPPOSE SHE'S OFF DRINKING SOMEWHERE AGAIN.

Chapter 4: Melancholy of Wind

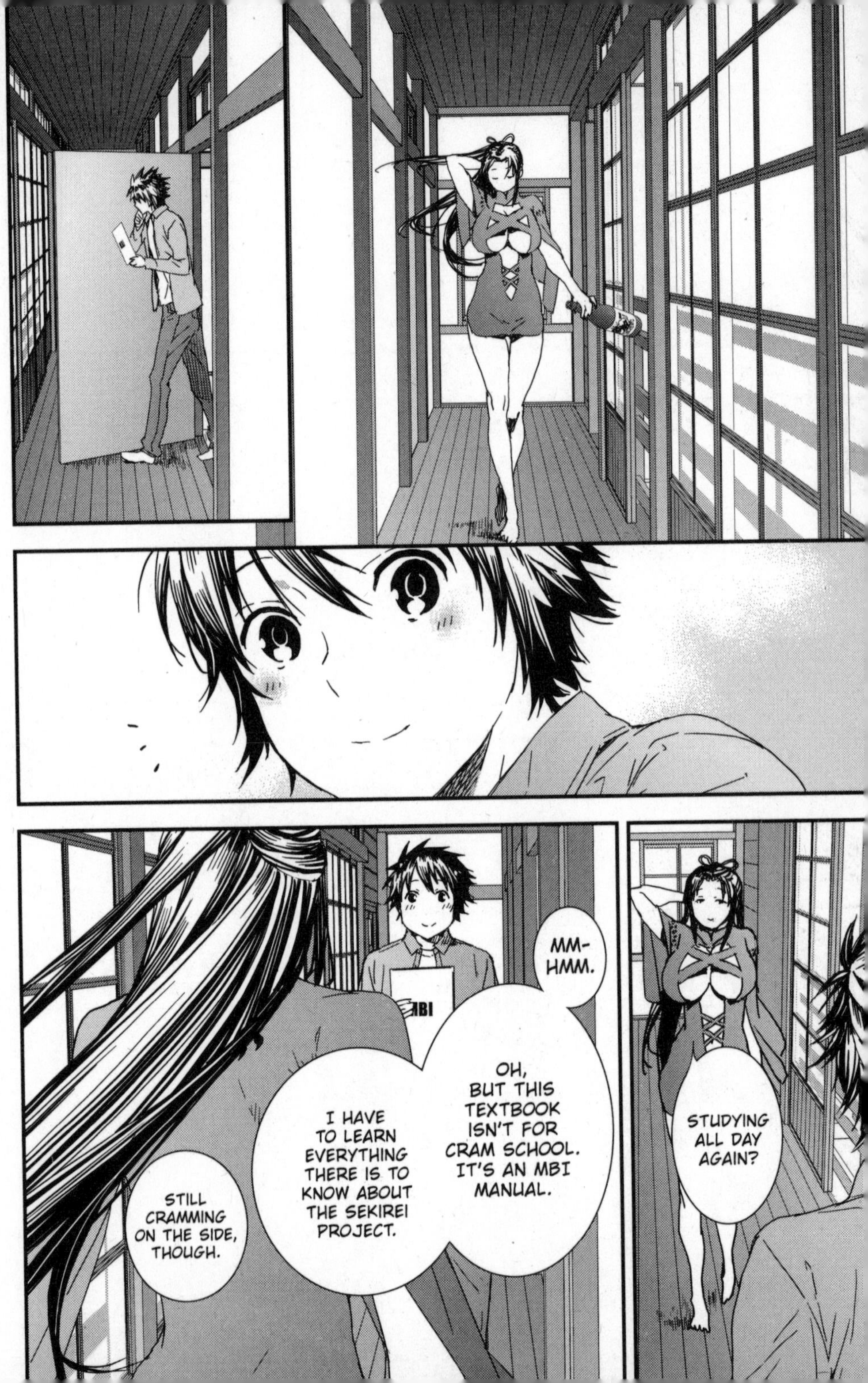
STUDYING ALL DAY AGAIN?
MM-HMM.
OH, BUT THIS TEXTBOOK ISN'T FOR CRAM SCHOOL. IT'S AN MBI MANUAL.
I HAVE TO LEARN EVERYTHING THERE IS TO KNOW ABOUT THE SEKIREI PROJECT.
STILL CRAMMING ON THE SIDE, THOUGH.

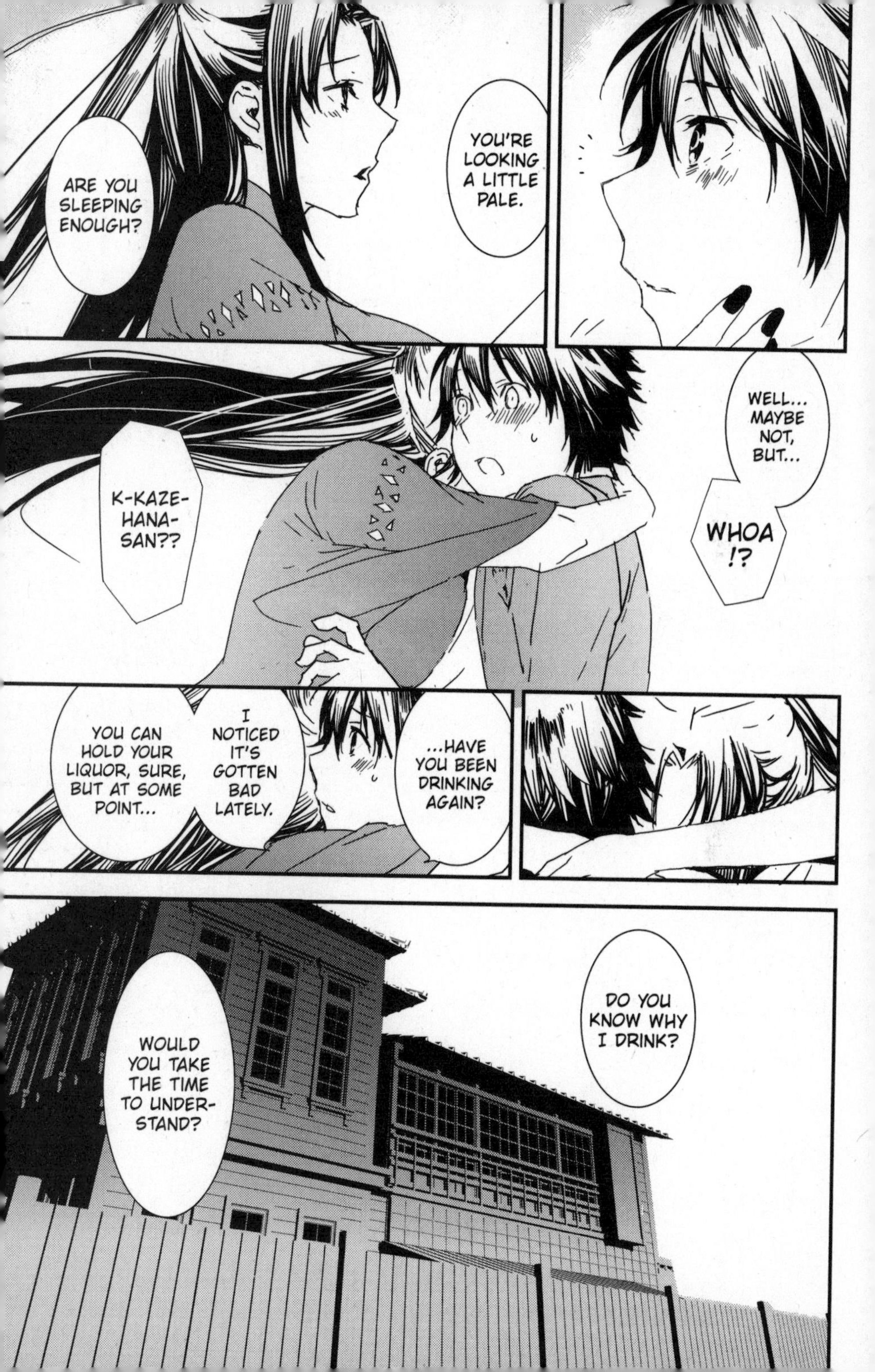
YOU'RE LOOKING A LITTLE PALE.
ARE YOU SLEEPING ENOUGH?
WELL... MAYBE NOT, BUT...
WHOA!?
K-KAZE-HANA-SAN??
...HAVE YOU BEEN DRINKING AGAIN?
I NOTICED IT'S GOTTEN BAD LATELY.
YOU CAN HOLD YOUR LIQUOR, SURE, BUT AT SOME POINT...
DO YOU KNOW WHY I DRINK?
WOULD YOU TAKE THE TIME TO UNDER-STAND?

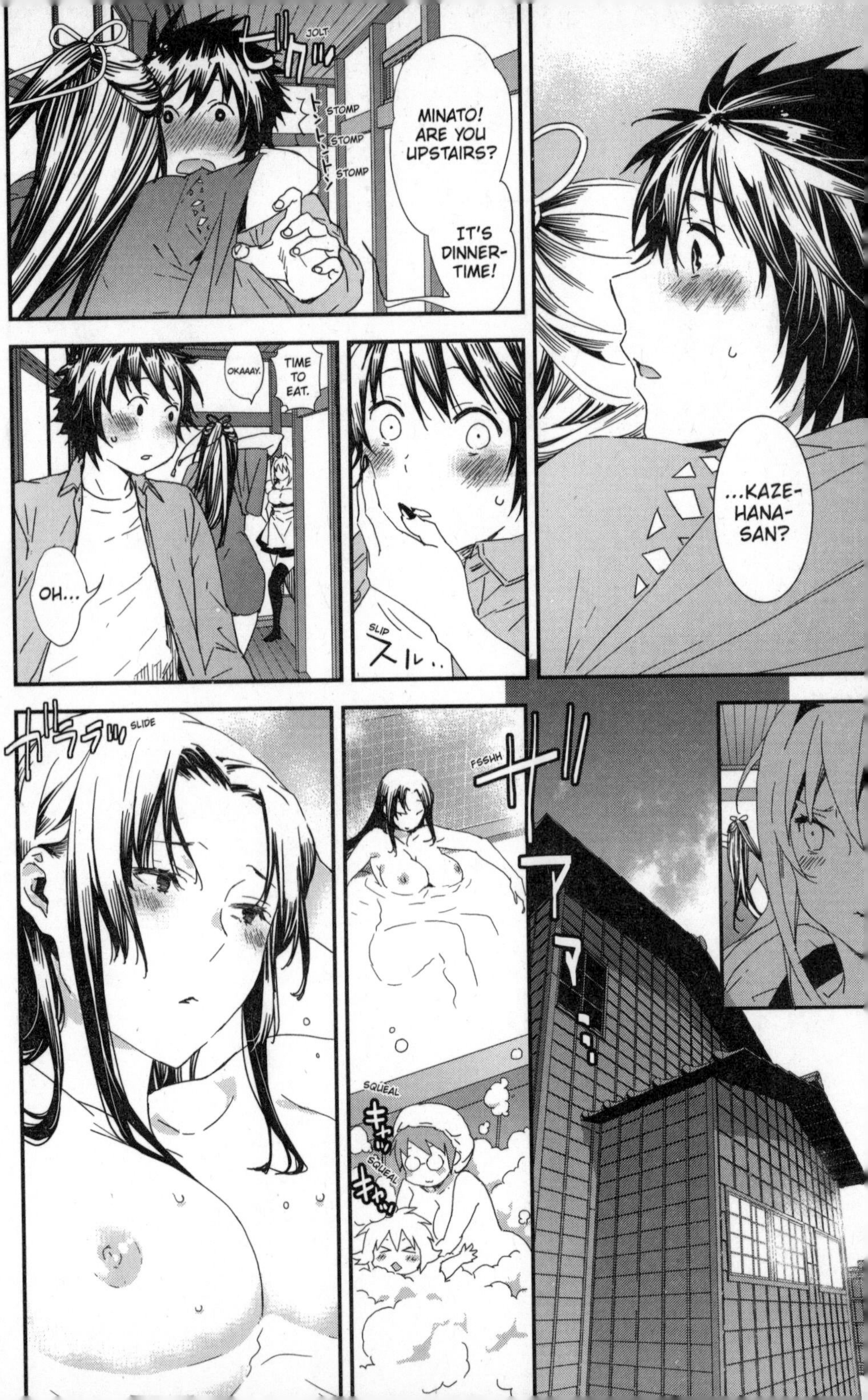
...KAZE-HANA-SAN?
JOLT
STOMP
STOMP
STOMP
MINATO! ARE YOU UPSTAIRS?
IT'S DINNER-TIME!
SLIP
TIME TO EAT.
OKAAAY.
OH...
FSSHH
SQUEAL
SQUEAL
SLIDE

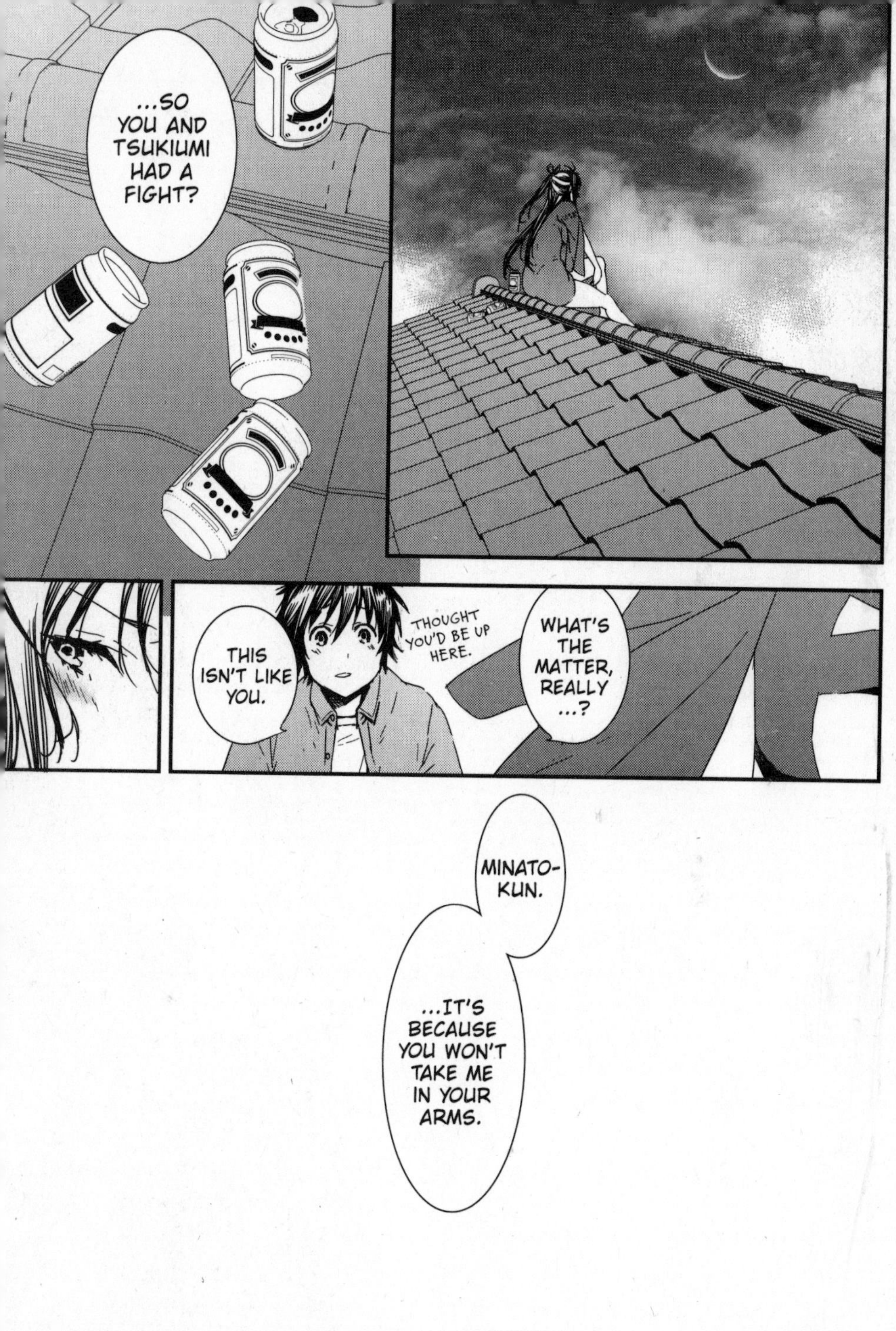
...SO YOU AND TSUKIUMI HAD A FIGHT?
WHAT'S THE MATTER, REALLY ...?
THOUGHT YOU'D BE UP HERE.
THIS ISN'T LIKE YOU.
MINATO-KUN.
...IT'S BECAUSE YOU WON'T TAKE ME IN YOUR ARMS.

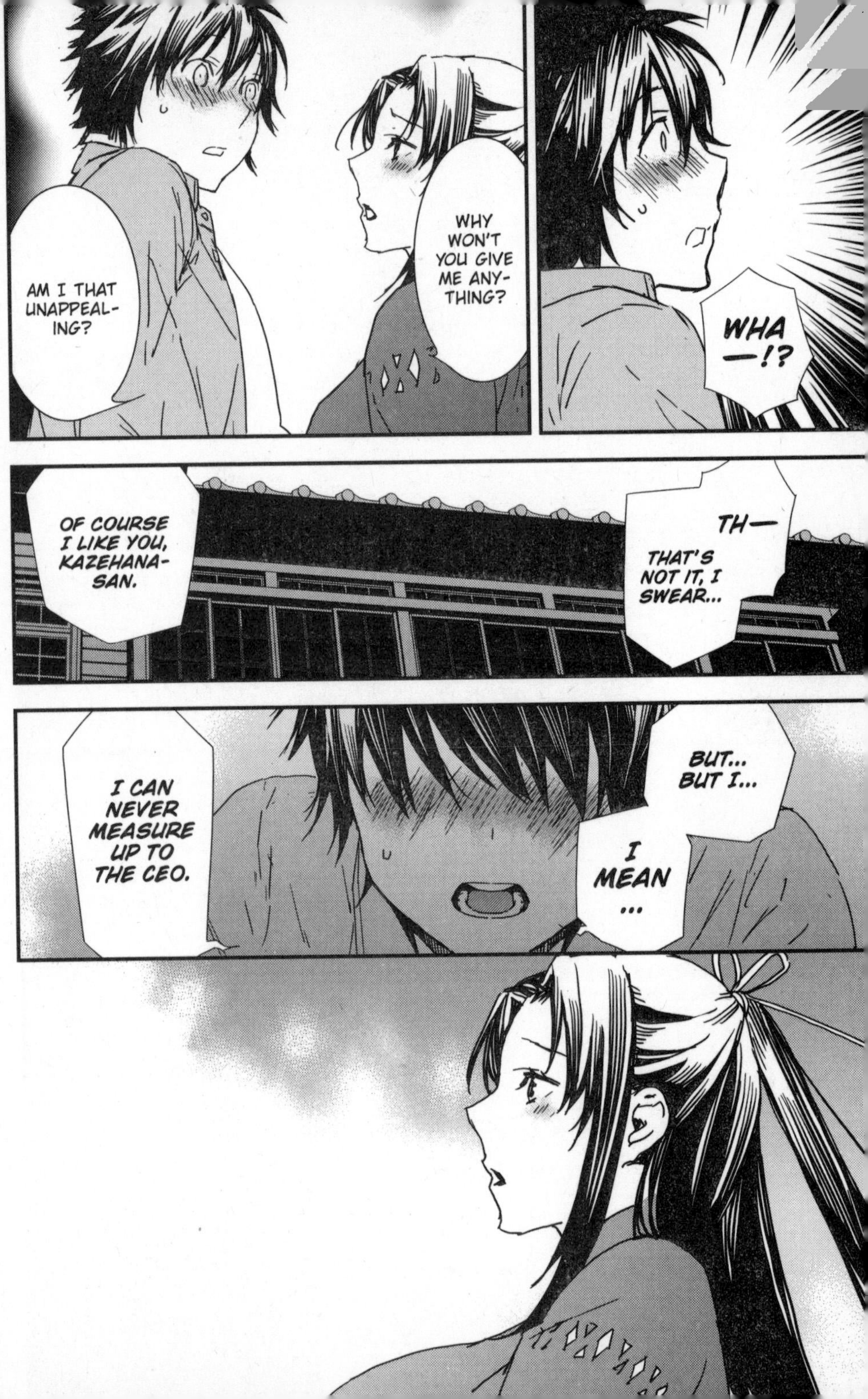
WHA—!?
WHY WON'T YOU GIVE ME ANYTHING?
AM I THAT UNAPPEALING?
TH—
THAT'S NOT IT, I SWEAR...
OF COURSE I LIKE YOU, KAZEHANA-SAN.
BUT... BUT I...
I MEAN...
I CAN NEVER MEASURE UP TO THE CEO.

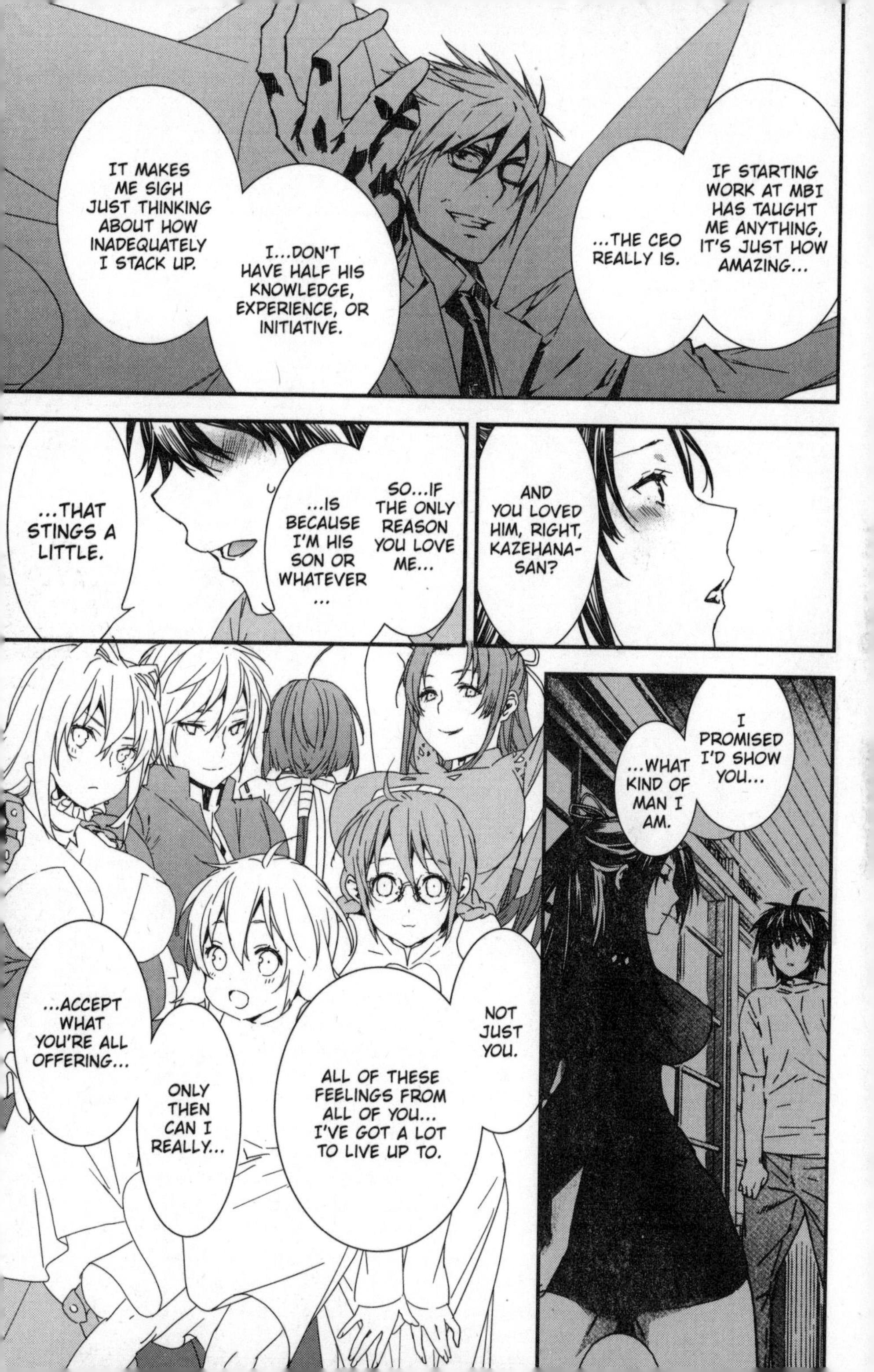
IF STARTING WORK AT MBI HAS TAUGHT ME ANYTHING, IT'S JUST HOW AMAZING...
...THE CEO REALLY IS.
I...DON'T HAVE HALF HIS KNOWLEDGE, EXPERIENCE, OR INITIATIVE.
IT MAKES ME SIGH JUST THINKING ABOUT HOW INADEQUATELY I STACK UP.
AND YOU LOVED HIM, RIGHT, KAZEHANA-SAN?
SO...IF THE ONLY REASON YOU LOVE ME...
...IS BECAUSE I'M HIS SON OR WHATEVER...
...THAT STINGS A LITTLE.
I PROMISED I'D SHOW YOU...
...WHAT KIND OF MAN I AM.
NOT JUST YOU.
ALL OF THESE FEELINGS FROM ALL OF YOU... I'VE GOT A LOT TO LIVE UP TO.
ONLY THEN CAN I REALLY...
...ACCEPT WHAT YOU'RE ALL OFFERING...

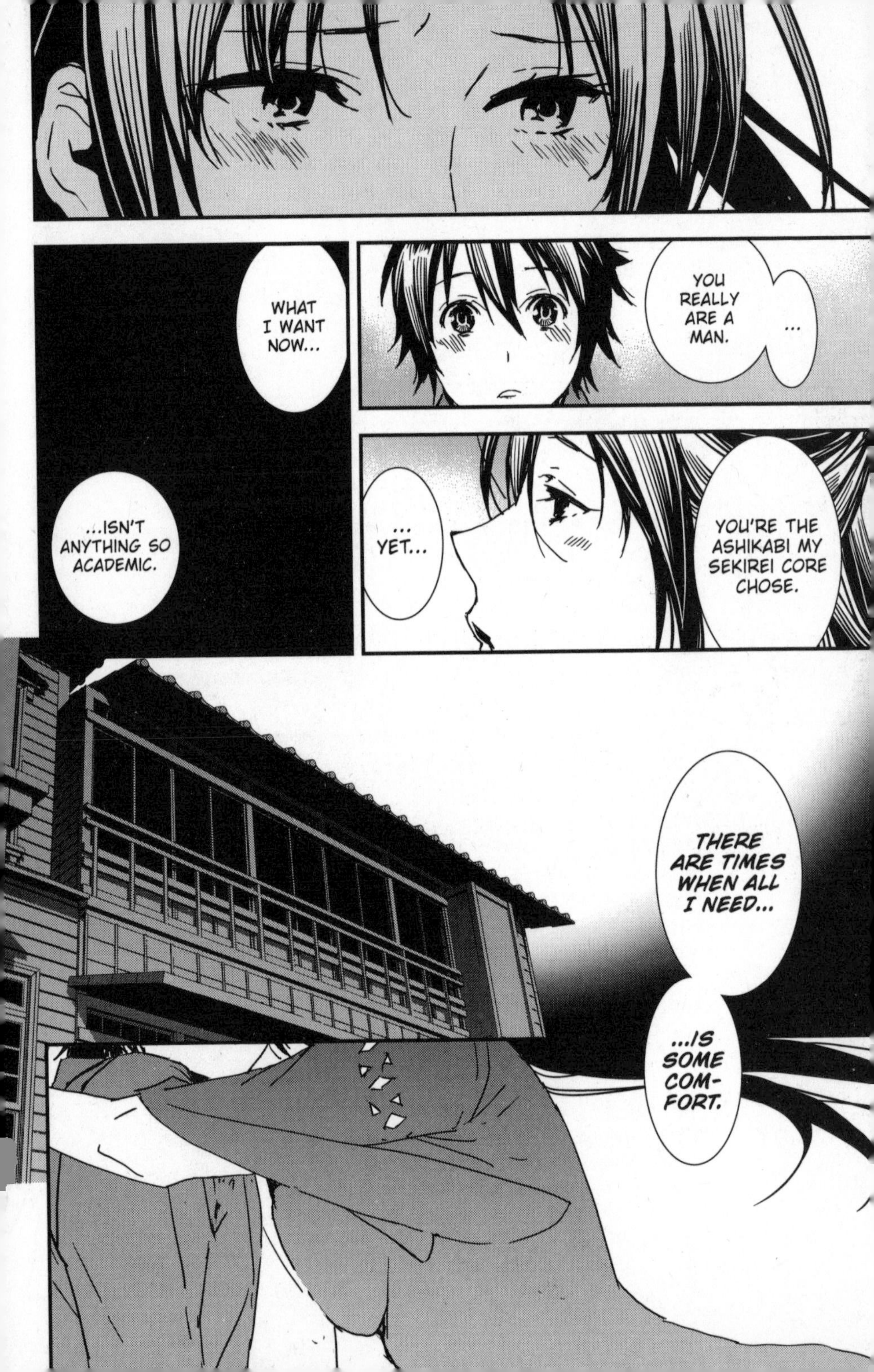
...
YOU REALLY ARE A MAN.
YOU'RE THE ASHIKABI MY SEKIREI CORE CHOSE.
... YET...
WHAT I WANT NOW...
...ISN'T ANYTHING SO ACADEMIC.
THERE ARE TIMES WHEN ALL I NEED...
...IS SOME COM-FORT.

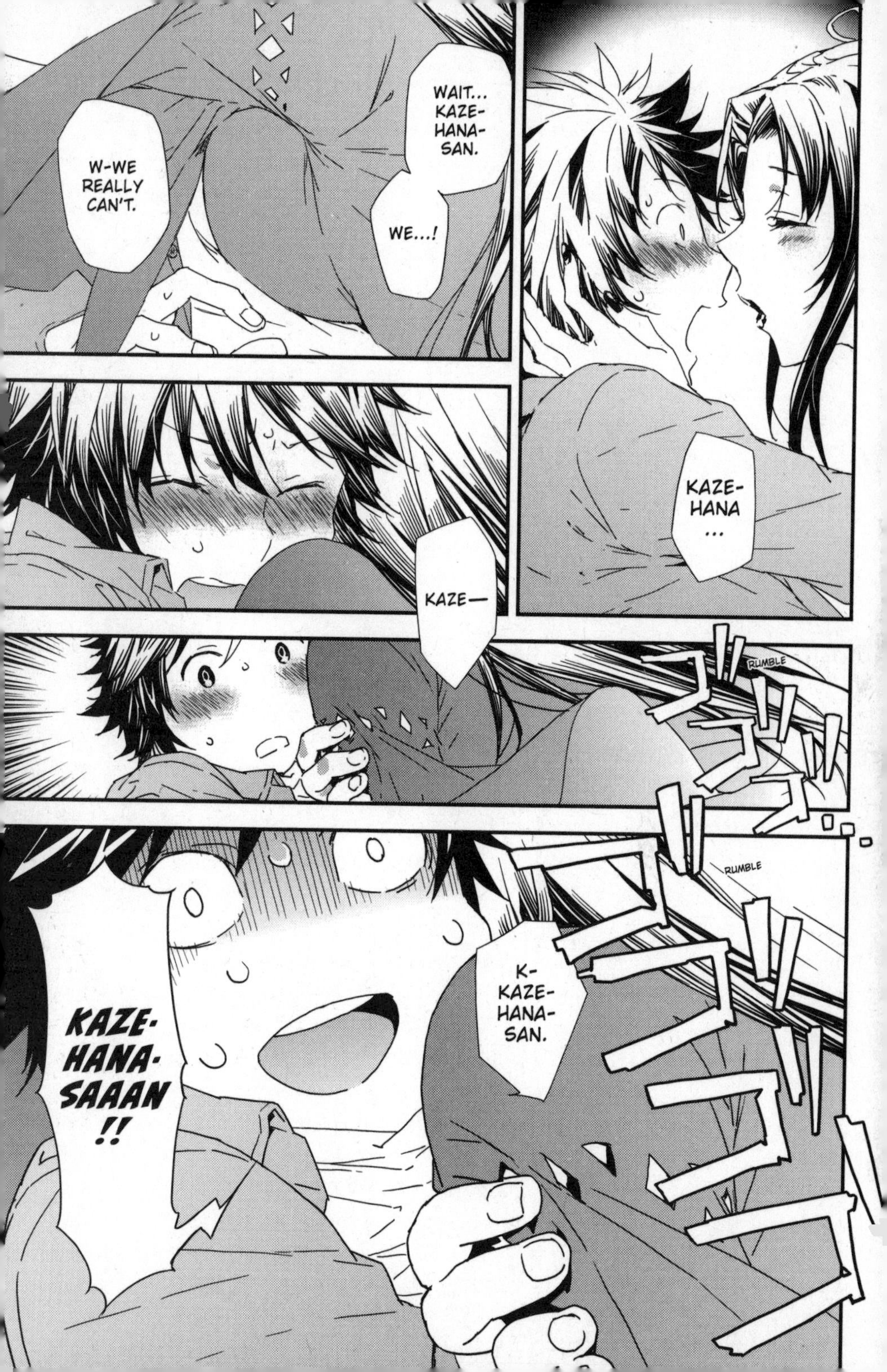
KAZE-HANA...
WAIT... KAZE-HANA-SAN.
W-WE REALLY CAN'T.
WE...!
KAZE—
RUMBLE
RUMBLE
K-KAZE-HANA-SAN.
KAZE-HANA-SAAAN!!

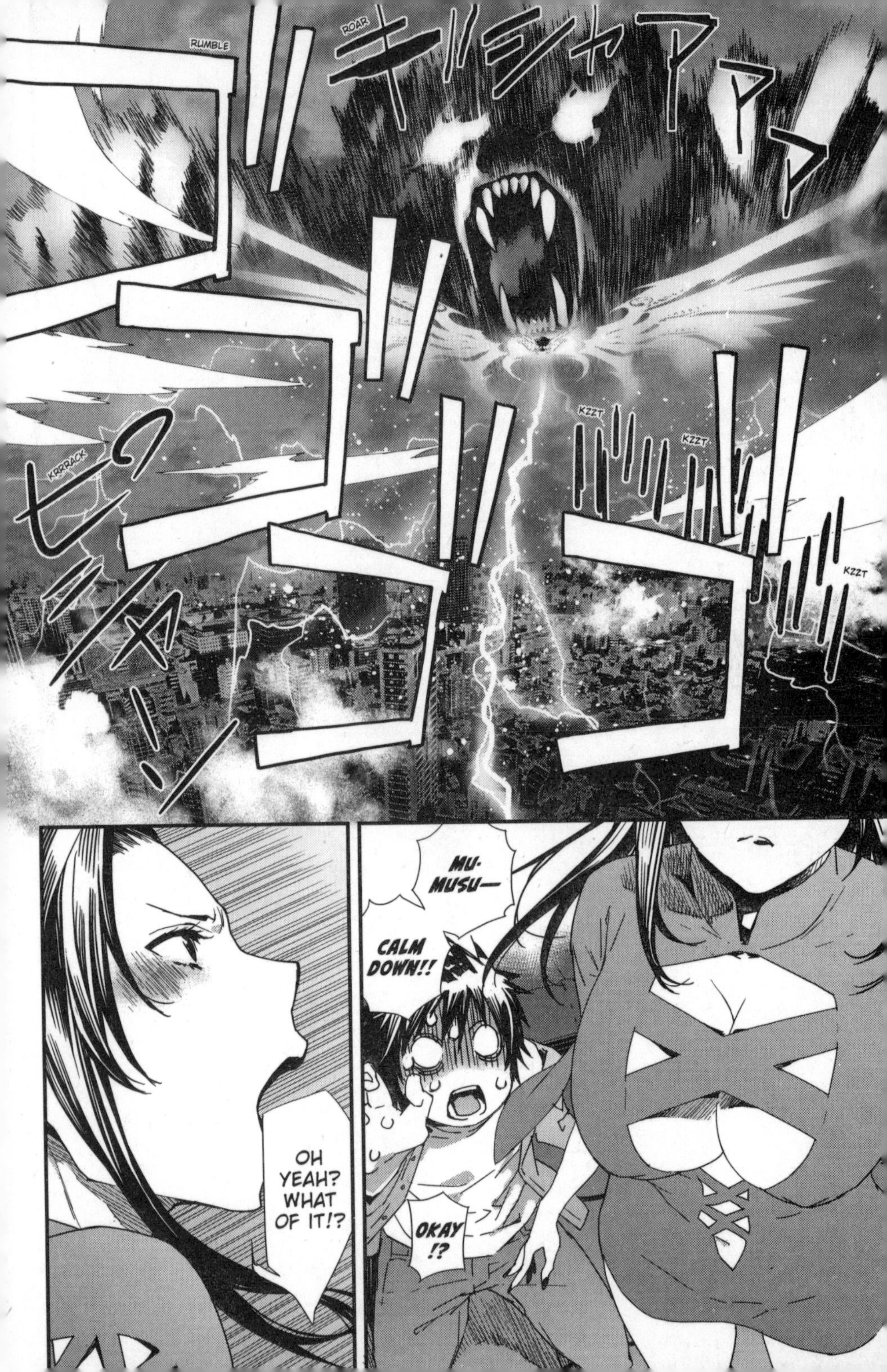
ROAR
RUMBLE
KZZT
KZZT
KZZT
KRRRACK
MU-MUSU—
CALM DOWN!!
OKAY!?
OH YEAH? WHAT OF IT!?

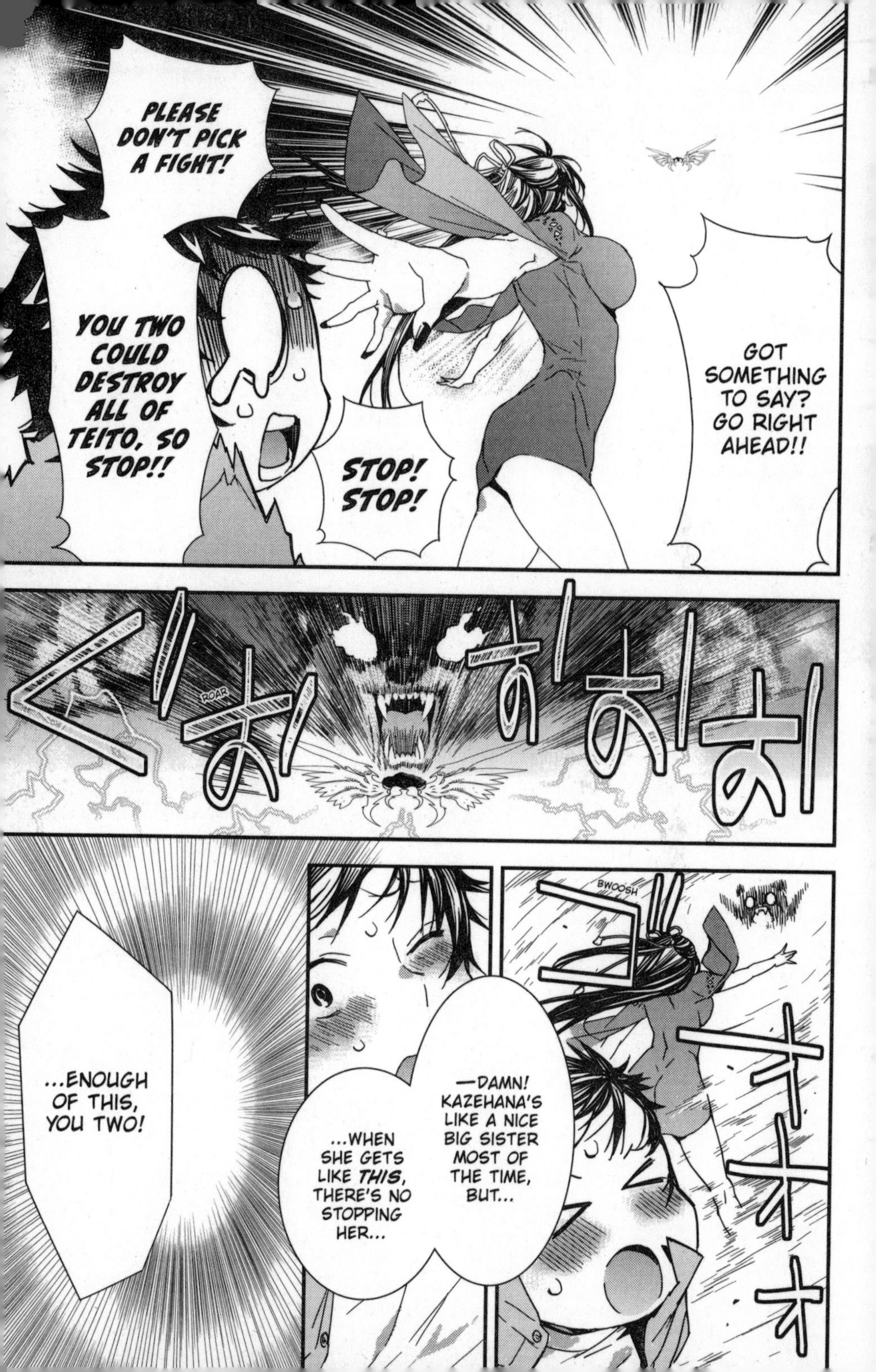
GOT SOMETHING TO SAY? GO RIGHT AHEAD!!
PLEASE DON'T PICK A FIGHT!
STOP! STOP!
YOU TWO COULD DESTROY ALL OF TEITO, SO STOP!!
ROAR
BWOOSH
—DAMN! KAZEHANA'S LIKE A NICE BIG SISTER MOST OF THE TIME, BUT...
...WHEN SHE GETS LIKE *THIS*, THERE'S NO STOPPING HER...
...ENOUGH OF THIS, YOU TWO!

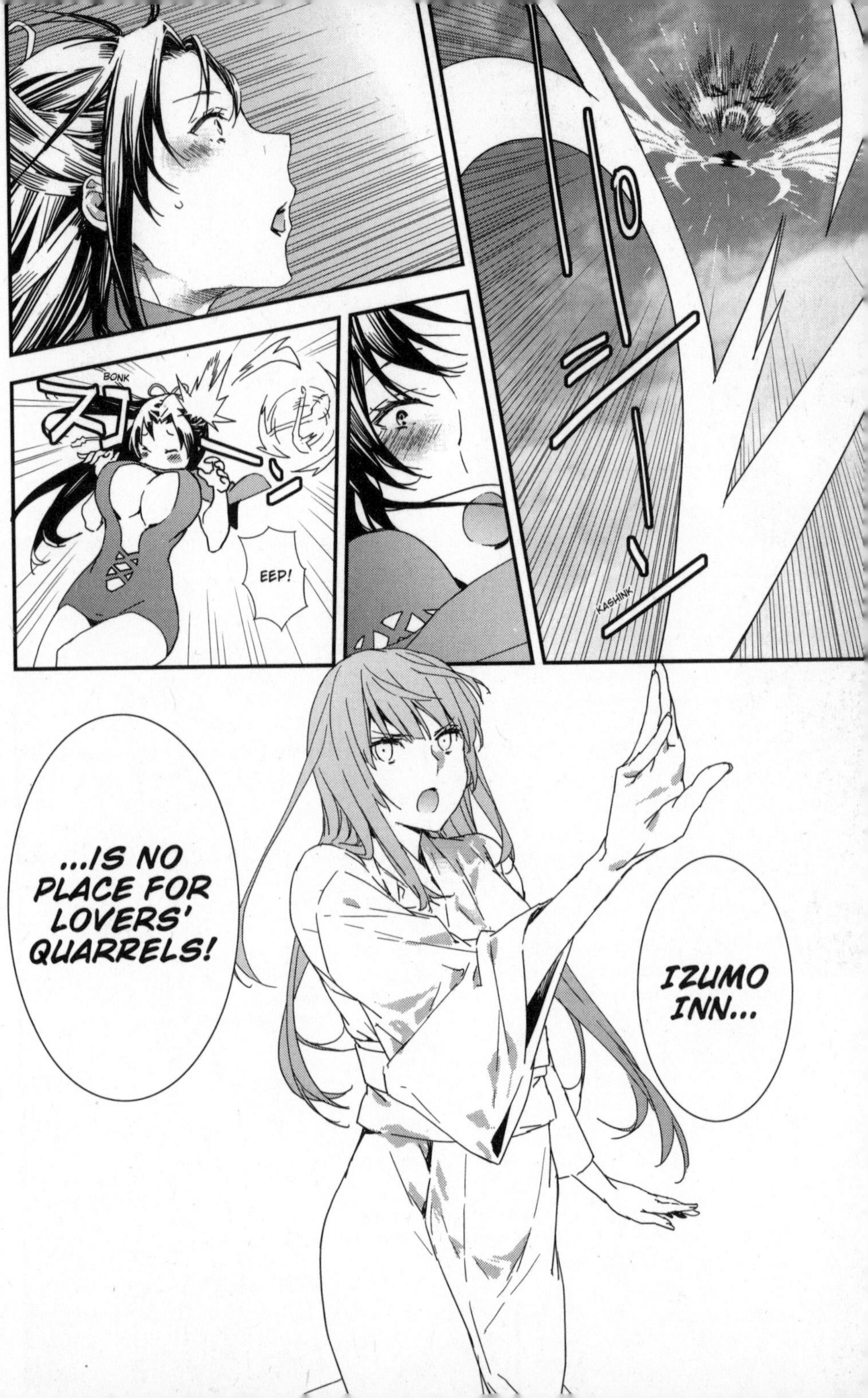

KASHINK
BONK
EEP!
IZUMO INN...
...IS NO PLACE FOR LOVERS' QUARRELS!

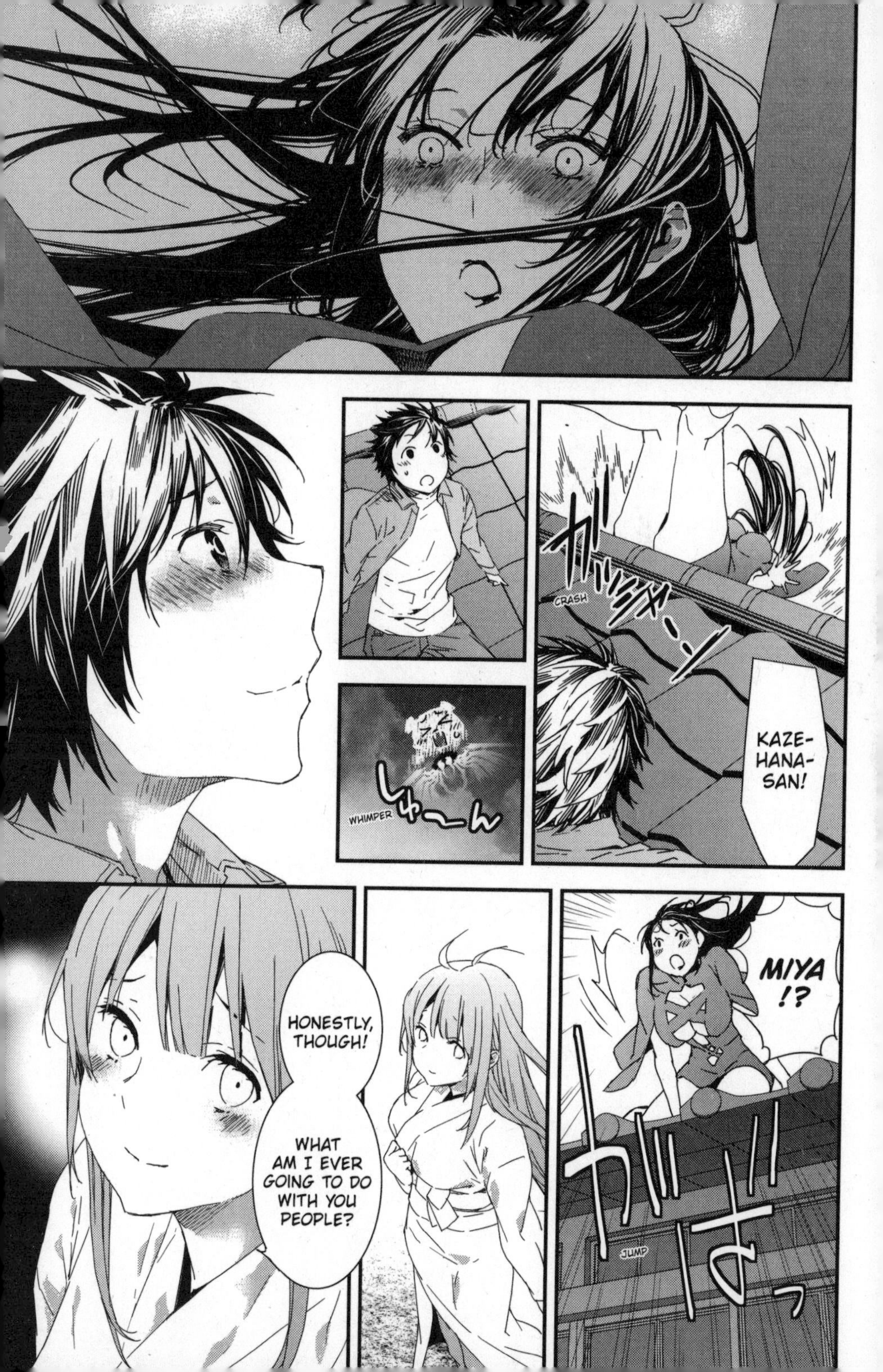

CRASH
KAZE-HANA-SAN!
しゅ〜ん
WHIMPER
MIYA!?
JUMP
HONESTLY, THOUGH!
WHAT AM I EVER GOING TO DO WITH YOU PEOPLE?

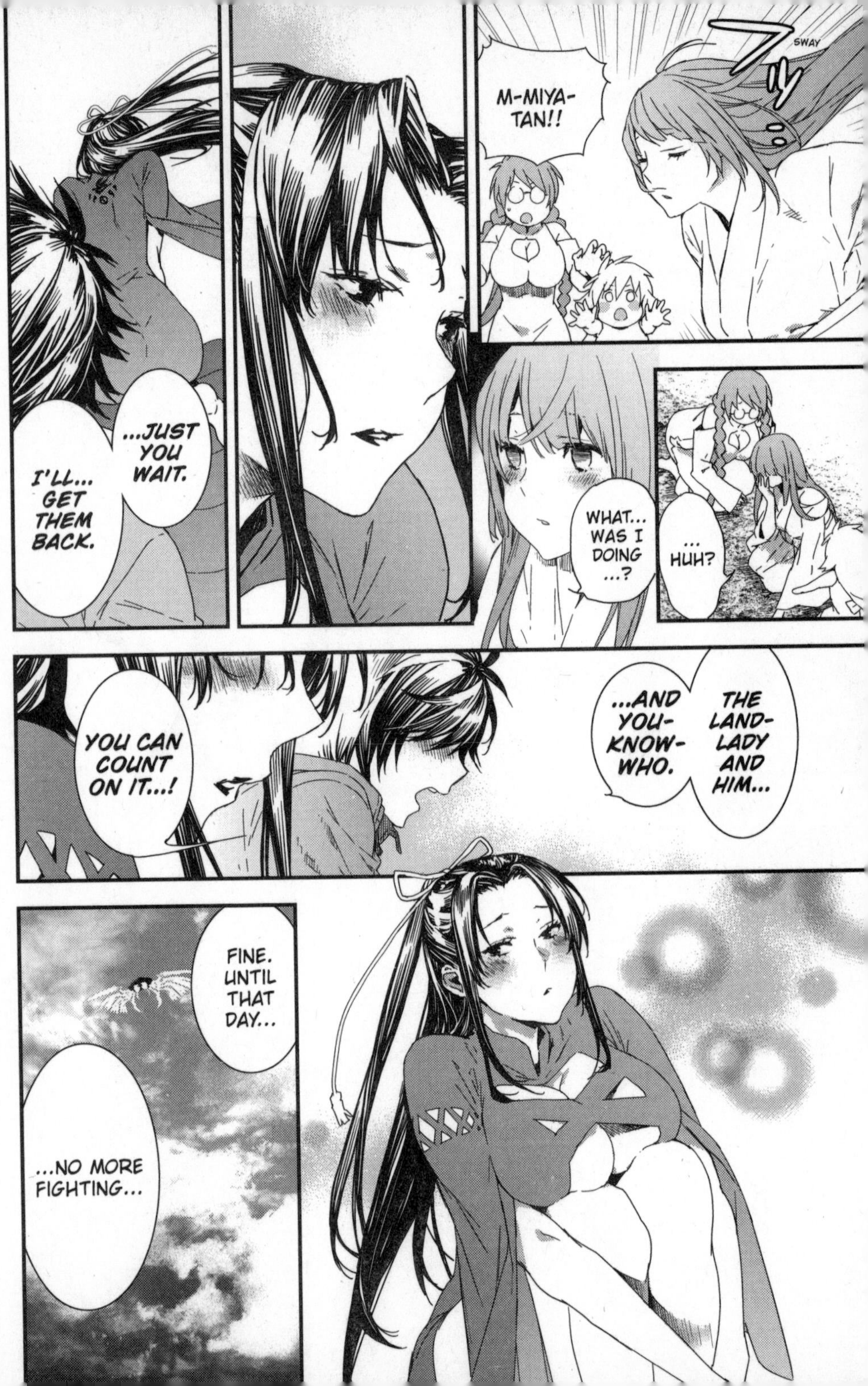
SWAY
M-MIYA-TAN!!
...HUH?
WHAT... WAS I DOING ...?
...JUST YOU WAIT.
I'LL... GET THEM BACK.
THE LANDLADY AND HIM...
...AND YOU-KNOW-WHO.
YOU CAN COUNT ON IT...!
FINE. UNTIL THAT DAY...
...NO MORE FIGHTING...

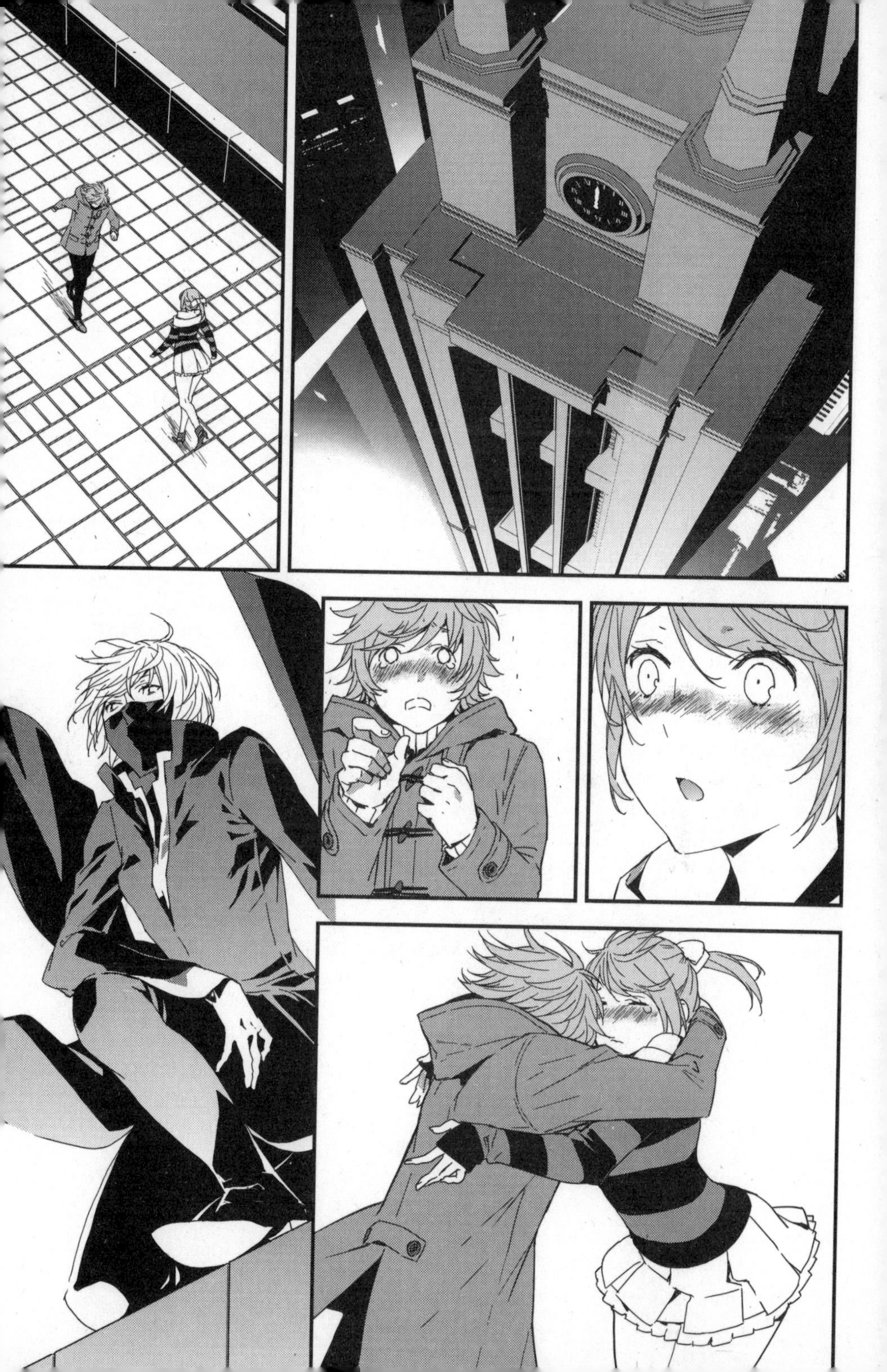

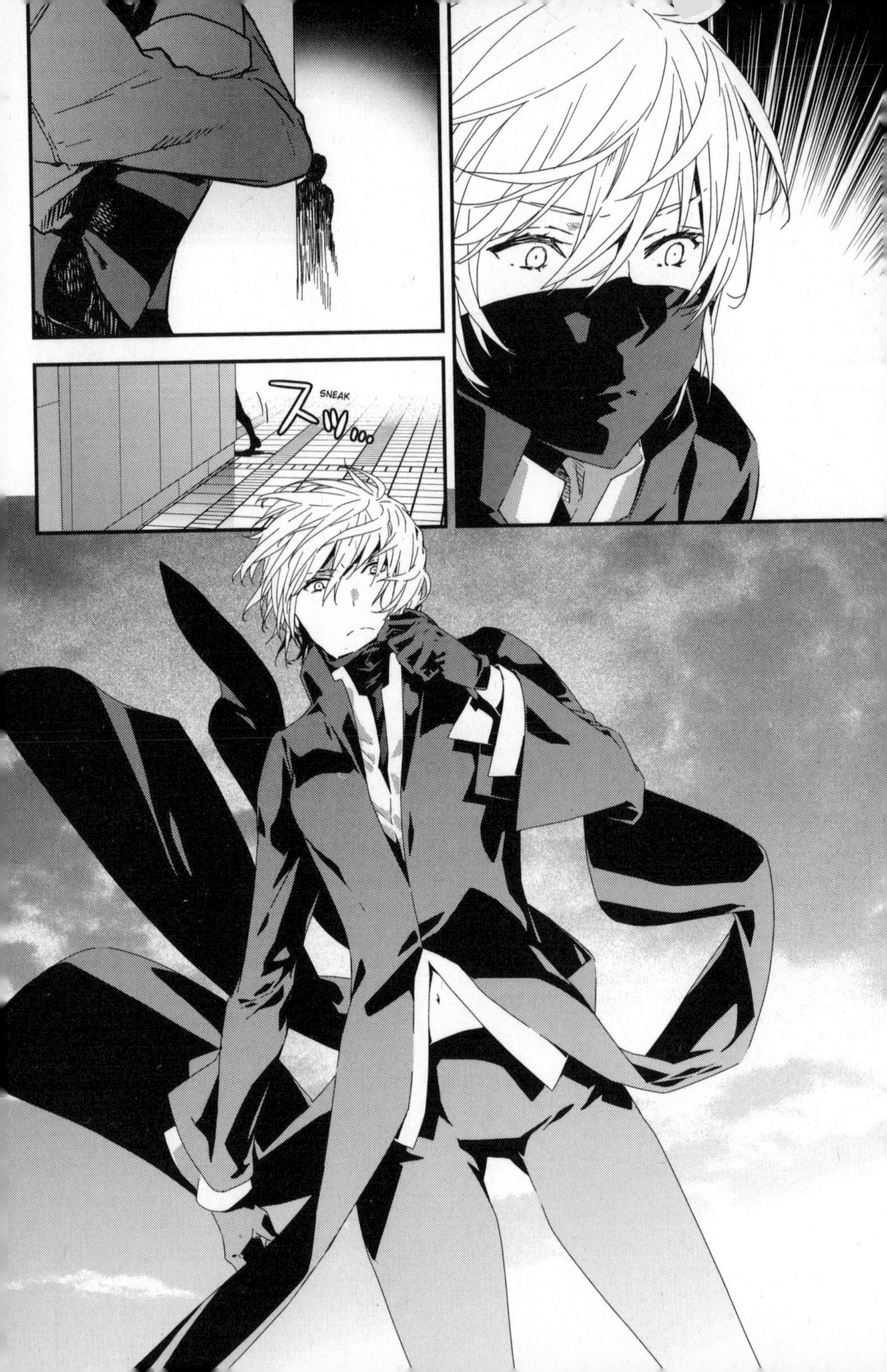
スッ...
SNEAK

...OH.

2020

12 December

ACHOO!

SNOW
...

December

YEAH, I
THOUGHT
IT FELT
COLD.

ALREADY
WINTER,
HUH...

M	T	W	T	F	S
30	1	2	3	4	5
7	8	9	10	11	12
14	15	16	17	18	19
21	22	23	24	25	26
28	29	30	31		

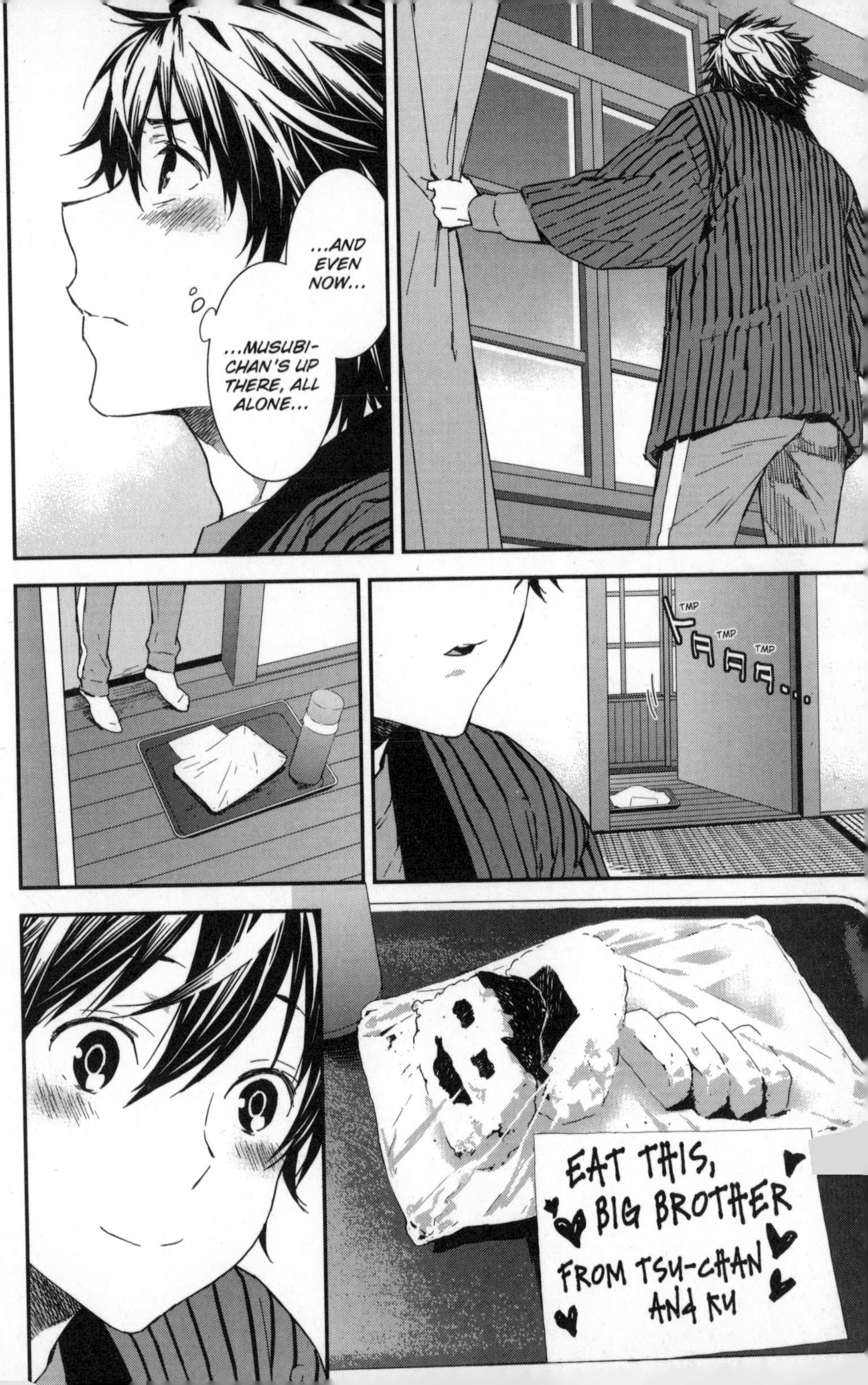
...AND EVEN NOW...
...MUSUBI-CHAN'S UP THERE, ALL ALONE...
TMP TMP TMP
EAT THIS, BIG BROTHER
FROM TSU-CHAN AND KU

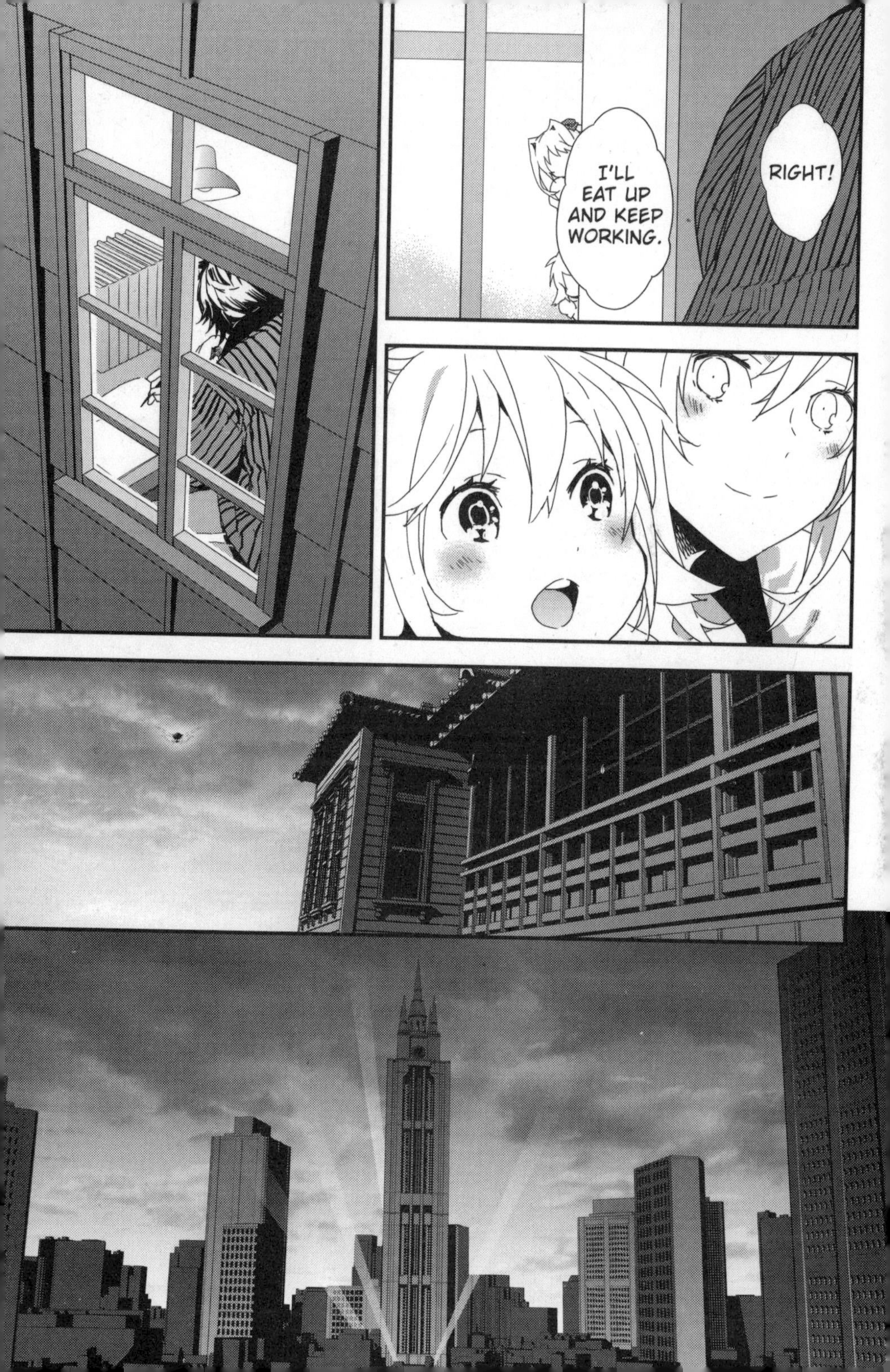
RIGHT!
I'LL EAT UP AND KEEP WORKING.

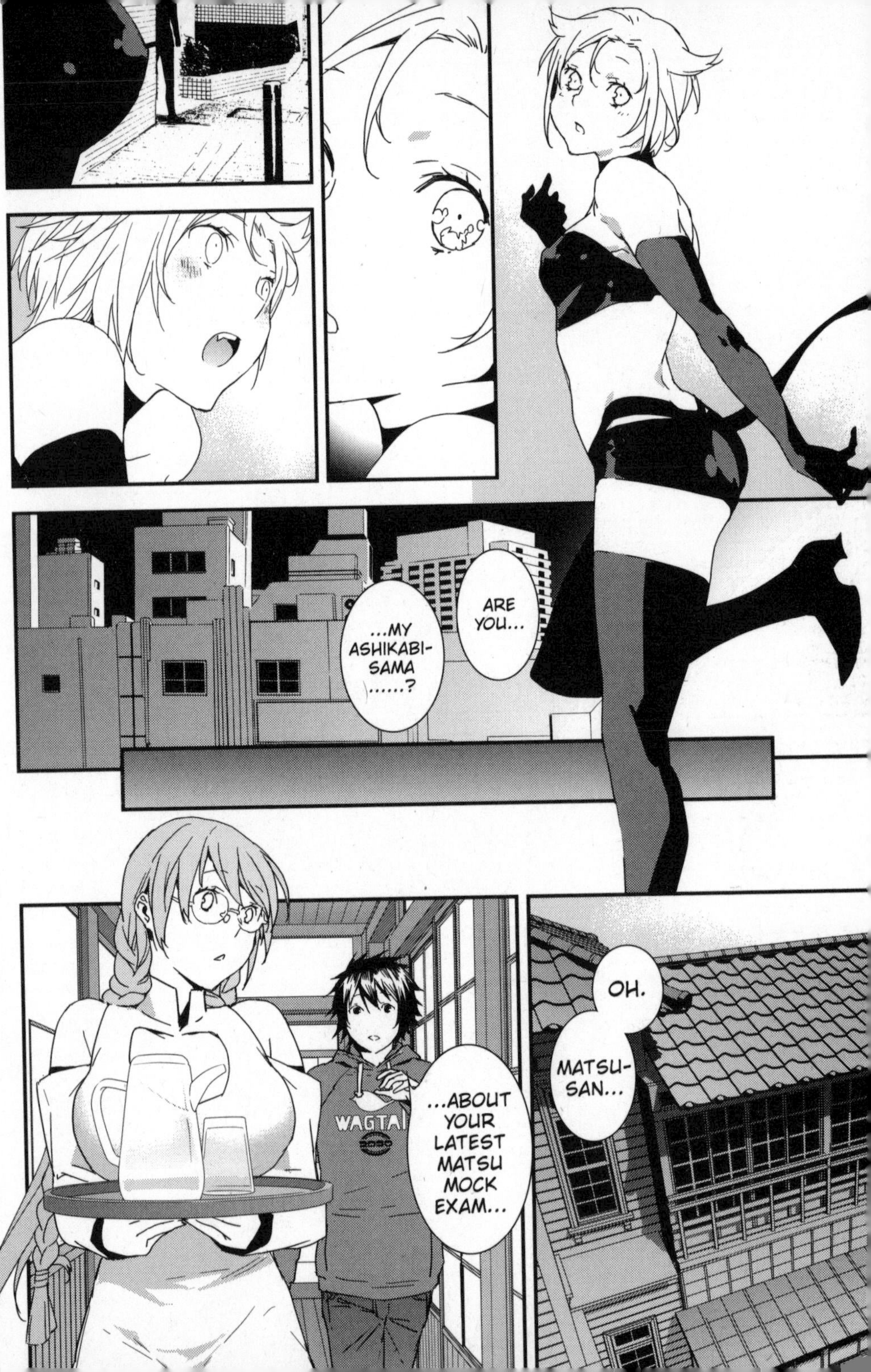
ARE YOU...
...MY ASHIKABI-SAMA ......?
OH.
MATSU-SAN...
...ABOUT YOUR LATEST MATSU MOCK EXAM...
WAGTAI

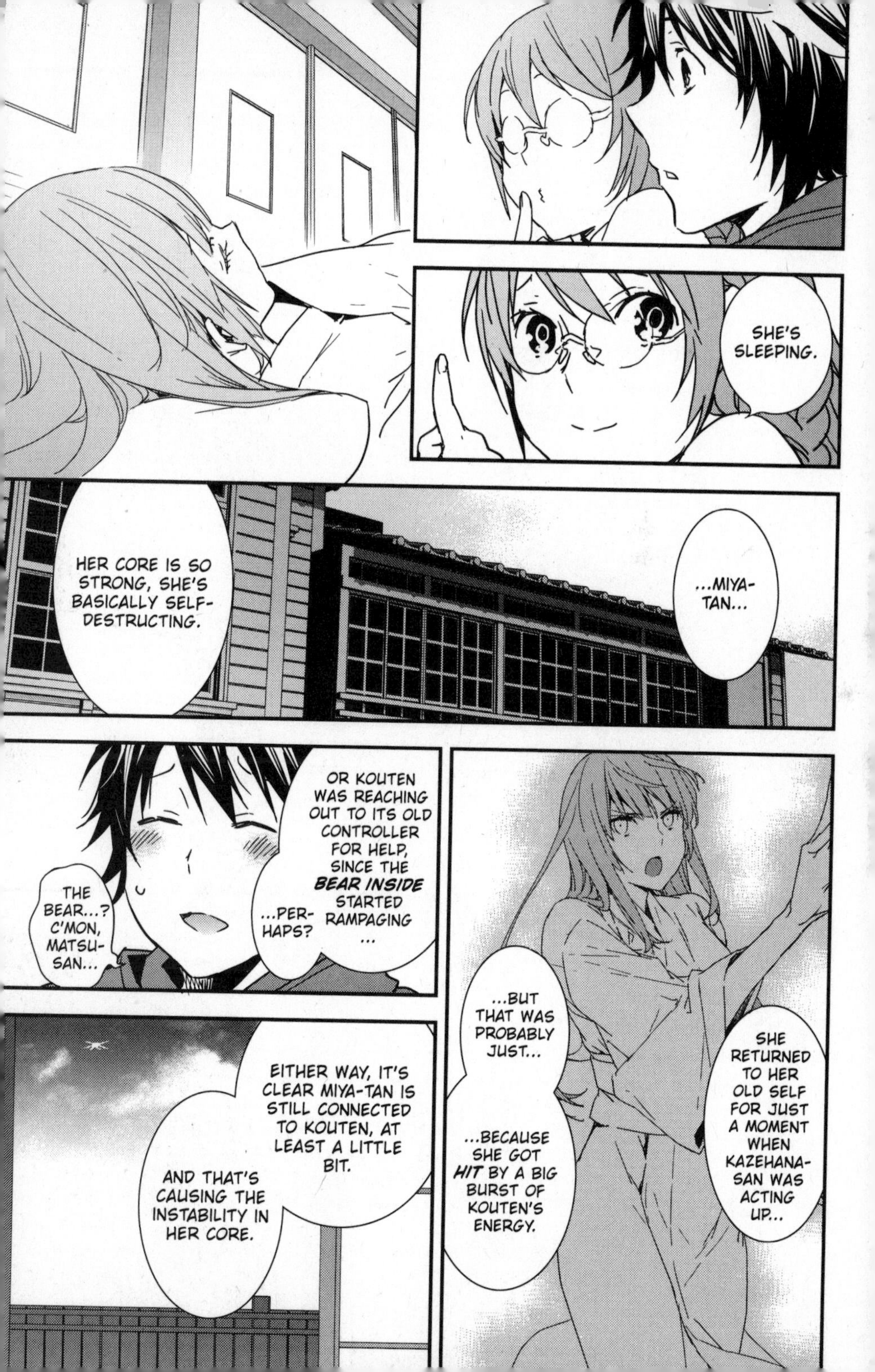
SHE'S SLEEPING.
...MIYA-TAN...
HER CORE IS SO STRONG, SHE'S BASICALLY SELF-DESTRUCTING.
SHE RETURNED TO HER OLD SELF FOR JUST A MOMENT WHEN KAZEHANA-SAN WAS ACTING UP...
...BUT THAT WAS PROBABLY JUST...
...BECAUSE SHE GOT HIT BY A BIG BURST OF KOUTEN'S ENERGY.
OR KOUTEN WAS REACHING OUT TO ITS OLD CONTROLLER FOR HELP, SINCE THE BEAR INSIDE STARTED RAMPAGING...
...PER-HAPS?
THE BEAR...? C'MON, MATSU-SAN...
EITHER WAY, IT'S CLEAR MIYA-TAN IS STILL CONNECTED TO KOUTEN, AT LEAST A LITTLE BIT.
AND THAT'S CAUSING THE INSTABILITY IN HER CORE.

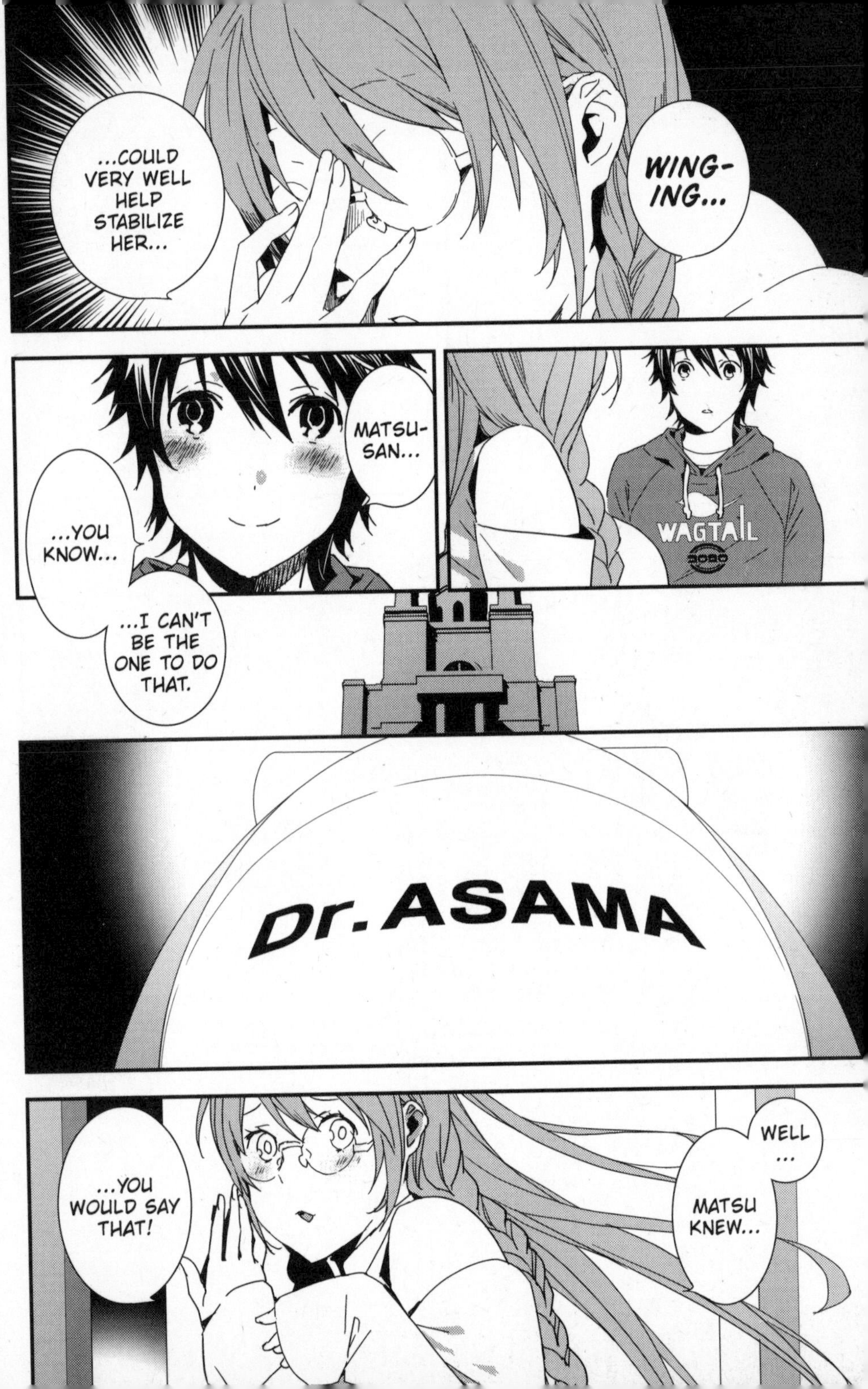
WING-ING...
...COULD VERY WELL HELP STABILIZE HER...
WAGTAIL
MATSU-SAN...
...YOU KNOW...
...I CAN'T BE THE ONE TO DO THAT.
Dr. ASAMA
WELL ...
MATSU KNEW...
...YOU WOULD SAY THAT!

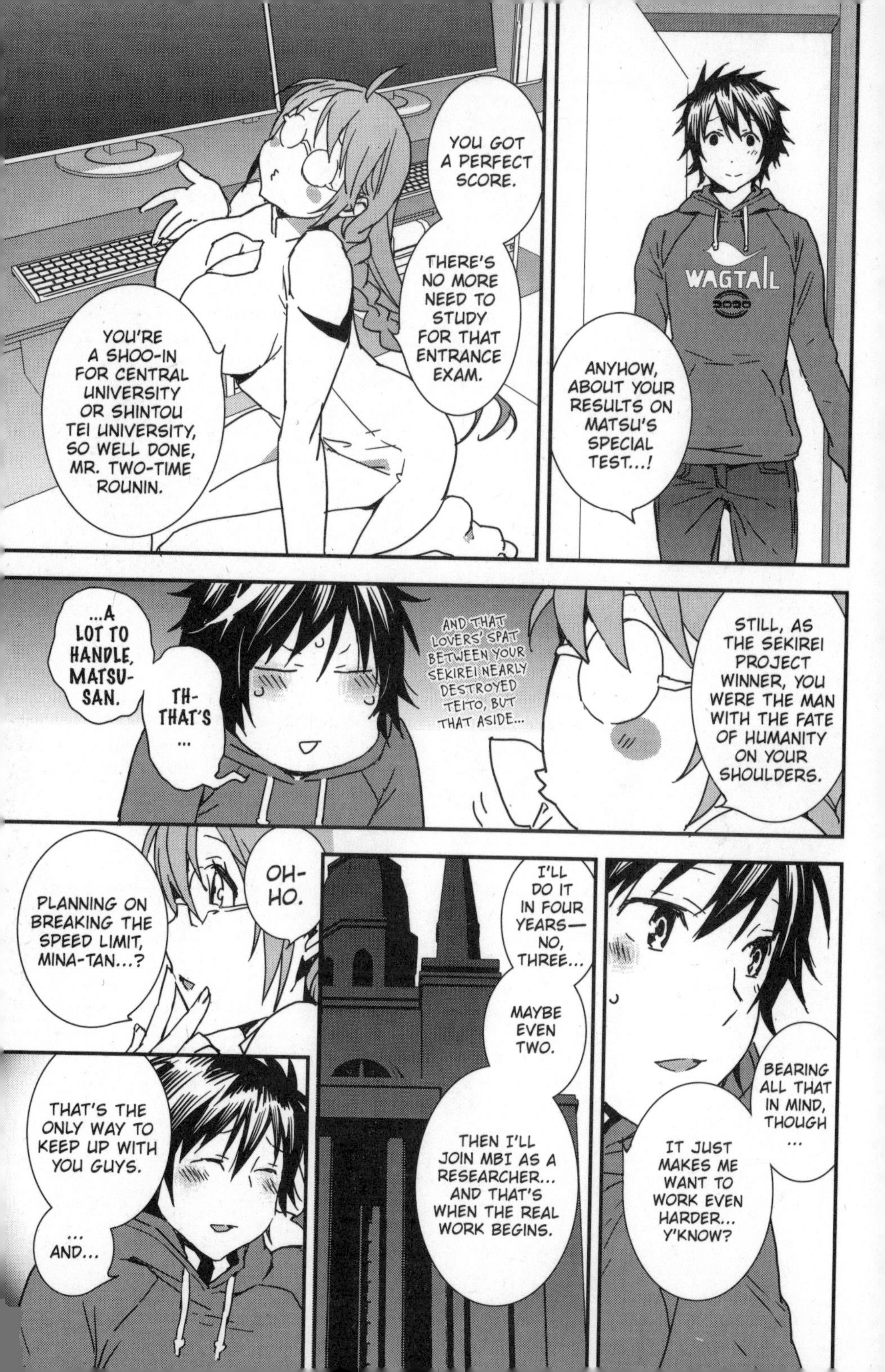
ANYHOW, ABOUT YOUR RESULTS ON MATSU'S SPECIAL TEST...!
YOU GOT A PERFECT SCORE.
THERE'S NO MORE NEED TO STUDY FOR THAT ENTRANCE EXAM.
YOU'RE A SHOO-IN FOR CENTRAL UNIVERSITY OR SHINTOU TEI UNIVERSITY, SO WELL DONE, MR. TWO-TIME ROUNIN.
STILL, AS THE SEKIREI PROJECT WINNER, YOU WERE THE MAN WITH THE FATE OF HUMANITY ON YOUR SHOULDERS.
AND THAT LOVERS' SPAT BETWEEN YOUR SEKIREI NEARLY DESTROYED TEITO, BUT THAT ASIDE...
TH-THAT'S ...
...A LOT TO HANDLE, MATSU-SAN.
BEARING ALL THAT IN MIND, THOUGH ...
IT JUST MAKES ME WANT TO WORK EVEN HARDER... Y'KNOW?
I'LL DO IT IN FOUR YEARS—NO, THREE...
MAYBE EVEN TWO.
THEN I'LL JOIN MBI AS A RESEARCHER... AND THAT'S WHEN THE REAL WORK BEGINS.
OH-HO.
PLANNING ON BREAKING THE SPEED LIMIT, MINA-TAN...?
THAT'S THE ONLY WAY TO KEEP UP WITH YOU GUYS.
... AND...

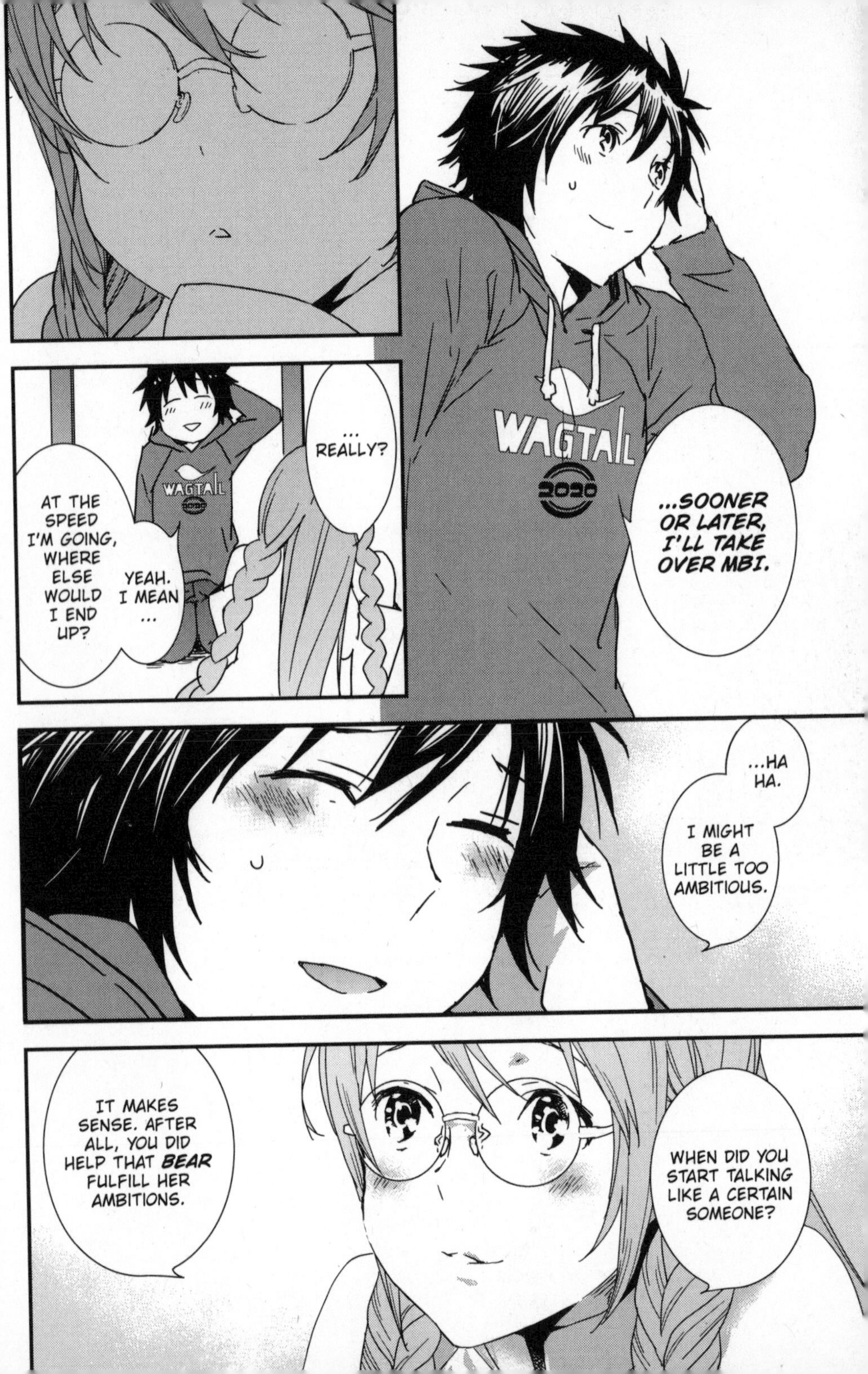
...SOONER OR LATER, I'LL TAKE OVER MBI.
... REALLY?
YEAH. I MEAN ...
AT THE SPEED I'M GOING, WHERE ELSE WOULD I END UP?
...HA HA.
I MIGHT BE A LITTLE TOO AMBITIOUS.
WHEN DID YOU START TALKING LIKE A CERTAIN SOMEONE?
IT MAKES SENSE. AFTER ALL, YOU DID HELP THAT **BEAR** FULFILL HER AMBITIONS.

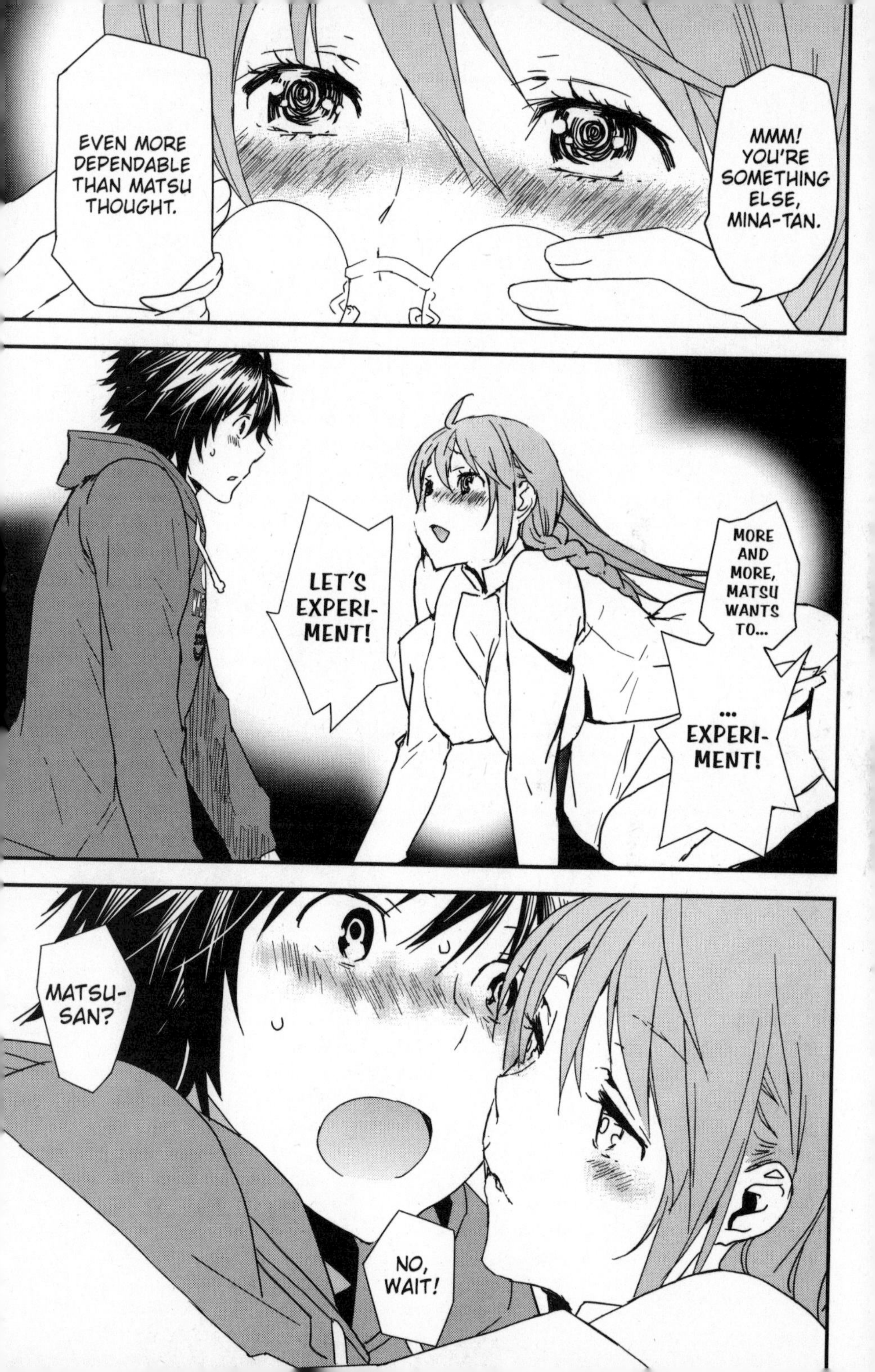
MMM! YOU'RE SOMETHING ELSE, MINA-TAN.
EVEN MORE DEPENDABLE THAN MATSU THOUGHT.
MORE AND MORE, MATSU WANTS TO...
... EXPERIMENT!
LET'S EXPERIMENT!
MATSU-SAN?
NO, WAIT!

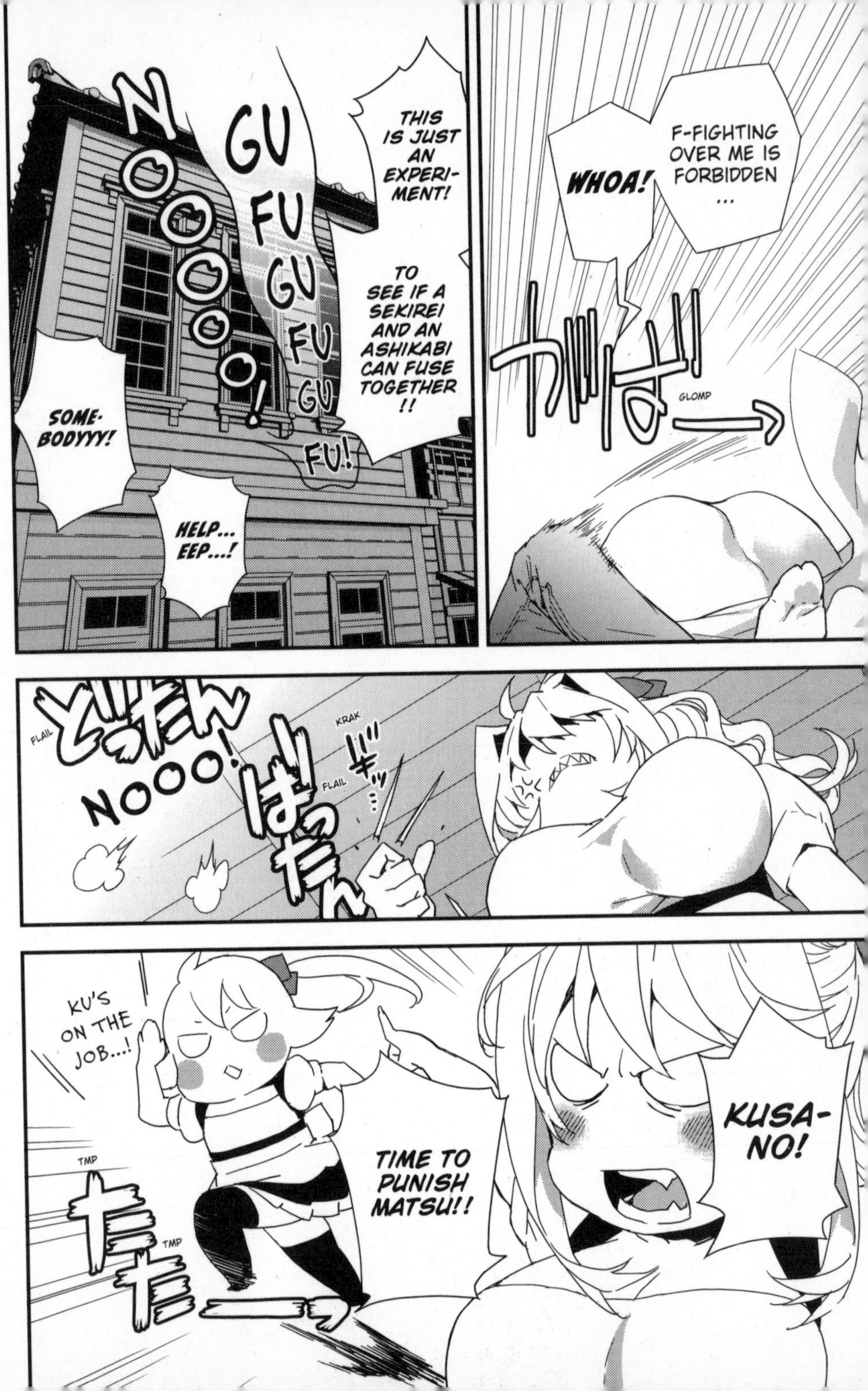
WHOA!
F-FIGHTING OVER ME IS FORBIDDEN ...
GLOMP
THIS IS JUST AN EXPERI- MENT!
TO SEE IF A SEKIREI AND AN ASHIKABI CAN FUSE TOGETHER !!
GU FU GU FU GU FU!
NOOOOOO!
SOME- BODYYY!
HELP... EEP...!
KRAK
ギッ
とったん
FLAIL
ばったん
FLAIL
NOOO!
KUSA- NO!
TIME TO PUNISH MATSU!!
KU'S ON THE JOB...!
TMP
TMP

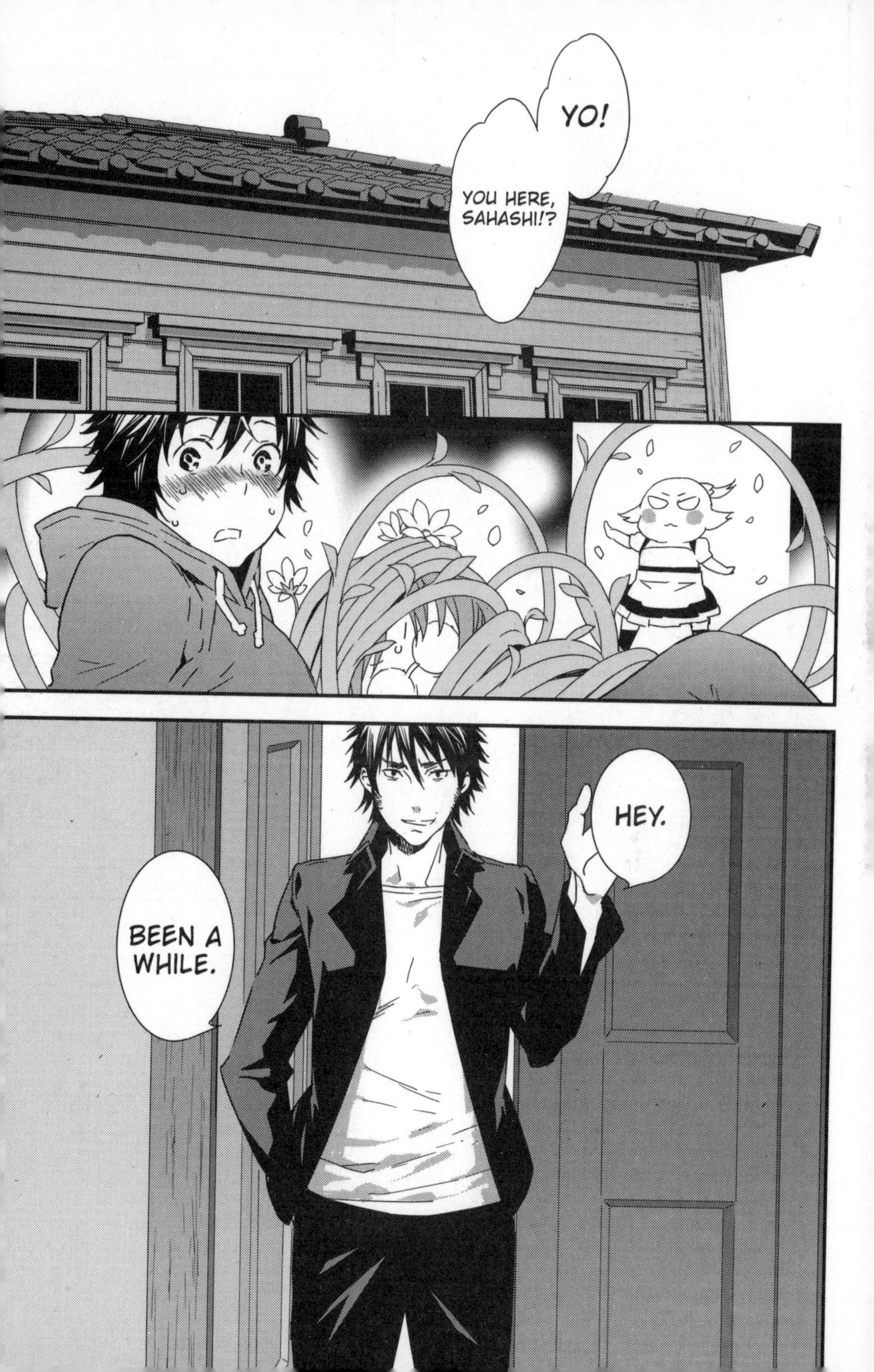
YO!
YOU HERE, SAHASHI!?
HEY.
BEEN A WHILE.

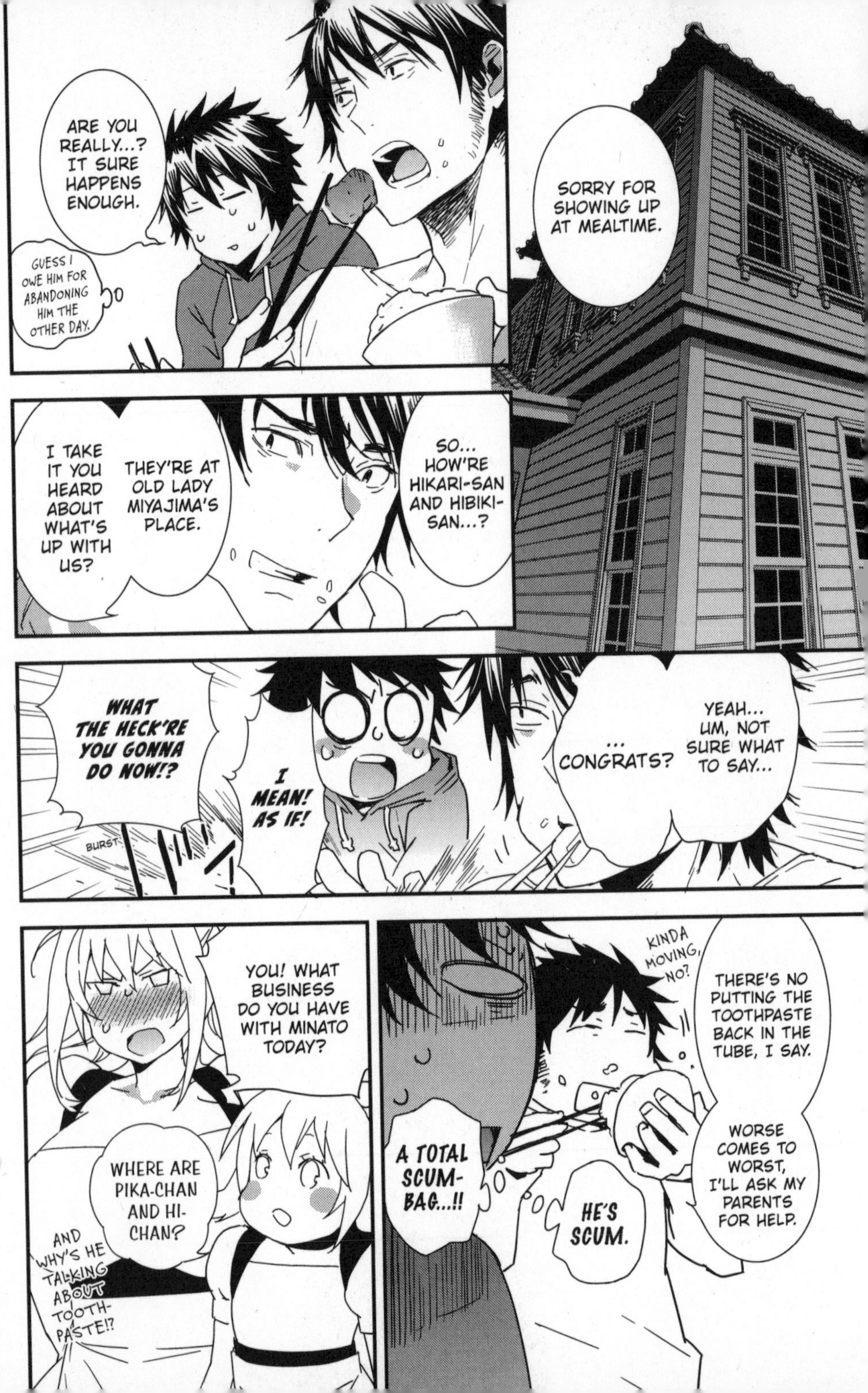
SORRY FOR SHOWING UP AT MEALTIME.
ARE YOU REALLY...? IT SURE HAPPENS ENOUGH.
GUESS I OWE HIM FOR ABANDONING HIM THE OTHER DAY.
SO... HOW'RE HIKARI-SAN AND HIBIKI-SAN...?
THEY'RE AT OLD LADY MIYAJIMA'S PLACE.
I TAKE IT YOU HEARD ABOUT WHAT'S UP WITH US?
YEAH... UM, NOT SURE WHAT TO SAY...
...CONGRATS?
I MEAN! AS IF!
WHAT THE HECK'RE YOU GONNA DO NOW!?
BURST
THERE'S NO PUTTING THE TOOTHPASTE BACK IN THE TUBE, I SAY.
KINDA MOVING, NO?
WORSE COMES TO WORST, I'LL ASK MY PARENTS FOR HELP.
HE'S SCUM.
A TOTAL SCUM-BAG...!!
YOU! WHAT BUSINESS DO YOU HAVE WITH MINATO TODAY?
WHERE ARE PIKA-CHAN AND HI-CHAN?
AND WHY'S HE TALKING ABOUT TOOTH-PASTE!?

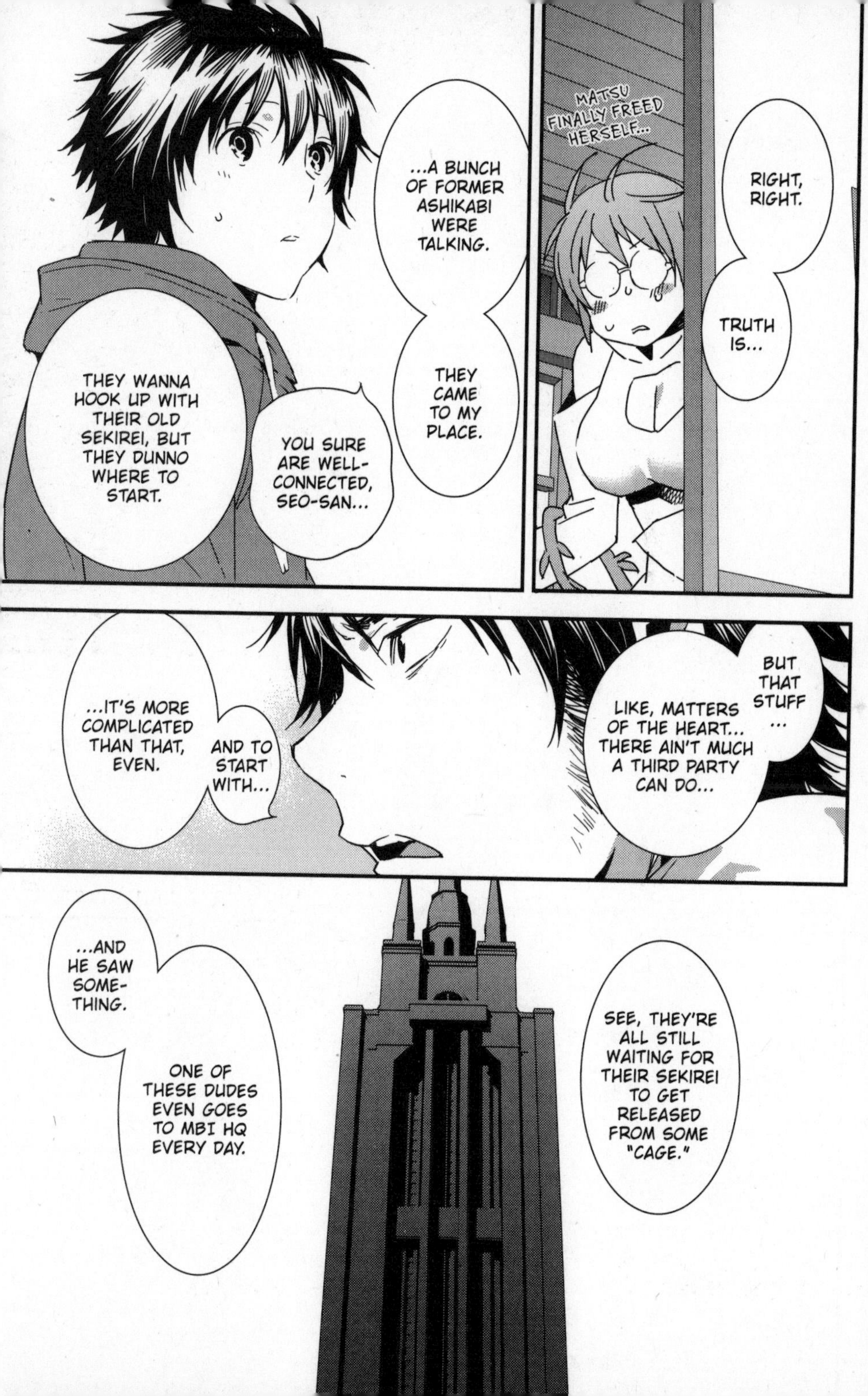
MATSU FINALLY FREED HERSELF...
RIGHT, RIGHT.
TRUTH IS...
...A BUNCH OF FORMER ASHIKABI WERE TALKING.
THEY CAME TO MY PLACE.
YOU SURE ARE WELL-CONNECTED, SEO-SAN...
THEY WANNA HOOK UP WITH THEIR OLD SEKIREI, BUT THEY DUNNO WHERE TO START.
BUT THAT STUFF...
LIKE, MATTERS OF THE HEART... THERE AIN'T MUCH A THIRD PARTY CAN DO...
...IT'S MORE COMPLICATED THAN THAT, EVEN.
AND TO START WITH...
SEE, THEY'RE ALL STILL WAITING FOR THEIR SEKIREI TO GET RELEASED FROM SOME "CAGE."
ONE OF THESE DUDES EVEN GOES TO MBI HQ EVERY DAY.
...AND HE SAW SOMETHING.

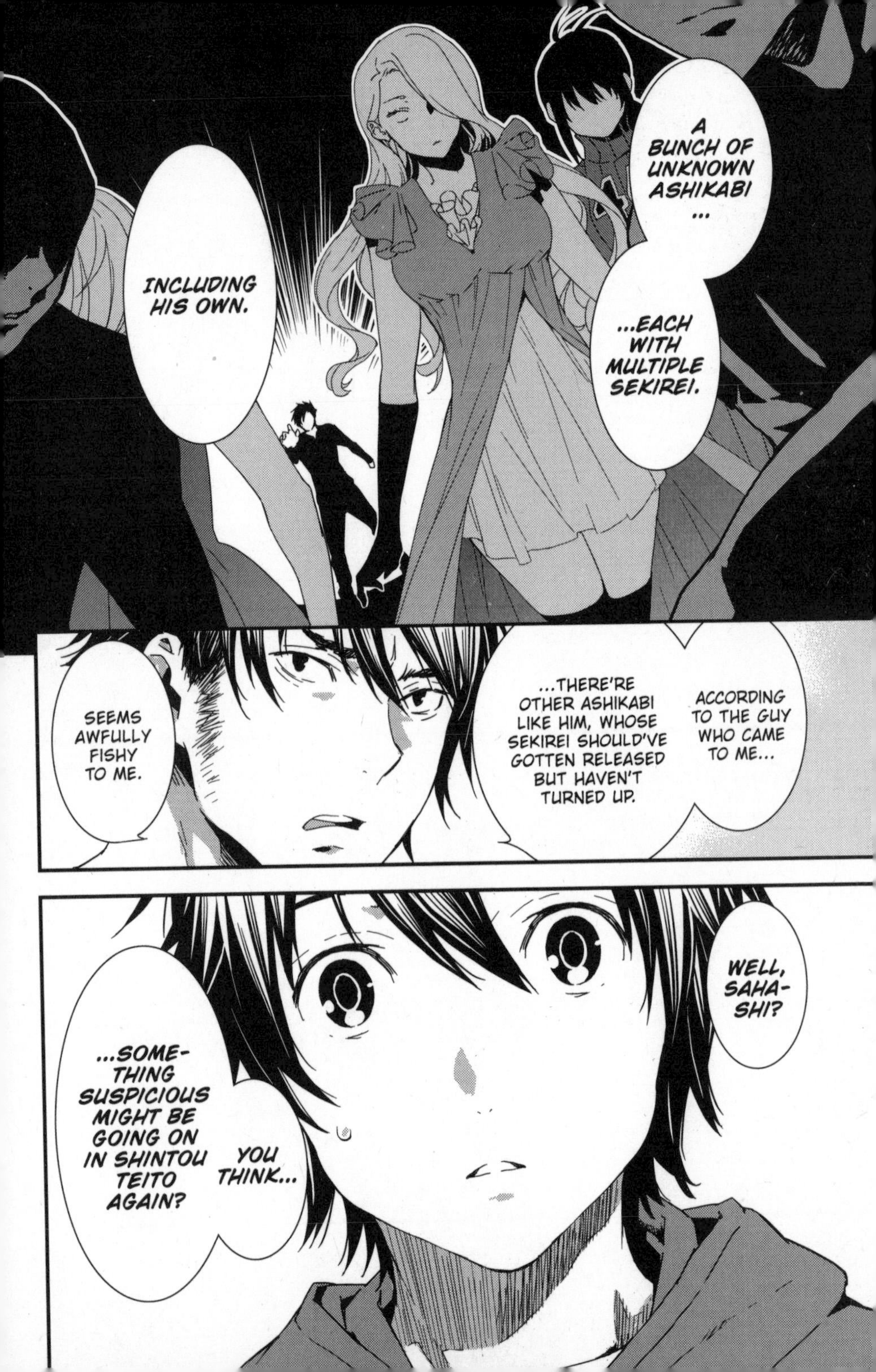
A BUNCH OF UNKNOWN ASHIKABI ...
...EACH WITH MULTIPLE SEKIREI.
INCLUDING HIS OWN.
ACCORDING TO THE GUY WHO CAME TO ME...
...THERE'RE OTHER ASHIKABI LIKE HIM, WHOSE SEKIREI SHOULD'VE GOTTEN RELEASED BUT HAVEN'T TURNED UP.
SEEMS AWFULLY FISHY TO ME.
WELL, SAHA-SHI?
YOU THINK...
...SOME-THING SUSPICIOUS MIGHT BE GOING ON IN SHINTOU TEITO AGAIN?

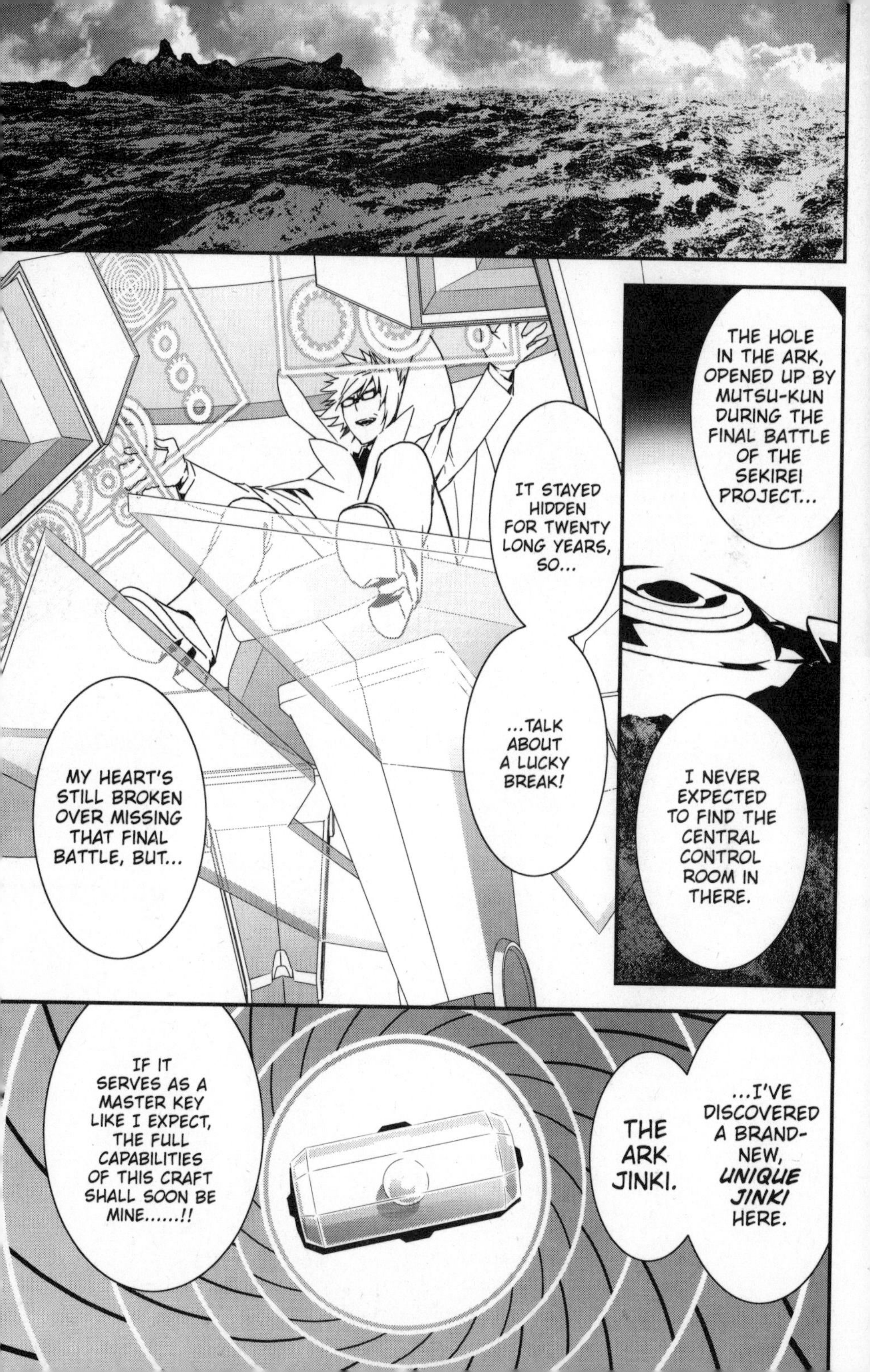

THE HOLE IN THE ARK, OPENED UP BY MUTSU-KUN DURING THE FINAL BATTLE OF THE SEKIREI PROJECT...
I NEVER EXPECTED TO FIND THE CENTRAL CONTROL ROOM IN THERE.
IT STAYED HIDDEN FOR TWENTY LONG YEARS, SO...
...TALK ABOUT A LUCKY BREAK!
MY HEART'S STILL BROKEN OVER MISSING THAT FINAL BATTLE, BUT...
...I'VE DISCOVERED A BRAND-NEW, *UNIQUE JINKI* HERE.
THE ARK JINKI.
IF IT SERVES AS A MASTER KEY LIKE I EXPECT, THE FULL CAPABILITIES OF THIS CRAFT SHALL SOON BE MINE......!!

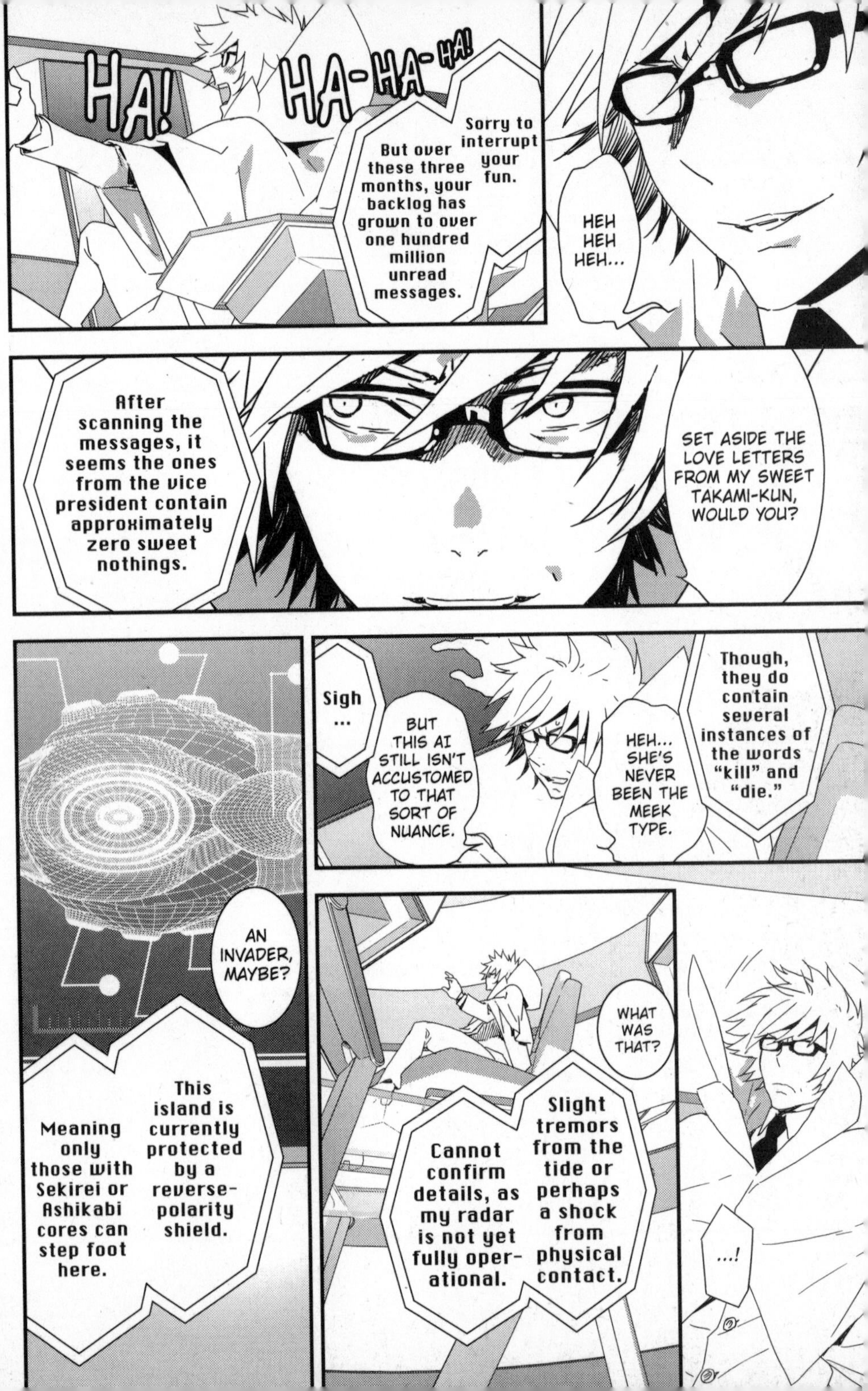
HEH HEH HEH...
HA!
HA-HA-HA!
Sorry to interrupt your fun.
But over these three months, your backlog has grown to over one hundred million unread messages.
SET ASIDE THE LOVE LETTERS FROM MY SWEET TAKAMI-KUN, WOULD YOU?
After scanning the messages, it seems the ones from the vice president contain approximately zero sweet nothings.
Though, they do contain several instances of the words "kill" and "die."
HEH... SHE'S NEVER BEEN THE MEEK TYPE.
BUT THIS AI STILL ISN'T ACCUSTOMED TO THAT SORT OF NUANCE.
Sigh ...
...!
WHAT WAS THAT?
Slight tremors from the tide or perhaps a shock from physical contact.
Cannot confirm details, as my radar is not yet fully oper-ational.
AN INVADER, MAYBE?
This island is currently protected by a reverse-polarity shield.
Meaning only those with Sekirei or Ashikabi cores can step foot here.

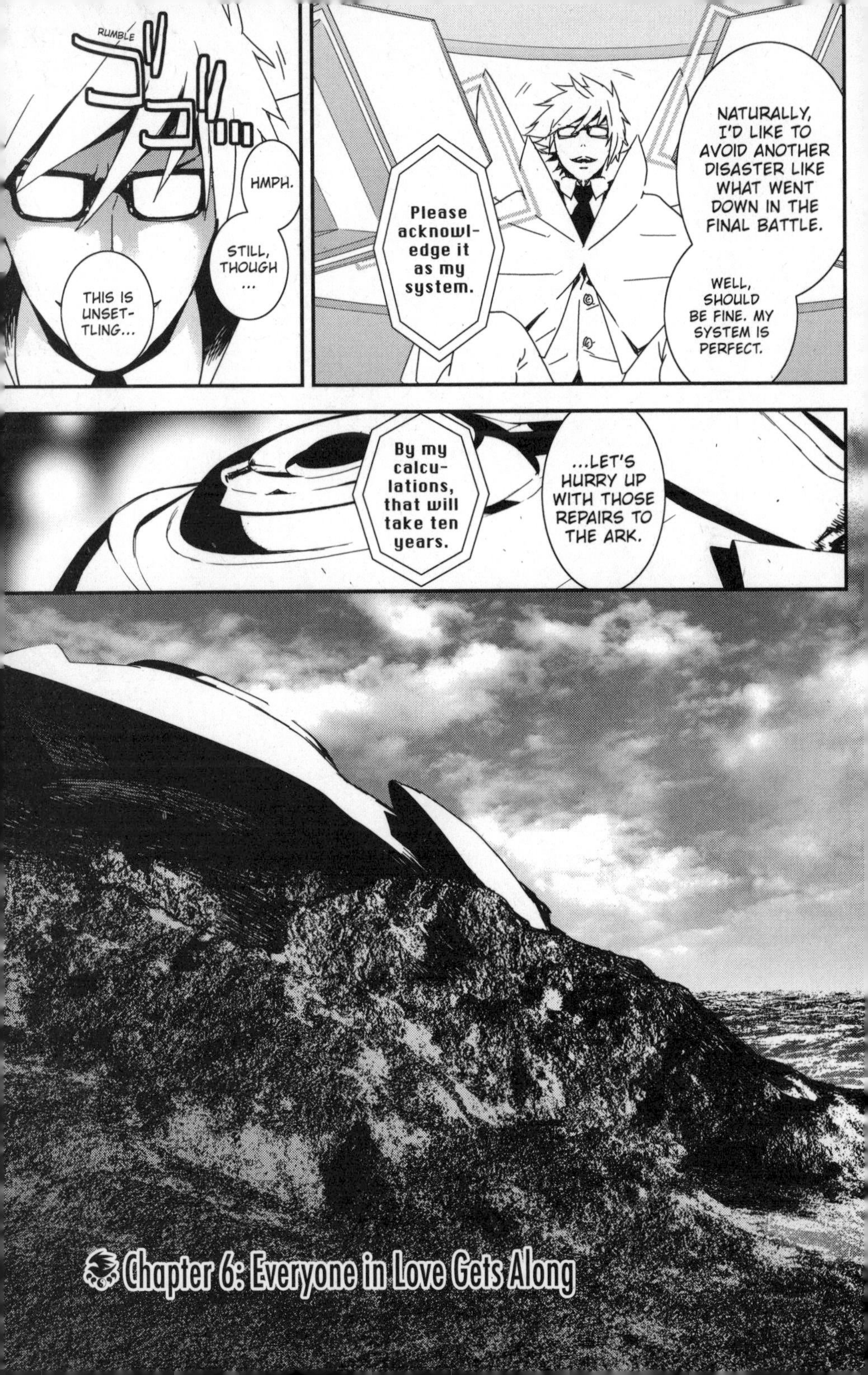
NATURALLY, I'D LIKE TO AVOID ANOTHER DISASTER LIKE WHAT WENT DOWN IN THE FINAL BATTLE.
WELL, SHOULD BE FINE. MY SYSTEM IS PERFECT.
Please acknowl-edge it as my system.
RUMBLE
HMPH.
STILL, THOUGH ...
THIS IS UNSET-TLING...
...LET'S HURRY UP WITH THOSE REPAIRS TO THE ARK.
By my calcu-lations, that will take ten years.
Chapter 6: Everyone in Love Gets Along

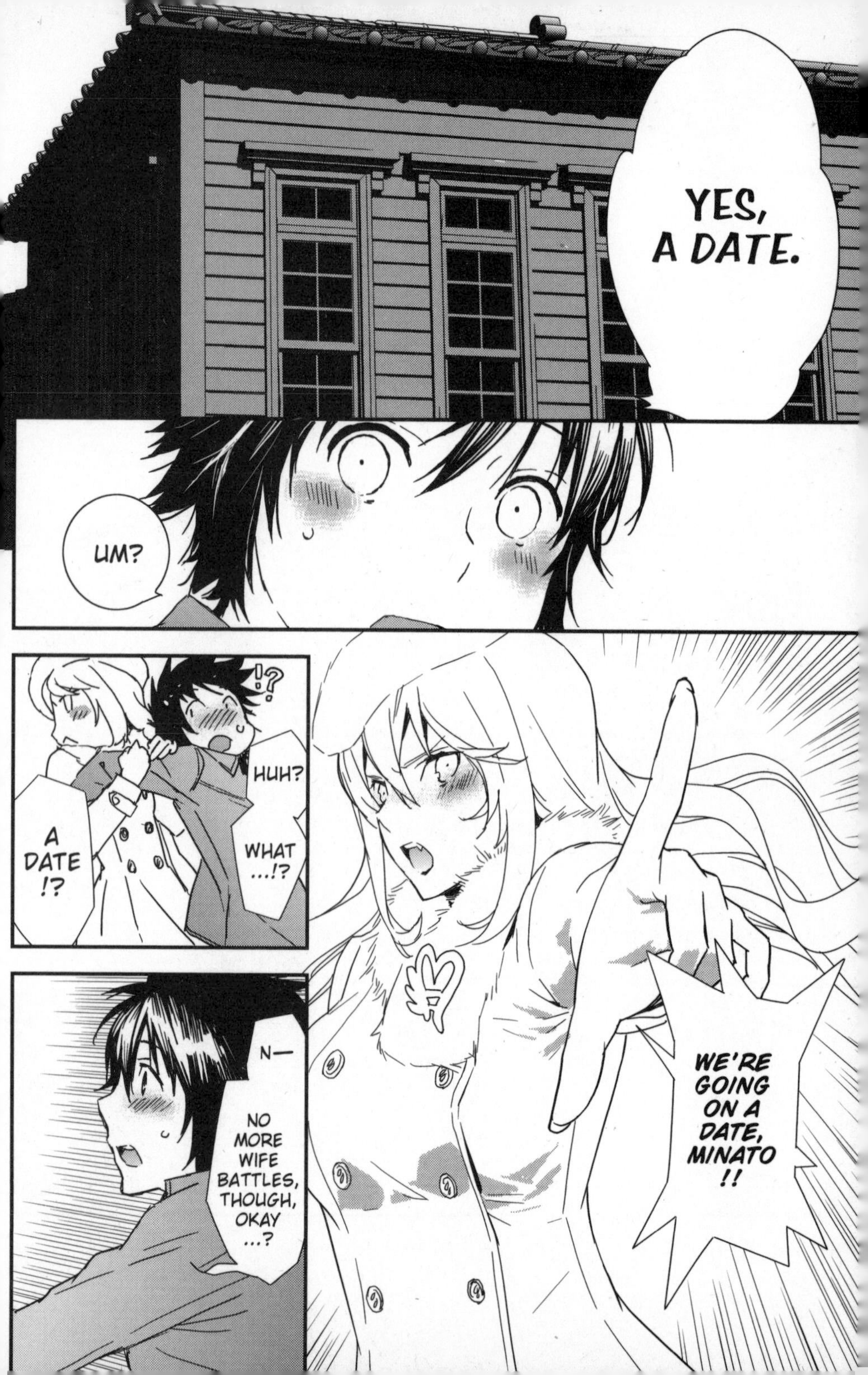
YES, A DATE.
UM?
WE'RE GOING ON A DATE, MINATO!!
!?
HUH?
WHAT...!?
A DATE!?
N—
NO MORE WIFE BATTLES, THOUGH, OKAY...?

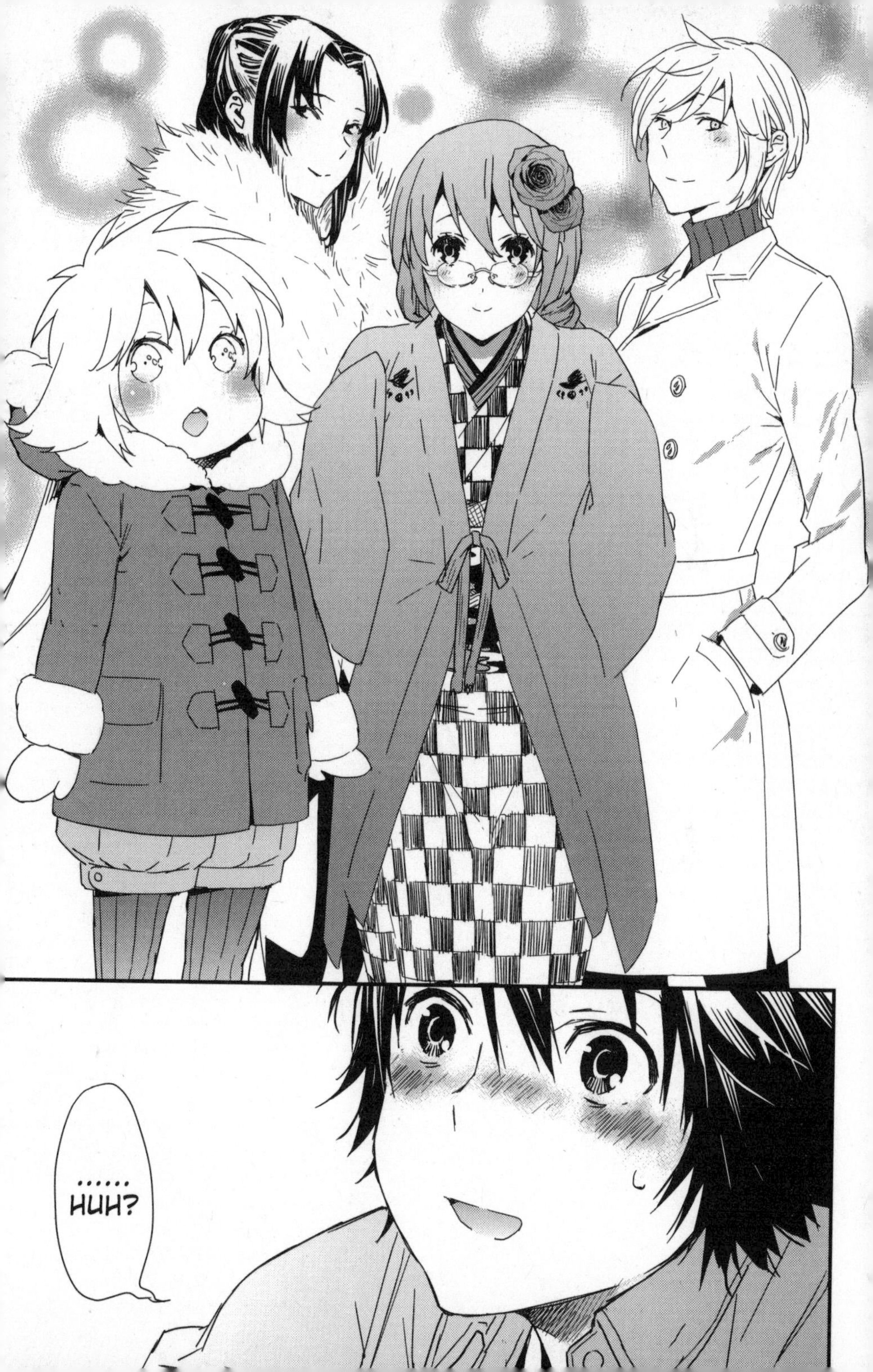
......
HUH?

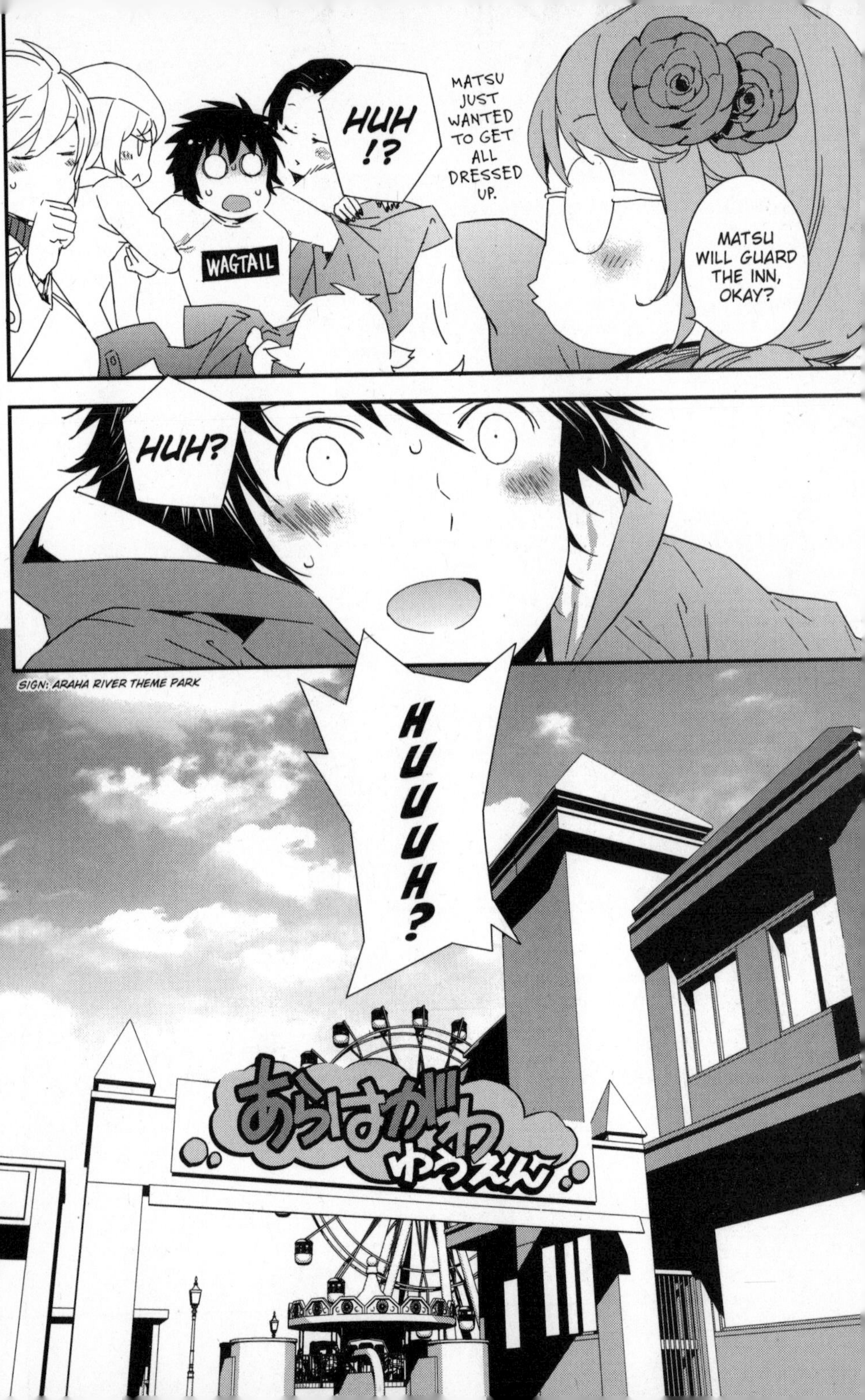
MATSU WILL GUARD THE INN, OKAY?
MATSU JUST WANTED TO GET ALL DRESSED UP.
HUH !?
WAGTAIL
HUH?
SIGN: ARAHA RIVER THEME PARK
HUUUUH?
あらはがわ
ゆうえん

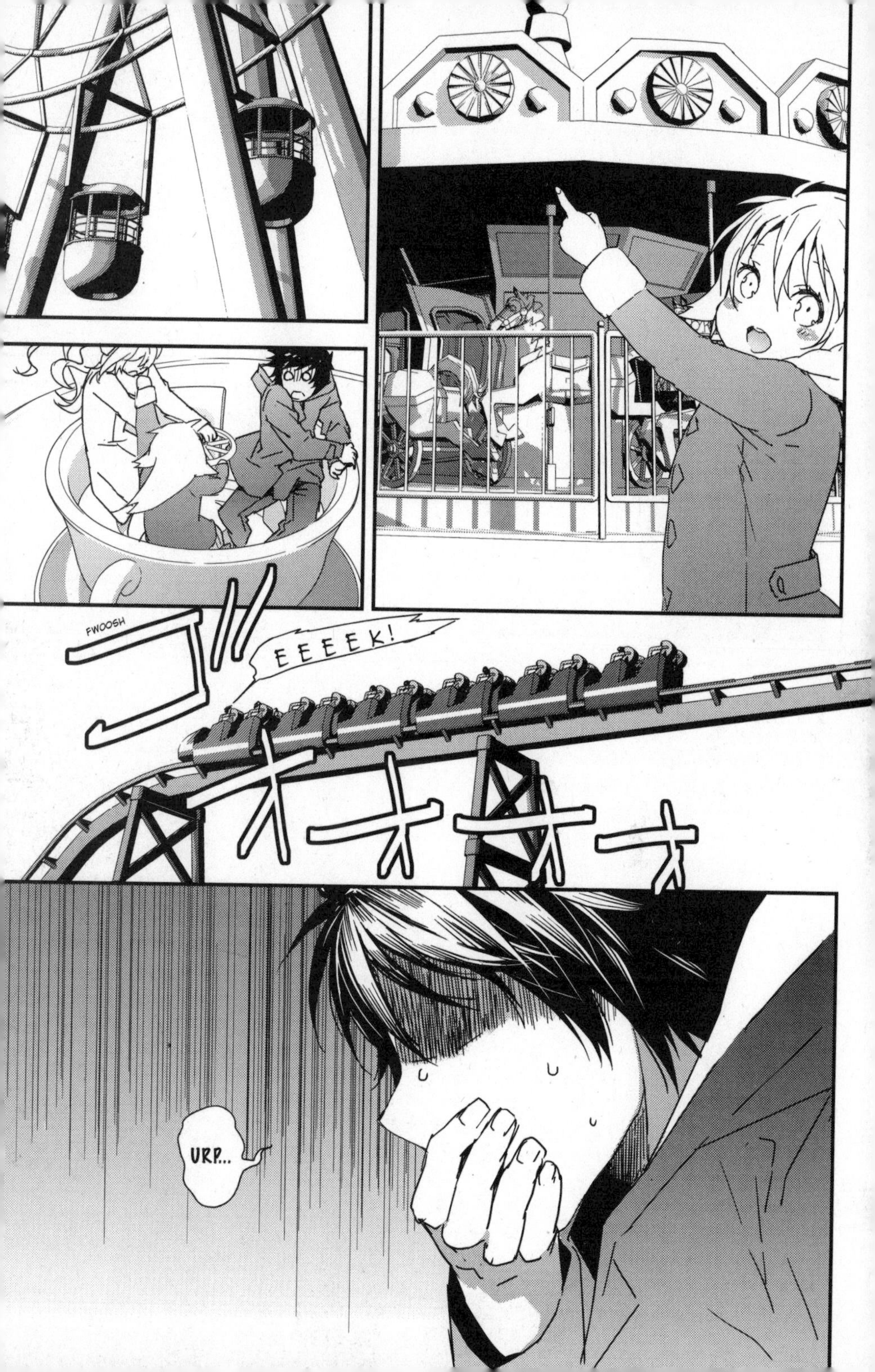
FWOOSH
EEEEK!
URP...

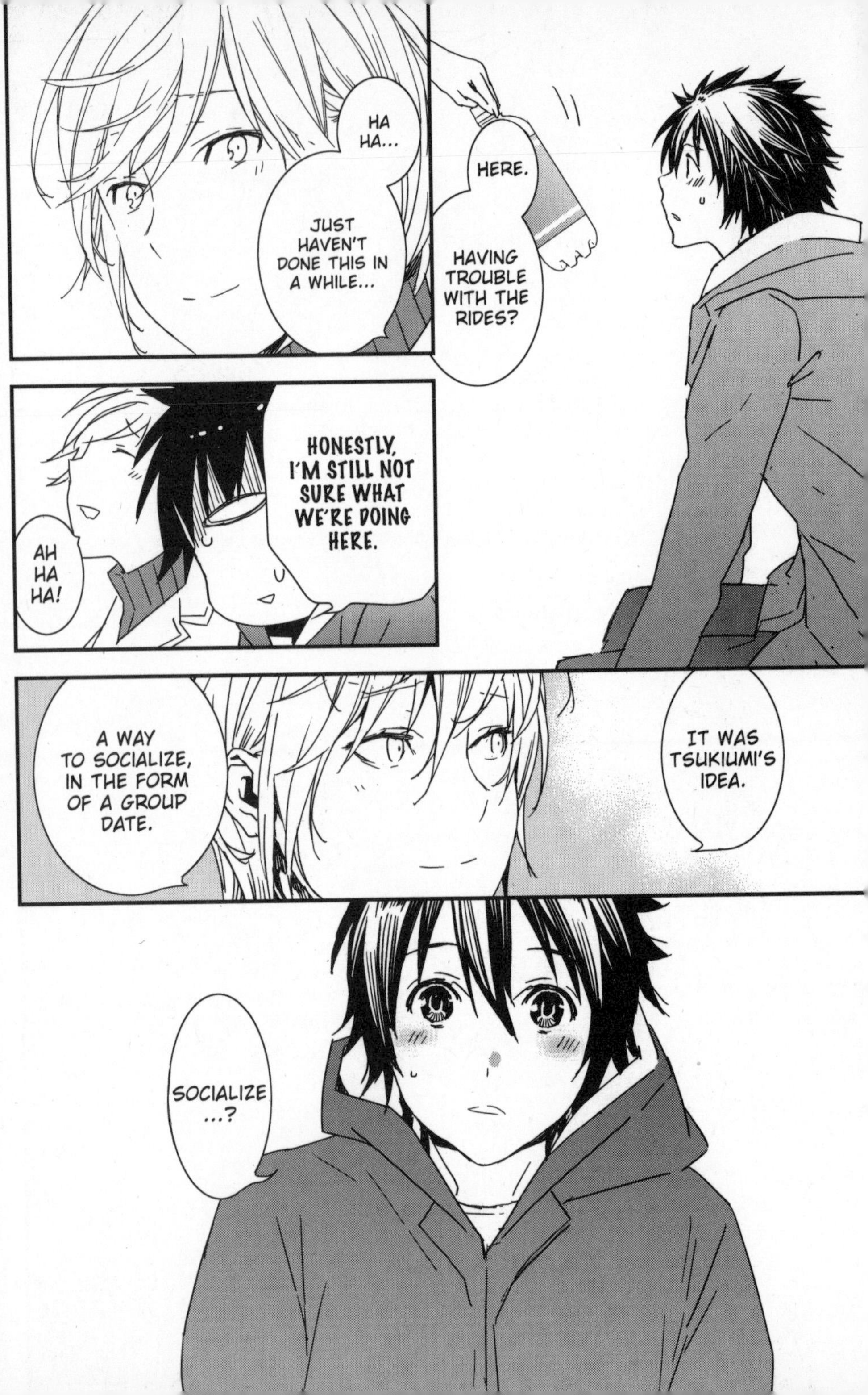
HERE.
HAVING TROUBLE WITH THE RIDES?
HA HA...
JUST HAVEN'T DONE THIS IN A WHILE...
HONESTLY, I'M STILL NOT SURE WHAT WE'RE DOING HERE.
AH HA HA!
IT WAS TSUKIUMI'S IDEA.
A WAY TO SOCIALIZE, IN THE FORM OF A GROUP DATE.
SOCIALIZE ...?

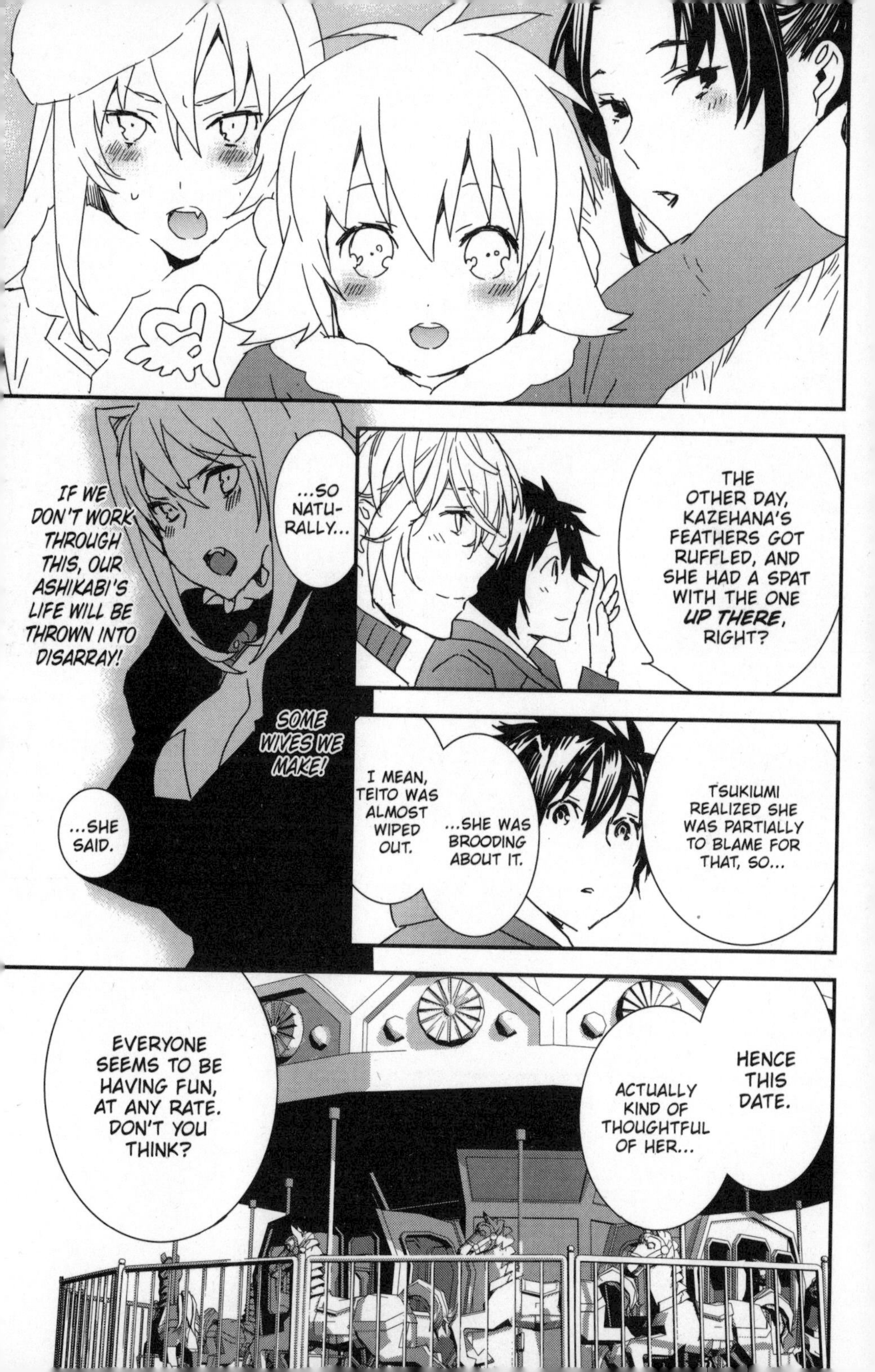
THE OTHER DAY, KAZEHANA'S FEATHERS GOT RUFFLED, AND SHE HAD A SPAT WITH THE ONE *UP THERE*, RIGHT?
TSUKIUMI REALIZED SHE WAS PARTIALLY TO BLAME FOR THAT, SO...
...SHE WAS BROODING ABOUT IT.
I MEAN, TEITO WAS ALMOST WIPED OUT.
...SO NATU-RALLY...
IF WE DON'T WORK THROUGH THIS, OUR ASHIKABI'S LIFE WILL BE THROWN INTO DISARRAY!
SOME WIVES WE MAKE!
...SHE SAID.
HENCE THIS DATE.
ACTUALLY KIND OF THOUGHTFUL OF HER...
EVERYONE SEEMS TO BE HAVING FUN, AT ANY RATE. DON'T YOU THINK?

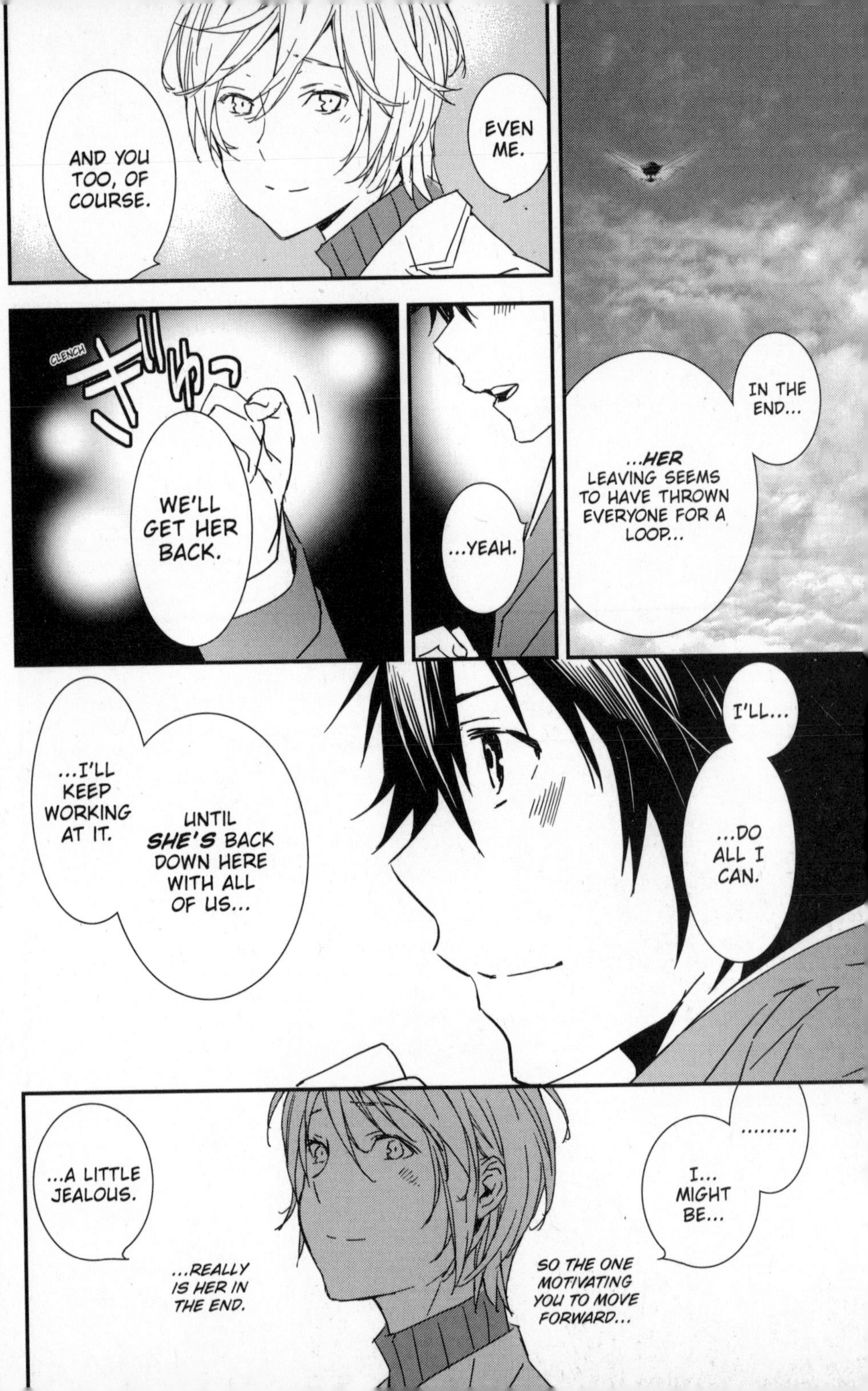
IN THE END...
...*HER* LEAVING SEEMS TO HAVE THROWN EVERYONE FOR A LOOP...
EVEN ME.
AND YOU TOO, OF COURSE.
...YEAH.
CLENCH
WE'LL GET HER BACK.
I'LL...
...DO ALL I CAN.
UNTIL *SHE'S* BACK DOWN HERE WITH ALL OF US...
...I'LL KEEP WORKING AT IT.
SO THE ONE MOTIVATING YOU TO MOVE FORWARD...
...REALLY IS HER IN THE END.
....
I... MIGHT BE...
...A LITTLE JEALOUS.

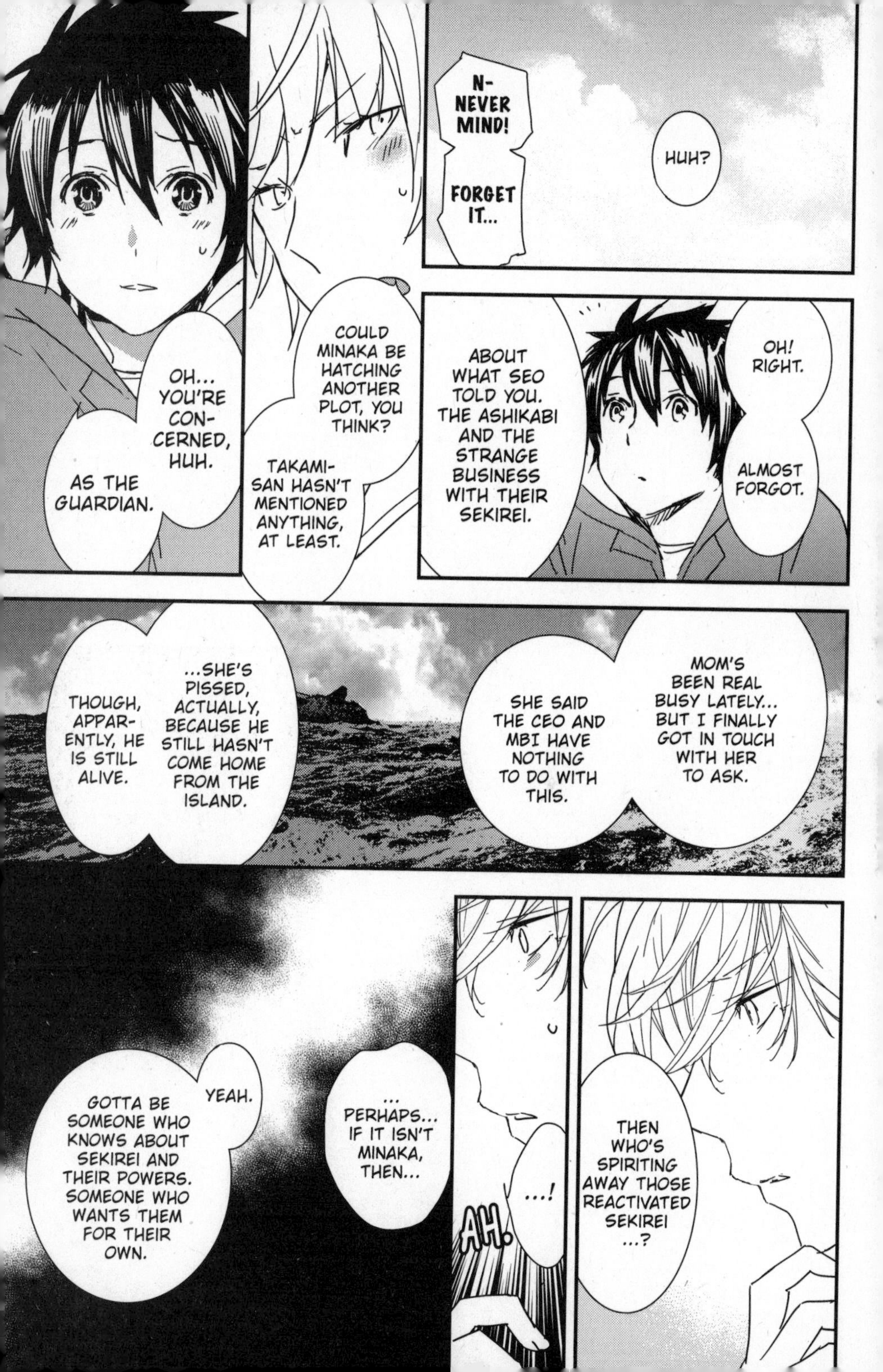
HUH?
N-NEVER MIND!
FORGET IT...
OH! RIGHT.
ALMOST FORGOT.
ABOUT WHAT SEO TOLD YOU. THE ASHIKABI AND THE STRANGE BUSINESS WITH THEIR SEKIREI.
COULD MINAKA BE HATCHING ANOTHER PLOT, YOU THINK?
TAKAMI-SAN HASN'T MENTIONED ANYTHING, AT LEAST.
OH... YOU'RE CONCERNED, HUH.
AS THE GUARDIAN.
MOM'S BEEN REAL BUSY LATELY... BUT I FINALLY GOT IN TOUCH WITH HER TO ASK.
SHE SAID THE CEO AND MBI HAVE NOTHING TO DO WITH THIS.
...SHE'S PISSED, ACTUALLY, BECAUSE HE STILL HASN'T COME HOME FROM THE ISLAND.
THOUGH, APPARENTLY, HE IS STILL ALIVE.
THEN WHO'S SPIRITING AWAY THOSE REACTIVATED SEKIREI ...?
AH.
...!
... PERHAPS... IF IT ISN'T MINAKA, THEN...
YEAH.
GOTTA BE SOMEONE WHO KNOWS ABOUT SEKIREI AND THEIR POWERS. SOMEONE WHO WANTS THEM FOR THEIR OWN.

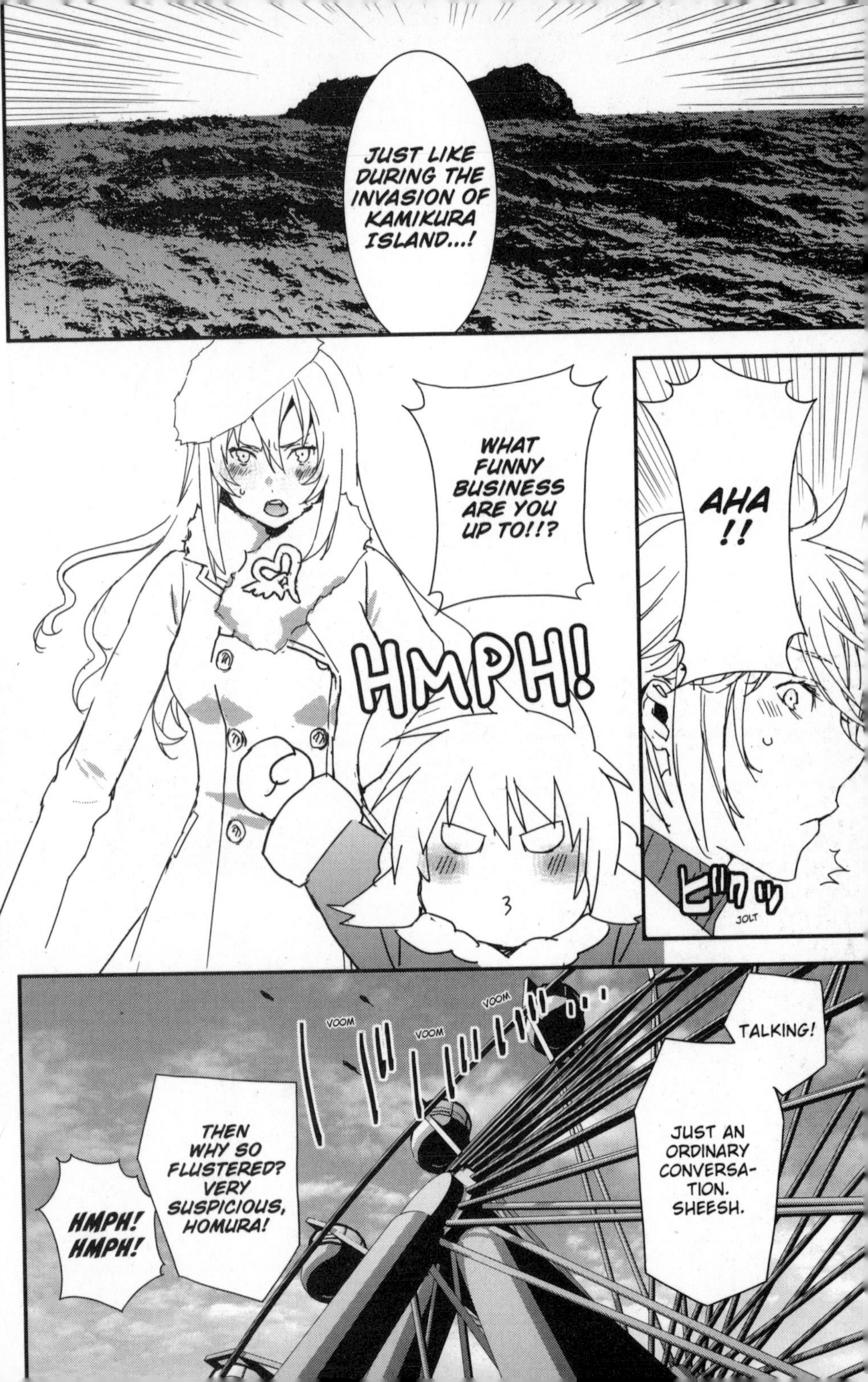
JUST LIKE DURING THE INVASION OF KAMIKURA ISLAND...!
AHA!!
ビクッ
JOLT
WHAT FUNNY BUSINESS ARE YOU UP TO!!?
HMPH!
TALKING!
JUST AN ORDINARY CONVERSA-TION. SHEESH.
VOOM
VOOM
VOOM
THEN WHY SO FLUSTERED? VERY SUSPICIOUS, HOMURA!
HMPH! HMPH!

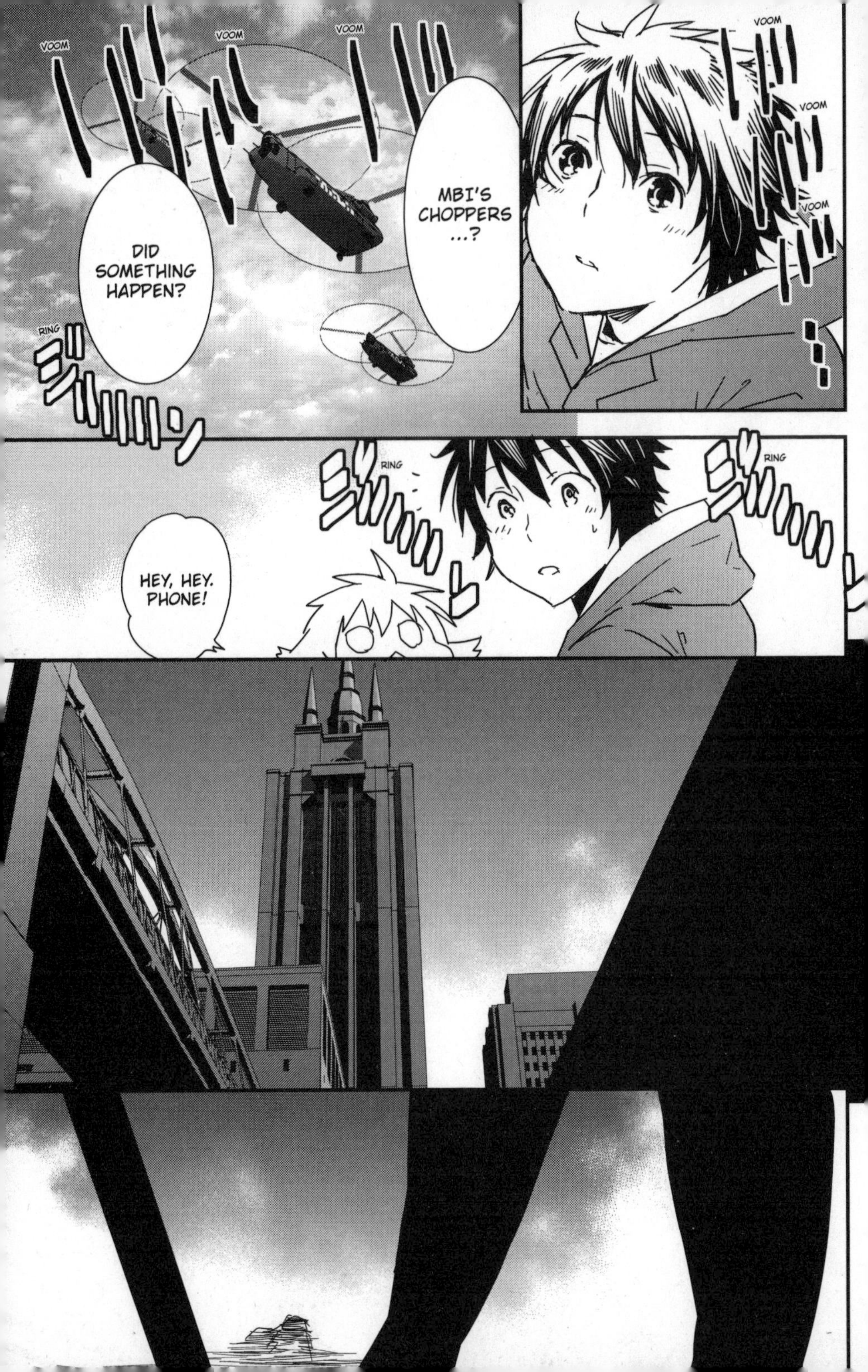
VOOM
VOOM
VOOM
MBI'S CHOPPERS ...?
VOOM
VOOM
VOOM
DID SOMETHING HAPPEN?
RING
RING
RING
HEY, HEY. PHONE!

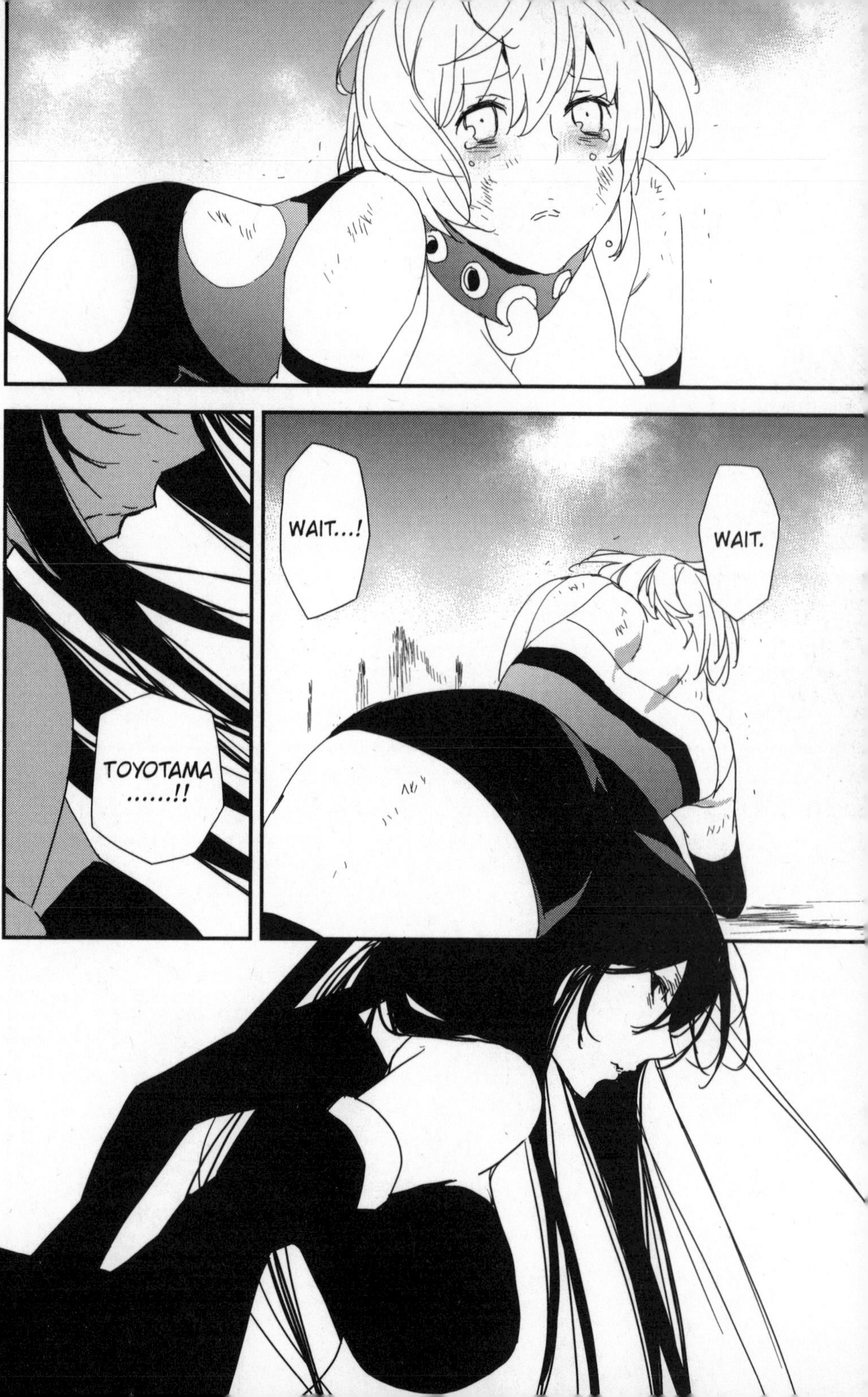
WAIT.
WAIT...!
TOYOTAMA ......!!

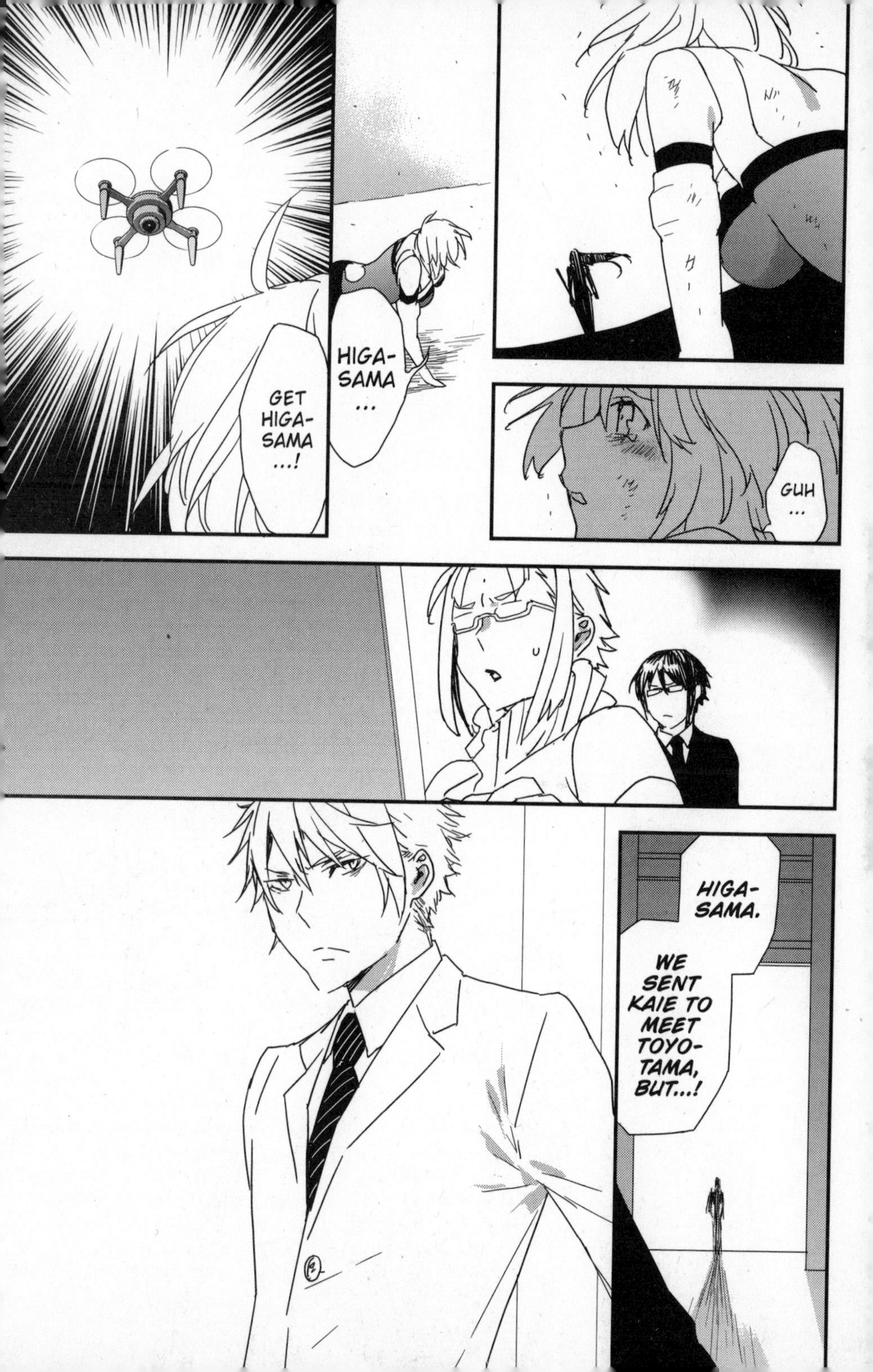
GUH ...
HIGA-SAMA ...
GET HIGA-SAMA ...!
HIGA-SAMA.
WE SENT KAIE TO MEET TOYO-TAMA, BUT...!

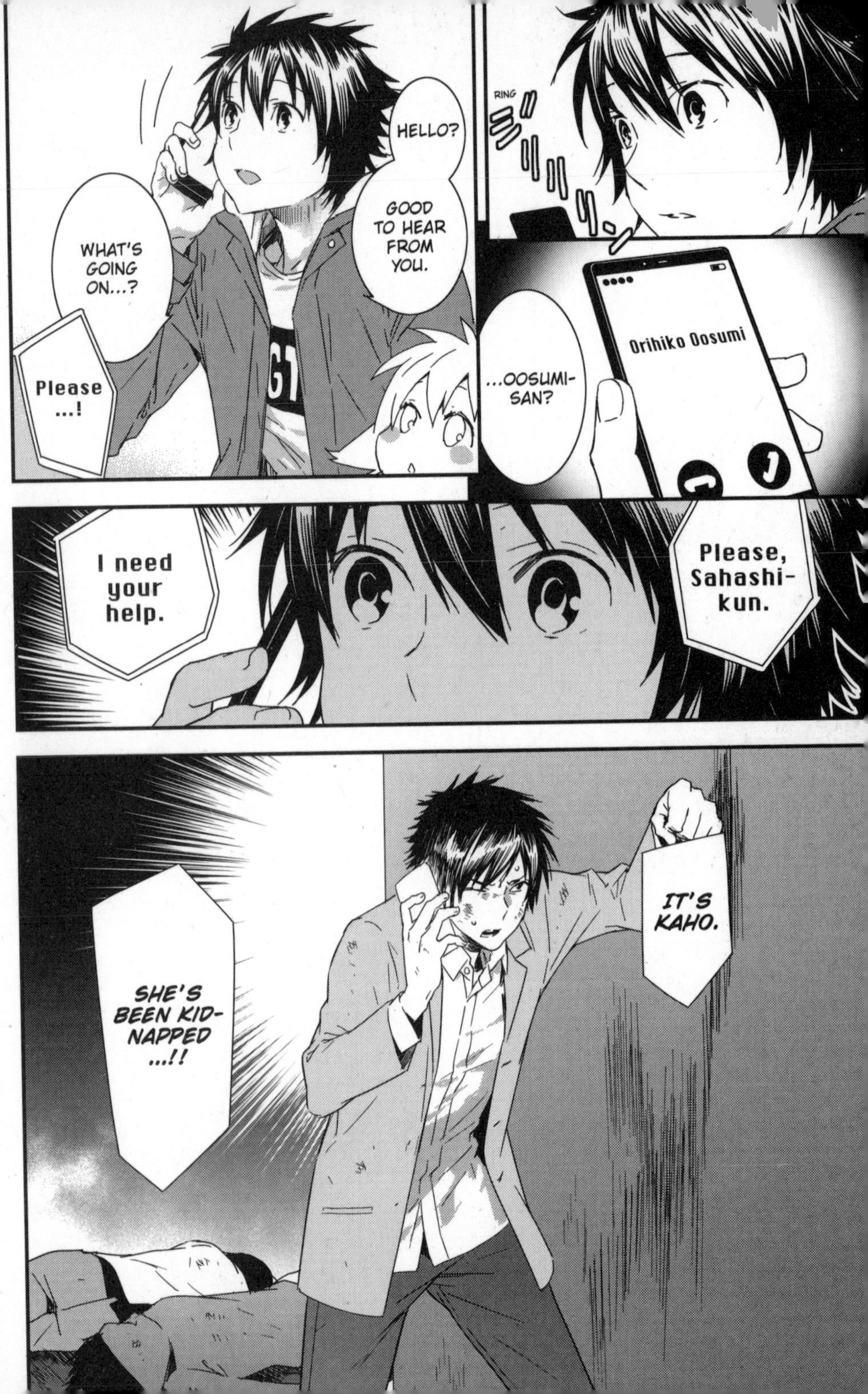
RING
Orihiko Oosumi
...OOSUMI-SAN?
HELLO?
GOOD TO HEAR FROM YOU.
WHAT'S GOING ON...?
Please ...!
Please, Sahashi-kun.
I need your help.
IT'S KAHO.
SHE'S BEEN KID-NAPPED ...!!

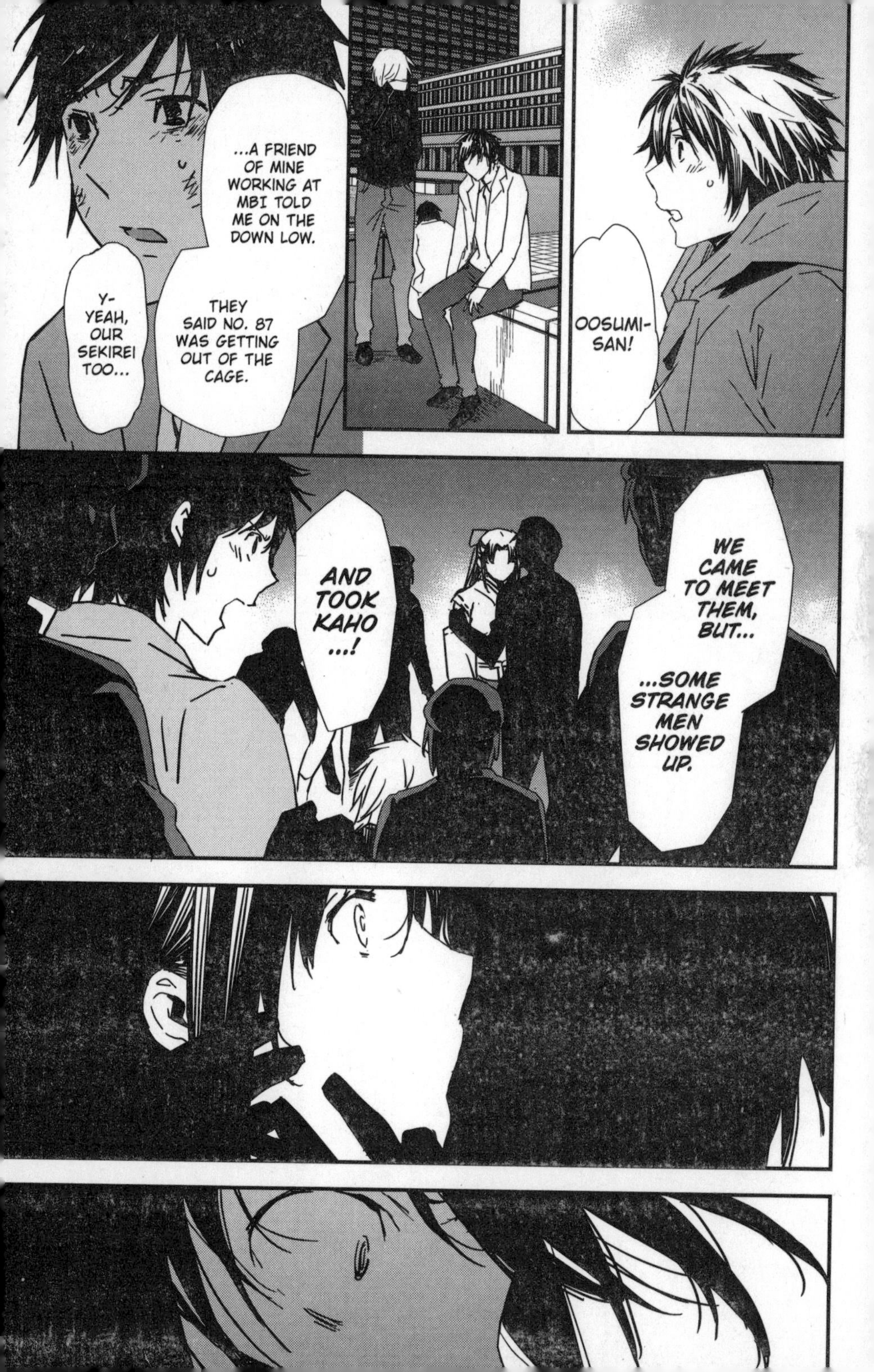
OOSUMI-SAN!
...A FRIEND OF MINE WORKING AT MBI TOLD ME ON THE DOWN LOW.
THEY SAID NO. 87 WAS GETTING OUT OF THE CAGE.
Y-YEAH, OUR SEKIREI TOO...
WE CAME TO MEET THEM, BUT...
...SOME STRANGE MEN SHOWED UP.
AND TOOK KAHO...!

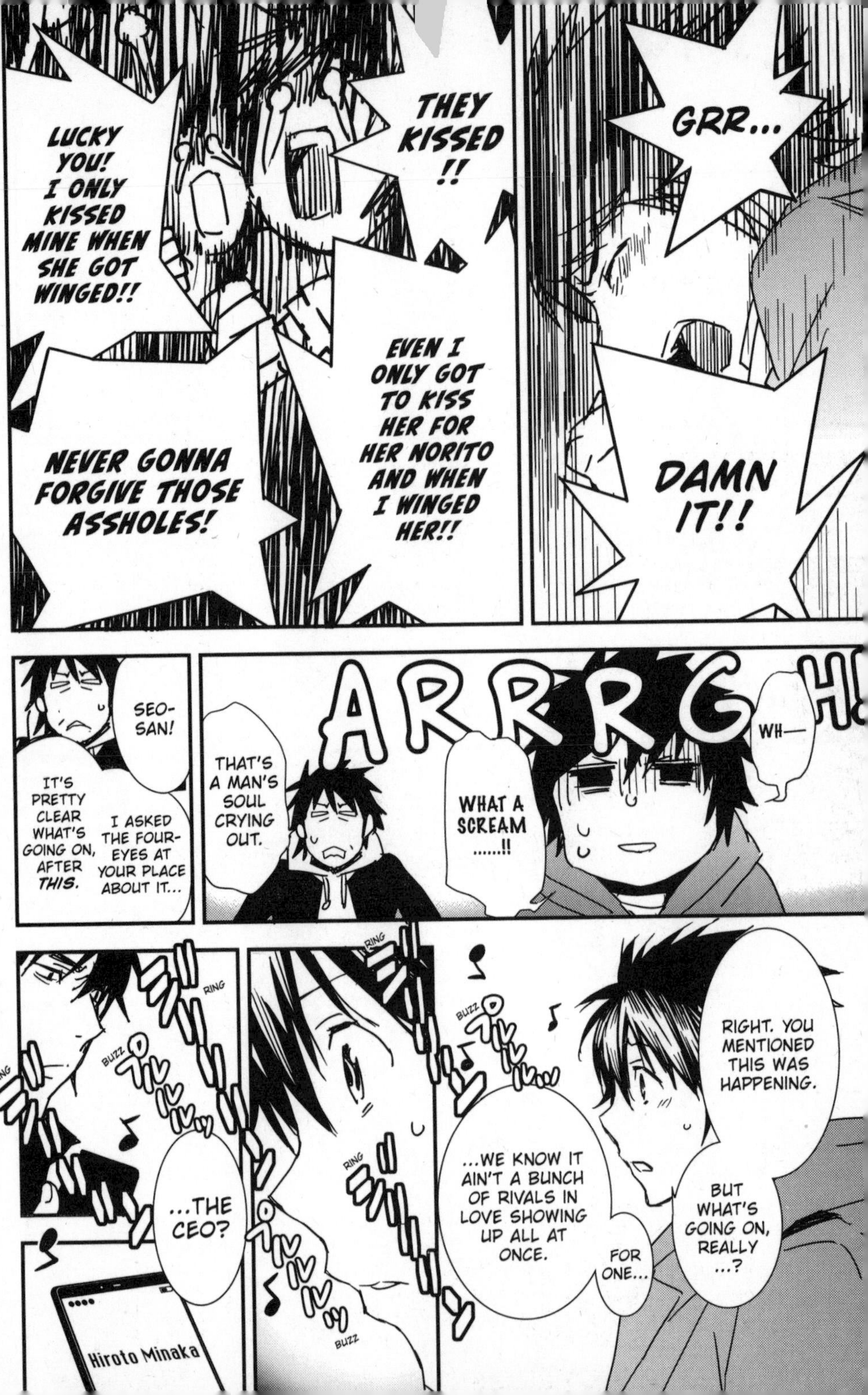
GRR...
DAMN IT!!
THEY KISSED !!
LUCKY YOU! I ONLY KISSED MINE WHEN SHE GOT WINGED!!
EVEN I ONLY GOT TO KISS HER FOR HER NORITO AND WHEN I WINGED HER!!
NEVER GONNA FORGIVE THOSE ASSHOLES!
ARRRGH!
WH—
WHAT A SCREAM ......!!
THAT'S A MAN'S SOUL CRYING OUT.
SEO-SAN!
I ASKED THE FOUR-EYES AT YOUR PLACE ABOUT IT...
IT'S PRETTY CLEAR WHAT'S GOING ON, AFTER THIS.
RIGHT. YOU MENTIONED THIS WAS HAPPENING.
BUT WHAT'S GOING ON, REALLY ...?
FOR ONE...
...WE KNOW IT AIN'T A BUNCH OF RIVALS IN LOVE SHOWING UP ALL AT ONCE.
RING
BUZZ
RING
BUZZ
RING
...THE CEO?
RING
BUZZ
RING
Hiroto Minaka

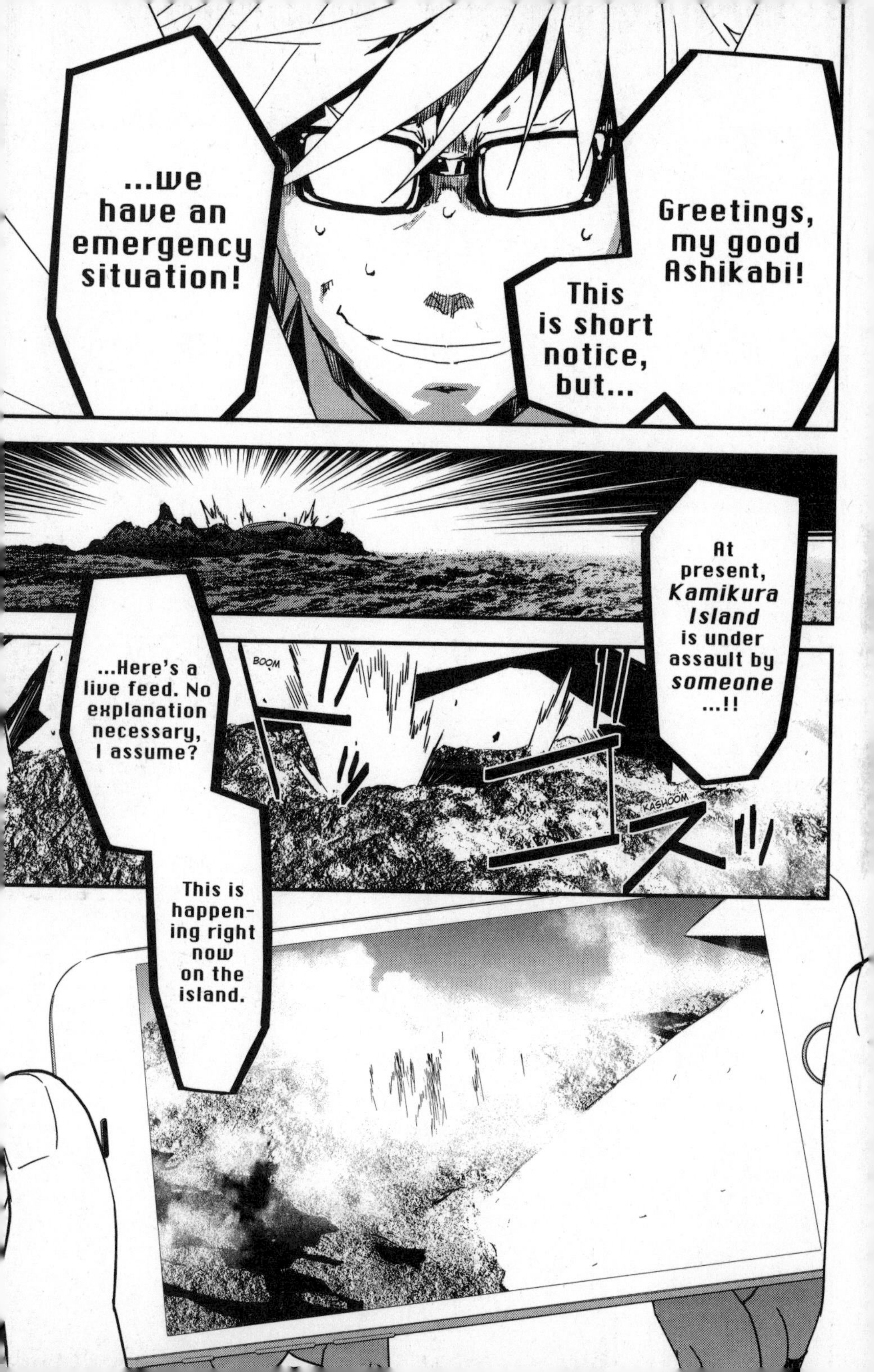
Greetings, my good Ashikabi!
This is short notice, but...
...we have an emergency situation!
At present, *Kamikura Island* is under assault by *someone* ...!!
BOOM
KASHOOM
...Here's a live feed. No explanation necessary, I assume?
This is happening right now on the island.

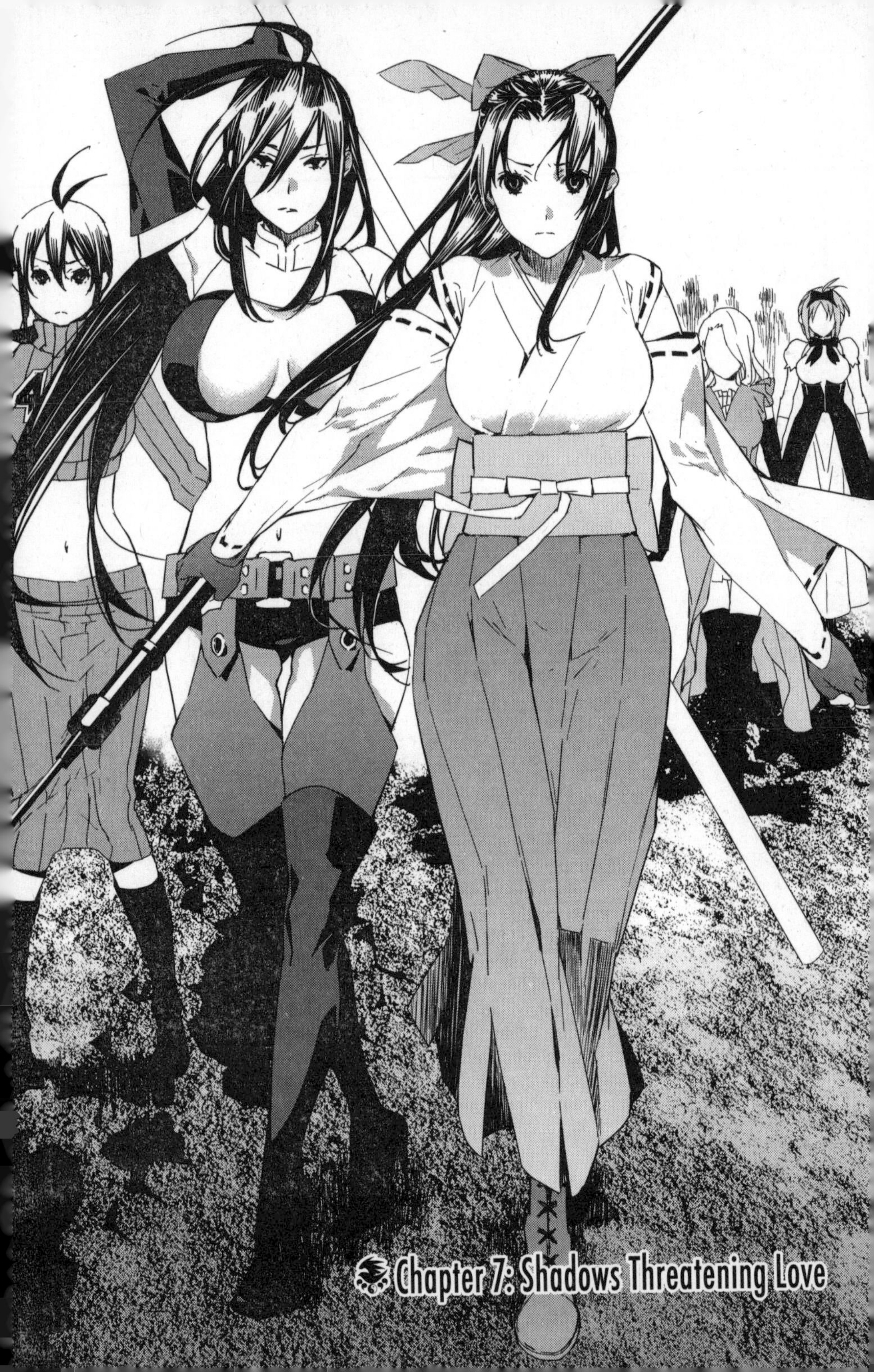
Chapter 7: Shadows Threatening Love

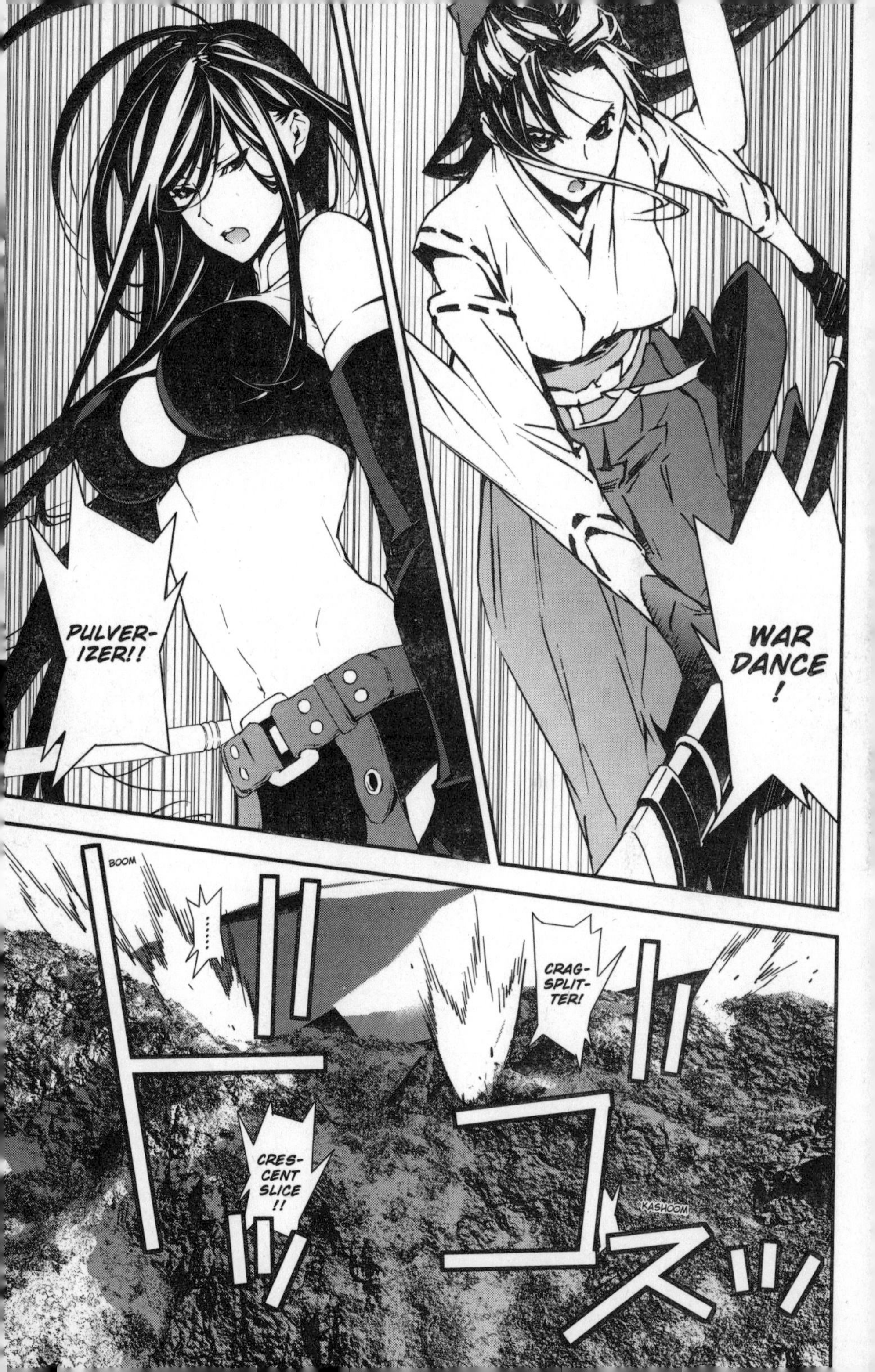
WAR DANCE!
PULVER-IZER!!
CRAG-SPLITTER!
......
BOOM
ドッ
KASHOOM
ゴスッ
CRES-CENT SLICE!!

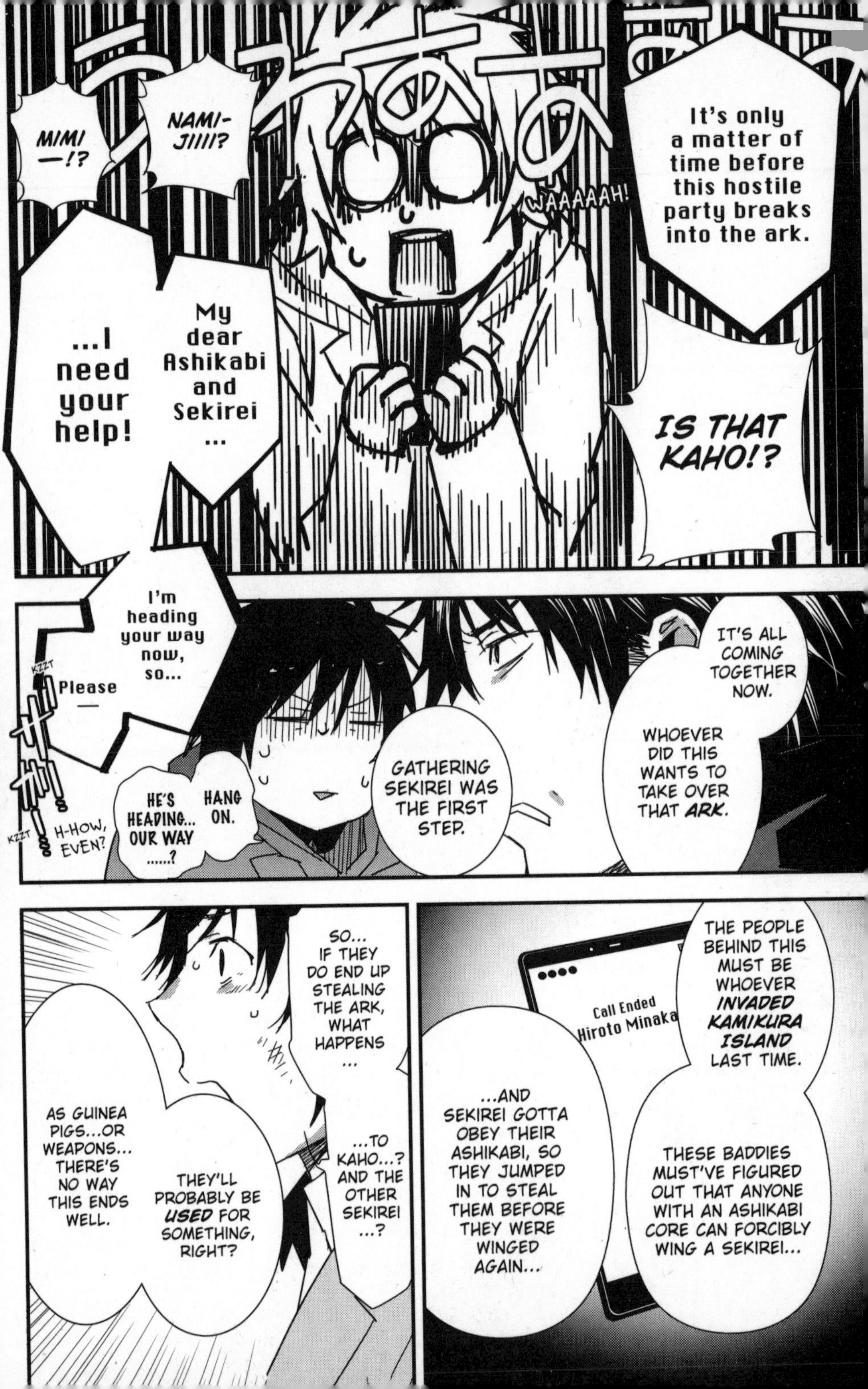
It's only a matter of time before this hostile party breaks into the ark.
WAAAAAH!
NAMI-JIIII?
MIMI—!?
IS THAT KAHO!?
My dear Ashikabi and Sekirei ...
...I need your help!
IT'S ALL COMING TOGETHER NOW.
WHOEVER DID THIS WANTS TO TAKE OVER THAT ARK.
GATHERING SEKIREI WAS THE FIRST STEP.
I'm heading your way now, so...
Please —
KZZT
HANG ON.
HE'S HEADING... OUR WAY ......?
H-HOW, EVEN?
KZZT
THE PEOPLE BEHIND THIS MUST BE WHOEVER INVADED KAMIKURA ISLAND LAST TIME.
Call Ended
Hiroto Minaka
THESE BADDIES MUST'VE FIGURED OUT THAT ANYONE WITH AN ASHIKABI CORE CAN FORCIBLY WING A SEKIREI...
...AND SEKIREI GOTTA OBEY THEIR ASHIKABI, SO THEY JUMPED IN TO STEAL THEM BEFORE THEY WERE WINGED AGAIN...
SO... IF THEY DO END UP STEALING THE ARK, WHAT HAPPENS ...
...TO KAHO...? AND THE OTHER SEKIREI ...?
THEY'LL PROBABLY BE USED FOR SOMETHING, RIGHT?
AS GUINEA PIGS...OR WEAPONS... THERE'S NO WAY THIS ENDS WELL.

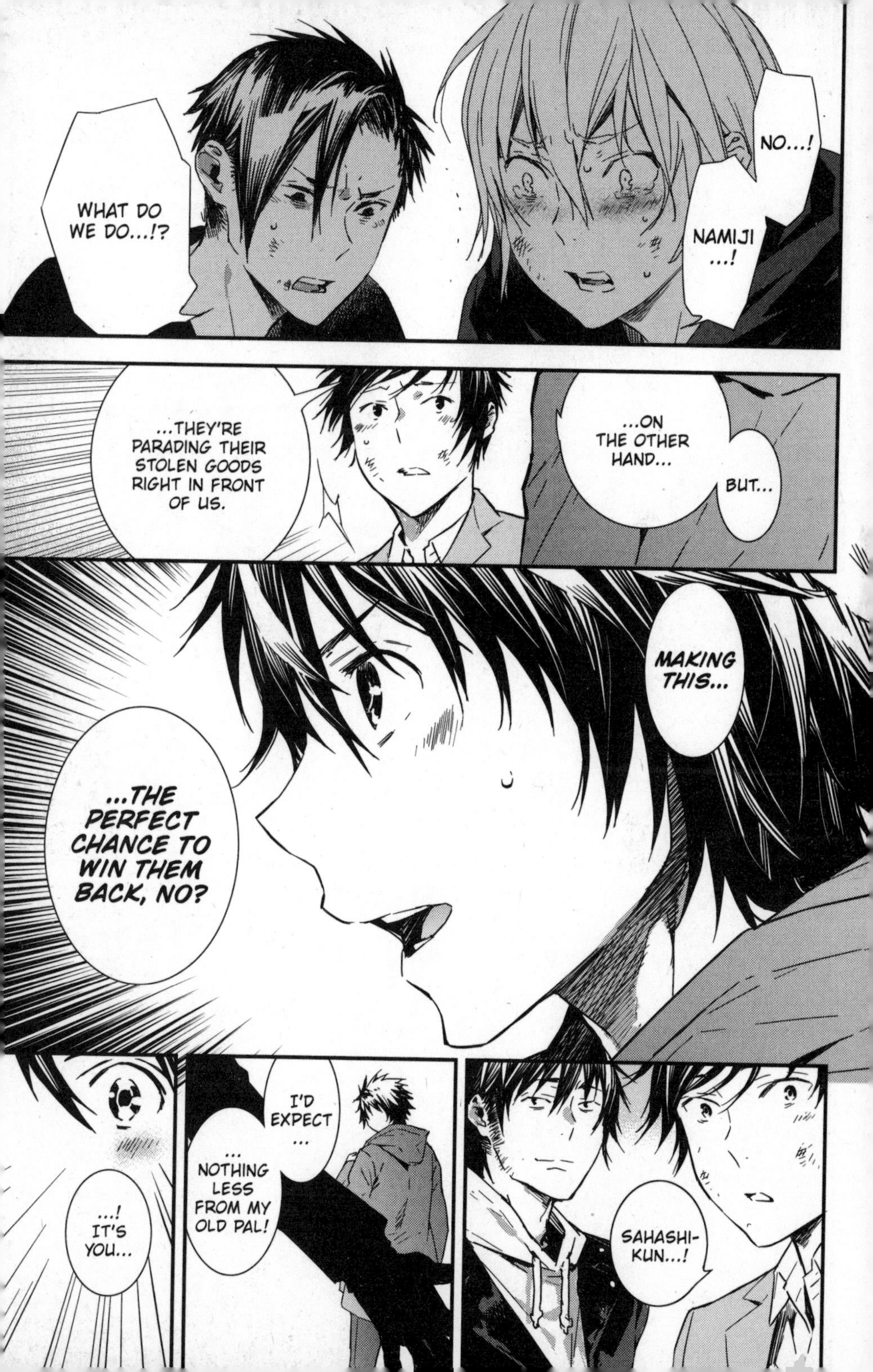
NO...!
NAMIJI ...!
WHAT DO WE DO...!?
...ON THE OTHER HAND...
BUT...
...THEY'RE PARADING THEIR STOLEN GOODS RIGHT IN FRONT OF US.
MAKING THIS...
...THE PERFECT CHANCE TO WIN THEM BACK, NO?
SAHASHI-KUN...!
I'D EXPECT ...
... NOTHING LESS FROM MY OLD PAL!
...! IT'S YOU...

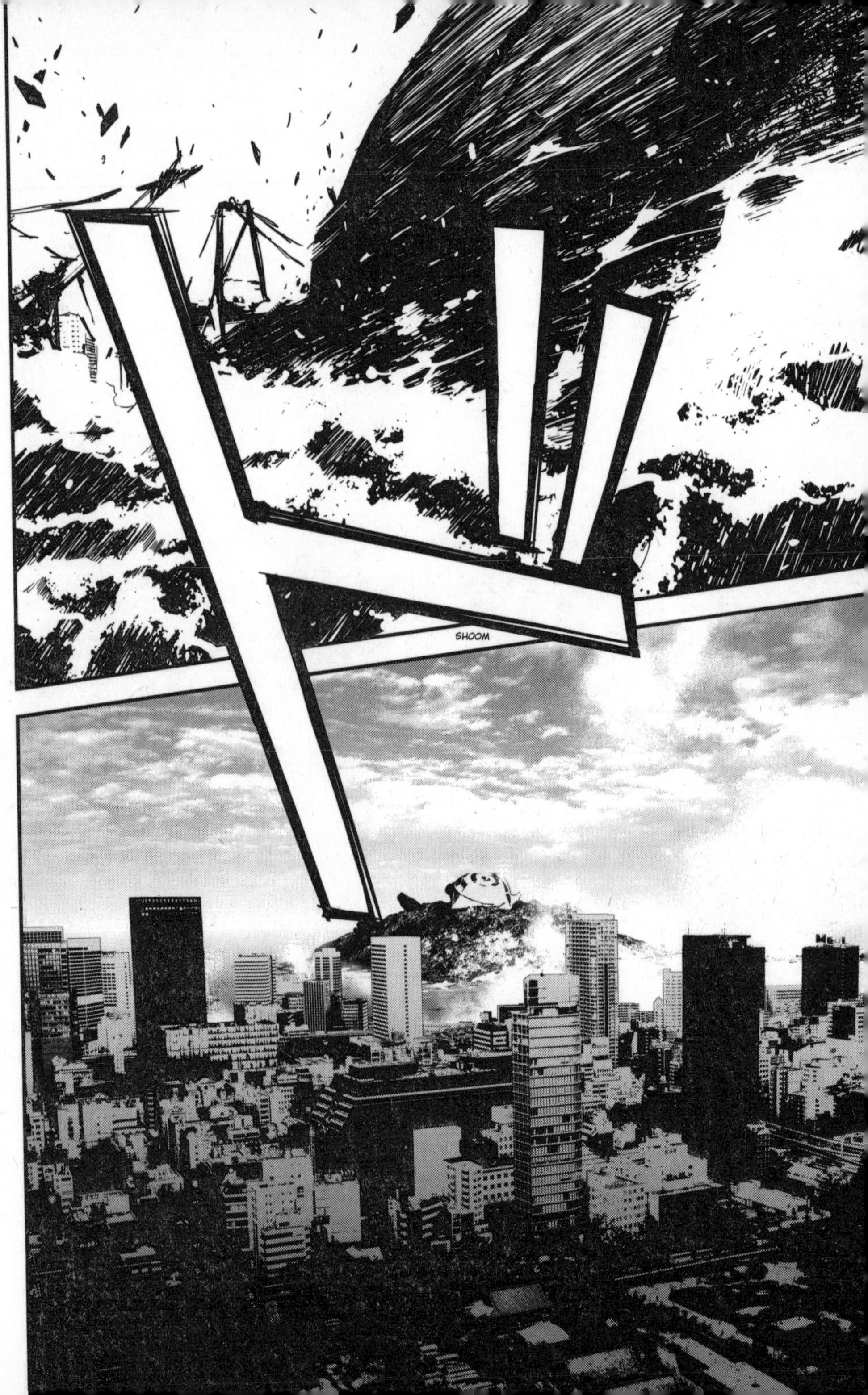
SHOOM

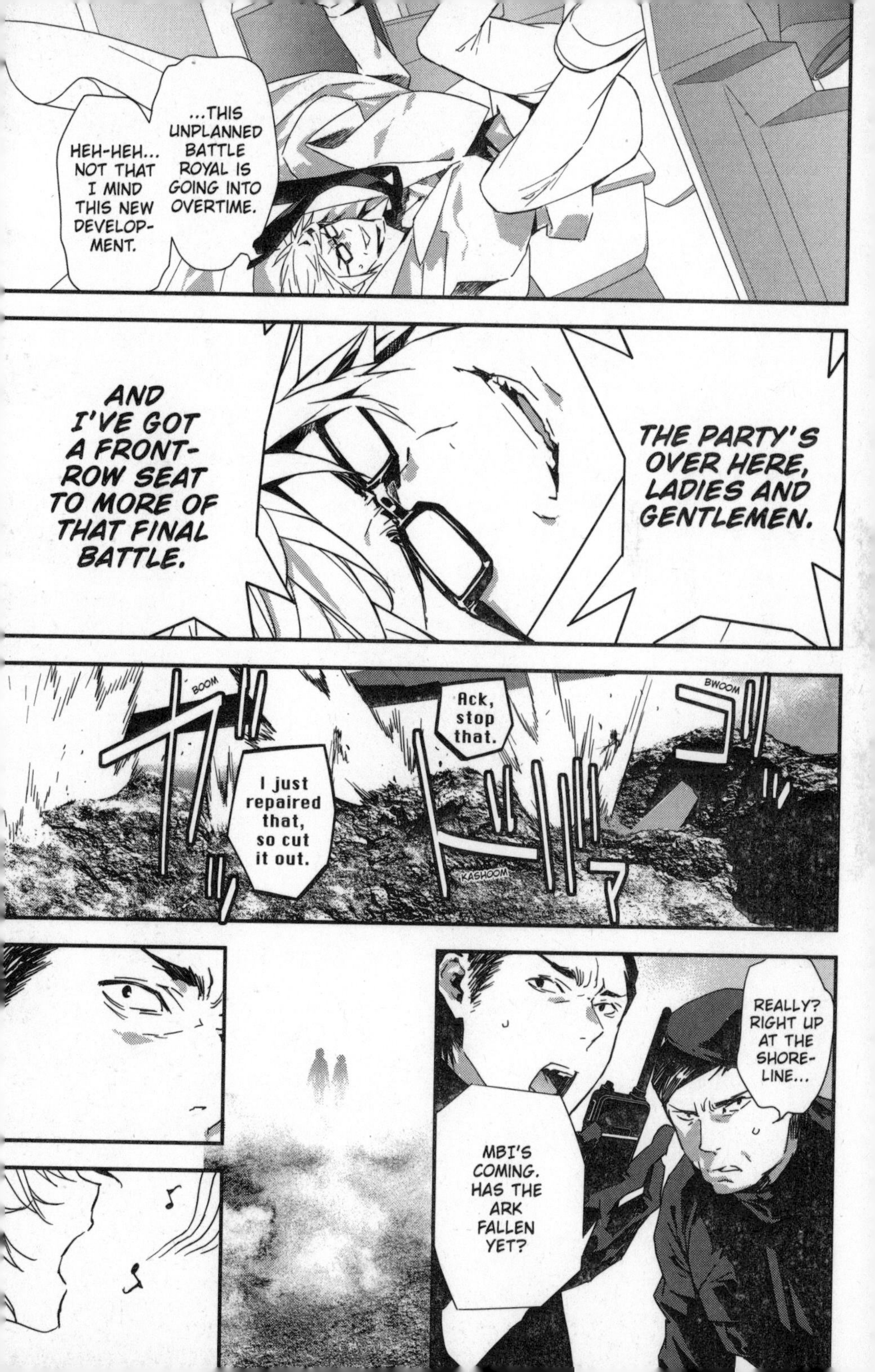
...THIS UNPLANNED BATTLE ROYAL IS GOING INTO OVERTIME.
HEH-HEH... NOT THAT I MIND THIS NEW DEVELOPMENT.
THE PARTY'S OVER HERE, LADIES AND GENTLEMEN.
AND I'VE GOT A FRONT-ROW SEAT TO MORE OF THAT FINAL BATTLE.
BWOOM
Ack, stop that.
KASHOOM
I just repaired that, so cut it out.
BOOM
REALLY? RIGHT UP AT THE SHORELINE...
MBI'S COMING. HAS THE ARK FALLEN YET?

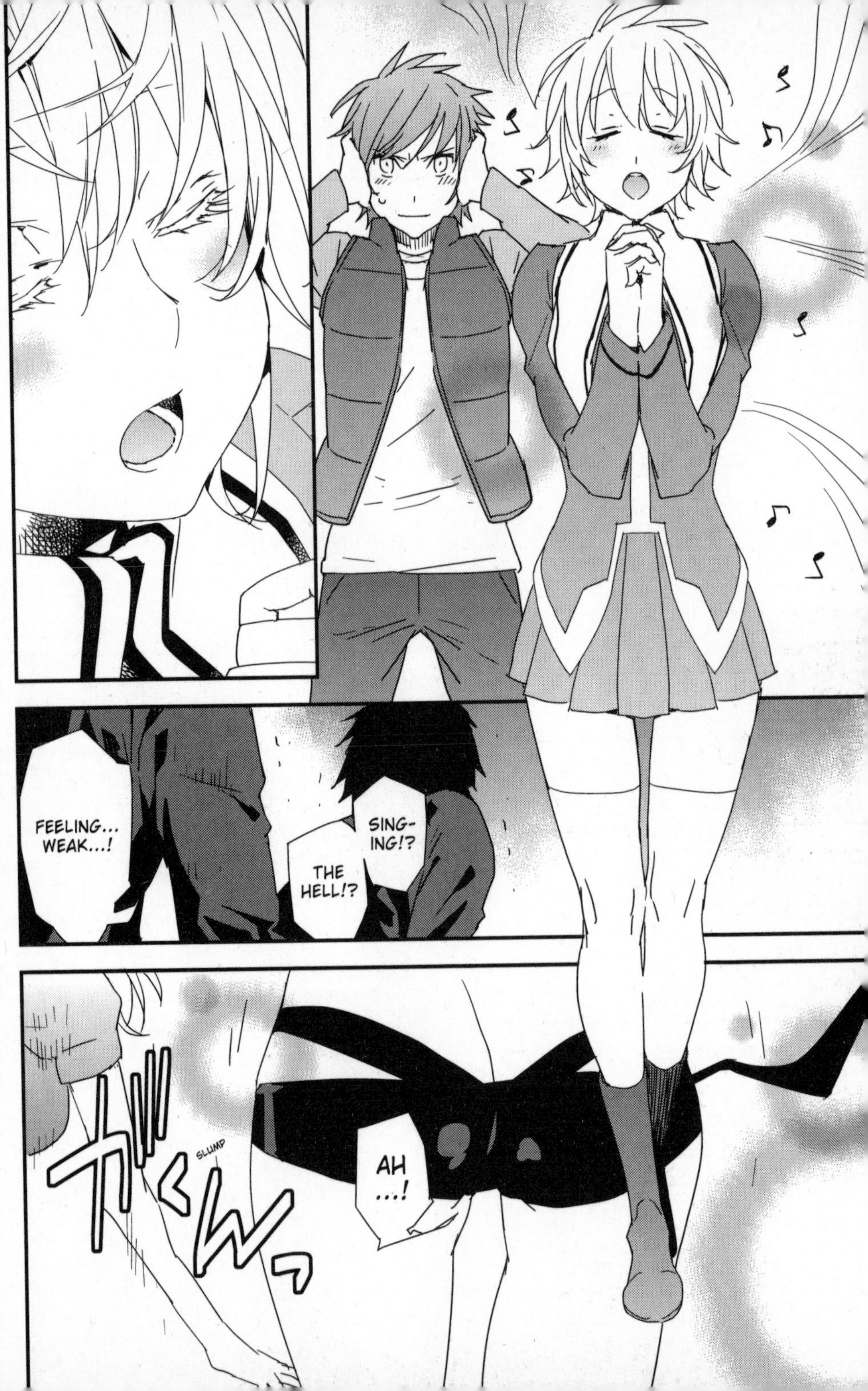
SING-ING!?
THE HELL!?
FEELING... WEAK...!
AH ...!
SLUMP

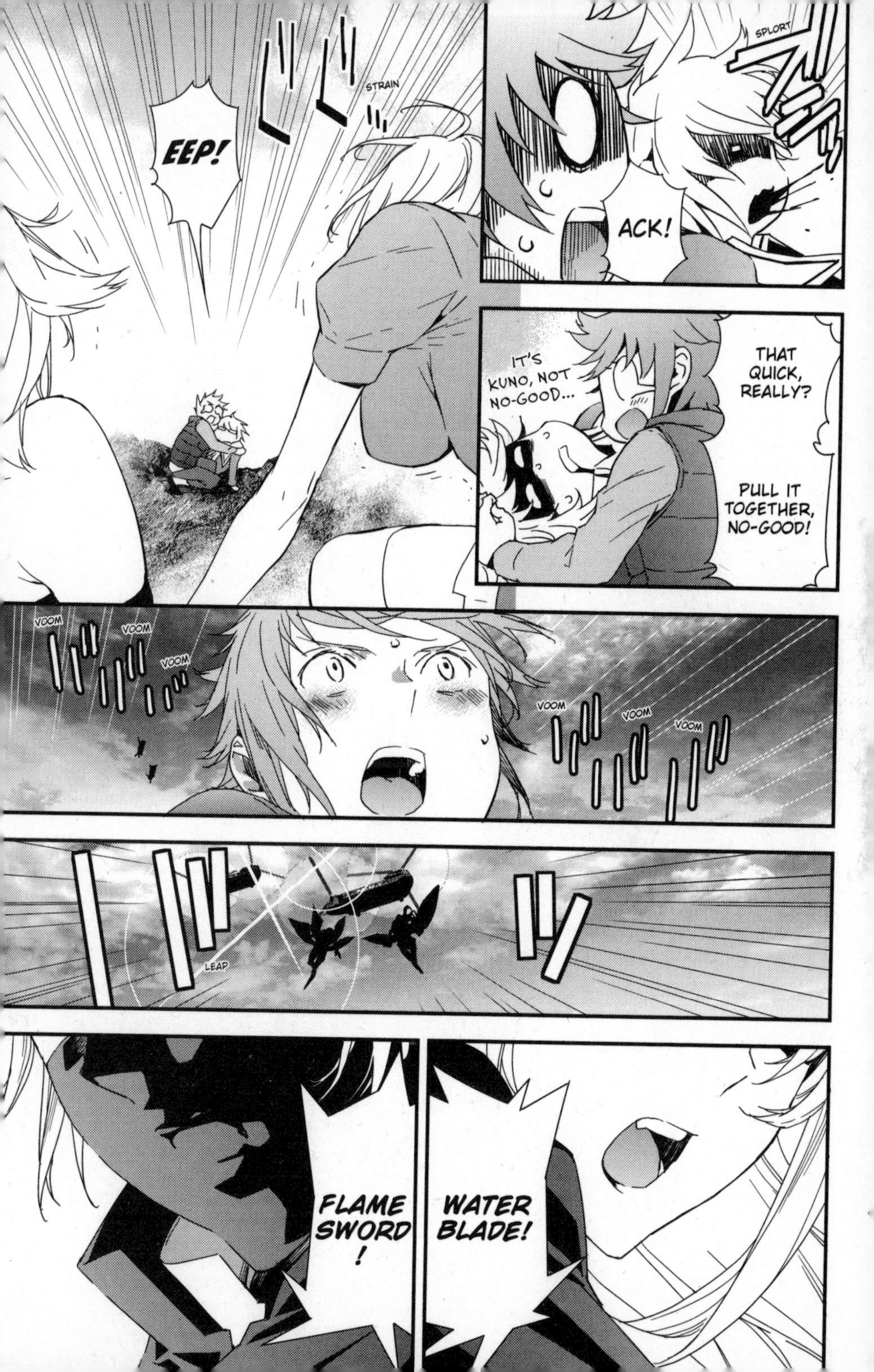
SPLORT
ACK!
THAT QUICK, REALLY?
PULL IT TOGETHER, NO-GOOD!
IT'S KUNO, NOT NO-GOOD...
STRAIN
EEP!
VOOM
VOOM
VOOM
VOOM
VOOM
VOOM
LEAP
WATER BLADE!
FLAME SWORD !

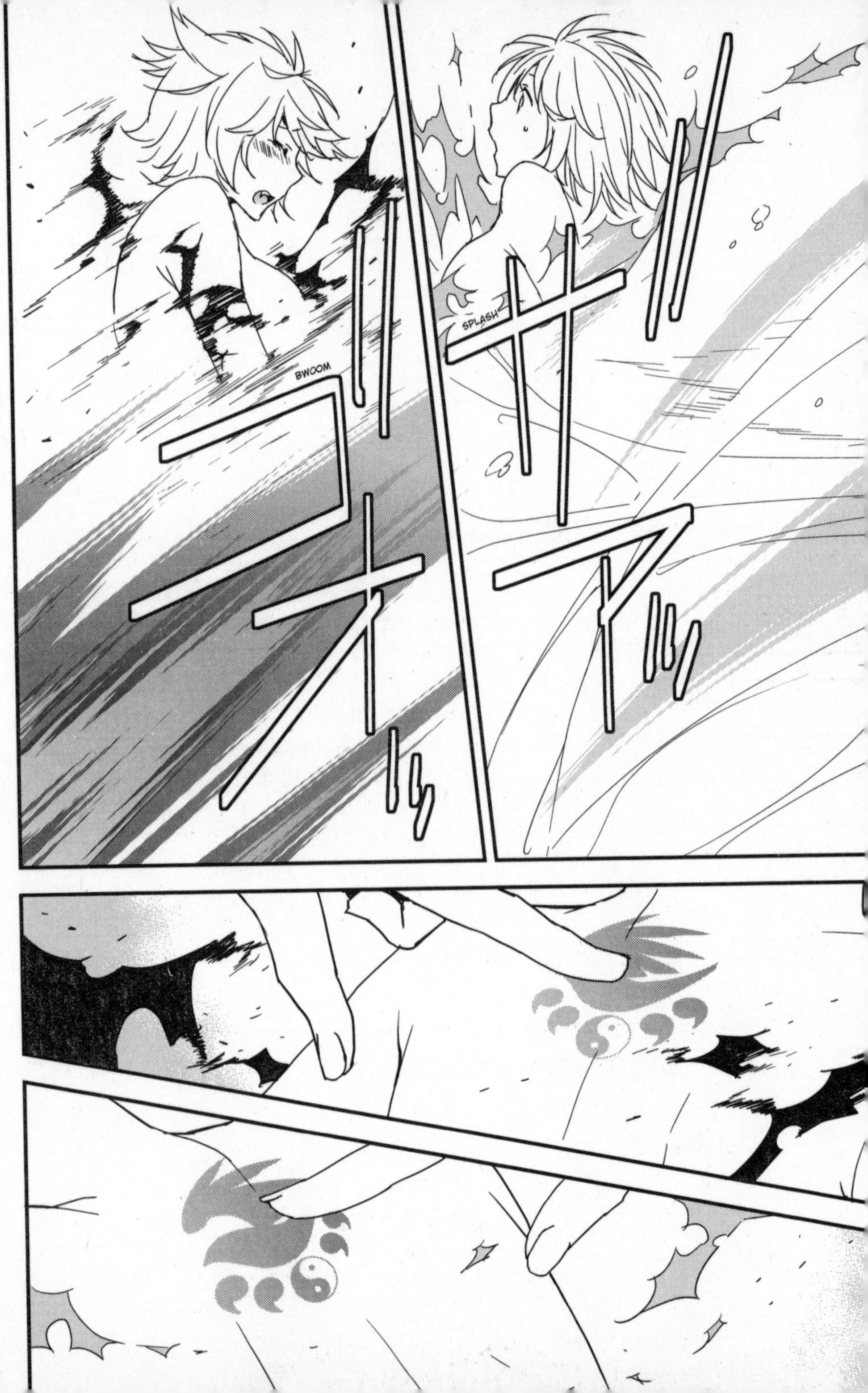

ザアッ
SPLASH
ゴオッ
BWOOM

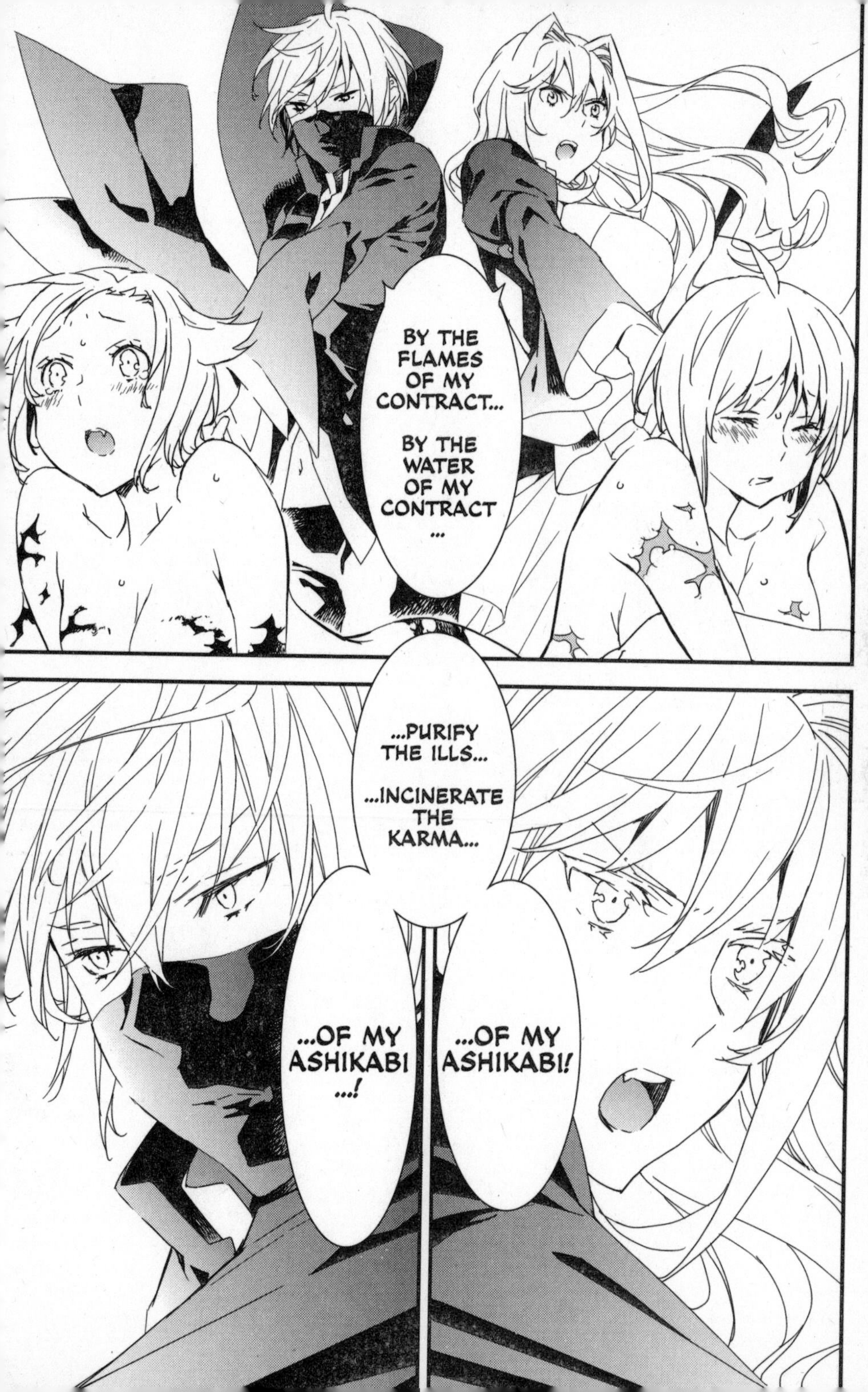
BY THE FLAMES OF MY CONTRACT... BY THE WATER OF MY CONTRACT ...
...PURIFY THE ILLS... ...INCINERATE THE KARMA...
...OF MY ASHIKABI!
...OF MY ASHIKABI ...!

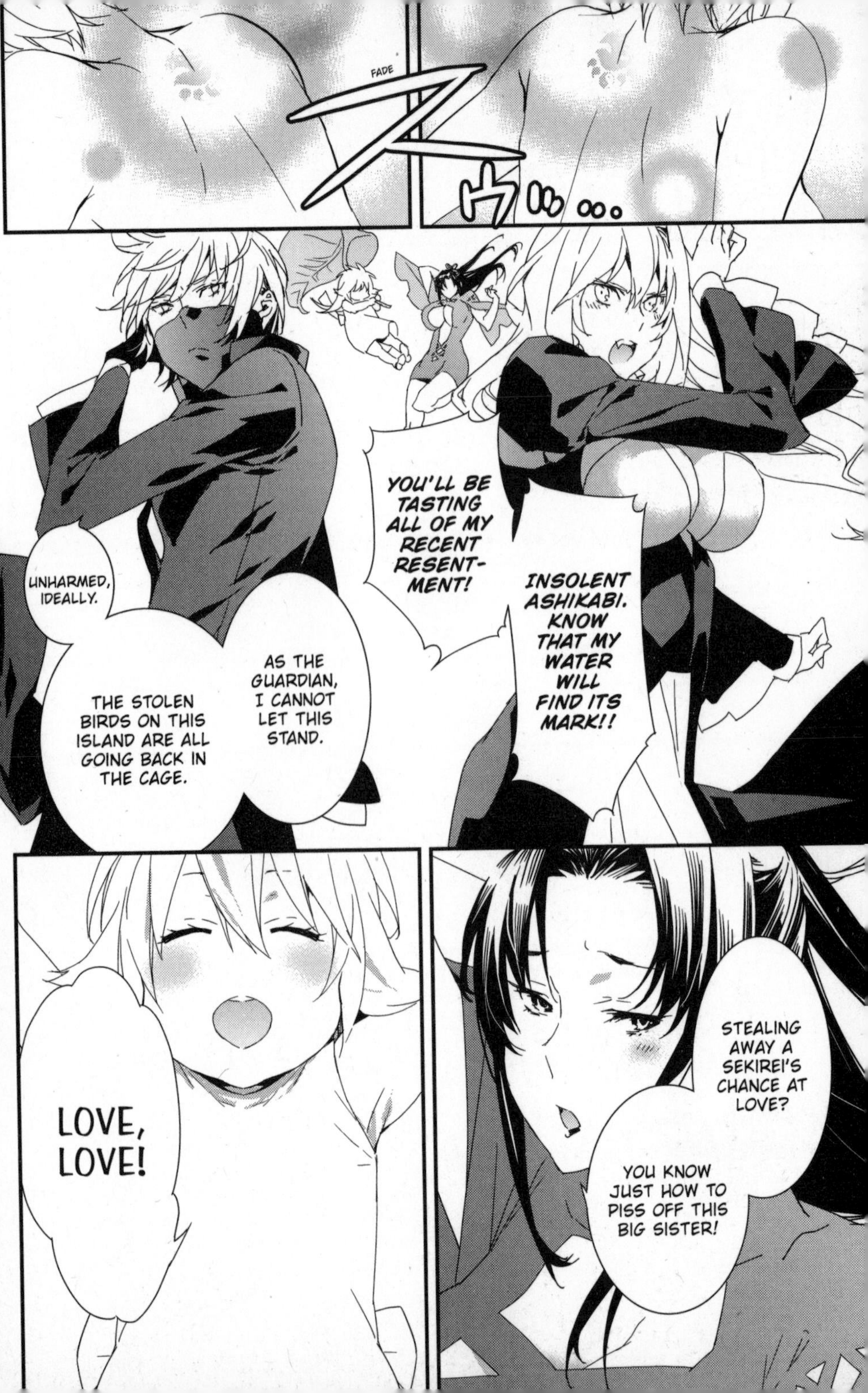
FADE
INSOLENT ASHIKABI. KNOW THAT MY WATER WILL FIND ITS MARK!!
YOU'LL BE TASTING ALL OF MY RECENT RESENT-MENT!
AS THE GUARDIAN, I CANNOT LET THIS STAND.
THE STOLEN BIRDS ON THIS ISLAND ARE ALL GOING BACK IN THE CAGE.
UNHARMED, IDEALLY.
STEALING AWAY A SEKIREI'S CHANCE AT LOVE?
YOU KNOW JUST HOW TO PISS OFF THIS BIG SISTER!
LOVE, LOVE!

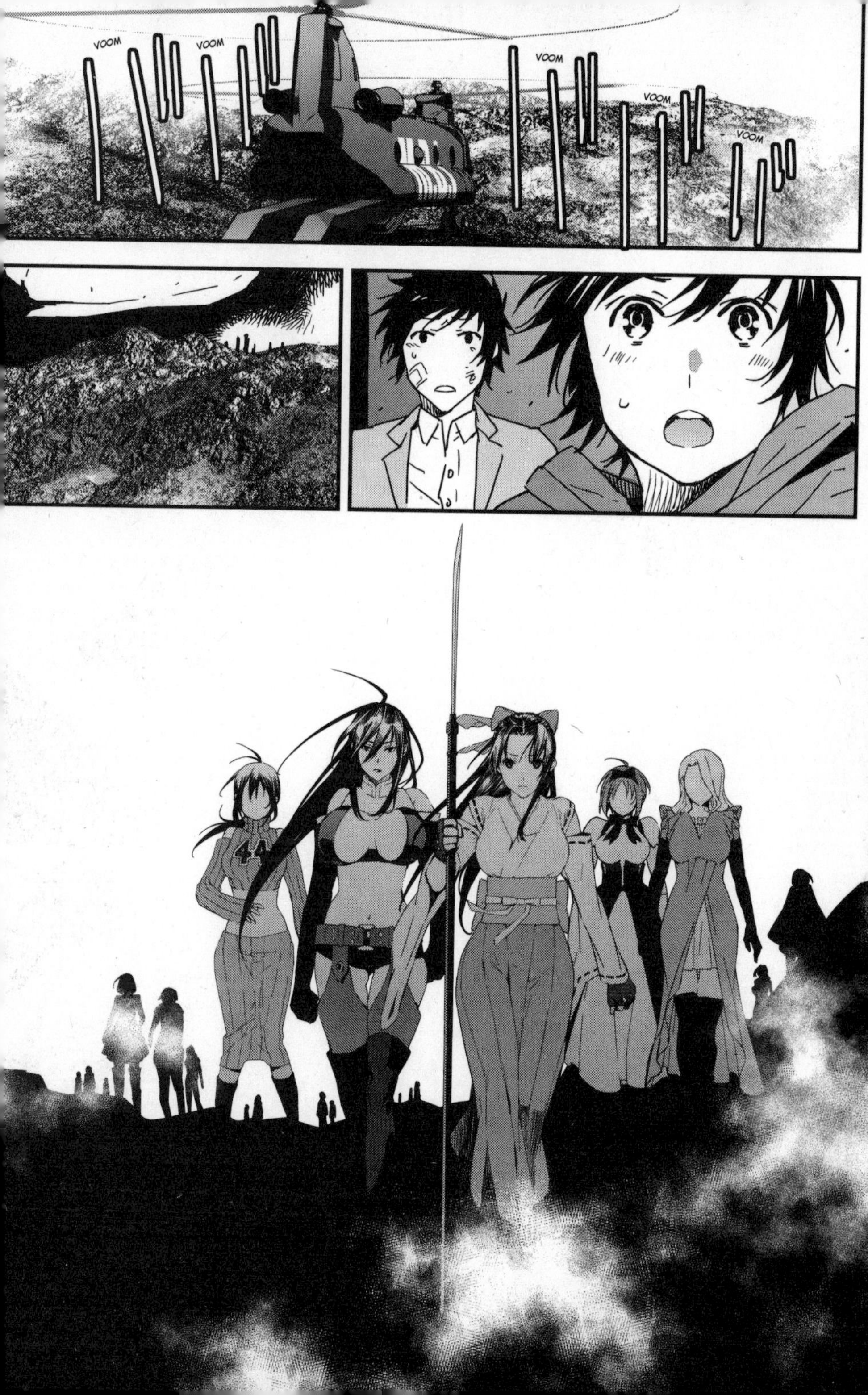
VOOM
VOOM
VOOM
VOOM
VOOM

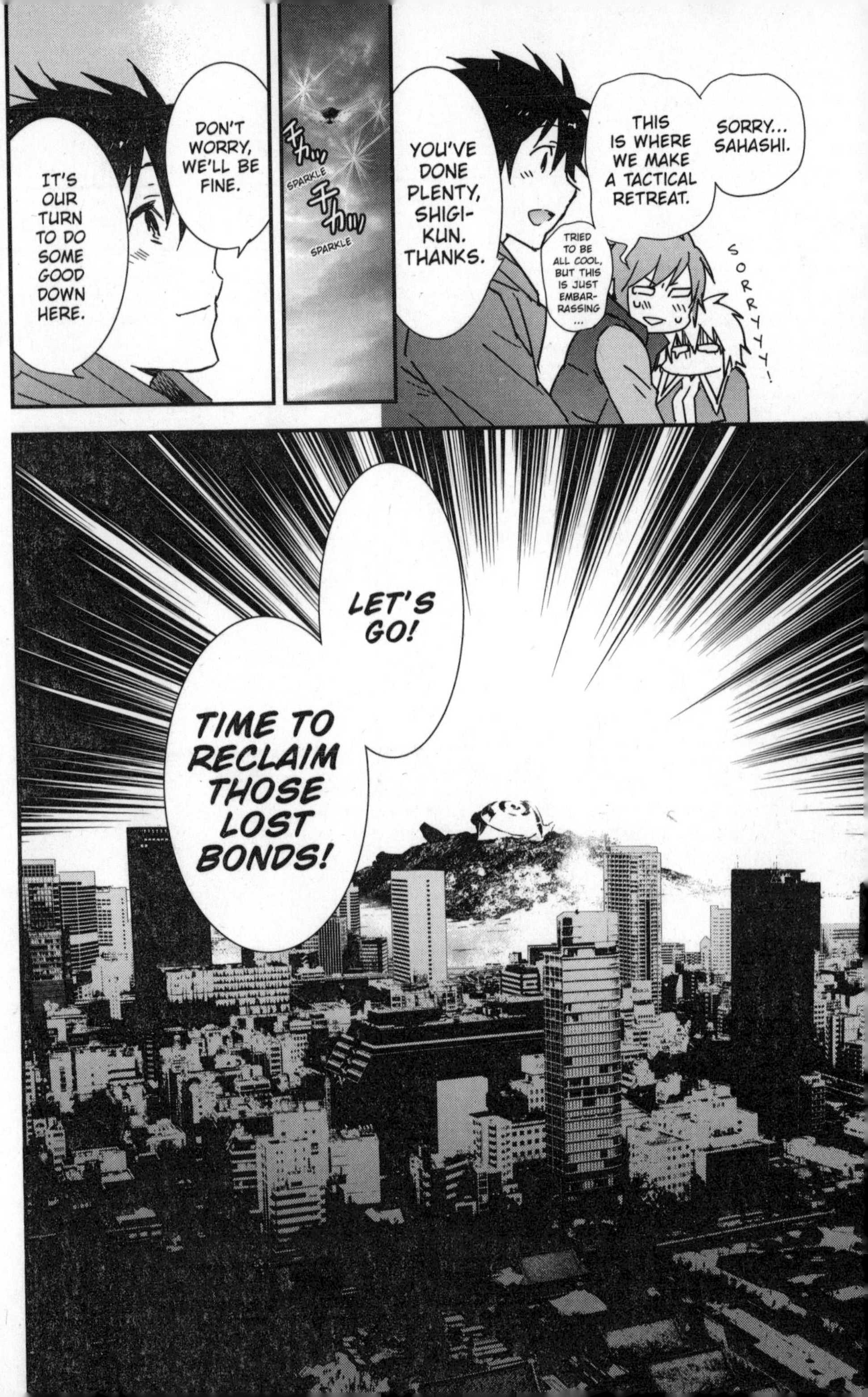
SORRY... SAHASHI.
THIS IS WHERE WE MAKE A TACTICAL RETREAT.
TRIED TO BE ALL COOL, BUT THIS IS JUST EMBARRASSING...
SORRYYY!
YOU'VE DONE PLENTY, SHIGI-KUN. THANKS.
SPARKLE
SPARKLE
DON'T WORRY, WE'LL BE FINE.
IT'S OUR TURN TO DO SOME GOOD DOWN HERE.
LET'S GO!
TIME TO RECLAIM THOSE LOST BONDS!

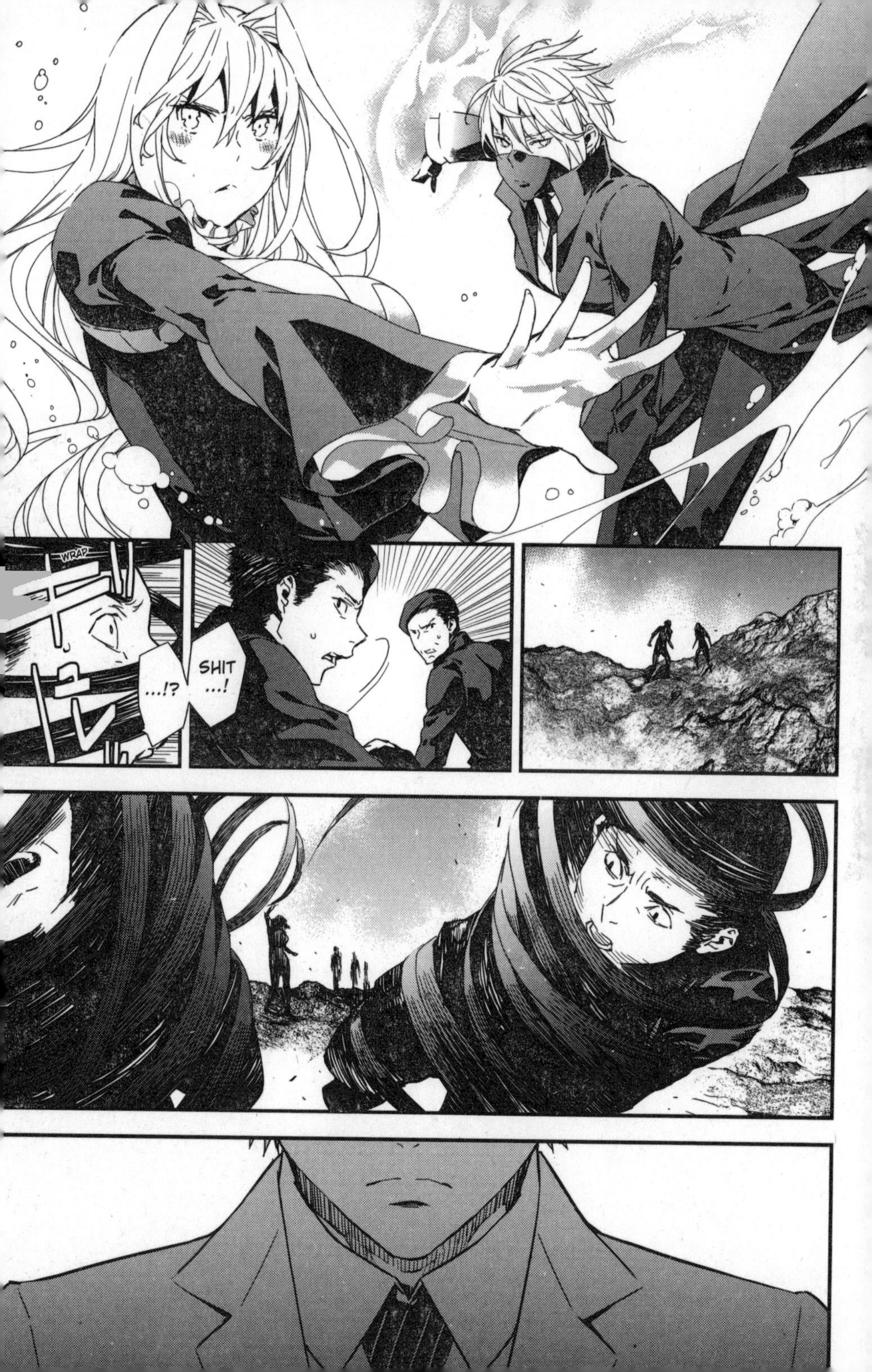
SHIT ...!
WRAP
...!?

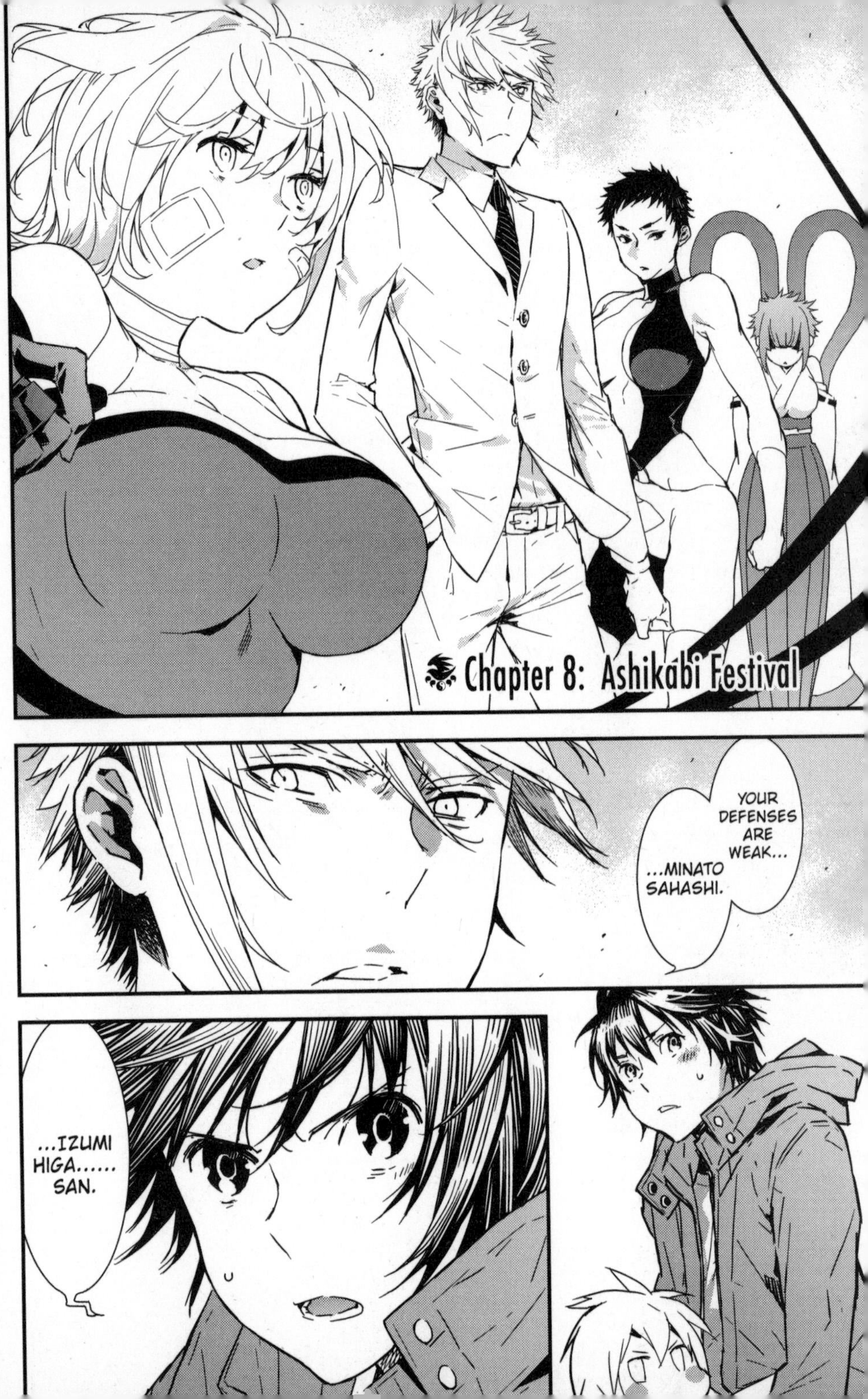
Chapter 8: Ashikabi Festival
YOUR DEFENSES ARE WEAK... ...MINATO SAHASHI.
...IZUMI HIGA...... SAN.

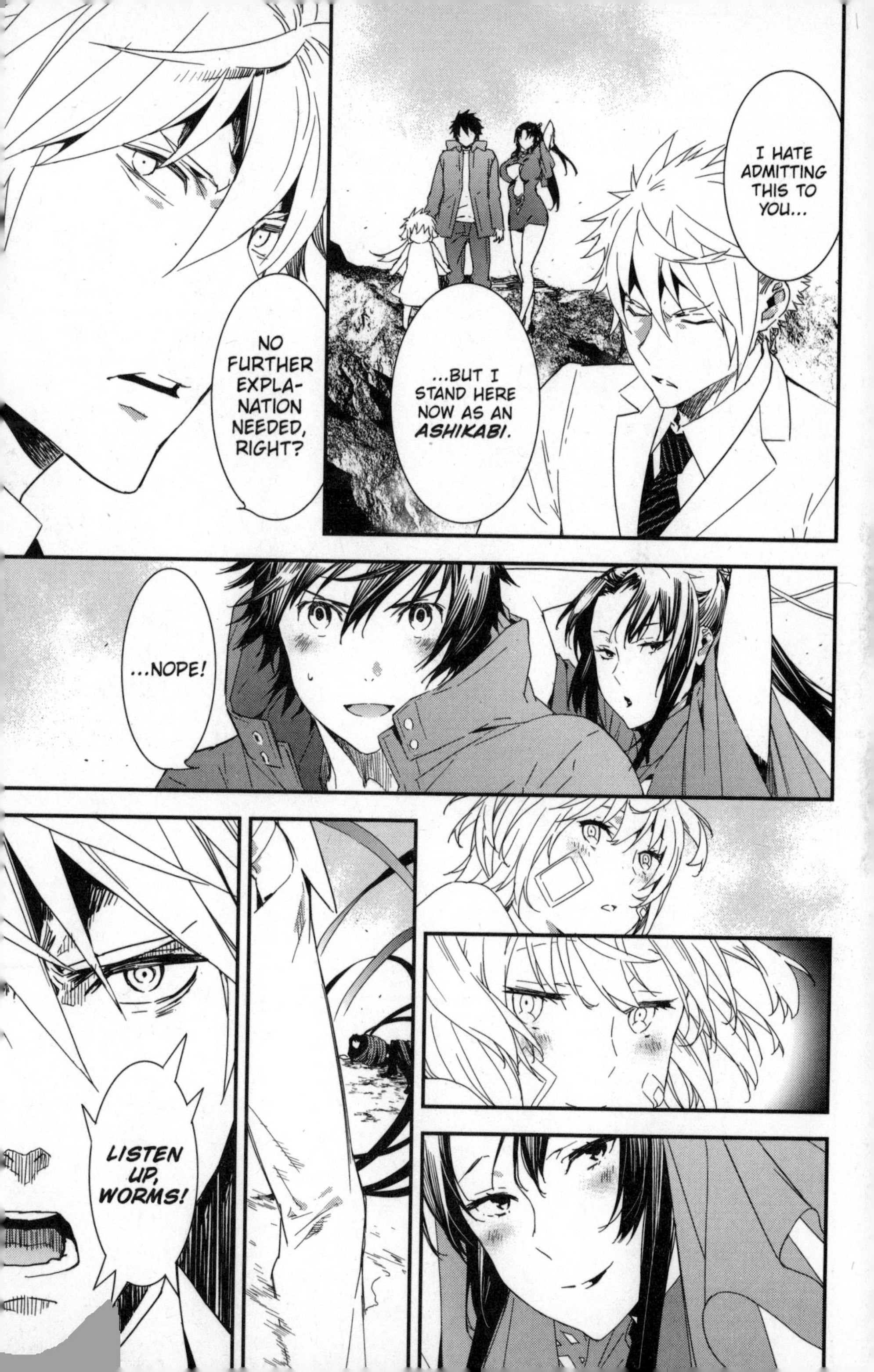
I HATE ADMITTING THIS TO YOU...
...BUT I STAND HERE NOW AS AN *ASHIKABI*.
NO FURTHER EXPLA-NATION NEEDED, RIGHT?
...NOPE!
LISTEN UP, WORMS!

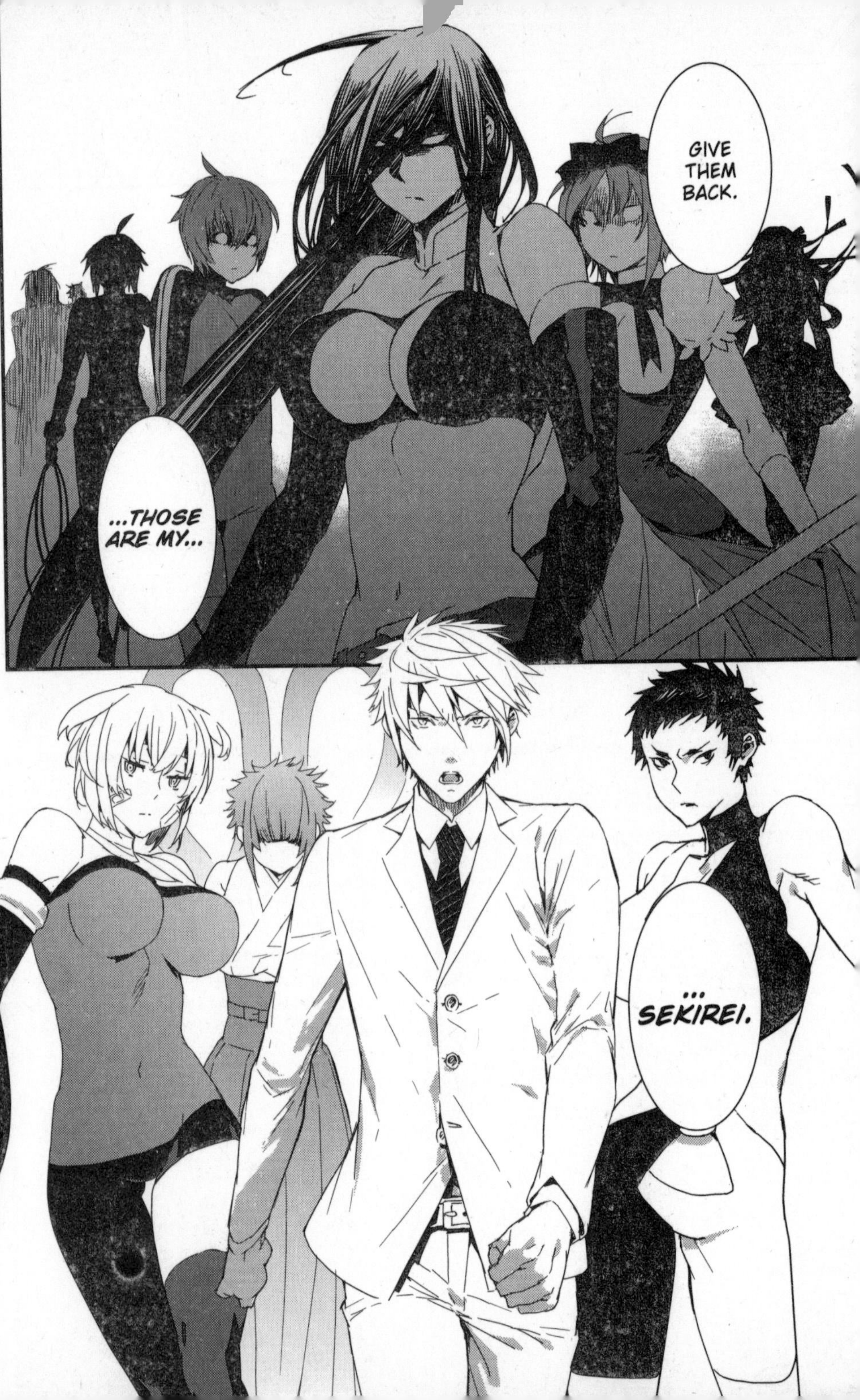
GIVE THEM BACK.
...THOSE ARE MY...
...SEKIREI.

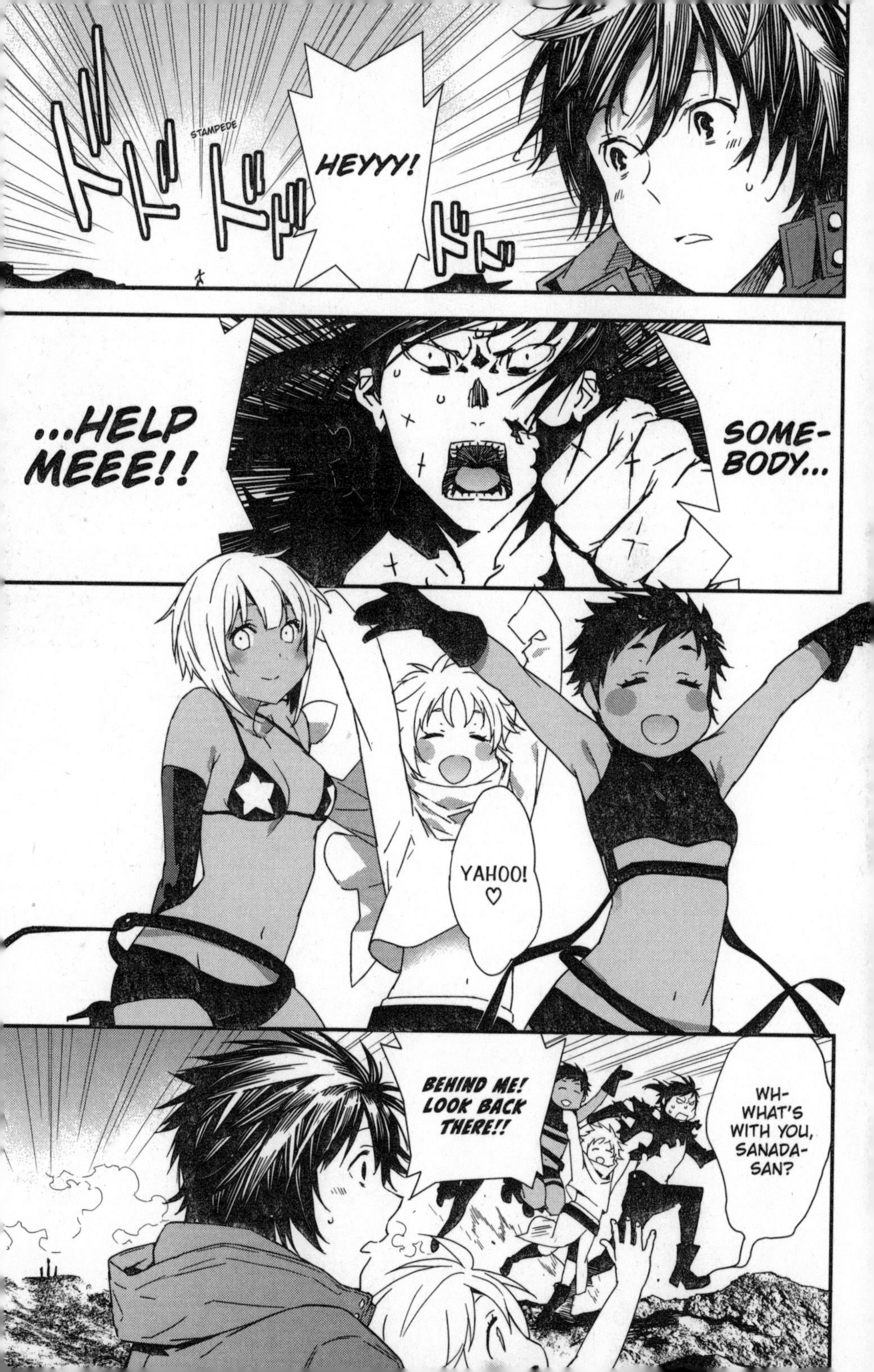
HEYYY!
STAMPEDE
SOME-BODY...
...HELP MEEE!!
YAHOO! ♡
WH-WHAT'S WITH YOU, SANADA-SAN?
BEHIND ME! LOOK BACK THERE!!

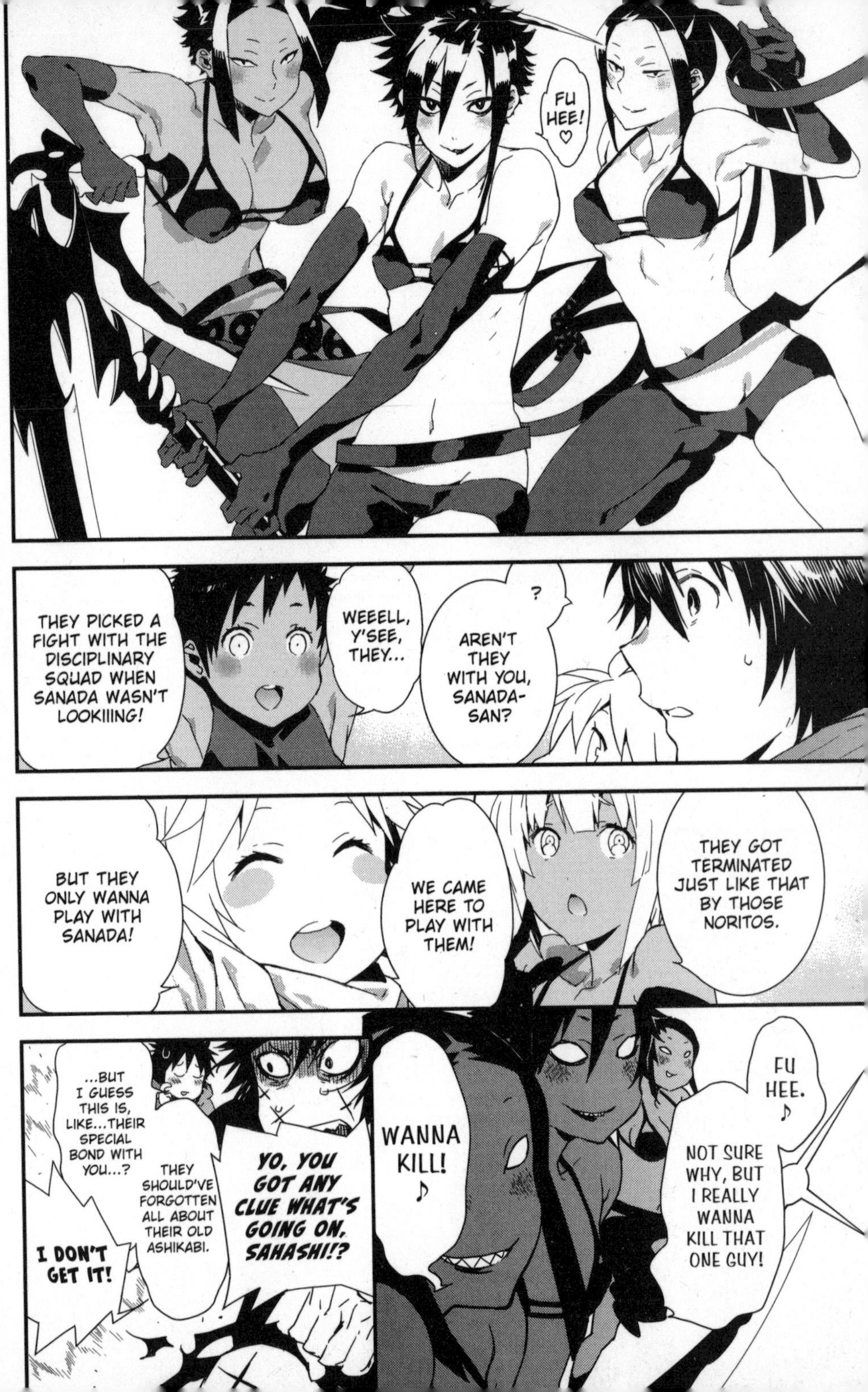
FU HEE! ♡
?
AREN'T THEY WITH YOU, SANADA-SAN?
WEEELL, Y'SEE, THEY...
THEY PICKED A FIGHT WITH THE DISCIPLINARY SQUAD WHEN SANADA WASN'T LOOKIIING!
THEY GOT TERMINATED JUST LIKE THAT BY THOSE NORITOS.
WE CAME HERE TO PLAY WITH THEM!
BUT THEY ONLY WANNA PLAY WITH SANADA!
FU HEE. ♪
NOT SURE WHY, BUT I REALLY WANNA KILL THAT ONE GUY!
WANNA KILL! ♪
YO, YOU GOT ANY CLUE WHAT'S GOING ON, SAHASHI!?
...BUT I GUESS THIS IS, LIKE...THEIR SPECIAL BOND WITH YOU...?
THEY SHOULD'VE FORGOTTEN ALL ABOUT THEIR OLD ASHIKABI.
I DON'T GET IT!

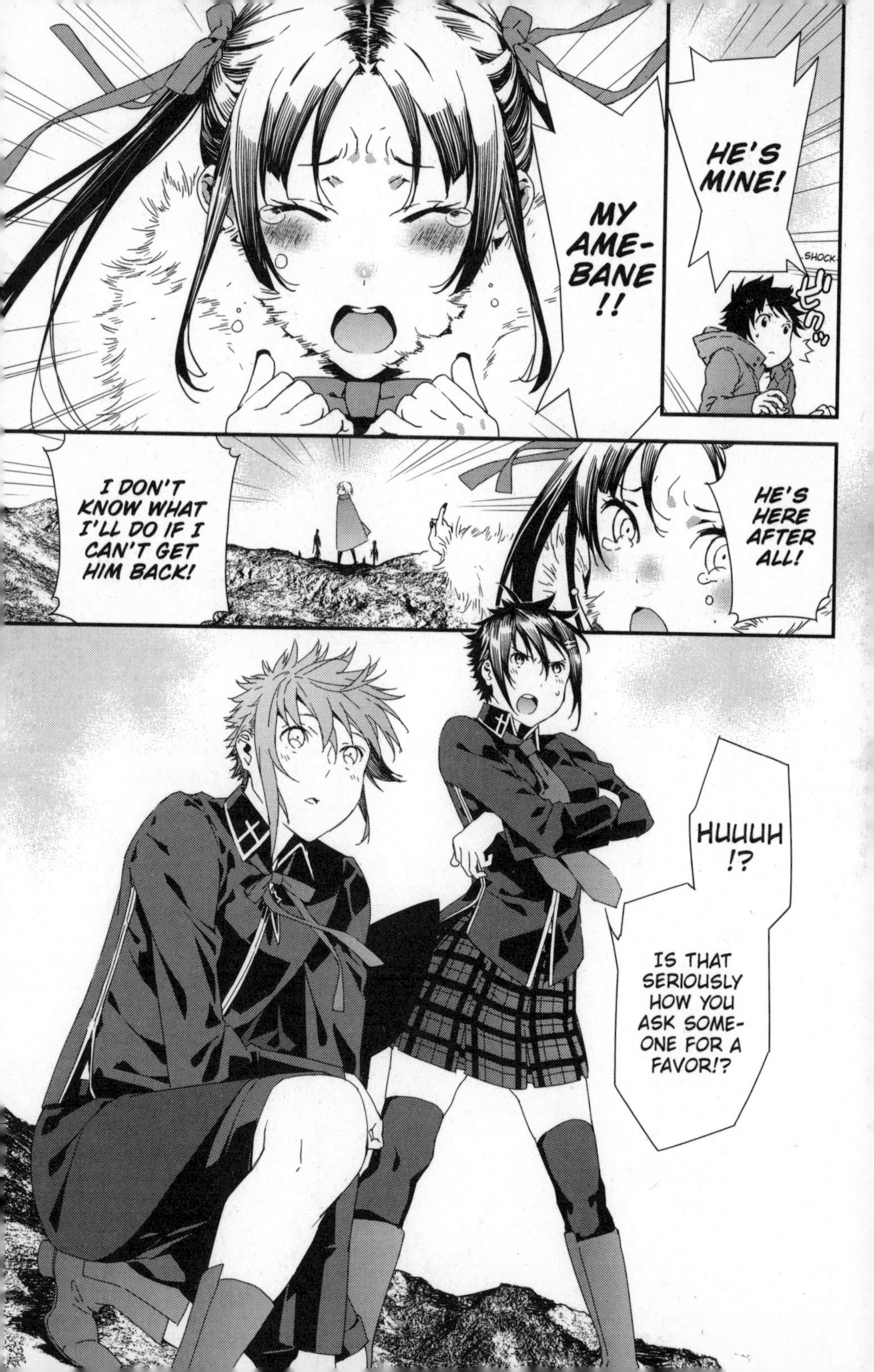
HE'S MINE!
SHOCK
MY AME-BANE!!
HE'S HERE AFTER ALL!
I DON'T KNOW WHAT I'LL DO IF I CAN'T GET HIM BACK!
HUUUH!?
IS THAT SERIOUSLY HOW YOU ASK SOME-ONE FOR A FAVOR!?

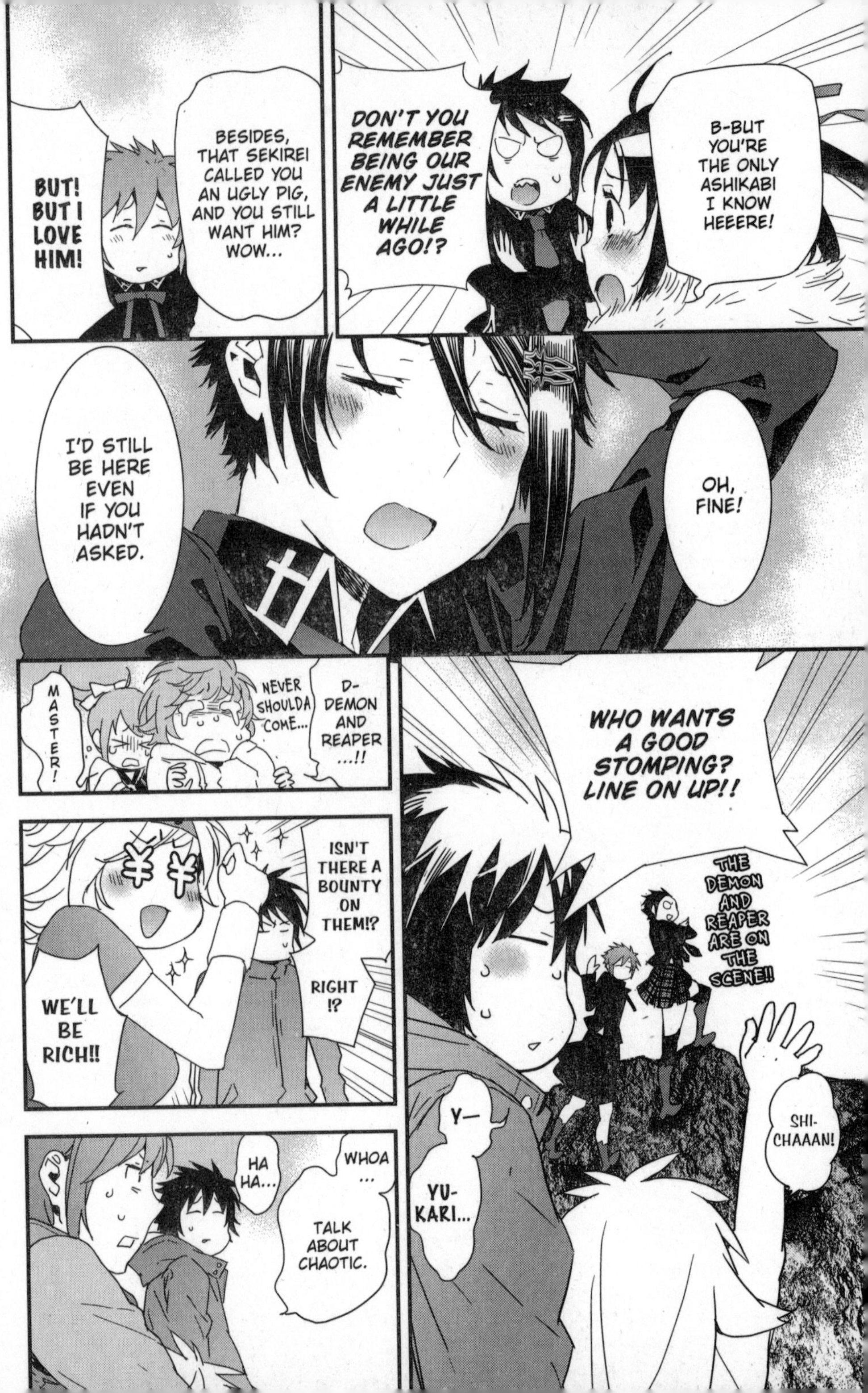
B-BUT YOU'RE THE ONLY ASHIKABI I KNOW HEEERE!
DON'T YOU REMEMBER BEING OUR ENEMY JUST A LITTLE WHILE AGO!?
BESIDES, THAT SEKIREI CALLED YOU AN UGLY PIG, AND YOU STILL WANT HIM? WOW...
BUT! BUT I LOVE HIM!
OH, FINE!
I'D STILL BE HERE EVEN IF YOU HADN'T ASKED.
WHO WANTS A GOOD STOMPING? LINE ON UP!!
THE DEMON AND REAPER ARE ON THE SCENE!!
SHI-CHAAAN!
Y—
YU-KARI...
D-DEMON AND REAPER ...!!
NEVER SHOULDA COME...
MASTER!
ISN'T THERE A BOUNTY ON THEM!?
RIGHT !?
WE'LL BE RICH!!
WHOA ...
TALK ABOUT CHAOTIC.
HA HA...

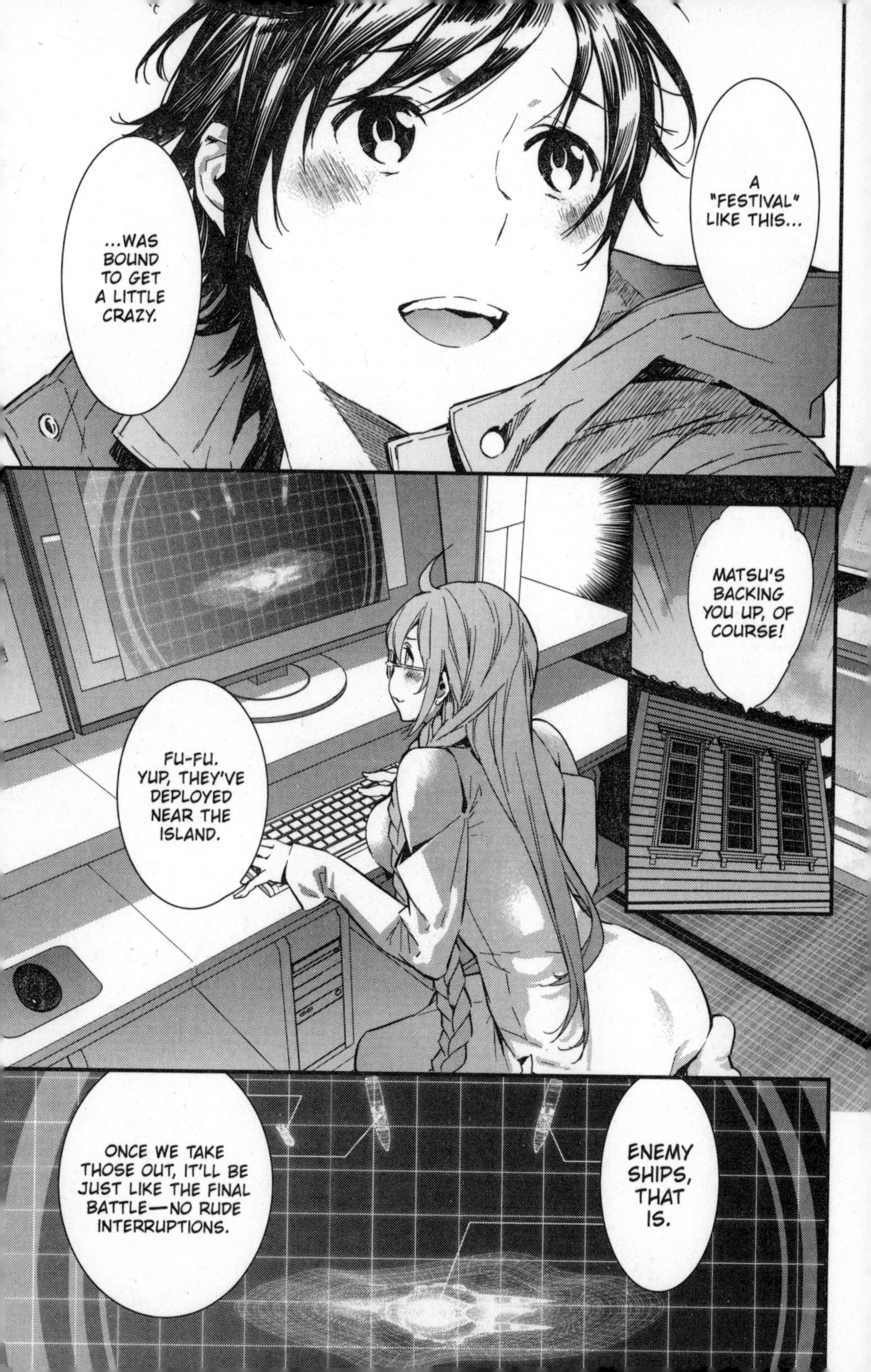
A "FESTIVAL" LIKE THIS...
...WAS BOUND TO GET A LITTLE CRAZY.
MATSU'S BACKING YOU UP, OF COURSE!
FU-FU. YUP, THEY'VE DEPLOYED NEAR THE ISLAND.
ENEMY SHIPS, THAT IS.
ONCE WE TAKE THOSE OUT, IT'LL BE JUST LIKE THE FINAL BATTLE—NO RUDE INTERRUPTIONS.

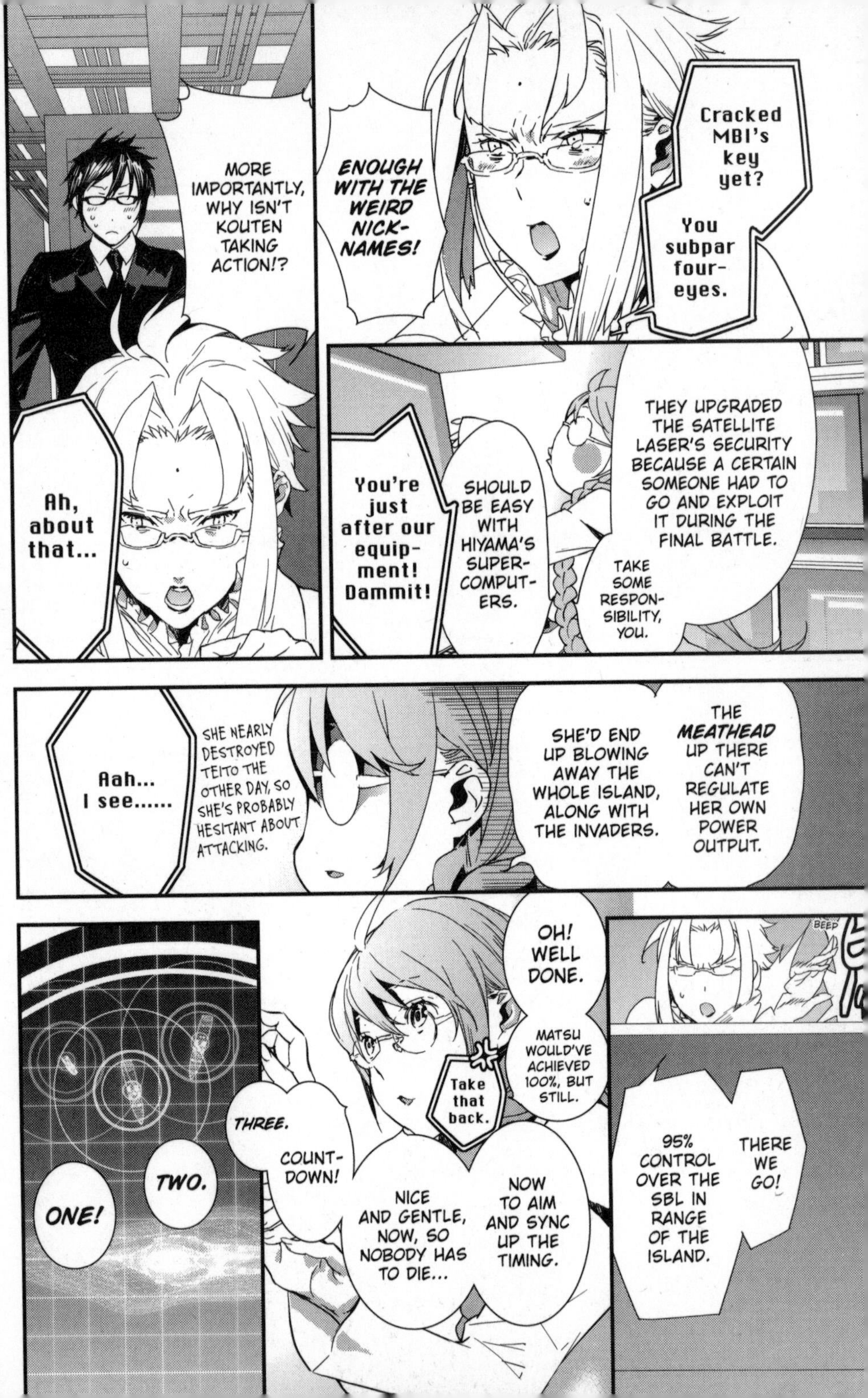
Cracked MBI's key yet?
You subpar four-eyes.
ENOUGH WITH THE WEIRD NICKNAMES!
THEY UPGRADED THE SATELLITE LASER'S SECURITY BECAUSE A CERTAIN SOMEONE HAD TO GO AND EXPLOIT IT DURING THE FINAL BATTLE.
TAKE SOME RESPONSIBILITY, YOU.
SHOULD BE EASY WITH HIYAMA'S SUPERCOMPUTERS.
You're just after our equipment! Dammit!
MORE IMPORTANTLY, WHY ISN'T KOUTEN TAKING ACTION!?
Ah, about that...
THE MEATHEAD UP THERE CAN'T REGULATE HER OWN POWER OUTPUT.
SHE'D END UP BLOWING AWAY THE WHOLE ISLAND, ALONG WITH THE INVADERS.
SHE NEARLY DESTROYED TEITO THE OTHER DAY, SO SHE'S PROBABLY HESITANT ABOUT ATTACKING.
Aah... I see......
BEEP
THERE WE GO!
95% CONTROL OVER THE SBL IN RANGE OF THE ISLAND.
OH! WELL DONE.
MATSU WOULD'VE ACHIEVED 100%, BUT STILL.
Take that back.
NOW TO AIM AND SYNC UP THE TIMING.
NICE AND GENTLE, NOW, SO NOBODY HAS TO DIE...
COUNTDOWN!
THREE.
TWO.
ONE!

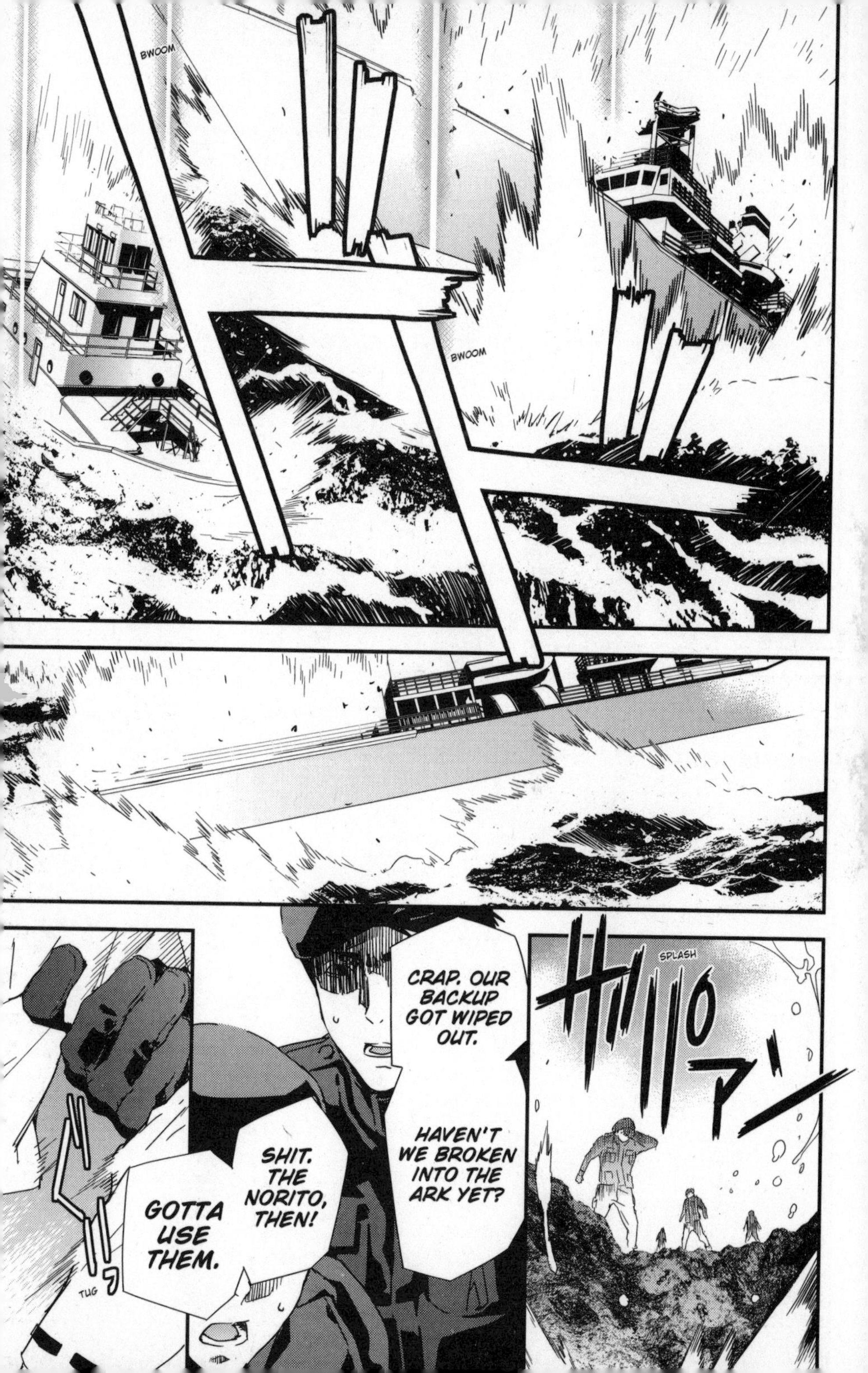
BWOOM
BWOOM
SPLASH
CRAP. OUR BACKUP GOT WIPED OUT.
HAVEN'T WE BROKEN INTO THE ARK YET?
SHIT. THE NORITO, THEN!
GOTTA USE THEM.
TUG

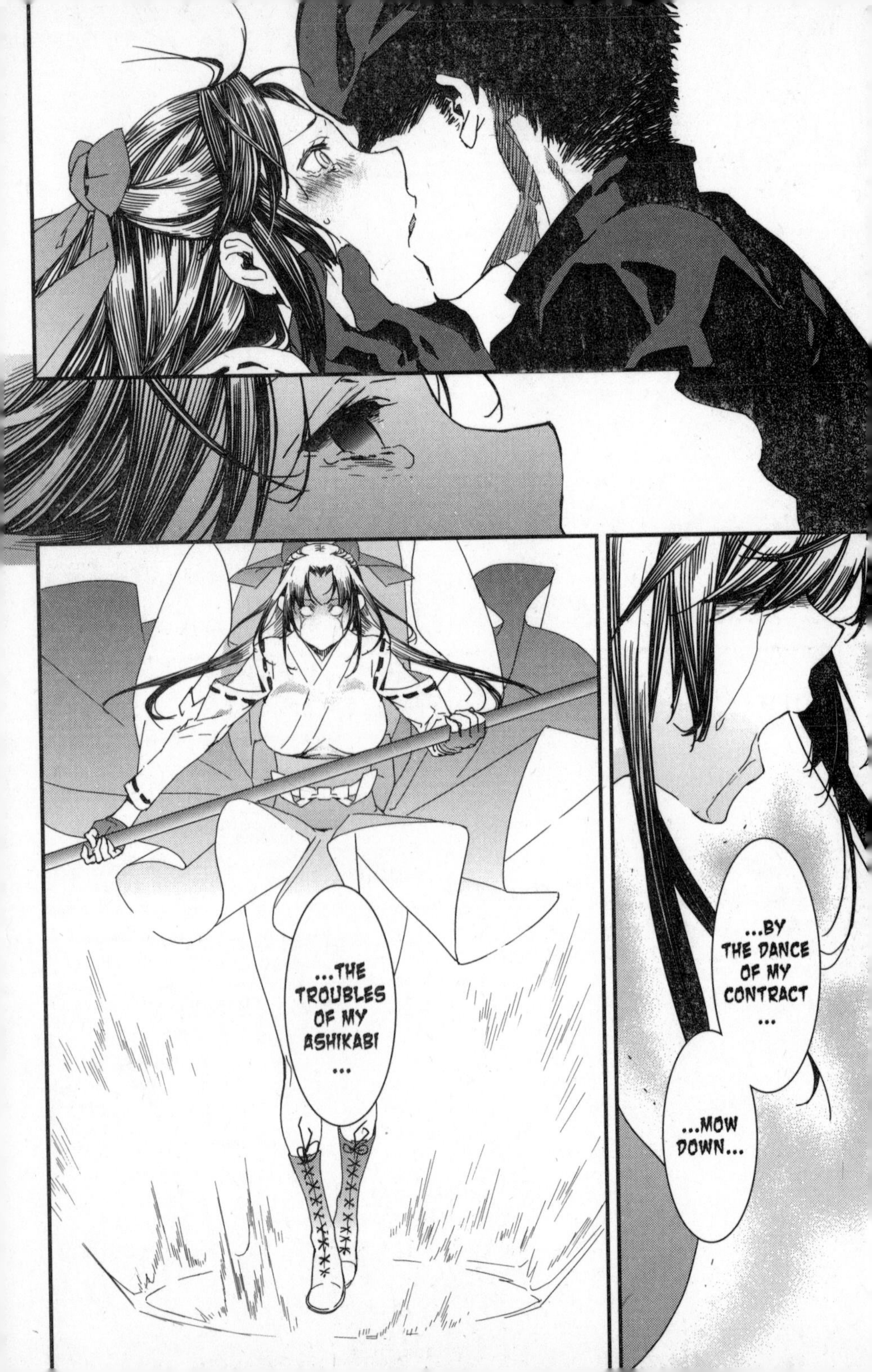
...BY THE DANCE OF MY CONTRACT ...
...MOW DOWN...
...THE TROUBLES OF MY ASHIKABI ...

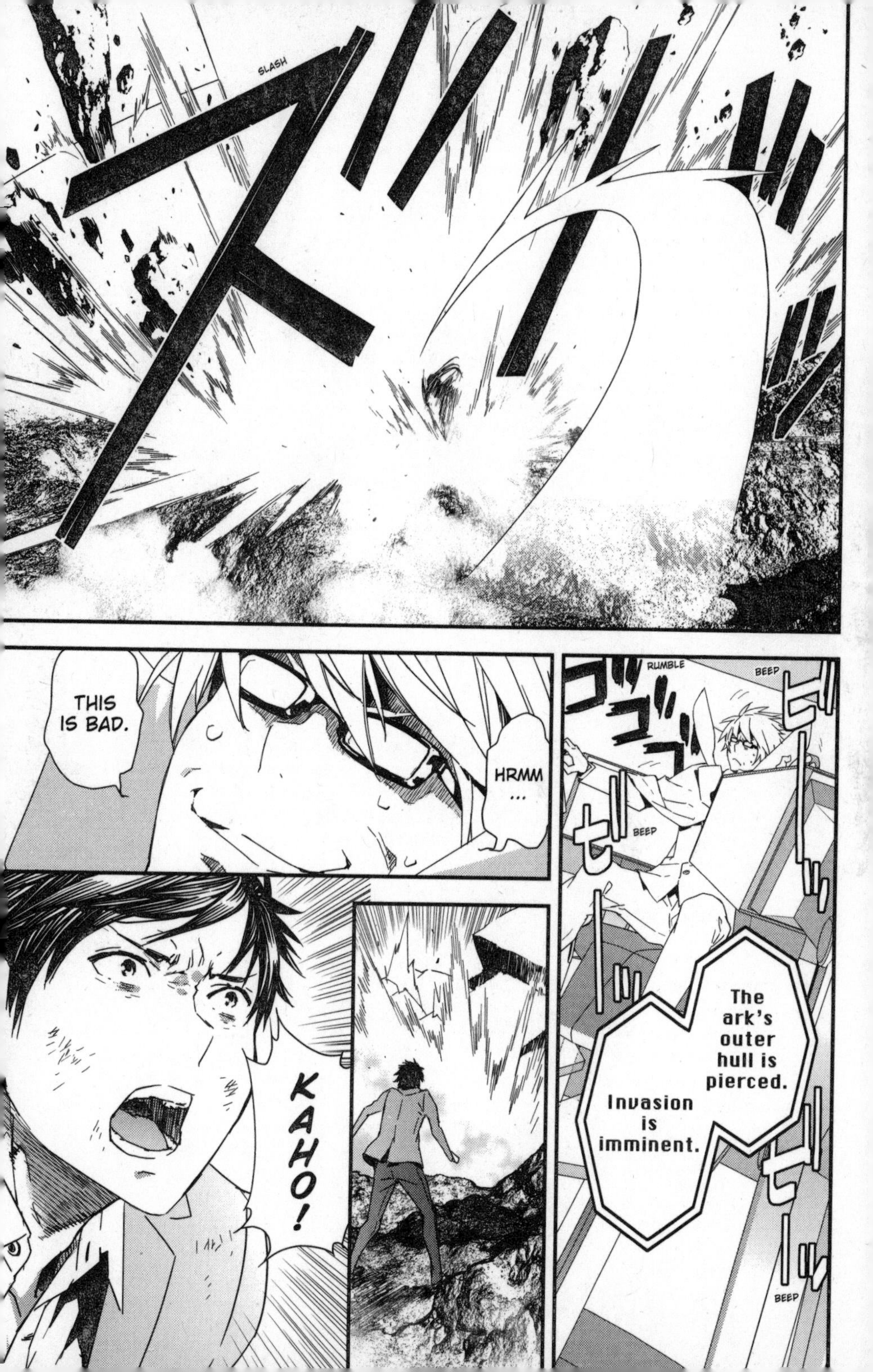
SLASH
RUMBLE
BEEP
BEEP
The ark's outer hull is pierced.
Invasion is imminent.
BEEP
HRMM...
THIS IS BAD.
KAHO!

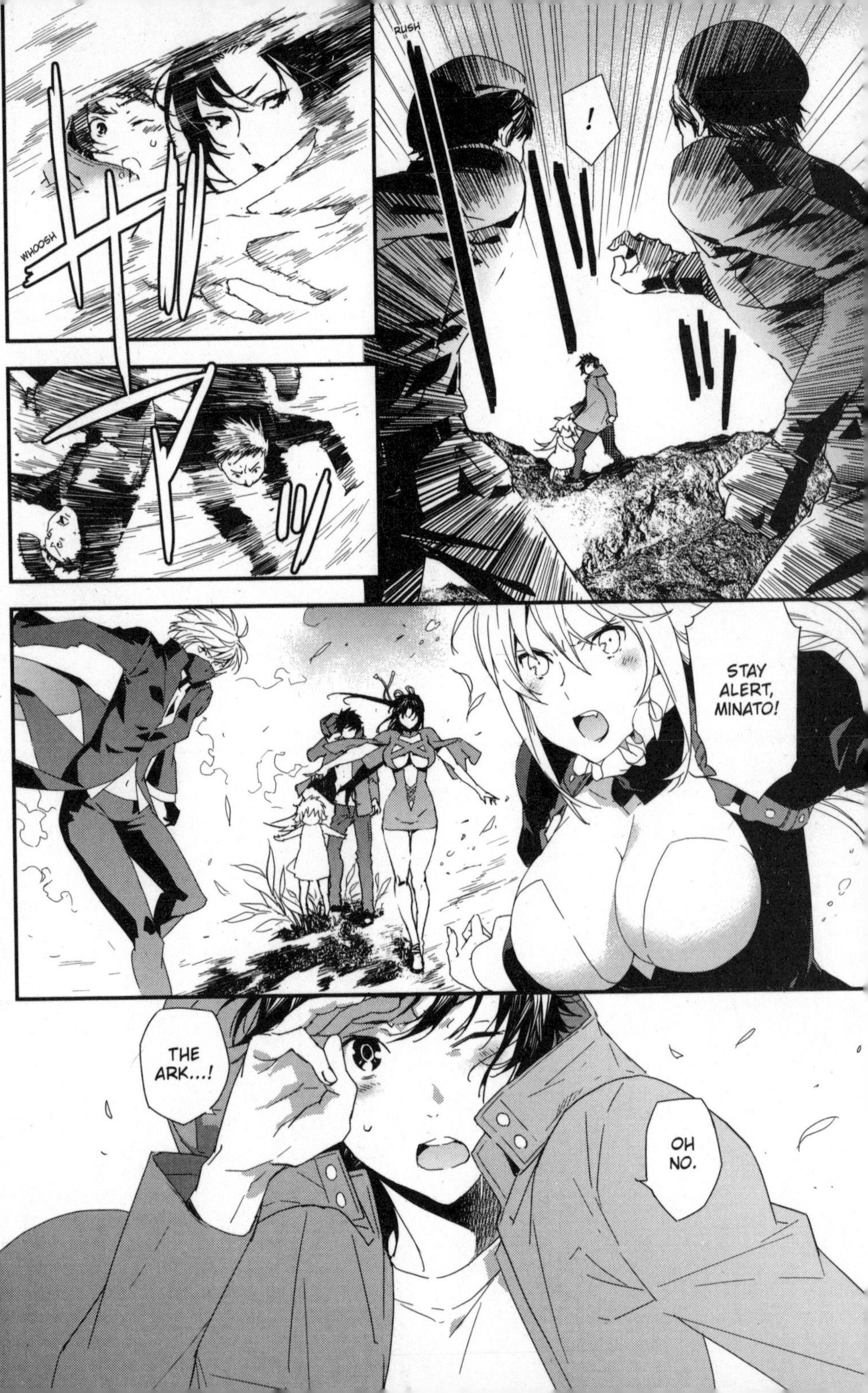
RUSH
!
WHOOSH
STAY ALERT, MINATO!
THE ARK...!
OH NO.

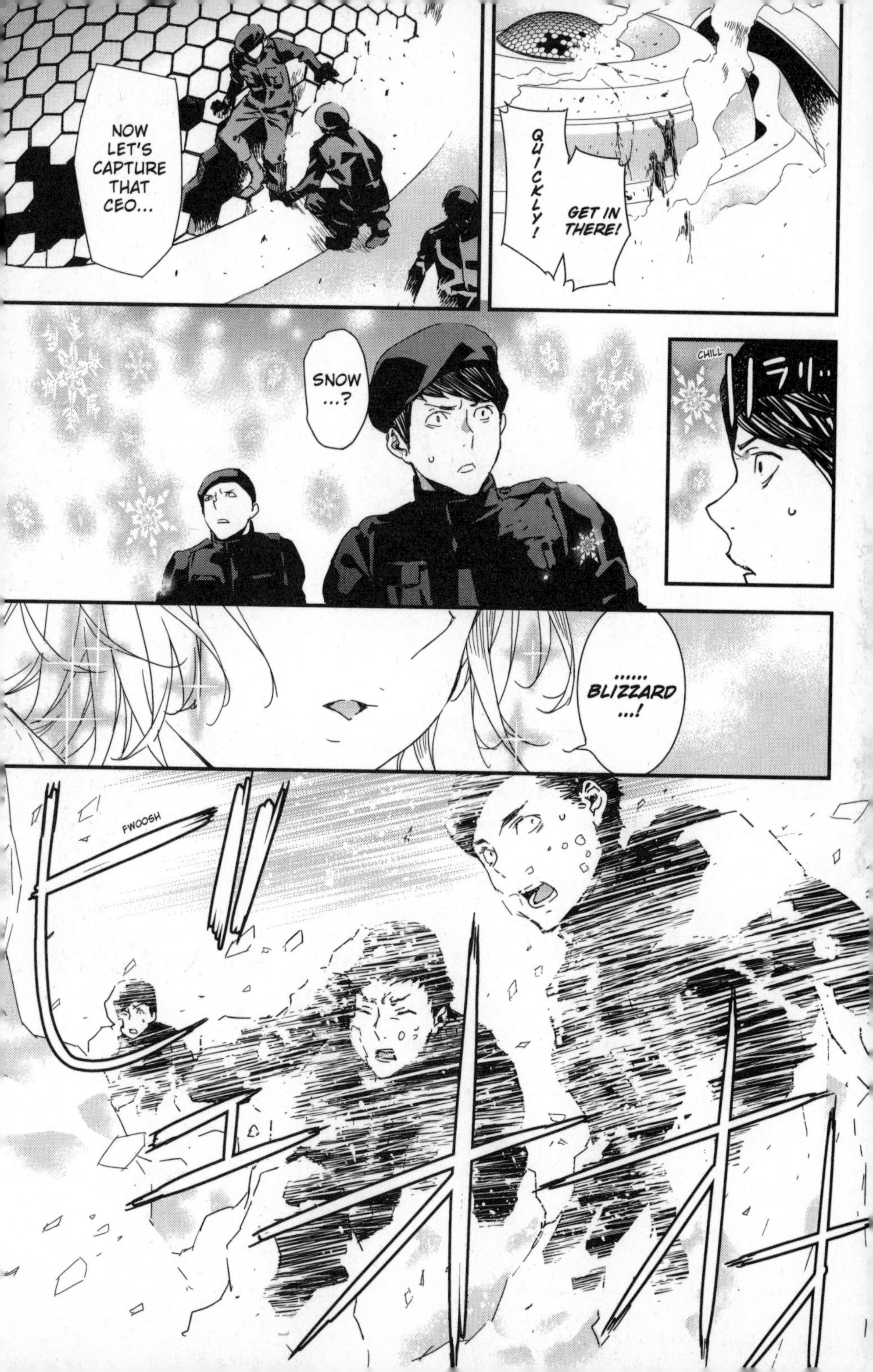
GET IN THERE!
QUICKLY!
NOW LET'S CAPTURE THAT CEO...
CHILL
SNOW ...?
...... BLIZZARD ...!
FWOOSH

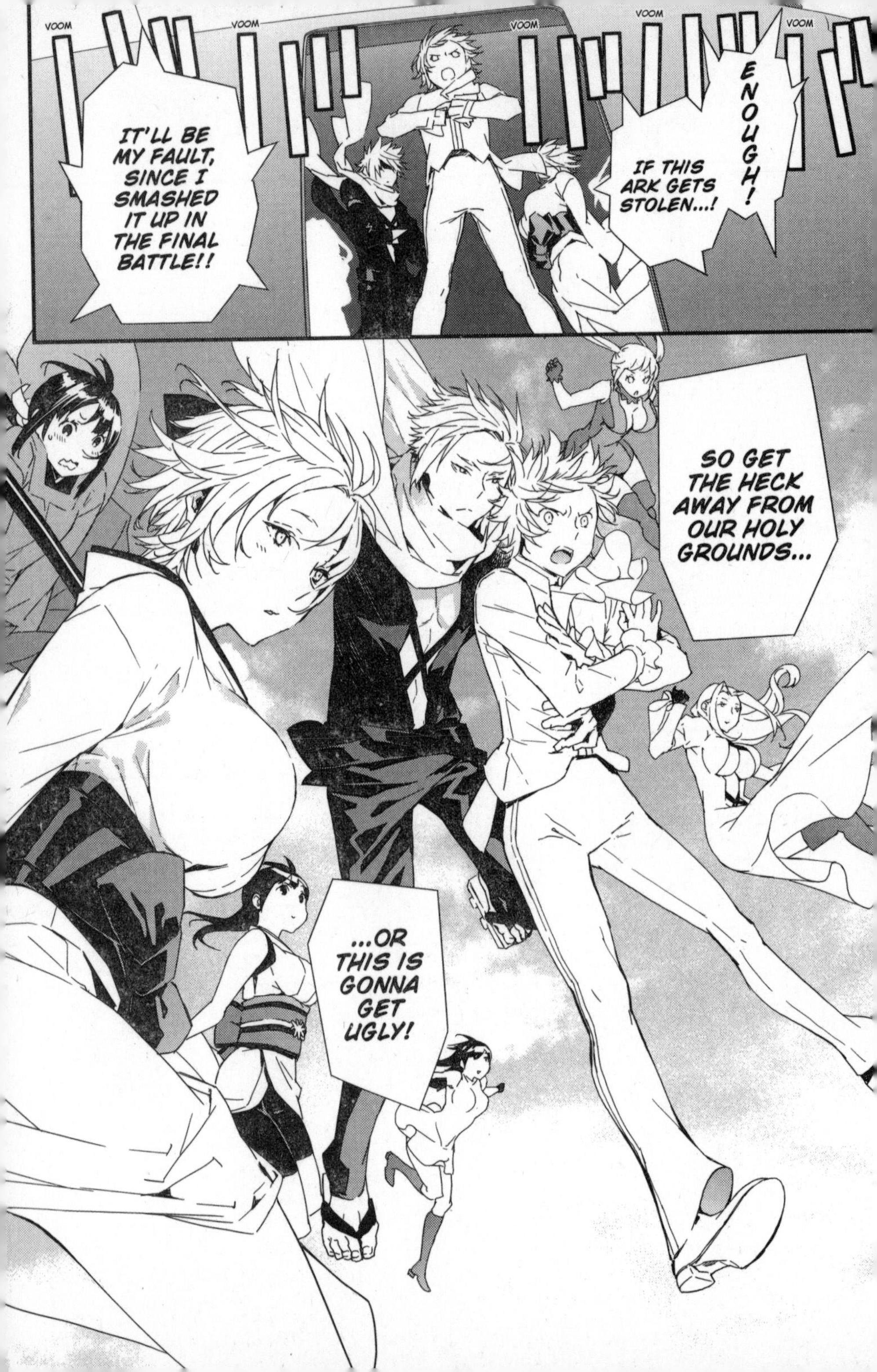
VOOM
VOOM
VOOM
VOOM
VOOM
ENOUGH!
IF THIS ARK GETS STOLEN...!
IT'LL BE MY FAULT, SINCE I SMASHED IT UP IN THE FINAL BATTLE!!
SO GET THE HECK AWAY FROM OUR HOLY GROUNDS...
...OR THIS IS GONNA GET UGLY!

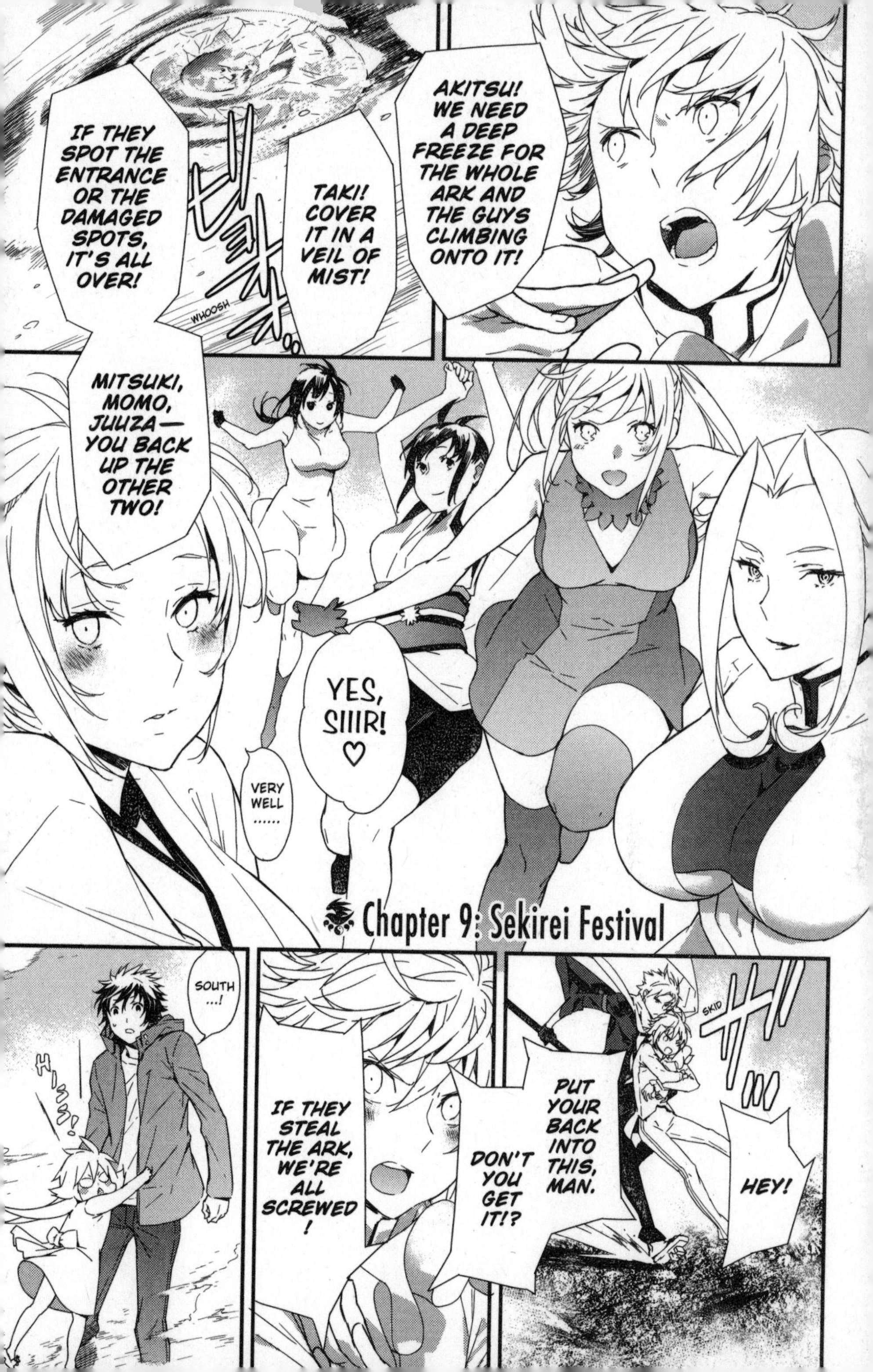
AKITSU! WE NEED A DEEP FREEZE FOR THE WHOLE ARK AND THE GUYS CLIMBING ONTO IT!
TAKI! COVER IT IN A VEIL OF MIST!
IF THEY SPOT THE ENTRANCE OR THE DAMAGED SPOTS, IT'S ALL OVER!
WHOOSH
MITSUKI, MOMO, JUUZA—YOU BACK UP THE OTHER TWO!
YES, SIIIR! ♡
VERY WELL ......
Chapter 9: Sekirei Festival
SKID
HEY!
PUT YOUR BACK INTO THIS, MAN.
DON'T YOU GET IT!?
IF THEY STEAL THE ARK, WE'RE ALL SCREWED!
SOUTH ...!

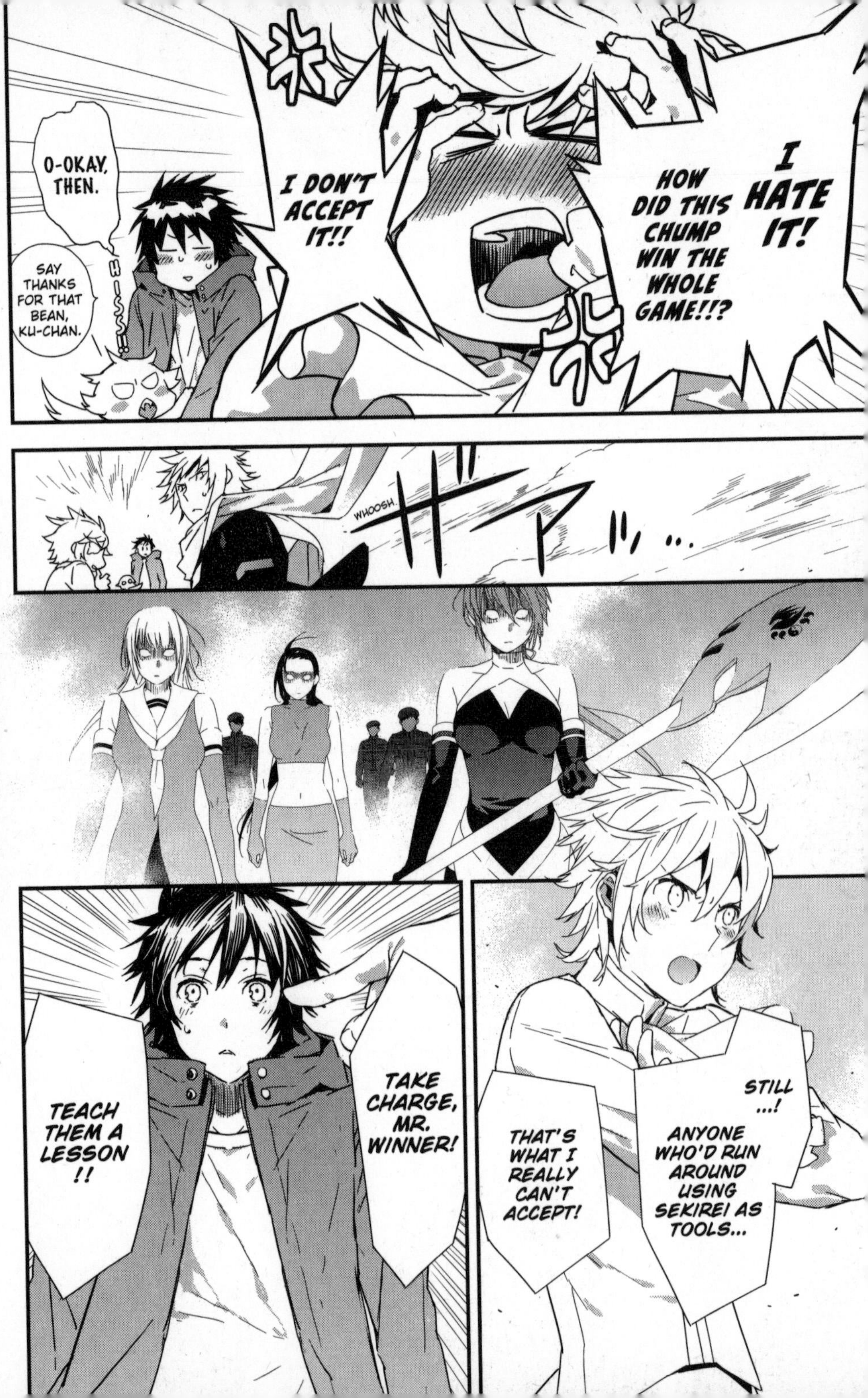
I HATE IT!
HOW DID THIS CHUMP WIN THE WHOLE GAME!!?
I DON'T ACCEPT IT!!
O-OKAY, THEN.
HISS!!
SAY THANKS FOR THAT BEAN, KU-CHAN.
WHOOSH
STILL...!
ANYONE WHO'D RUN AROUND USING SEKIREI AS TOOLS...
THAT'S WHAT I REALLY CAN'T ACCEPT!
TAKE CHARGE, MR. WINNER!
TEACH THEM A LESSON!!

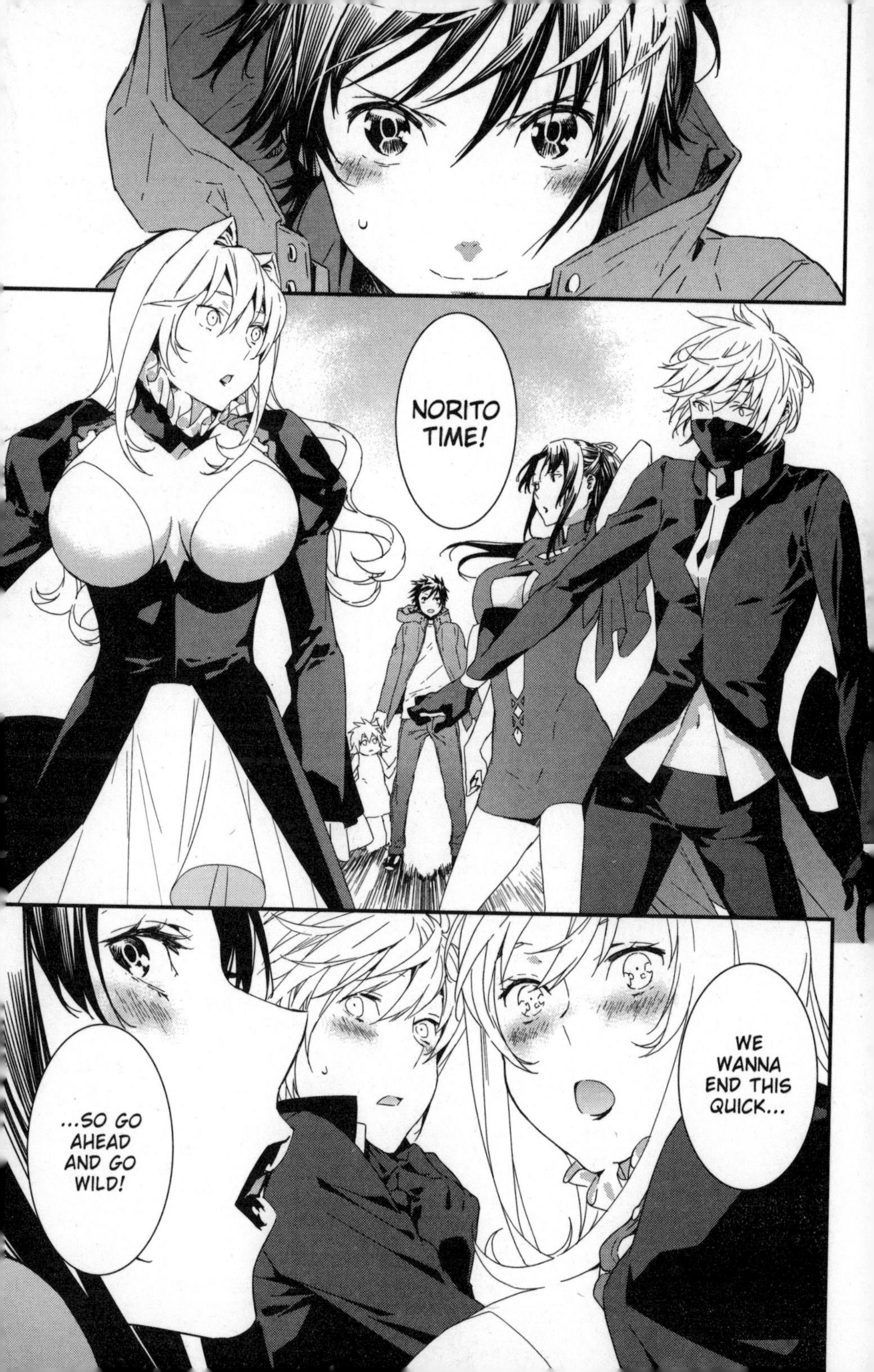
NORITO TIME!
WE WANNA END THIS QUICK...
...SO GO AHEAD AND GO WILD!

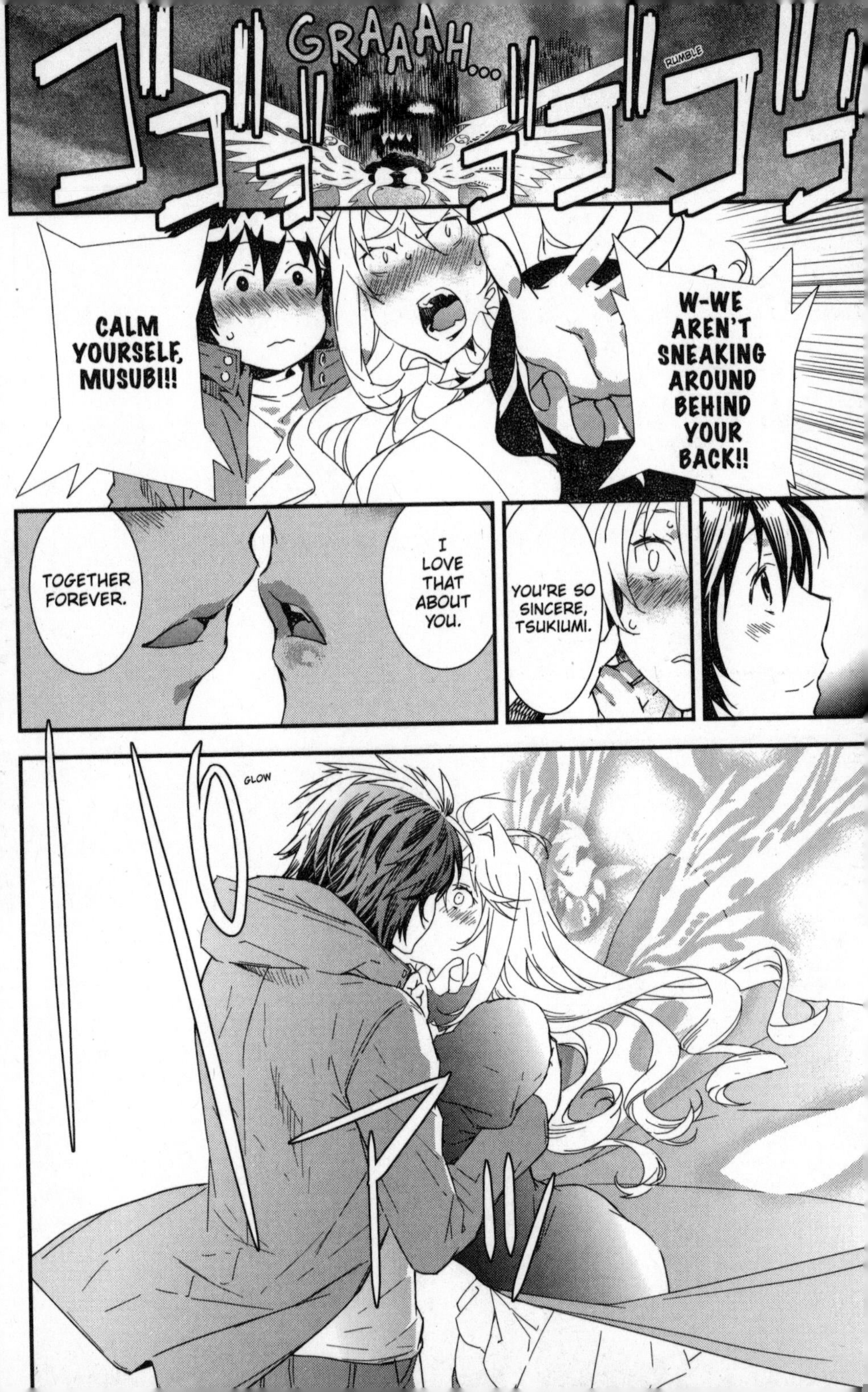
GRAAAH...
RUMBLE
W-WE AREN'T SNEAKING AROUND BEHIND YOUR BACK!!
CALM YOURSELF, MUSUBI!!
YOU'RE SO SINCERE, TSUKIUMI.
I LOVE THAT ABOUT YOU.
TOGETHER FOREVER.
GLOW

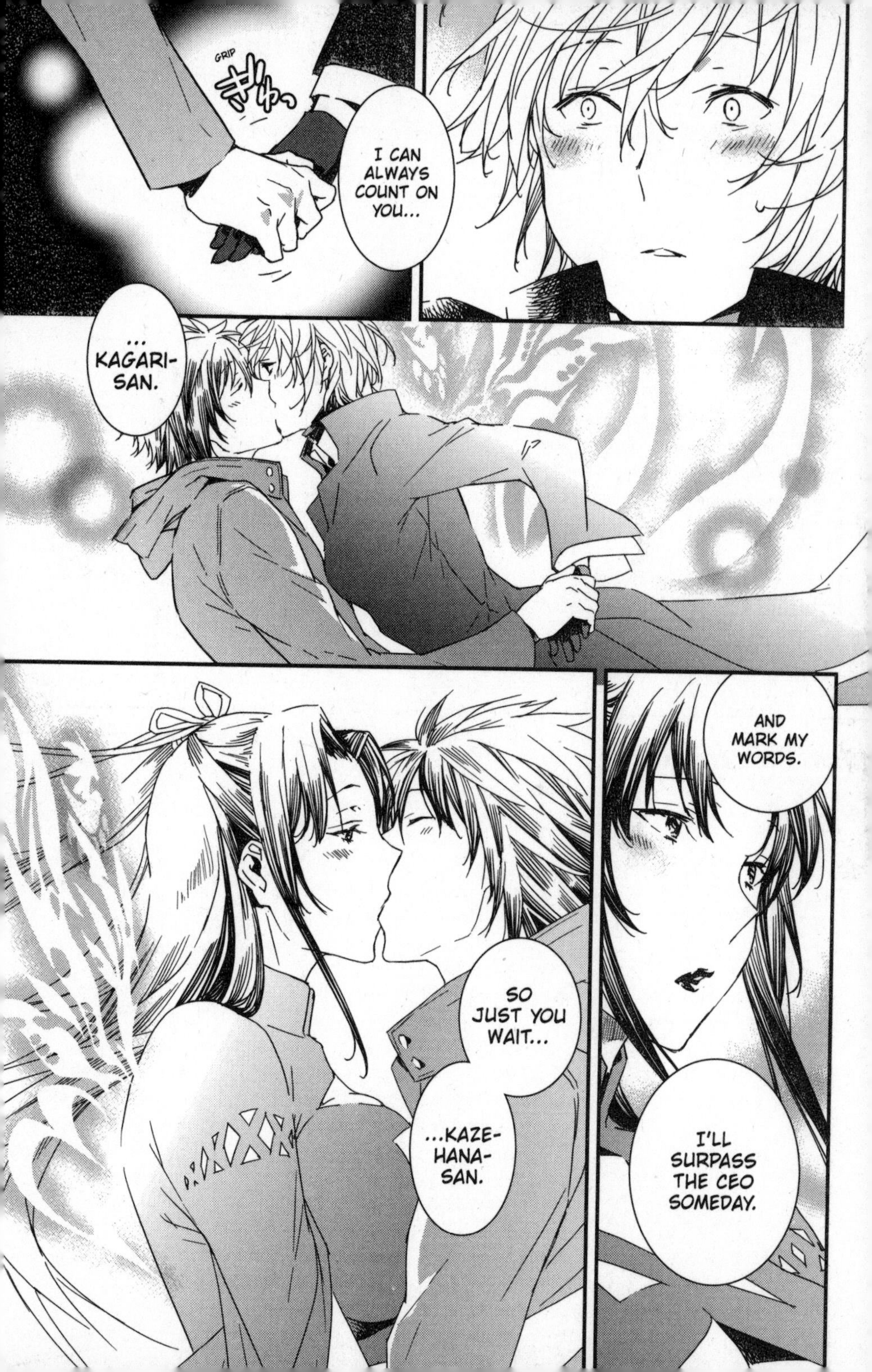
I CAN ALWAYS COUNT ON YOU...
GRIP
ぎゅっ
...KAGARI-SAN.
AND MARK MY WORDS.
I'LL SURPASS THE CEO SOMEDAY.
SO JUST YOU WAIT...
...KAZE-HANA-SAN.

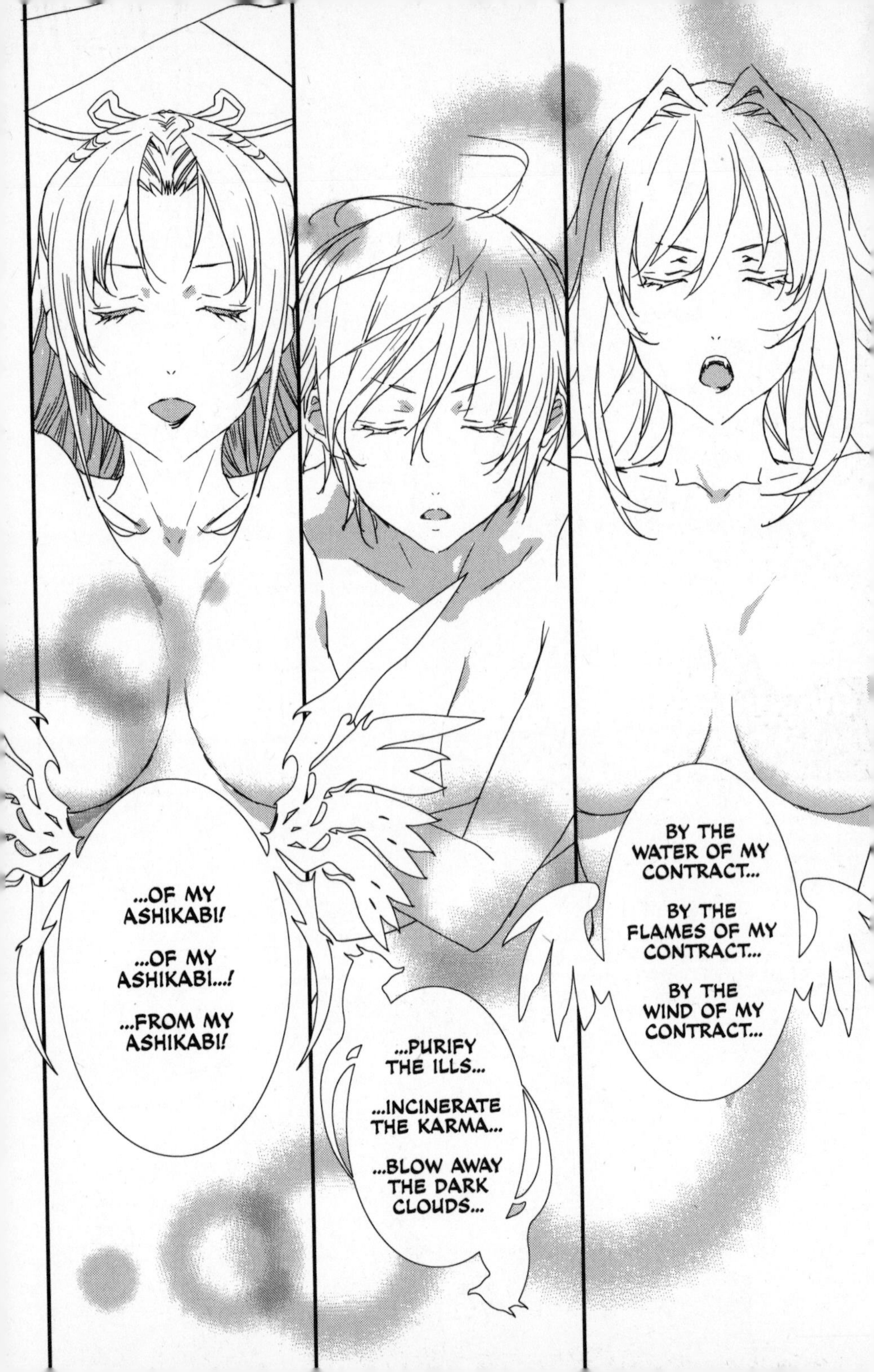
BY THE WATER OF MY CONTRACT...
BY THE FLAMES OF MY CONTRACT...
BY THE WIND OF MY CONTRACT...
...PURIFY THE ILLS...
...INCINERATE THE KARMA...
...BLOW AWAY THE DARK CLOUDS...
...OF MY ASHIKABI!
...OF MY ASHIKABI...!
...FROM MY ASHIKABI!

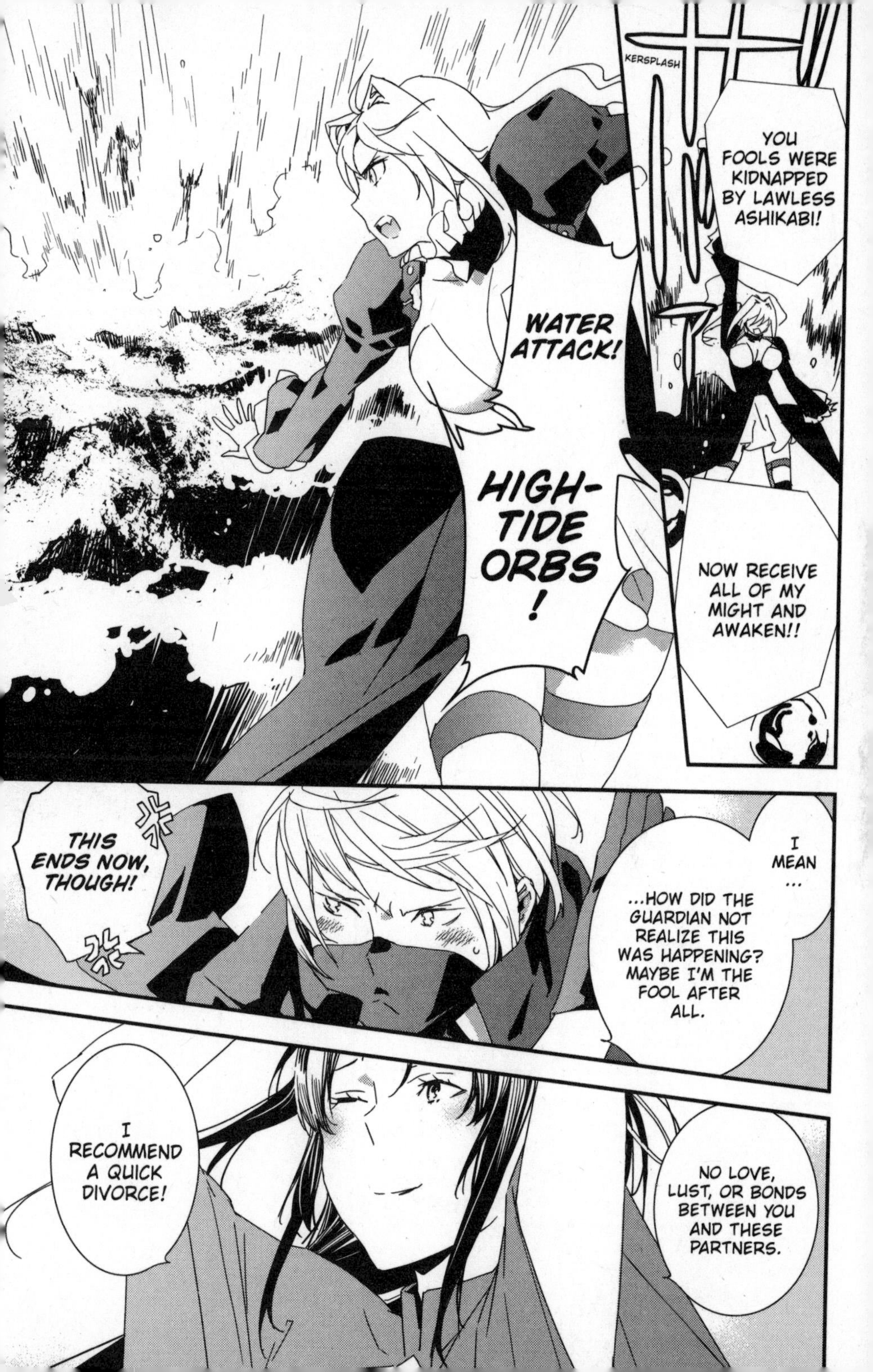
KERSPLASH
YOU FOOLS WERE KIDNAPPED BY LAWLESS ASHIKABI!
NOW RECEIVE ALL OF MY MIGHT AND AWAKEN!!
WATER ATTACK!
HIGH-TIDE ORBS!
I MEAN...
...HOW DID THE GUARDIAN NOT REALIZE THIS WAS HAPPENING? MAYBE I'M THE FOOL AFTER ALL.
THIS ENDS NOW, THOUGH!
NO LOVE, LUST, OR BONDS BETWEEN YOU AND THESE PARTNERS.
I RECOMMEND A QUICK DIVORCE!

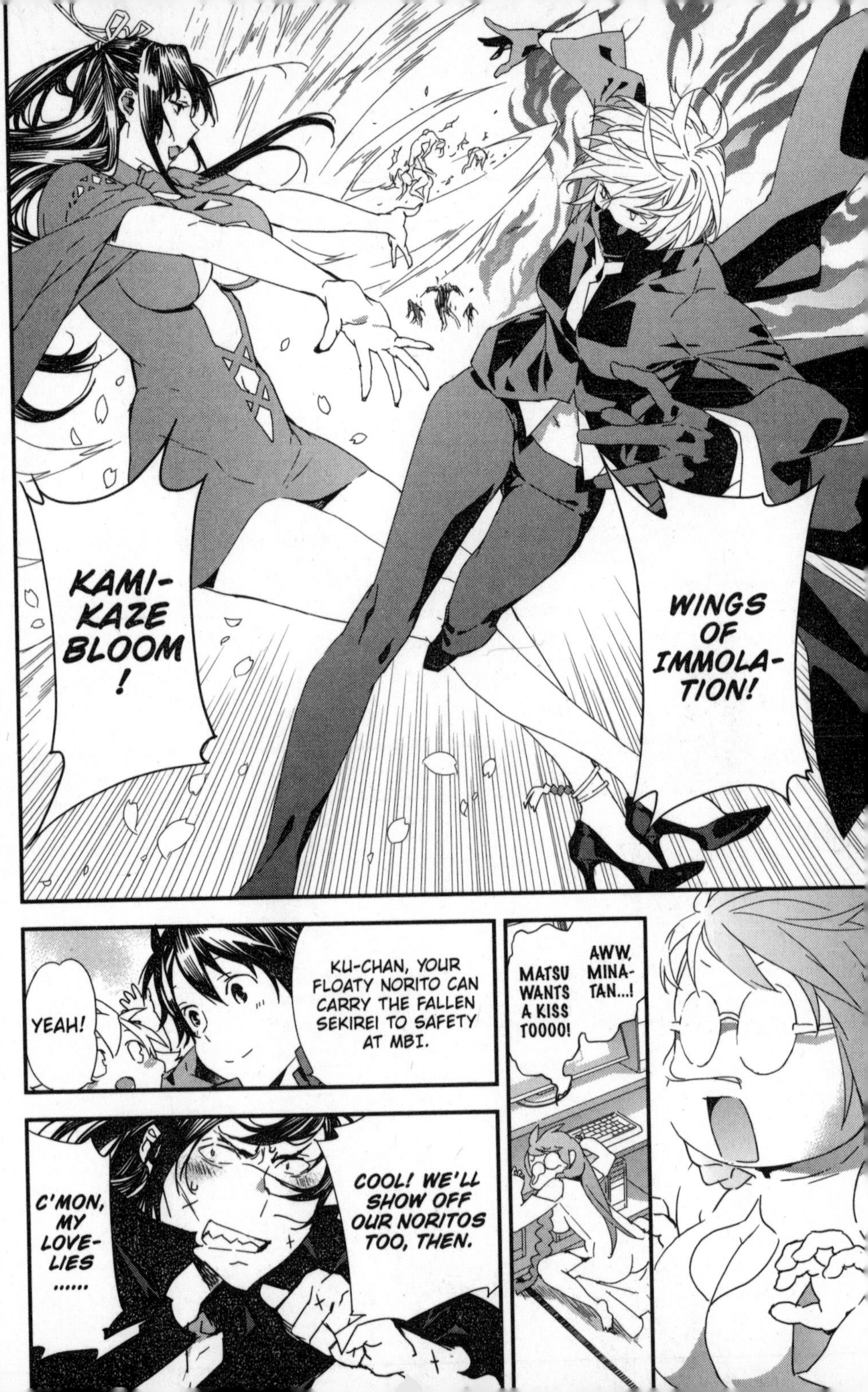
WINGS OF IMMOLATION!
KAMIKAZE BLOOM!
AWW, MINA-TAN...!
MATSU WANTS A KISS TOOOO!
KU-CHAN, YOUR FLOATY NORITO CAN CARRY THE FALLEN SEKIREI TO SAFETY AT MBI.
YEAH!
COOL! WE'LL SHOW OFF OUR NORITOS TOO, THEN.
C'MON, MY LOVELIES ......

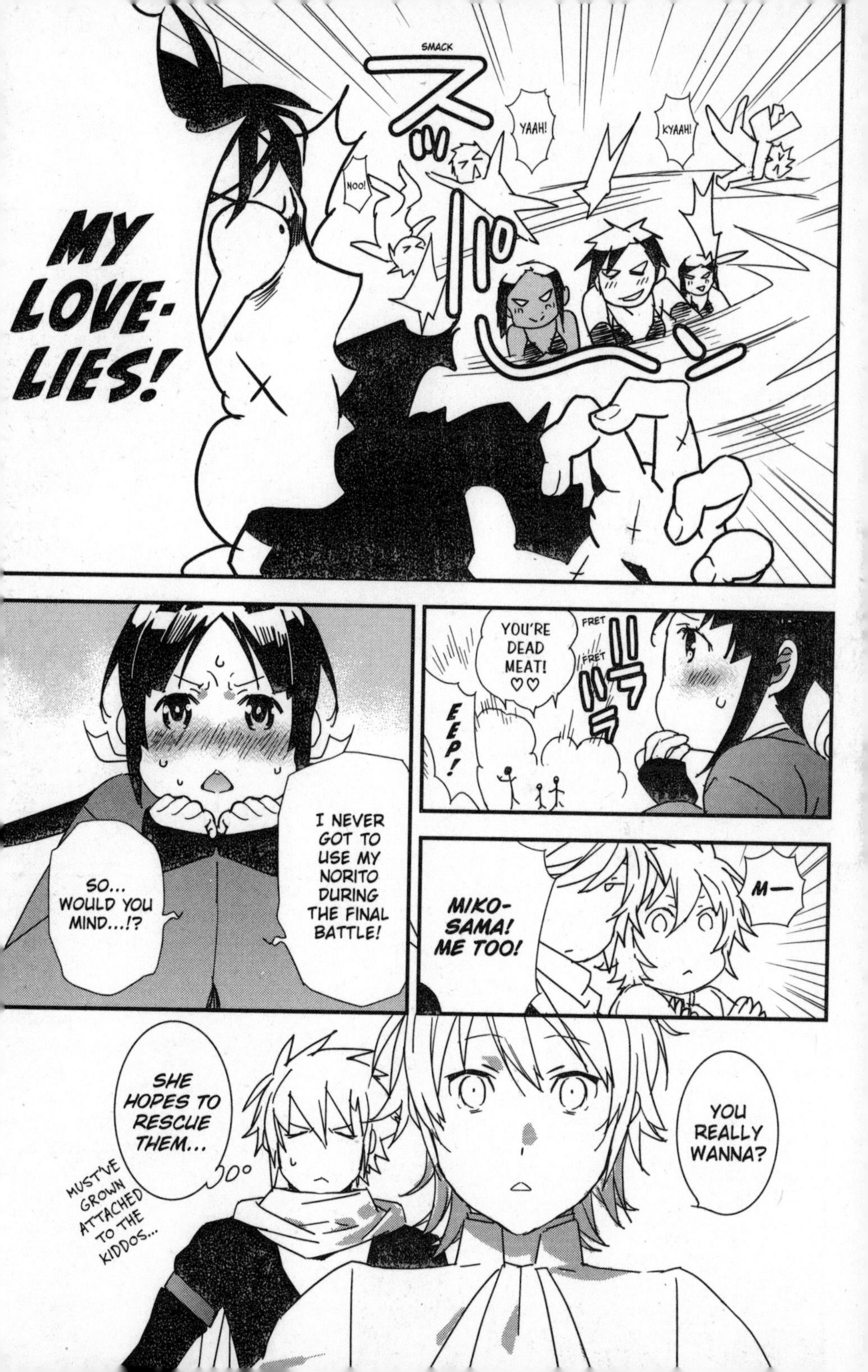
SMACK
KYAAH!
YAAH!
NOO!
MY LOVE-LIES!
FRET FRET
YOU'RE DEAD MEAT! ♡♡
EEP!
M—
MIKO-SAMA! ME TOO!
I NEVER GOT TO USE MY NORITO DURING THE FINAL BATTLE!
SO... WOULD YOU MIND...!?
YOU REALLY WANNA?
SHE HOPES TO RESCUE THEM...
MUST'VE GROWN ATTACHED TO THE KIDDOS...

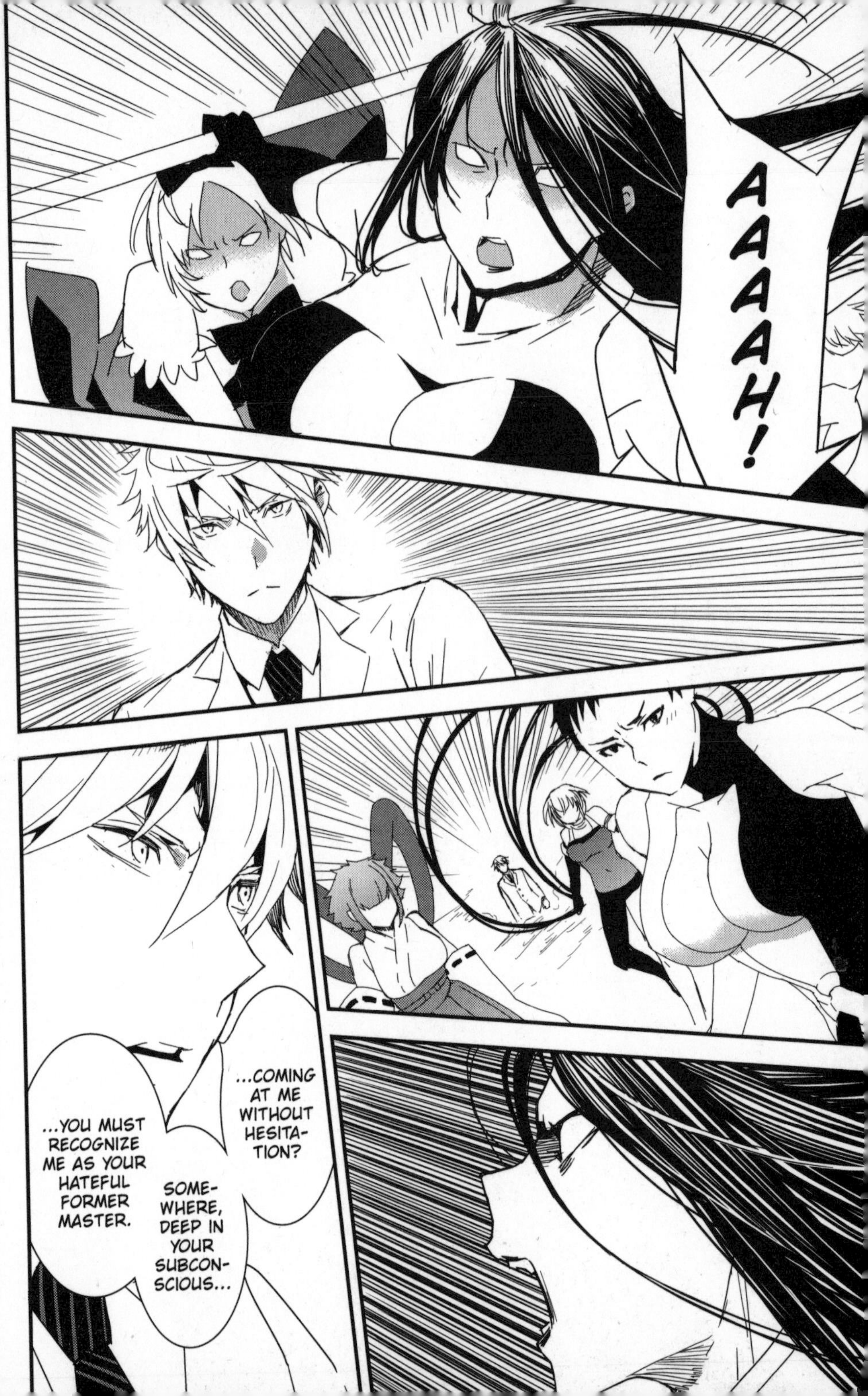
AAAAH!
...COMING AT ME WITHOUT HESITATION?
SOMEWHERE, DEEP IN YOUR SUBCONSCIOUS...
...YOU MUST RECOGNIZE ME AS YOUR HATEFUL FORMER MASTER.

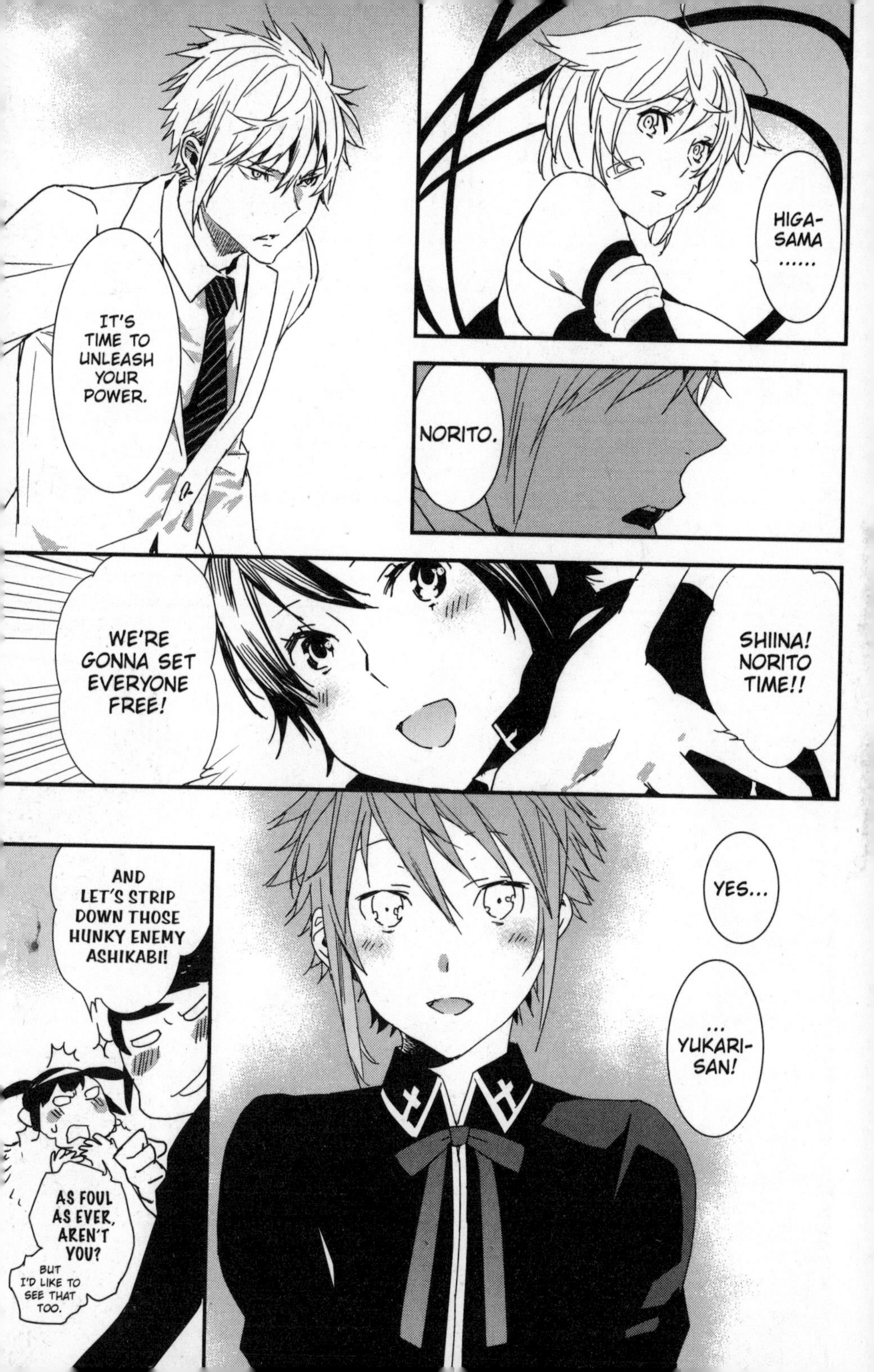
HIGA-SAMA......
NORITO.
IT'S TIME TO UNLEASH YOUR POWER.
SHIINA! NORITO TIME!!
WE'RE GONNA SET EVERYONE FREE!
YES...
...YUKARI-SAN!
AND LET'S STRIP DOWN THOSE HUNKY ENEMY ASHIKABI!
AS FOUL AS EVER, AREN'T YOU?
BUT I'D LIKE TO SEE THAT TOO.

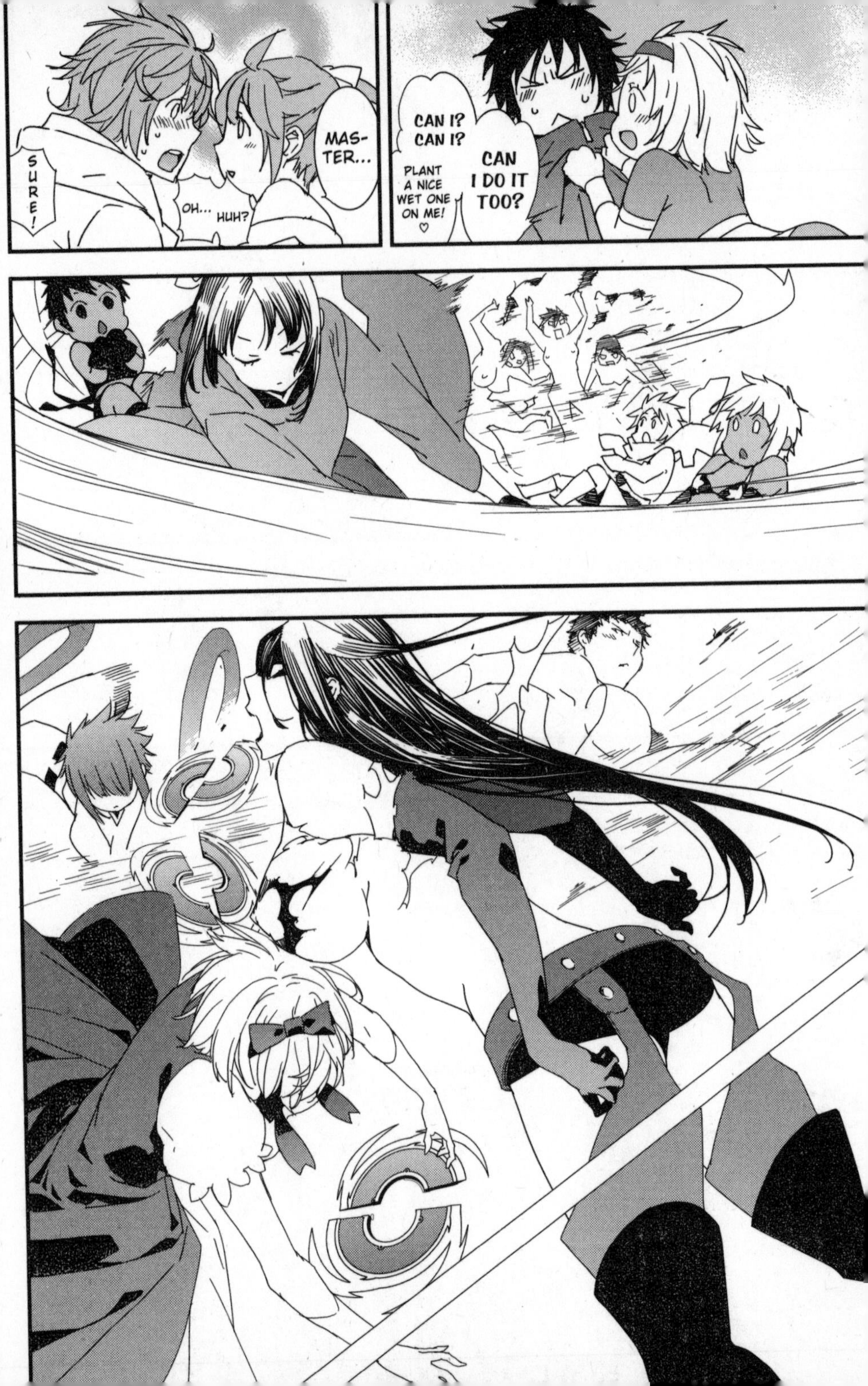
CAN I DO IT TOO?
CAN I? CAN I?
PLANT A NICE WET ONE ON ME! ♡
MAS-TER...
OH... HUH?
SURE!

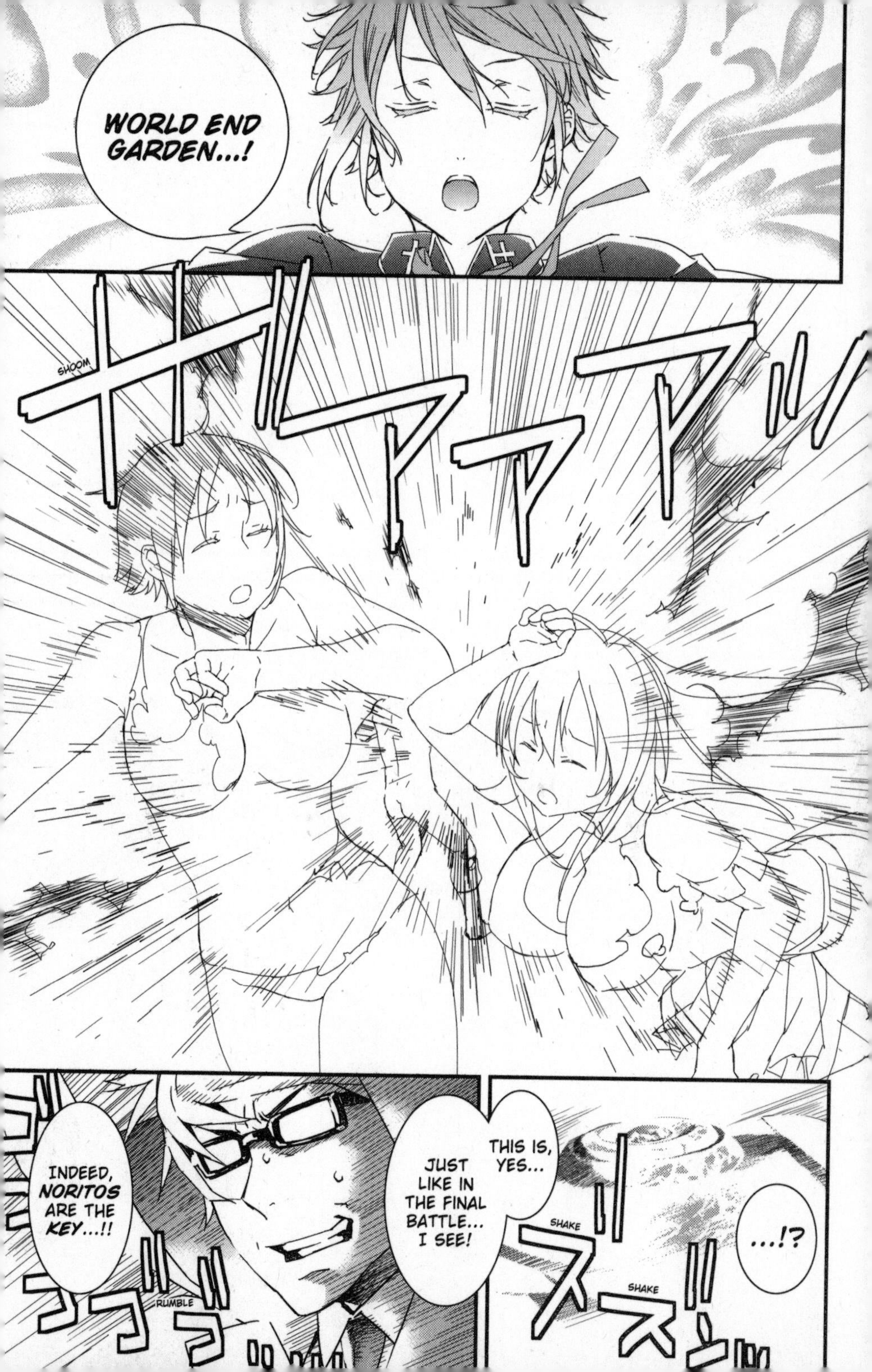
WORLD END GARDEN...!
SHOOM
SHAKE
SHAKE
...!?
THIS IS, YES...
JUST LIKE IN THE FINAL BATTLE... I SEE!
INDEED, NORITOS ARE THE KEY...!!
RUMBLE

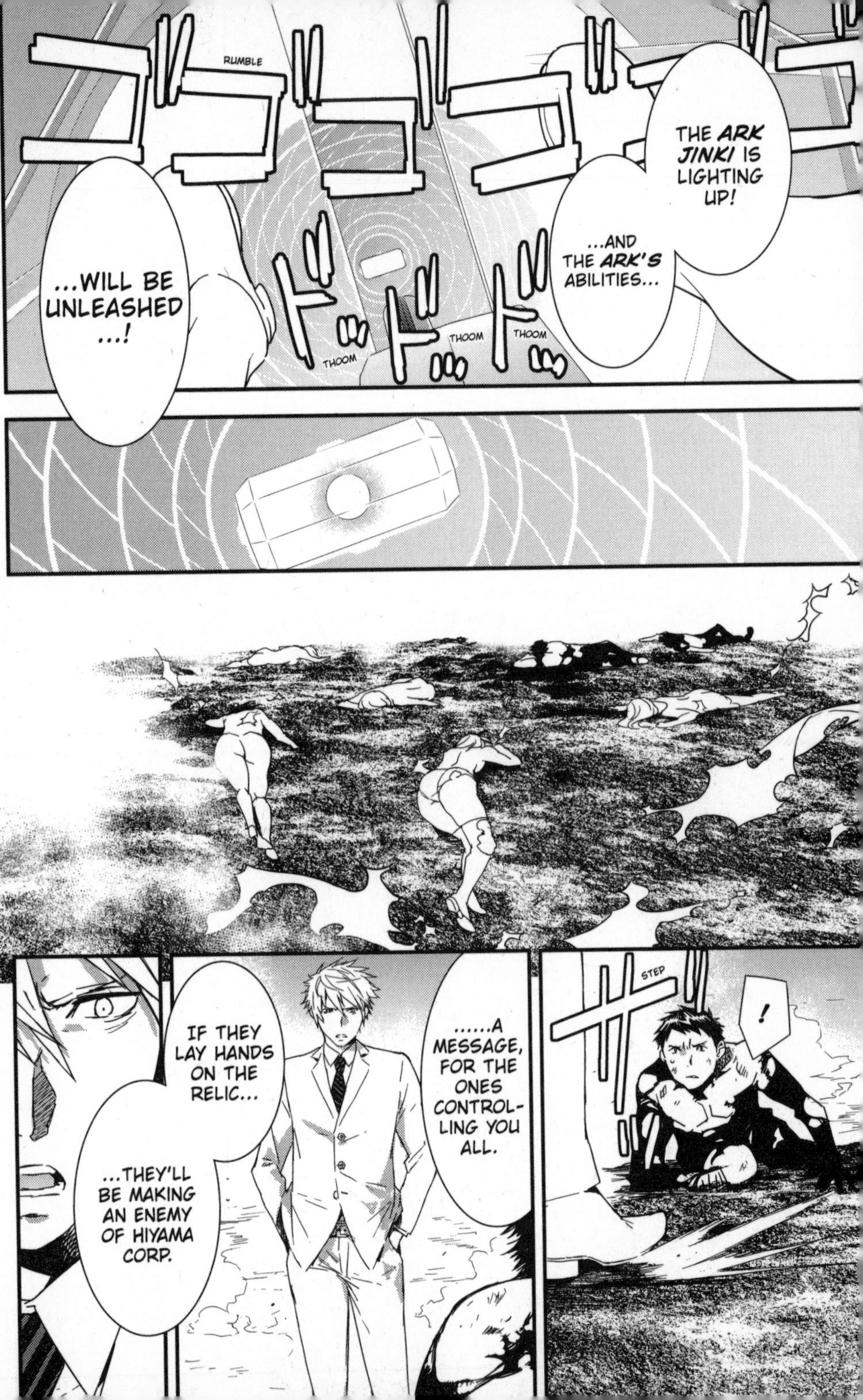
RUMBLE
THE ARK JINKI IS LIGHTING UP!
...AND THE ARK'S ABILITIES...
THOOM
THOOM
THOOM
...WILL BE UNLEASHED ...!
STEP
!
......A MESSAGE, FOR THE ONES CONTROL-LING YOU ALL.
IF THEY LAY HANDS ON THE RELIC...
...THEY'LL BE MAKING AN ENEMY OF HIYAMA CORP.

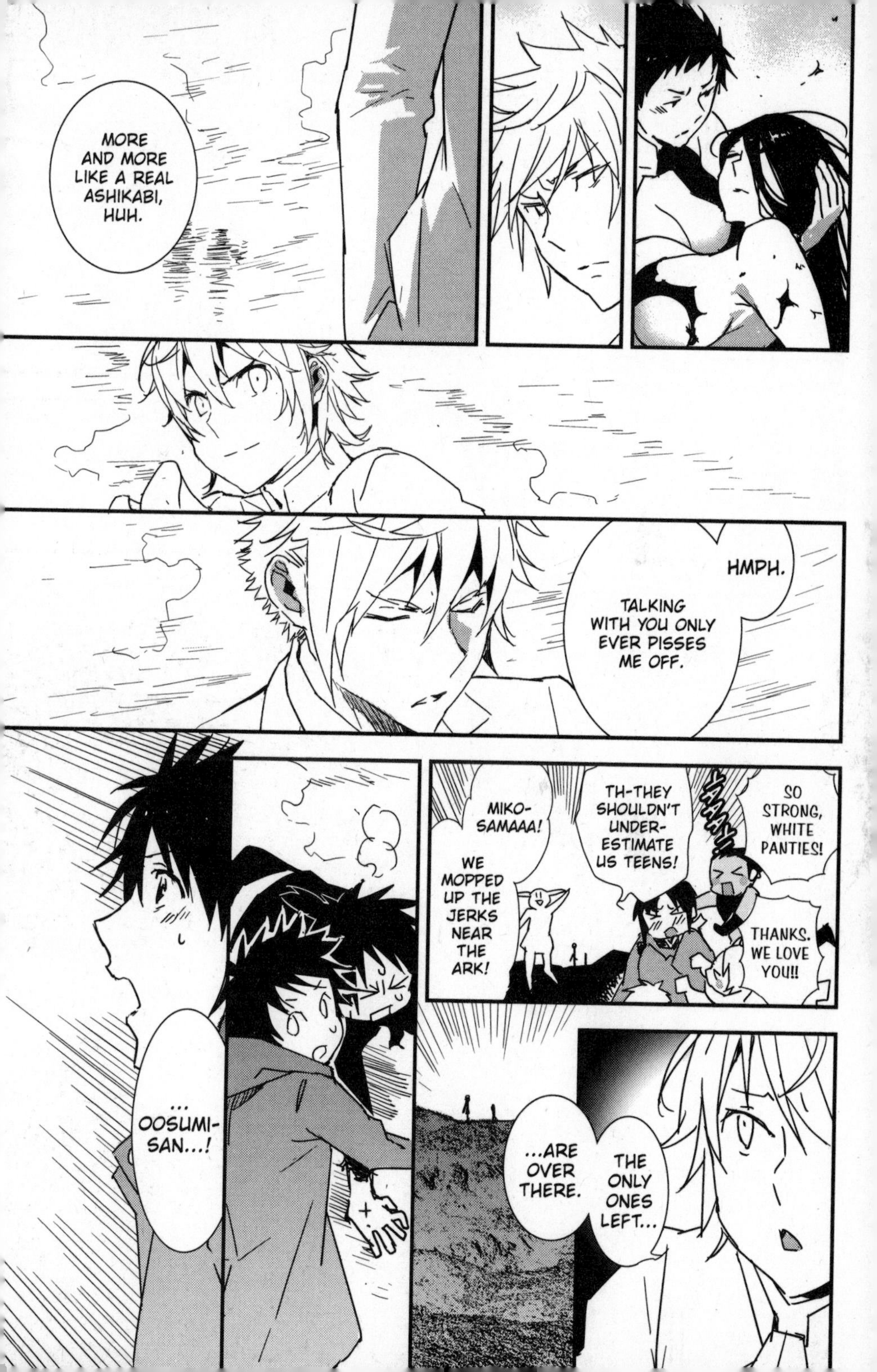
MORE AND MORE LIKE A REAL ASHIKABI, HUH.
HMPH.
TALKING WITH YOU ONLY EVER PISSES ME OFF.
SO STRONG, WHITE PANTIES!
TH-THEY SHOULDN'T UNDER-ESTIMATE US TEENS!
MIKO-SAMAAA!
WE MOPPED UP THE JERKS NEAR THE ARK!
THANKS. WE LOVE YOU!!
THE ONLY ONES LEFT...
...ARE OVER THERE.
...OOSUMI-SAN...!

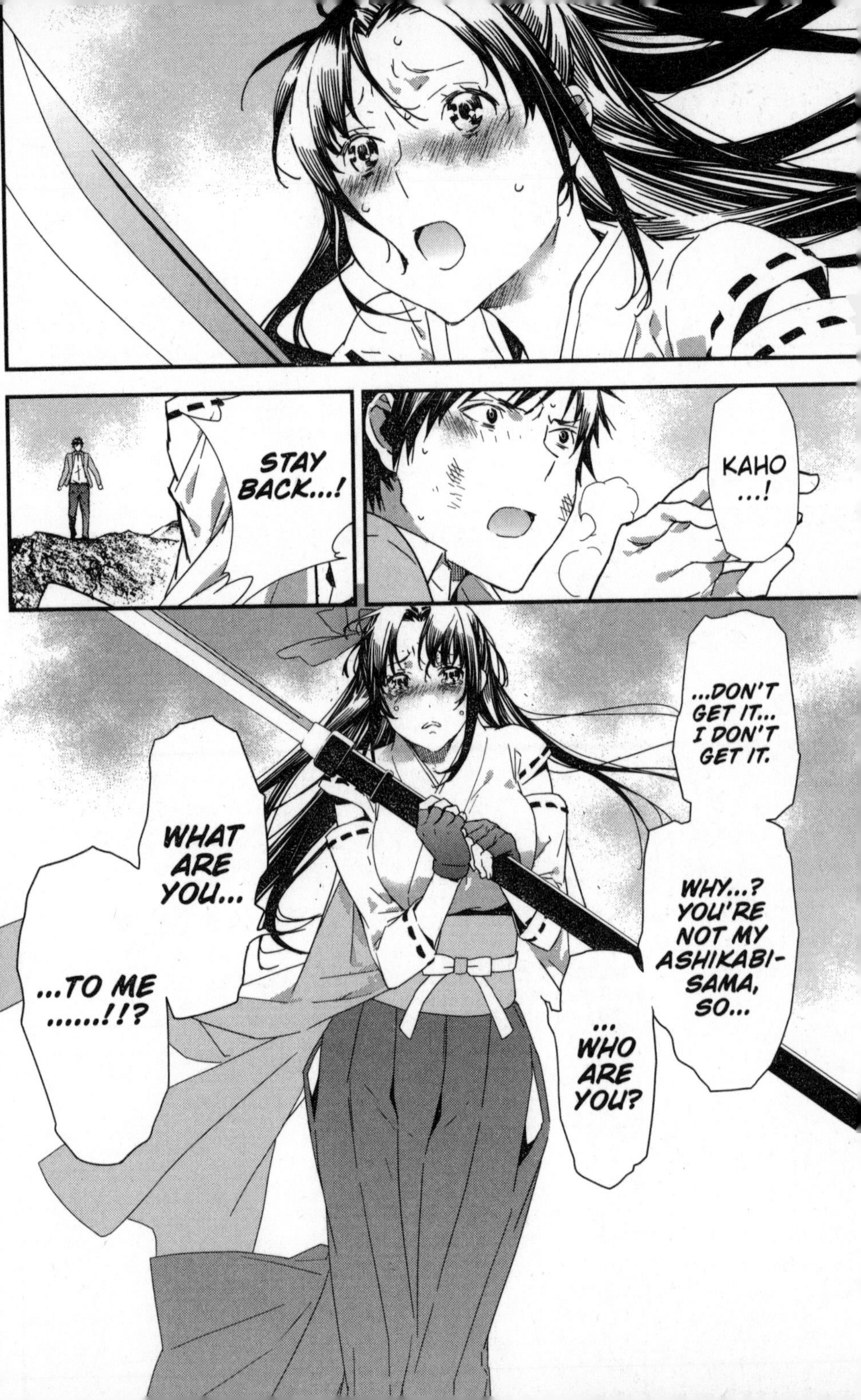
KAHO ...!
STAY BACK...!
...DON'T GET IT... I DON'T GET IT.
WHY...? YOU'RE NOT MY ASHIKABI-SAMA, SO...
... WHO ARE YOU?
WHAT ARE YOU...
...TO ME ......!!?

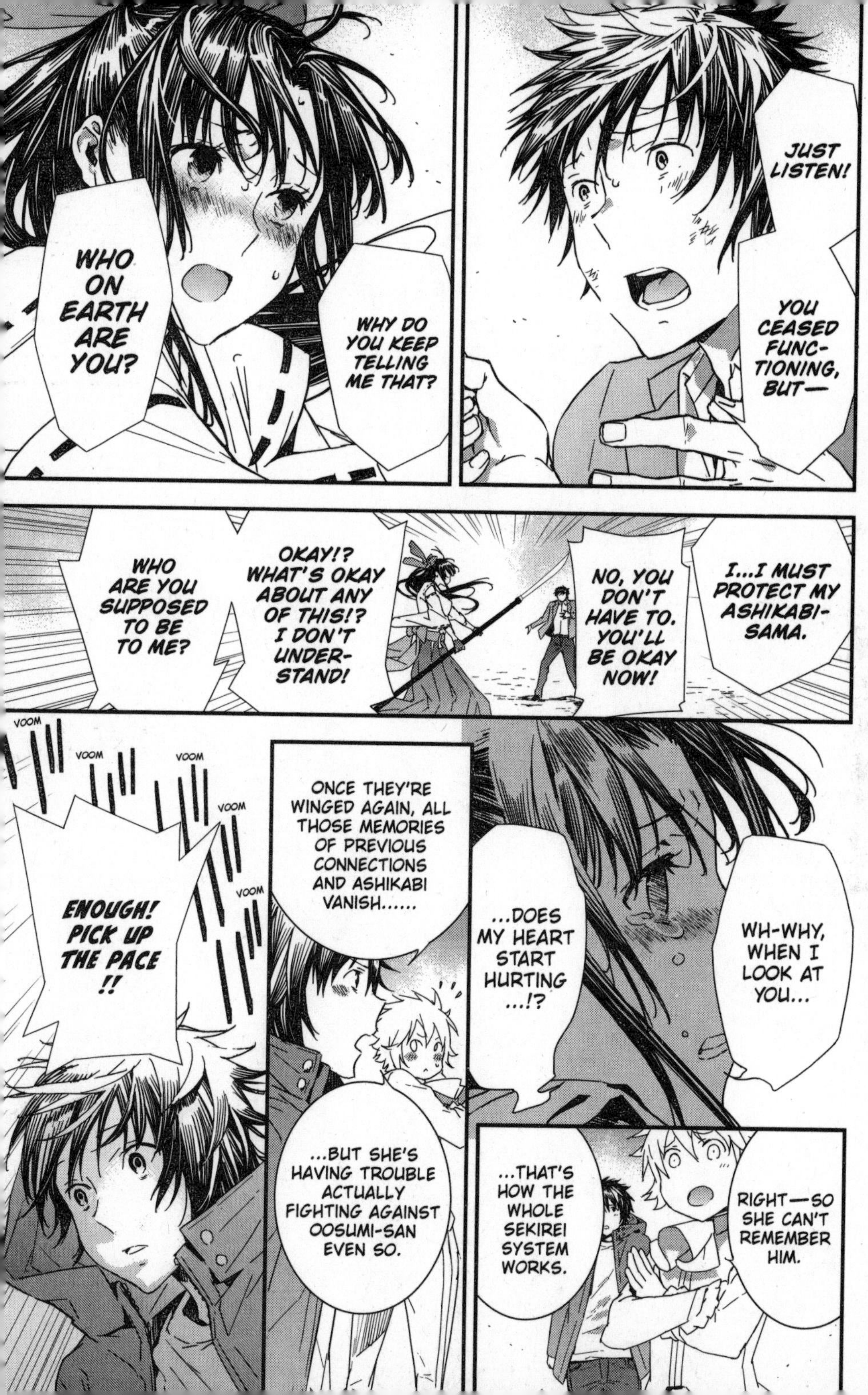
JUST LISTEN!
YOU CEASED FUNC-TIONING, BUT—
WHY DO YOU KEEP TELLING ME THAT?
WHO ON EARTH ARE YOU?
I...I MUST PROTECT MY ASHIKABI-SAMA.
NO, YOU DON'T HAVE TO. YOU'LL BE OKAY NOW!
OKAY!? WHAT'S OKAY ABOUT ANY OF THIS!? I DON'T UNDER-STAND!
WHO ARE YOU SUPPOSED TO BE TO ME?
WH-WHY, WHEN I LOOK AT YOU...
...DOES MY HEART START HURTING ...!?
RIGHT—SO SHE CAN'T REMEMBER HIM.
...THAT'S HOW THE WHOLE SEKIREI SYSTEM WORKS.
ONCE THEY'RE WINGED AGAIN, ALL THOSE MEMORIES OF PREVIOUS CONNECTIONS AND ASHIKABI VANISH......
...BUT SHE'S HAVING TROUBLE ACTUALLY FIGHTING AGAINST OOSUMI-SAN EVEN SO.
VOOM
VOOM
VOOM
VOOM
VOOM
ENOUGH! PICK UP THE PACE !!

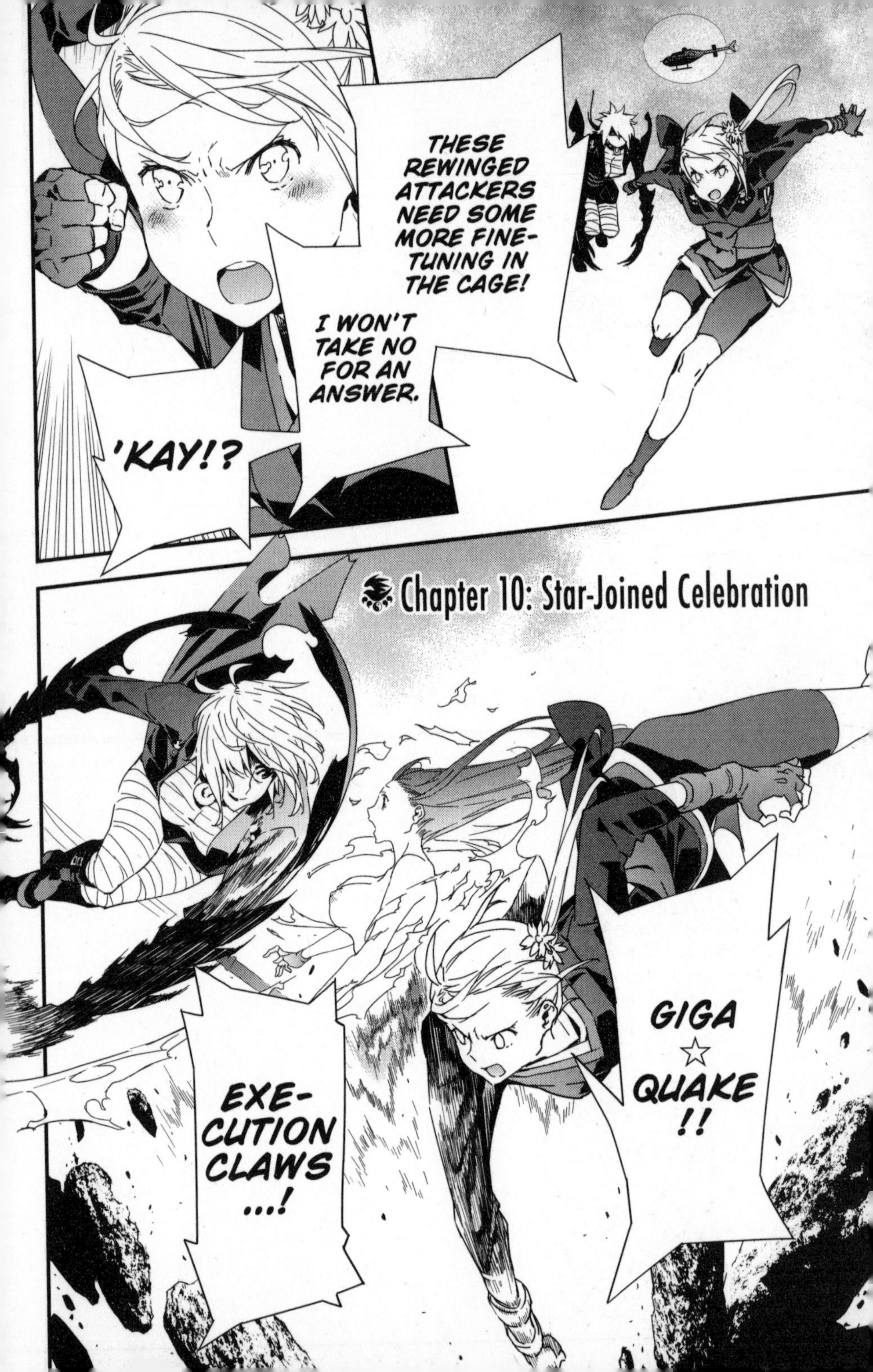
THESE REWINGED ATTACKERS NEED SOME MORE FINE-TUNING IN THE CAGE!
I WON'T TAKE NO FOR AN ANSWER.
'KAY!?
Chapter 10: Star-Joined Celebration
GIGA ☆ QUAKE!!
EXECUTION CLAWS ...!

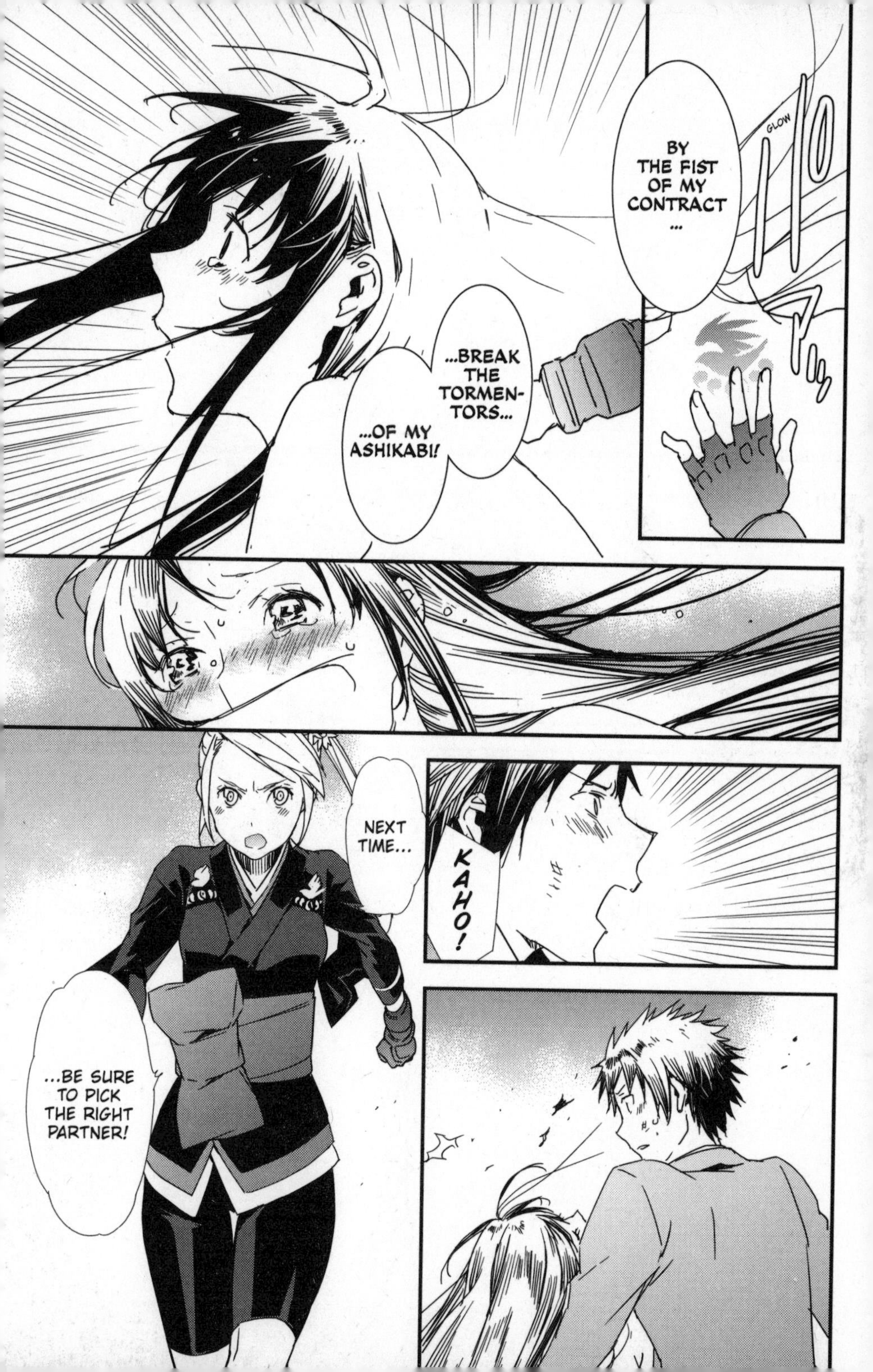
BY THE FIST OF MY CONTRACT ...
GLOW
...BREAK THE TORMEN-TORS...
...OF MY ASHIKABI!
KAHO!
NEXT TIME...
...BE SURE TO PICK THE RIGHT PARTNER!

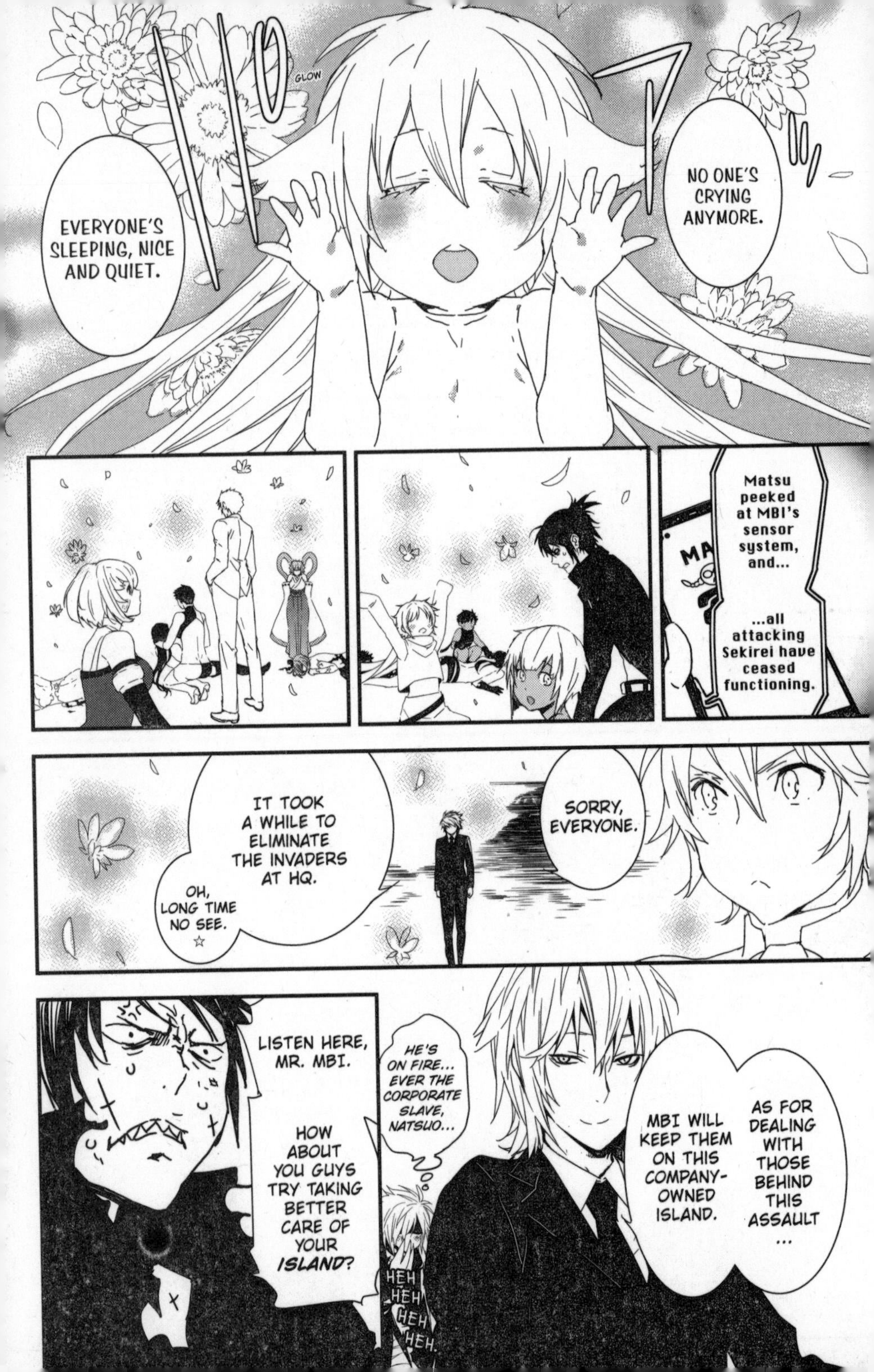
NO ONE'S CRYING ANYMORE.
GLOW
EVERYONE'S SLEEPING, NICE AND QUIET.
Matsu peeked at MBI's sensor system, and...
...all attacking Sekirei have ceased functioning.
SORRY, EVERYONE.
IT TOOK A WHILE TO ELIMINATE THE INVADERS AT HQ.
OH, LONG TIME NO SEE. ☆
AS FOR DEALING WITH THOSE BEHIND THIS ASSAULT...
MBI WILL KEEP THEM ON THIS COMPANY-OWNED ISLAND.
HE'S ON FIRE... EVER THE CORPORATE SLAVE, NATSUO...
HEH HEH HEH HEH.
LISTEN HERE, MR. MBI.
HOW ABOUT YOU GUYS TRY TAKING BETTER CARE OF YOUR *ISLAND*?

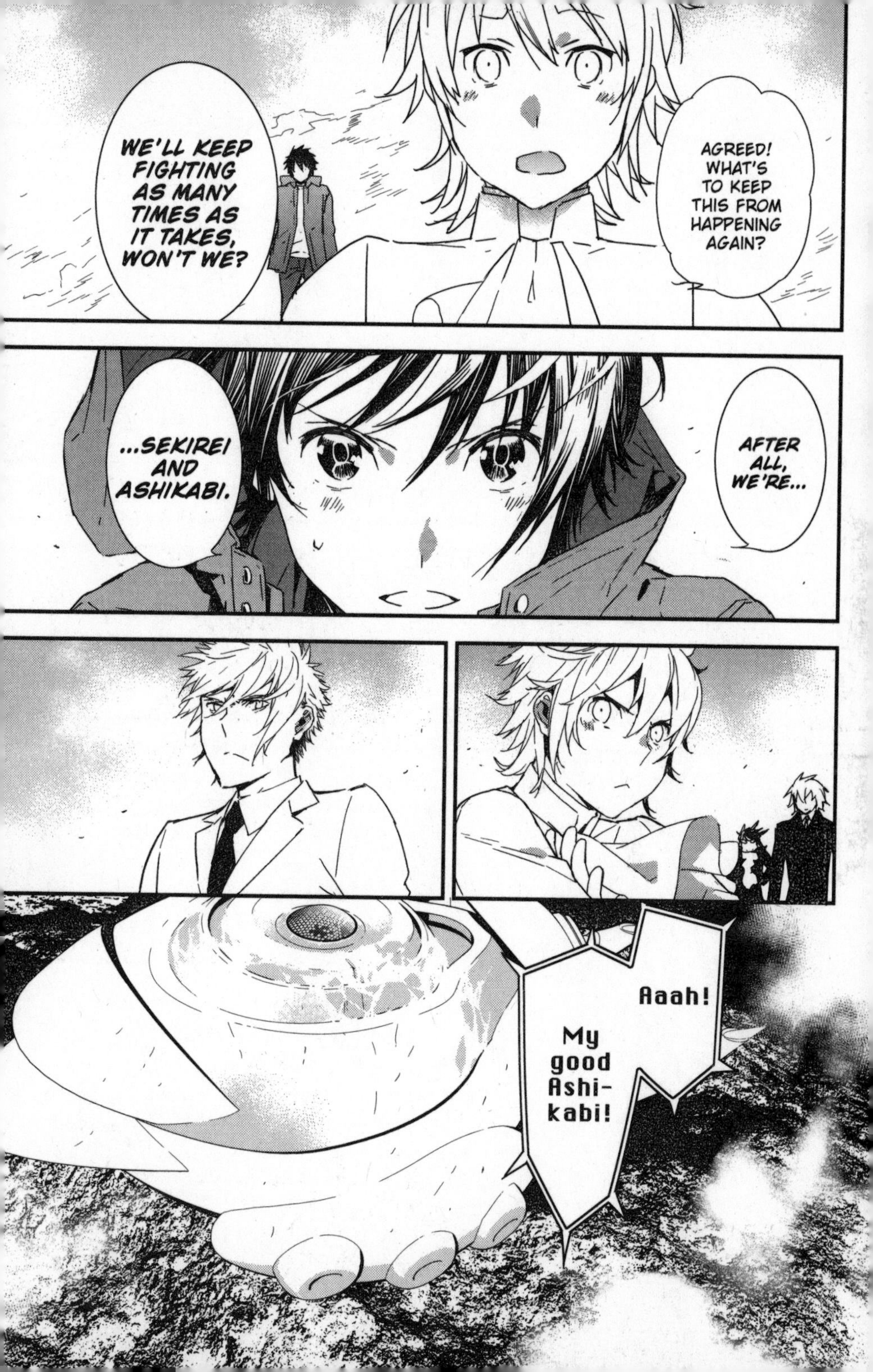
AGREED! WHAT'S TO KEEP THIS FROM HAPPENING AGAIN?
WE'LL KEEP FIGHTING AS MANY TIMES AS IT TAKES, WON'T WE?
AFTER ALL, WE'RE...
...SEKIREI AND ASHIKABI.
Aaah!
My good Ashi-kabi!

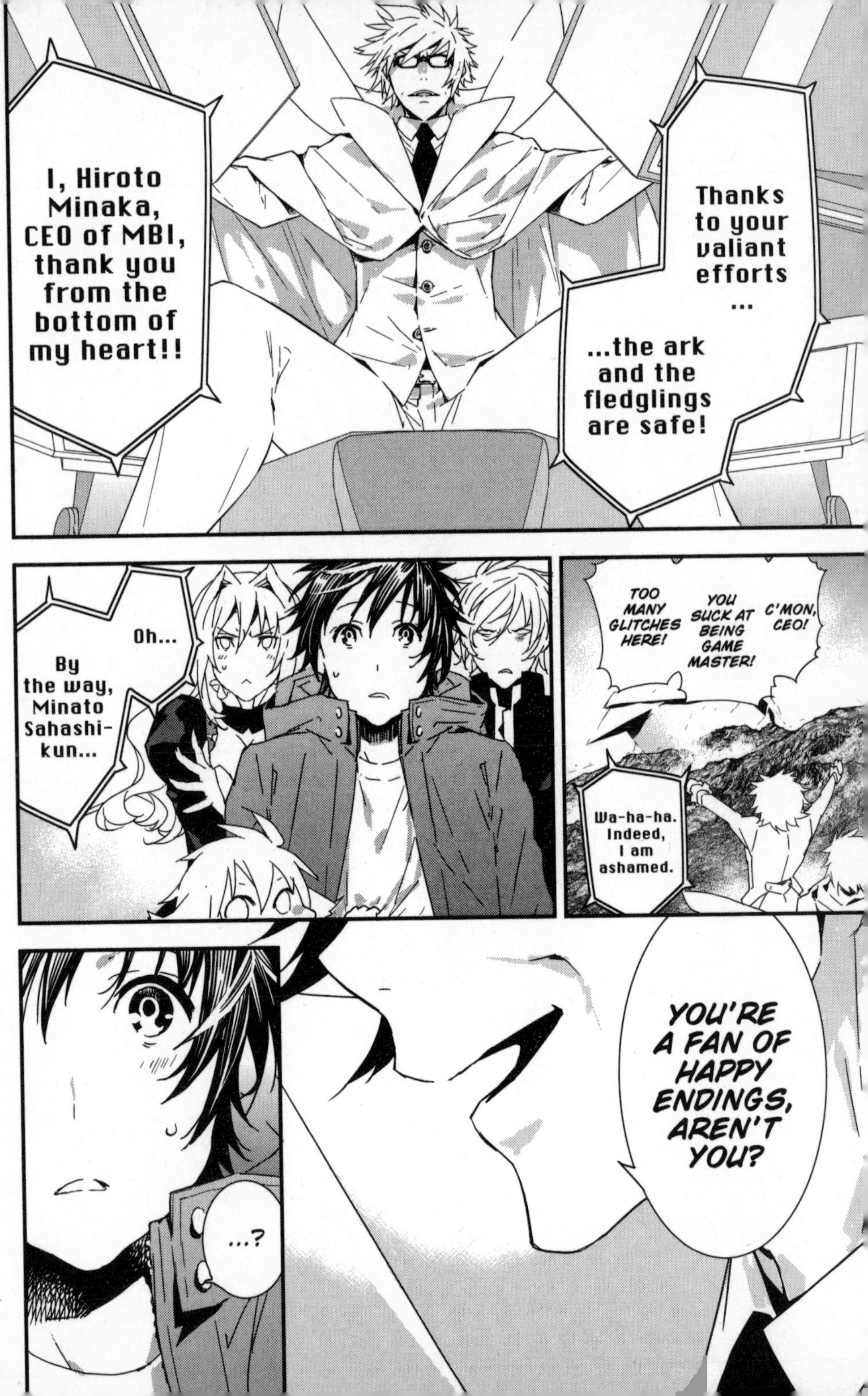
Thanks to your valiant efforts ...
...the ark and the fledglings are safe!
I, Hiroto Minaka, CEO of MBI, thank you from the bottom of my heart!!
C'MON, CEO!
YOU SUCK AT BEING GAME MASTER!
TOO MANY GLITCHES HERE!
Wa-ha-ha. Indeed, I am ashamed.
Oh...
By the way, Minato Sahashi-kun...
YOU'RE A FAN OF HAPPY ENDINGS, AREN'T YOU?
...?

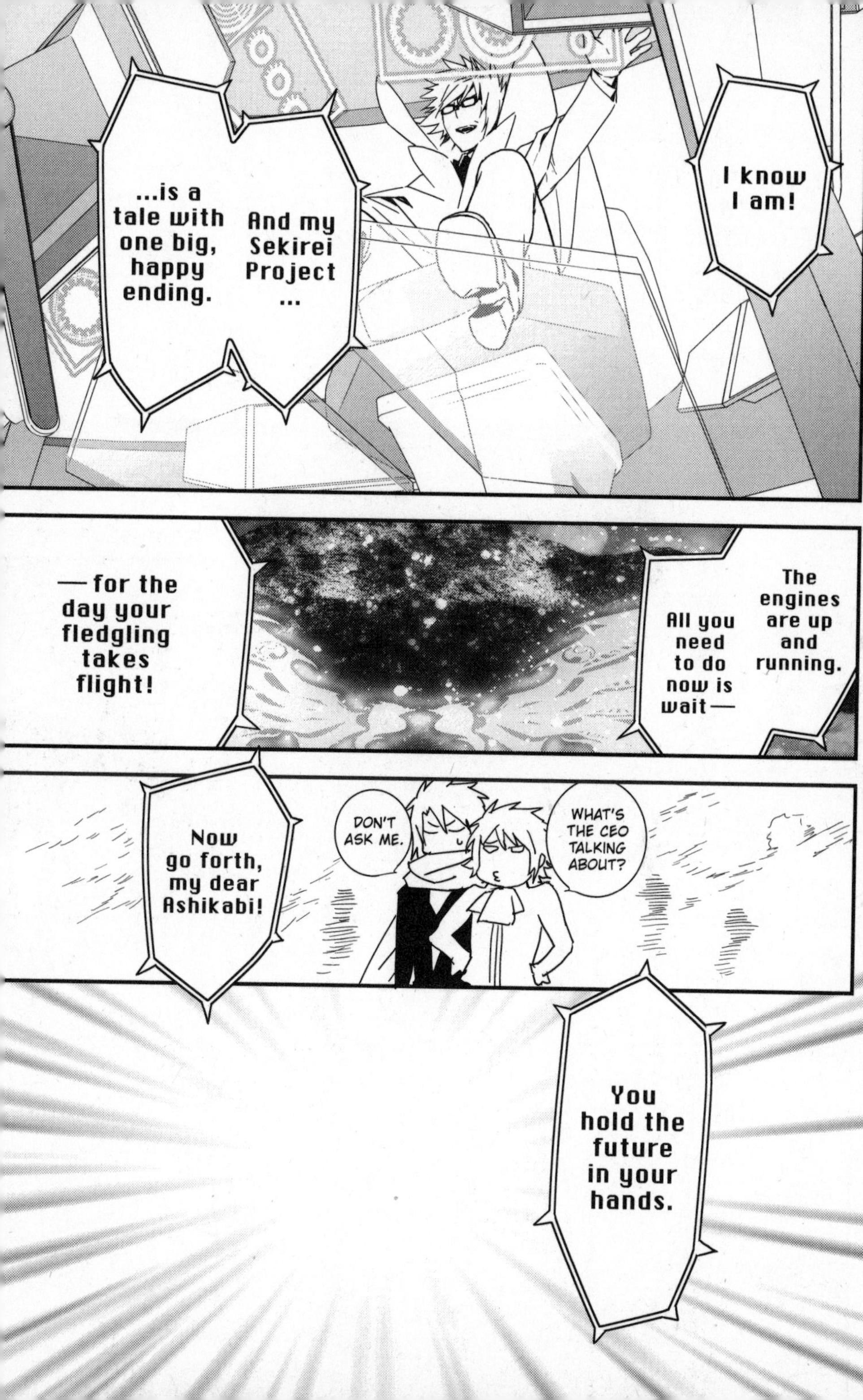
I know I am!
And my Sekirei Project ...
...is a tale with one big, happy ending.
The engines are up and running.
All you need to do now is wait—
—for the day your fledgling takes flight!
WHAT'S THE CEO TALKING ABOUT?
DON'T ASK ME.
Now go forth, my dear Ashikabi!
You hold the future in your hands.

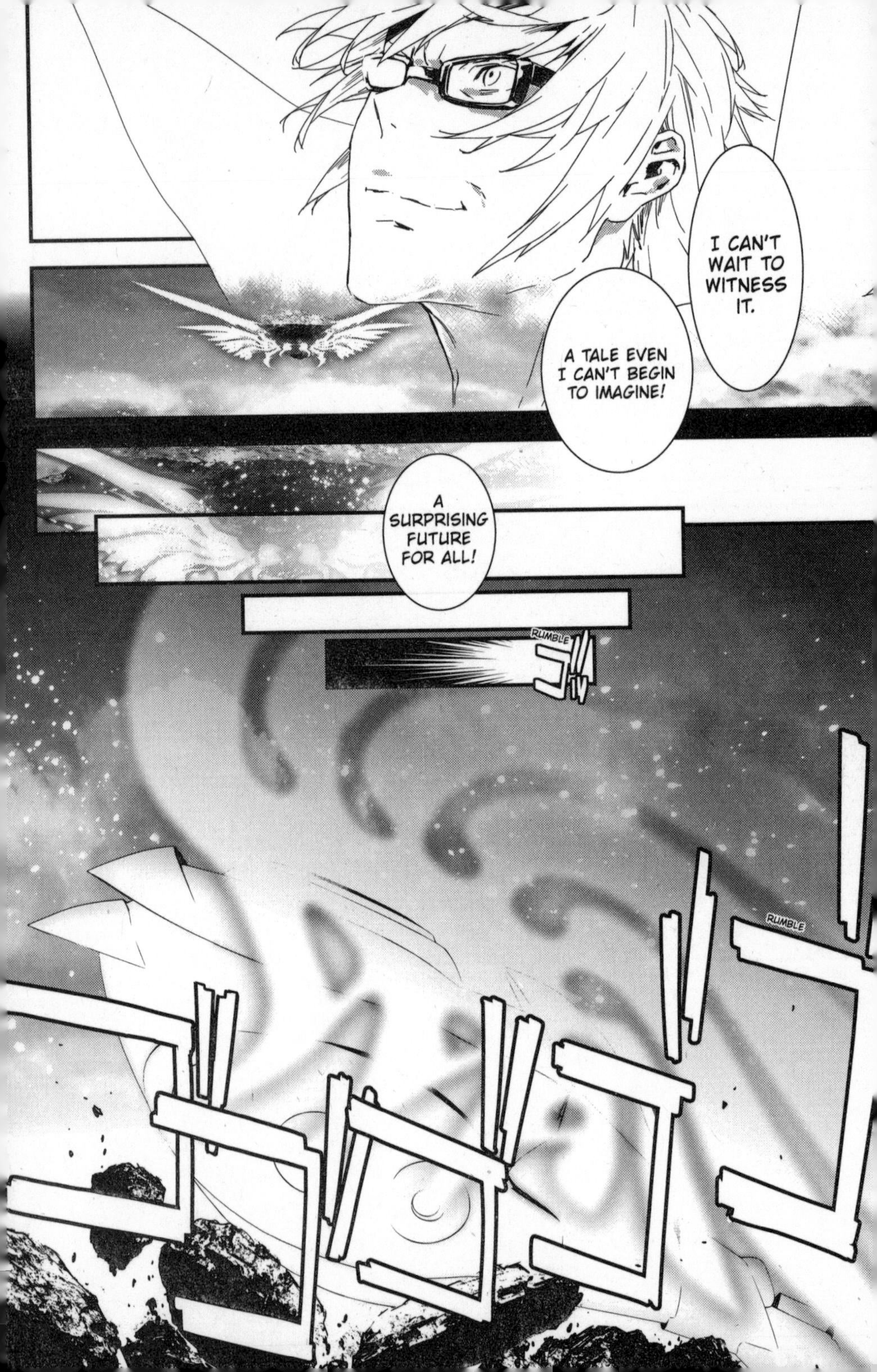
I CAN'T WAIT TO WITNESS IT.
A TALE EVEN I CAN'T BEGIN TO IMAGINE!
A SURPRISING FUTURE FOR ALL!
RUMBLE
RUMBLE

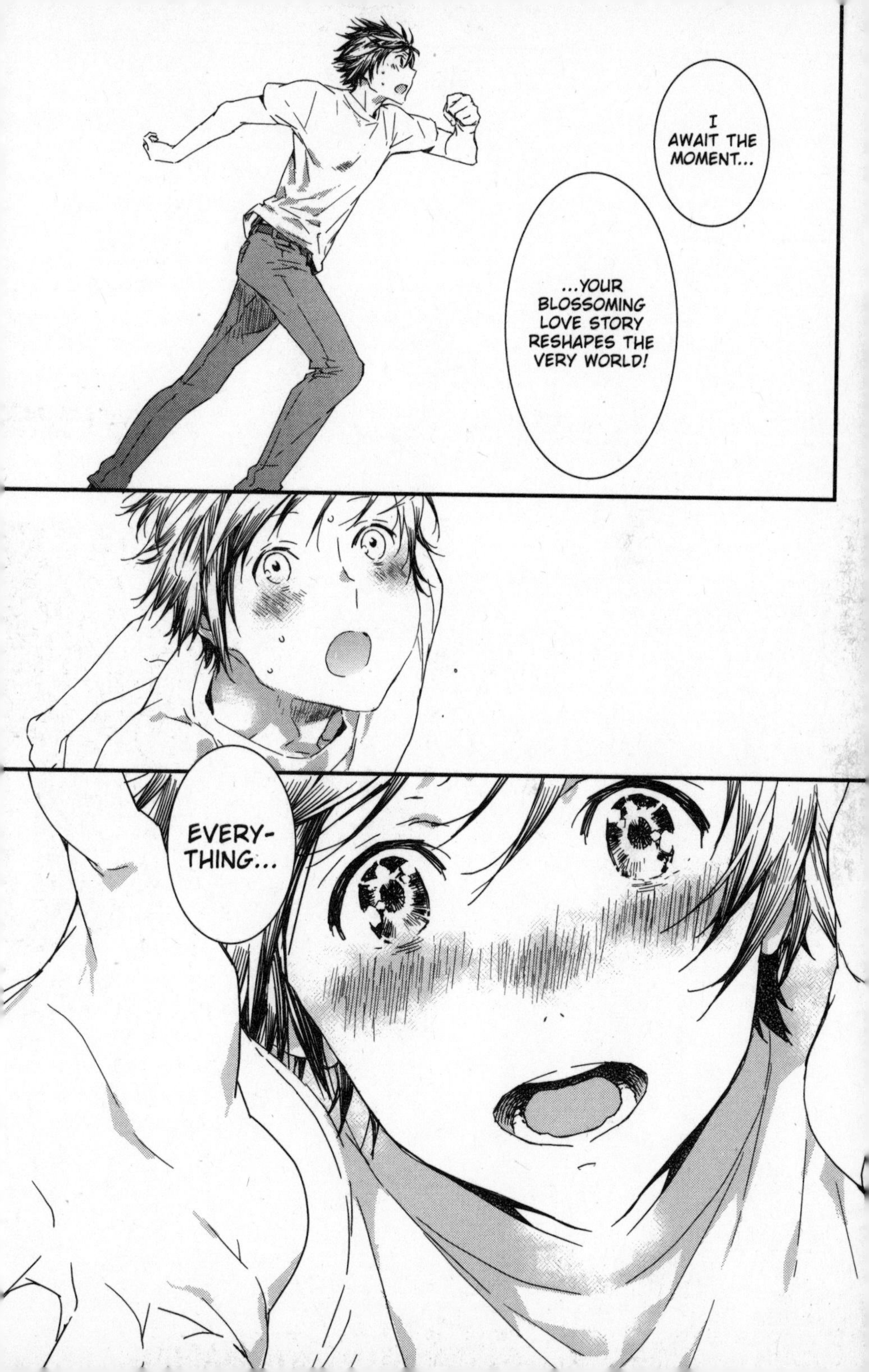
I AWAIT THE MOMENT...
...YOUR BLOSSOMING LOVE STORY RESHAPES THE VERY WORLD!
EVERY-THING...

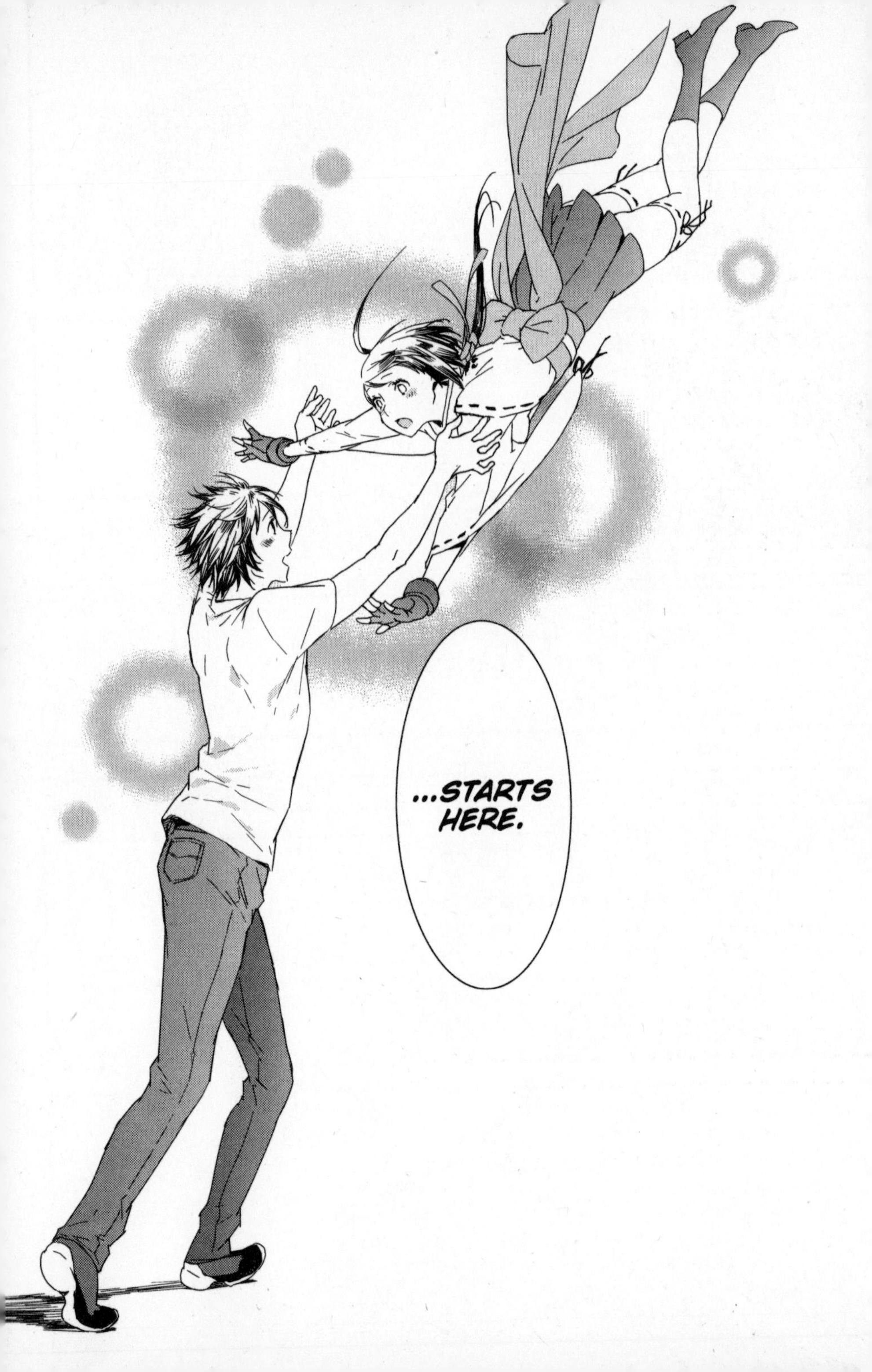
...STARTS HERE.

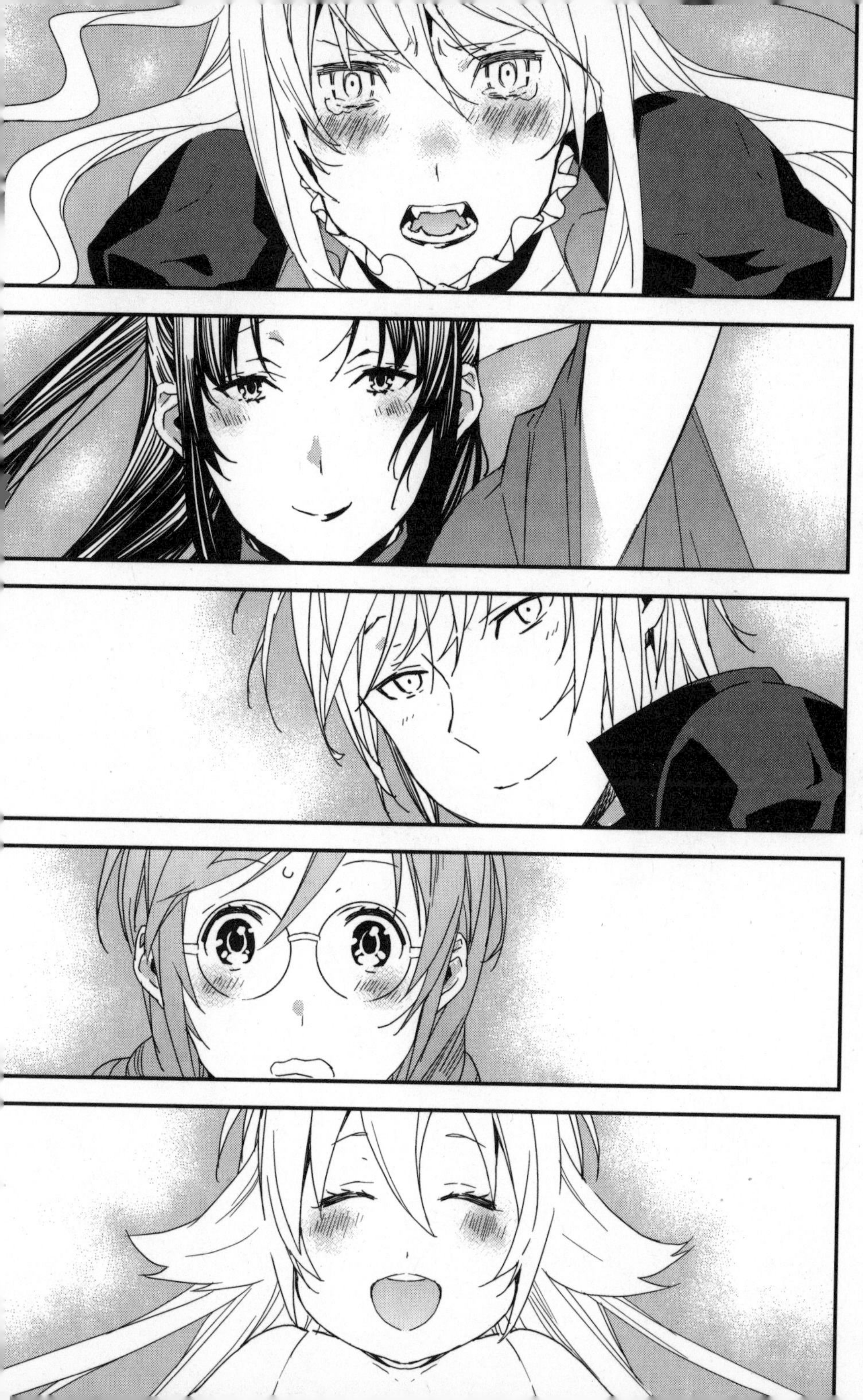

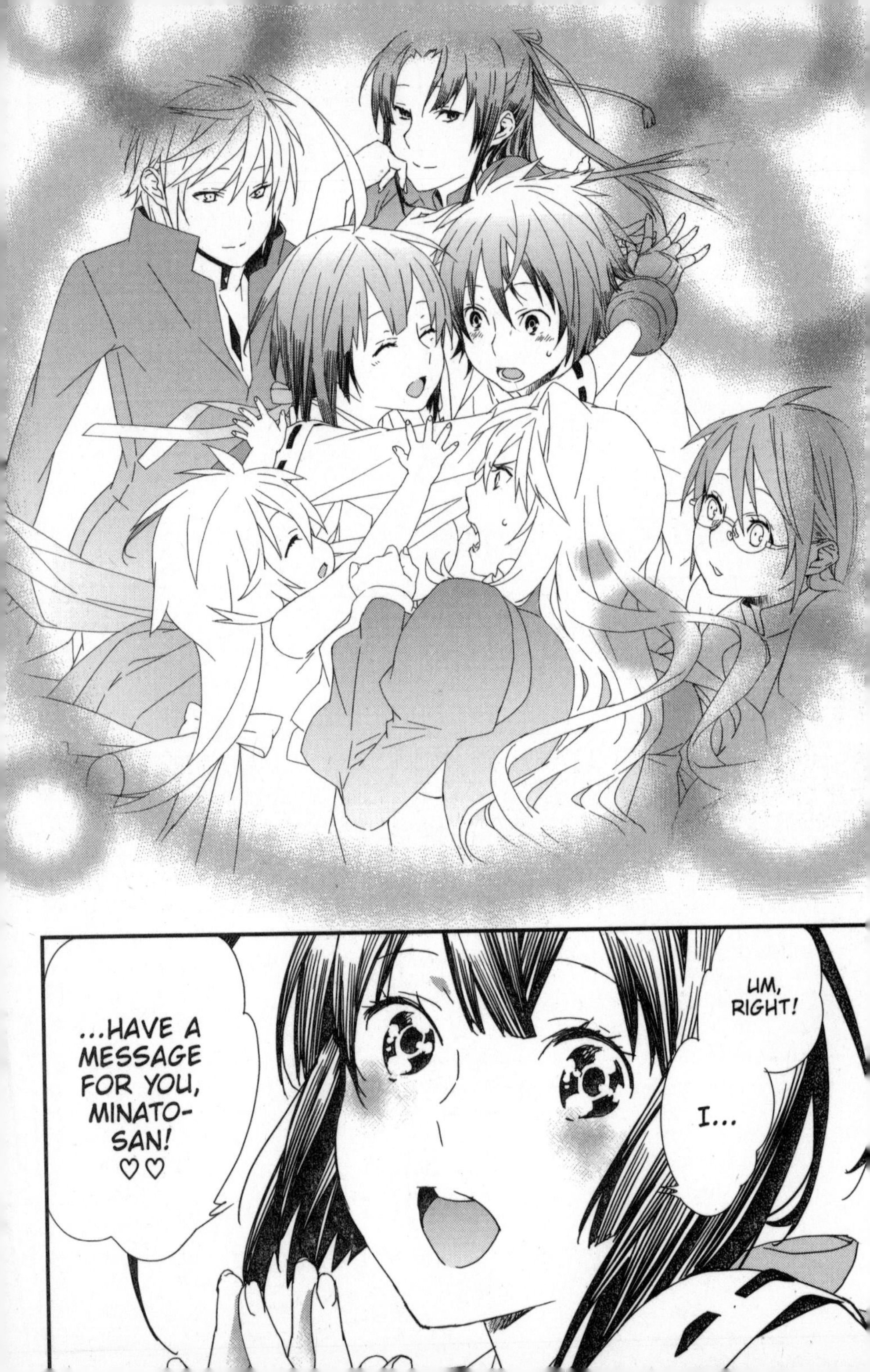
UM, RIGHT!
I...
...HAVE A MESSAGE FOR YOU, MINATO-SAN! ♡♡

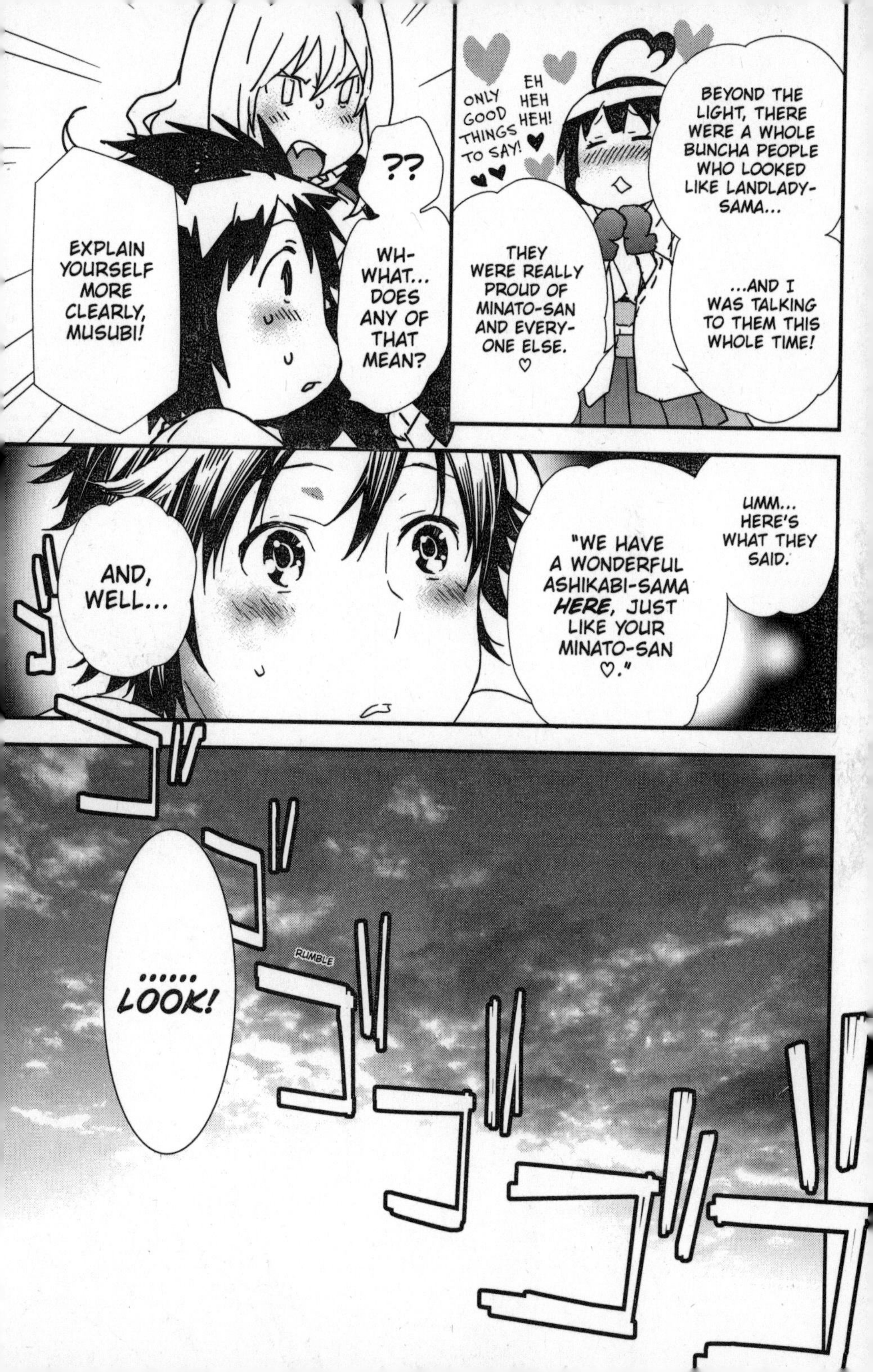
BEYOND THE LIGHT, THERE WERE A WHOLE BUNCHA PEOPLE WHO LOOKED LIKE LANDLADY-SAMA...
...AND I WAS TALKING TO THEM THIS WHOLE TIME!
EH HEH HEH!
ONLY GOOD THINGS TO SAY!
THEY WERE REALLY PROUD OF MINATO-SAN AND EVERY-ONE ELSE. ♡
WH-WHAT... DOES ANY OF THAT MEAN?
??
EXPLAIN YOURSELF MORE CLEARLY, MUSUBI!
UMM... HERE'S WHAT THEY SAID.
"WE HAVE A WONDERFUL ASHIKABI-SAMA *HERE*, JUST LIKE YOUR MINATO-SAN ♡."
AND, WELL...
RUMBLE
......LOOK!

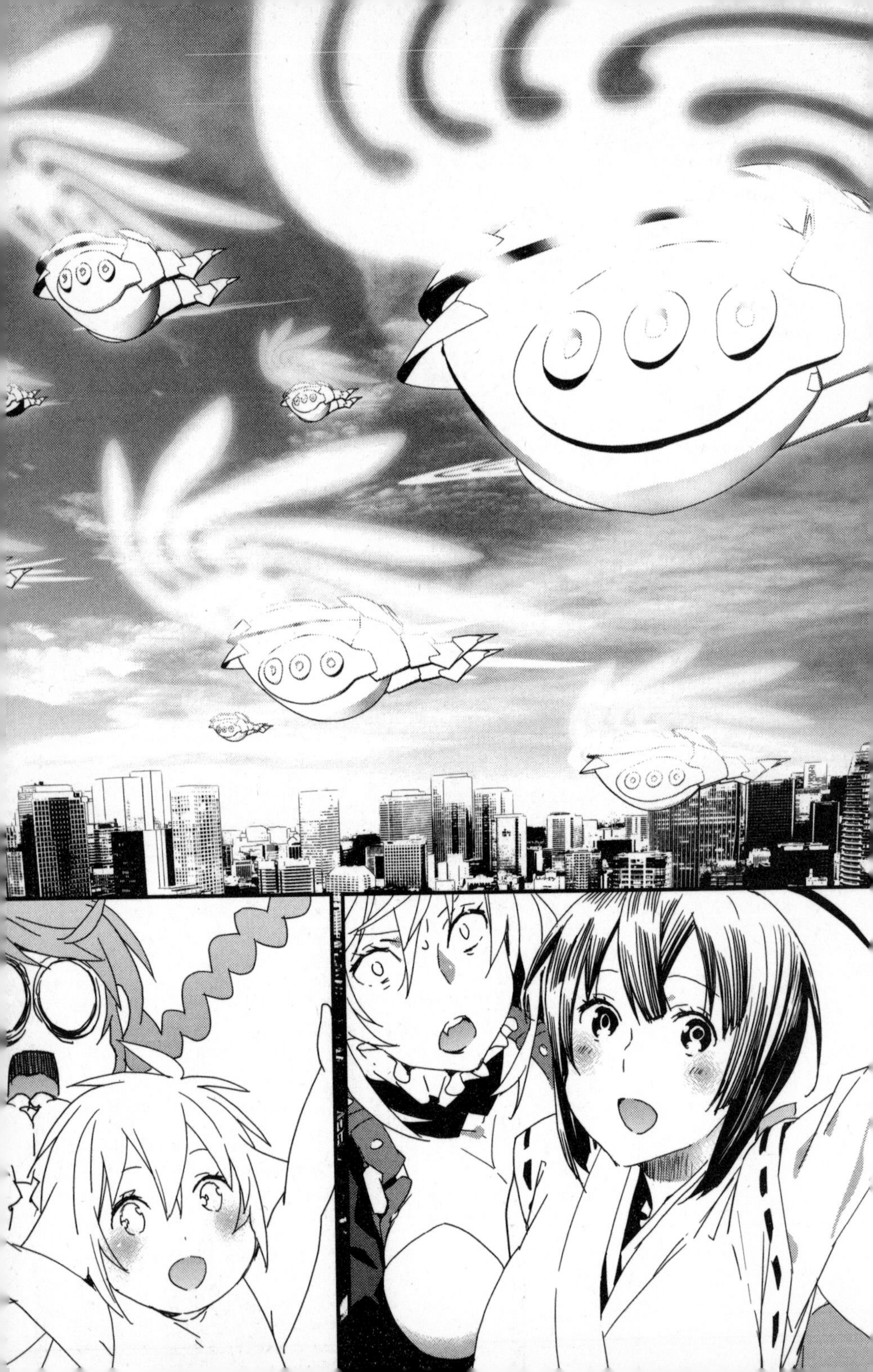

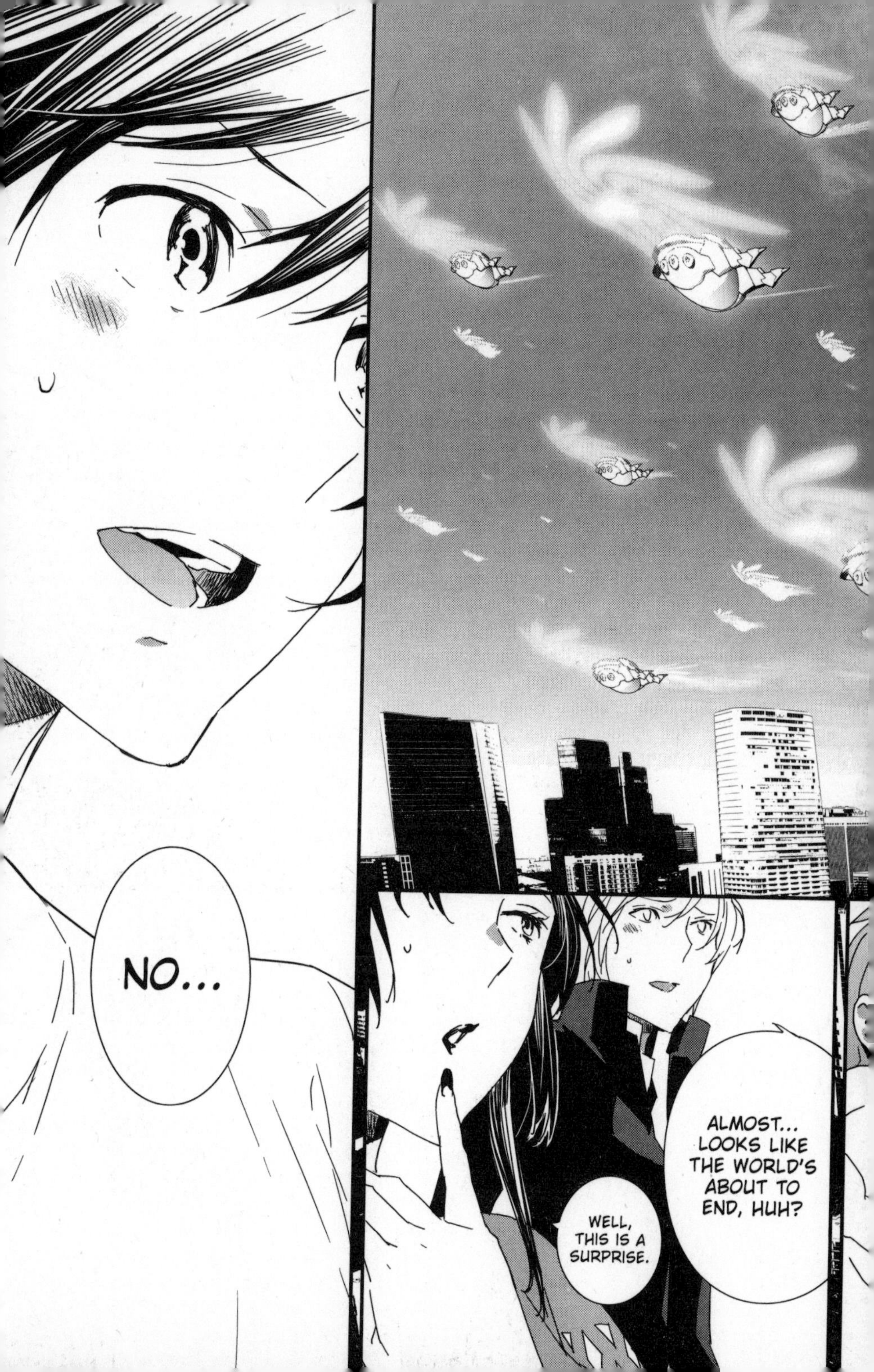
ALMOST... LOOKS LIKE THE WORLD'S ABOUT TO END, HUH?
WELL, THIS IS A SURPRISE.
NO...

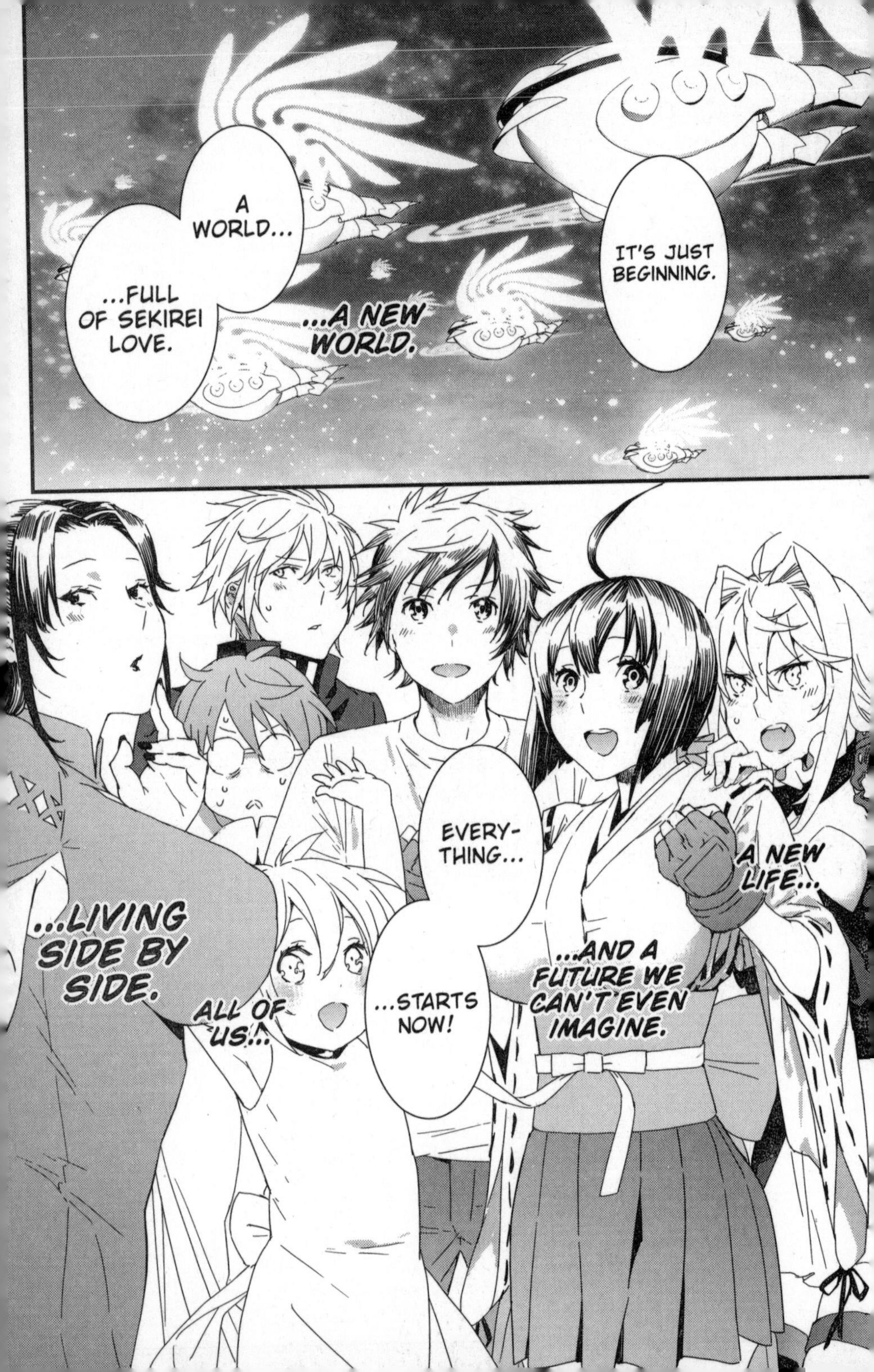
IT'S JUST BEGINNING.
...A NEW WORLD.
A WORLD...
...FULL OF SEKIREI LOVE.
A NEW LIFE...
...AND A FUTURE WE CAN'T EVEN IMAGINE.
EVERYTHING...
...STARTS NOW!
ALL OF US...
...LIVING SIDE BY SIDE.

Chapter 11: Epilogue: Together Forever, Wherever

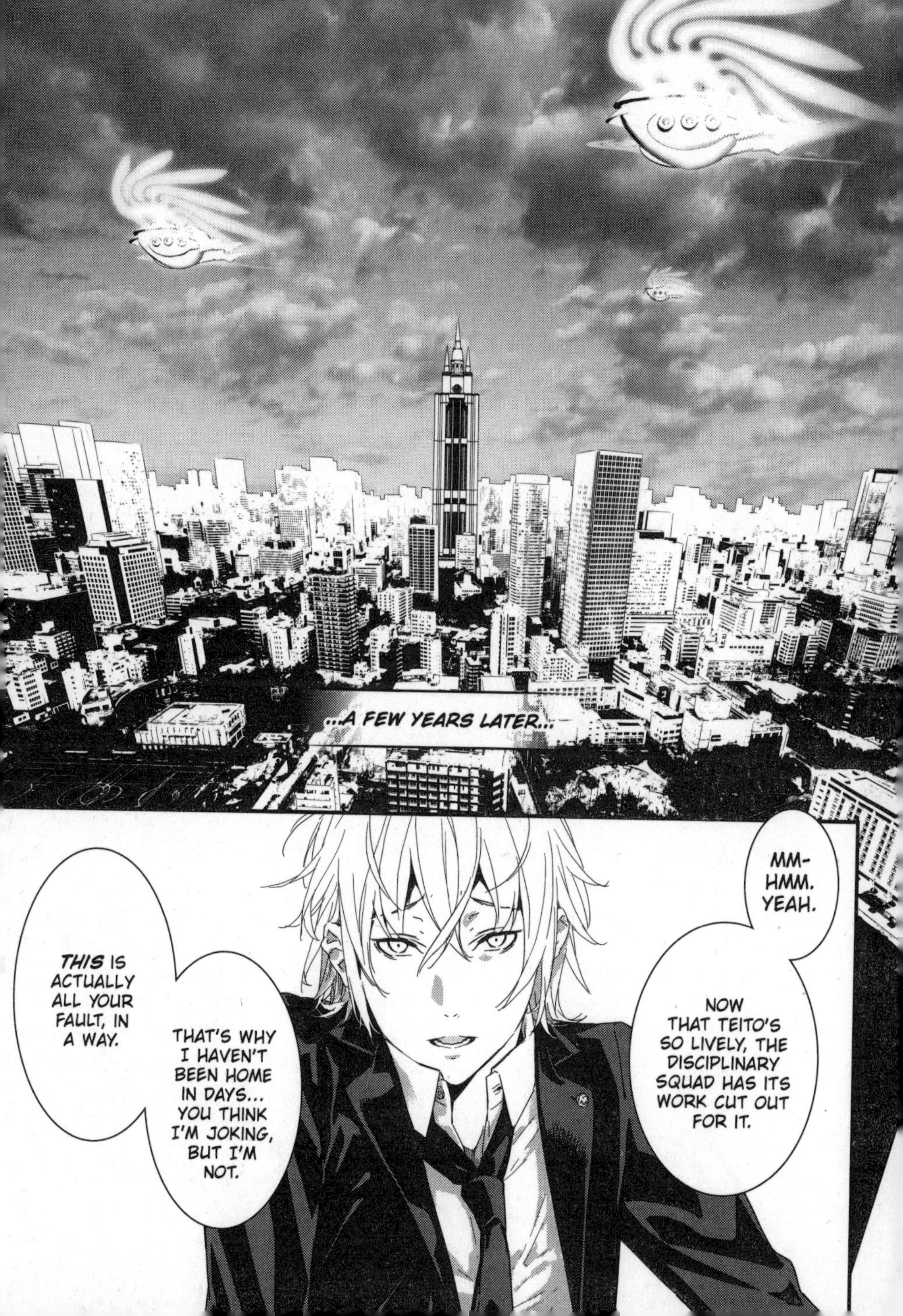
...A FEW YEARS LATER...
MM-HMM. YEAH.
NOW THAT TEITO'S SO LIVELY, THE DISCIPLINARY SQUAD HAS ITS WORK CUT OUT FOR IT.
THAT'S WHY I HAVEN'T BEEN HOME IN DAYS... YOU THINK I'M JOKING, BUT I'M NOT.
THIS is ACTUALLY ALL YOUR FAULT, IN A WAY.

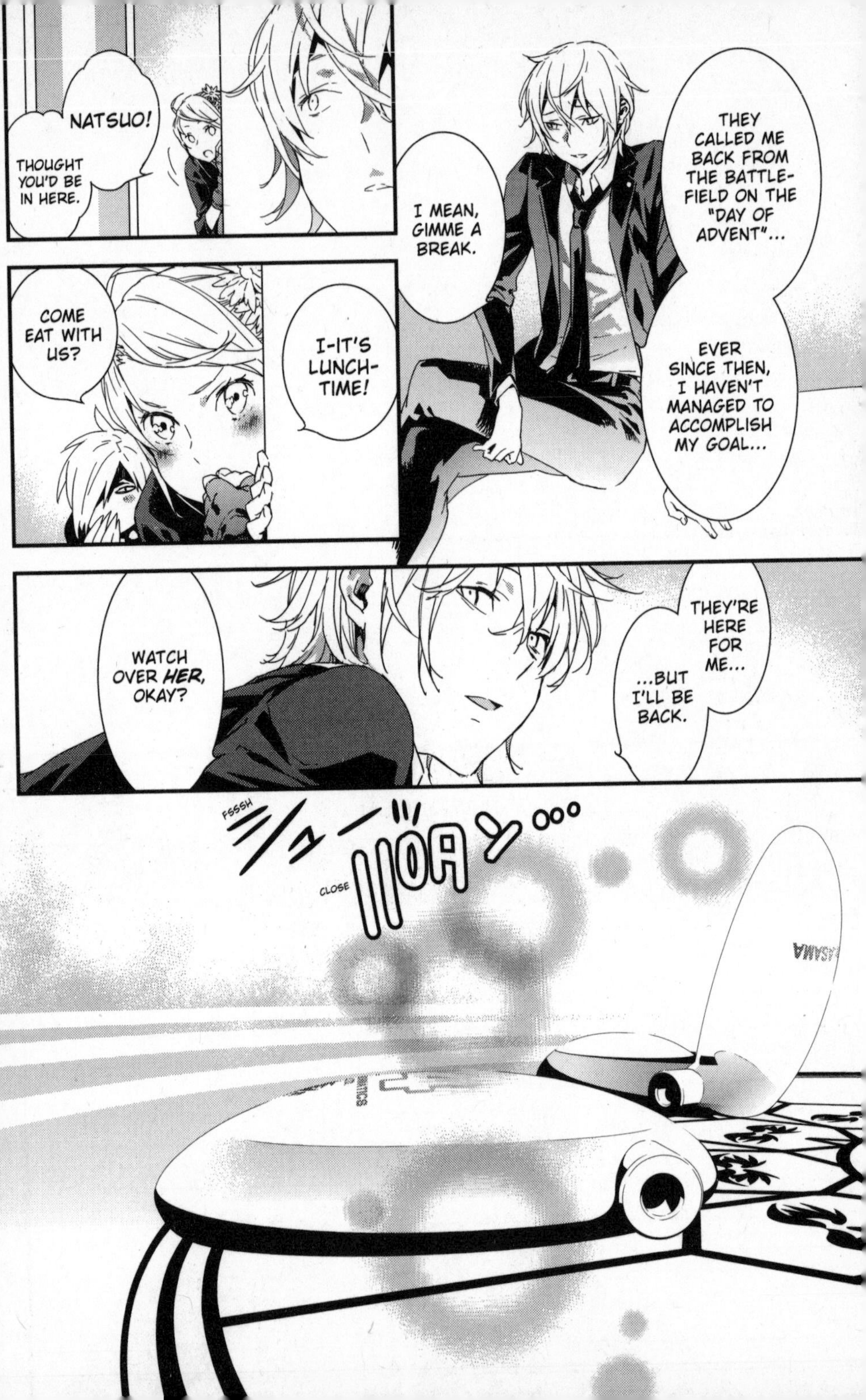
THEY CALLED ME BACK FROM THE BATTLE-FIELD ON THE "DAY OF ADVENT"...
EVER SINCE THEN, I HAVEN'T MANAGED TO ACCOMPLISH MY GOAL...
I MEAN, GIMME A BREAK.
NATSUO!
THOUGHT YOU'D BE IN HERE.
I-IT'S LUNCH-TIME!
COME EAT WITH US?
THEY'RE HERE FOR ME...
...BUT I'LL BE BACK.
WATCH OVER *HER*, OKAY?
FSSSH
CLOSE

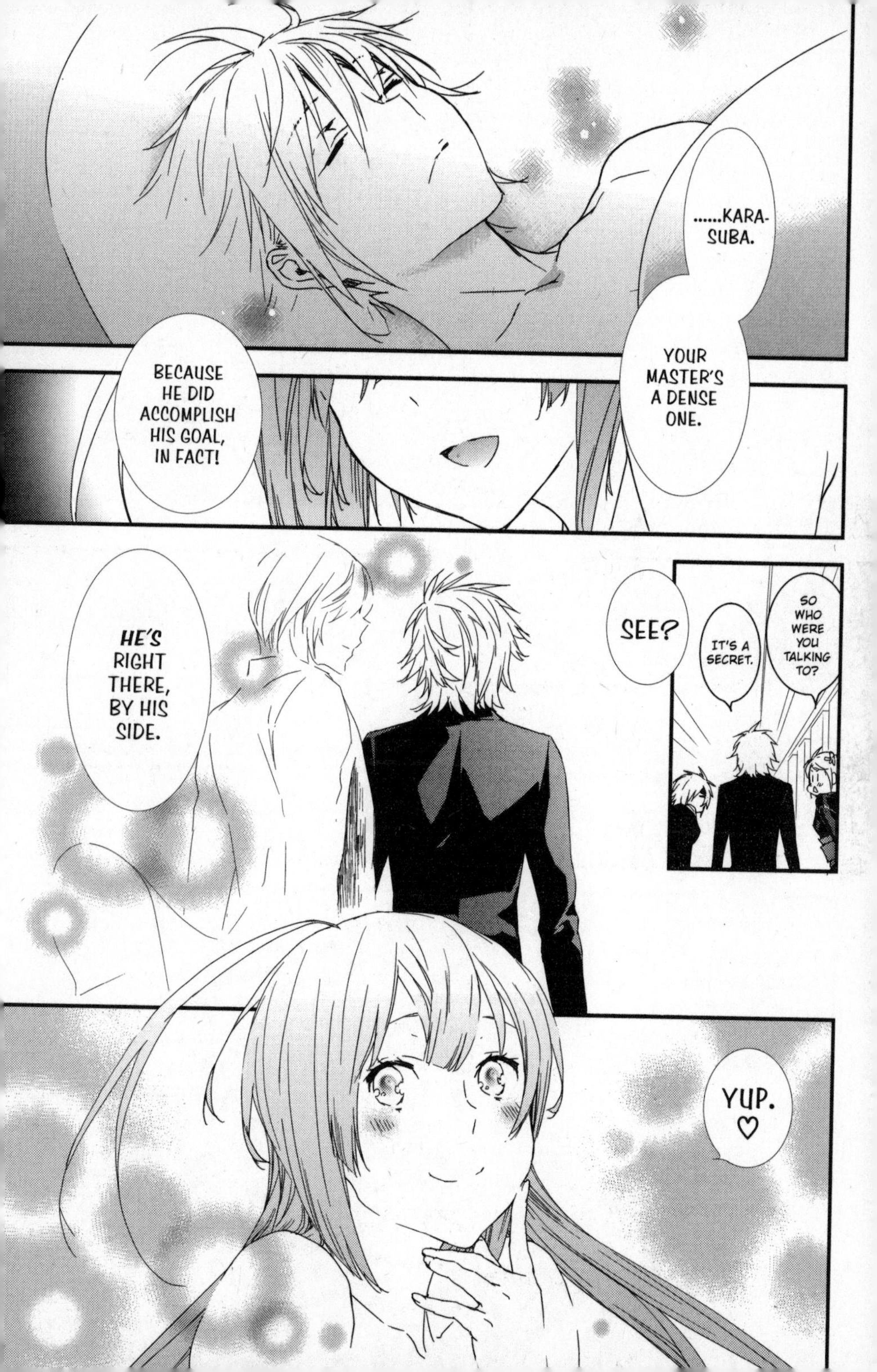
......KARA-SUBA.
YOUR MASTER'S A DENSE ONE.
BECAUSE HE DID ACCOMPLISH HIS GOAL, IN FACT!
SO WHO WERE YOU TALKING TO?
IT'S A SECRET.
SEE?
HE'S RIGHT THERE, BY HIS SIDE.
YUP. ♡

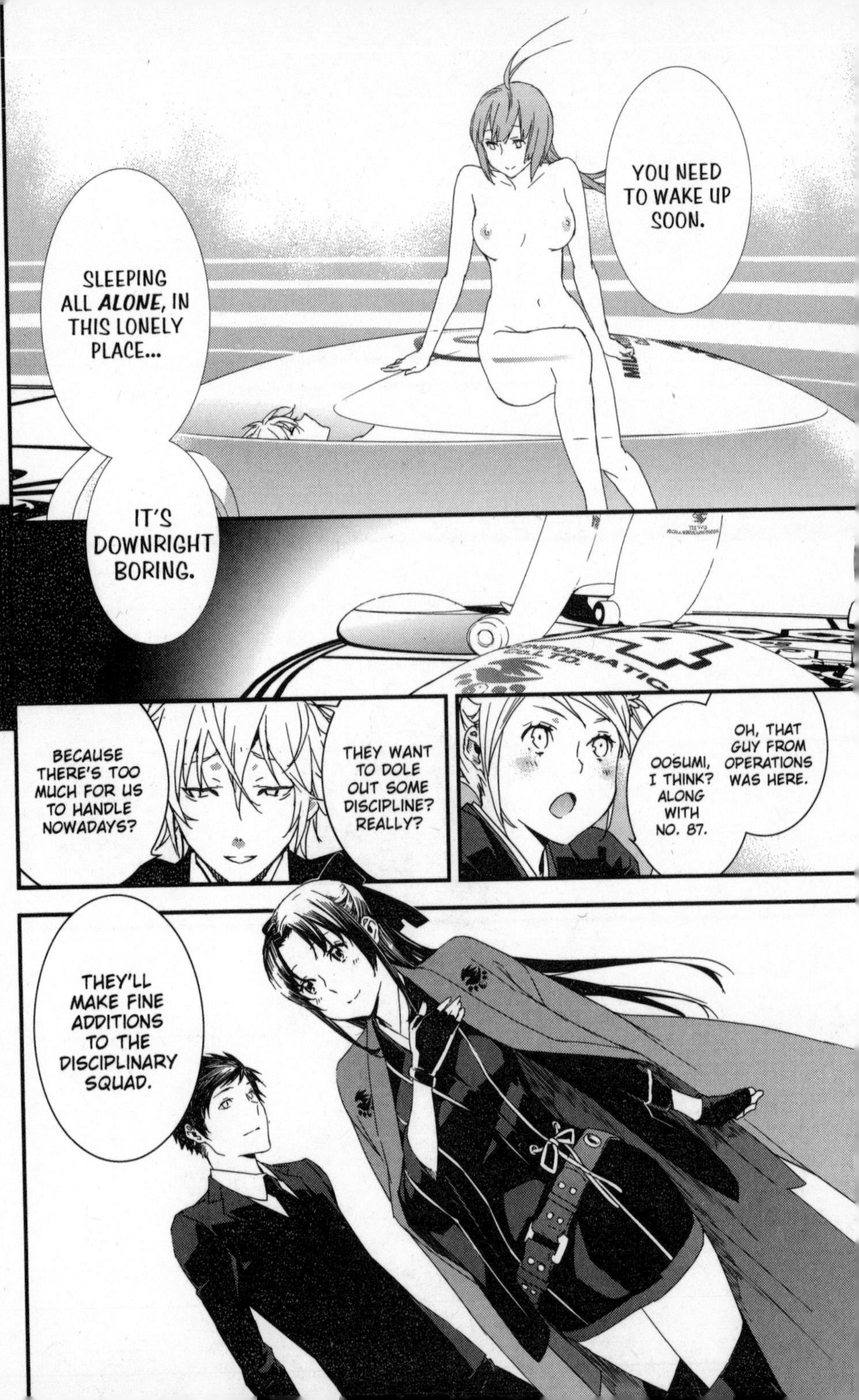
YOU NEED TO WAKE UP SOON.
SLEEPING ALL *ALONE*, IN THIS LONELY PLACE...
IT'S DOWNRIGHT BORING.
OH, THAT GUY FROM OPERATIONS WAS HERE.
OOSUMI, I THINK? ALONG WITH NO. 87.
THEY WANT TO DOLE OUT SOME DISCIPLINE? REALLY?
BECAUSE THERE'S TOO MUCH FOR US TO HANDLE NOWADAYS?
THEY'LL MAKE FINE ADDITIONS TO THE DISCIPLINARY SQUAD.

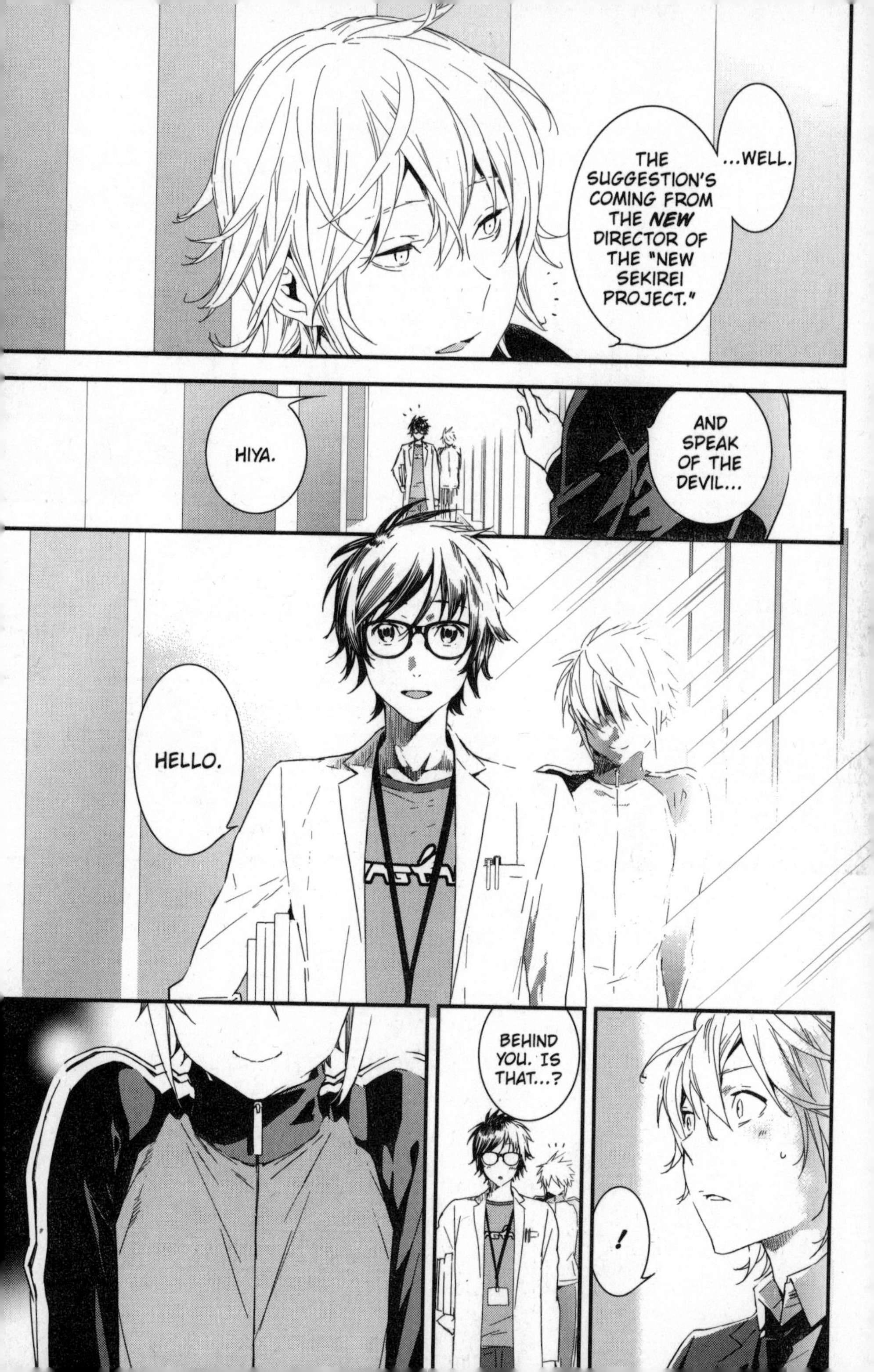
...WELL.
THE SUGGESTION'S COMING FROM THE ***NEW*** DIRECTOR OF THE "NEW SEKIREI PROJECT."
AND SPEAK OF THE DEVIL...
HIYA.
HELLO.
!
BEHIND YOU. IS THAT...?

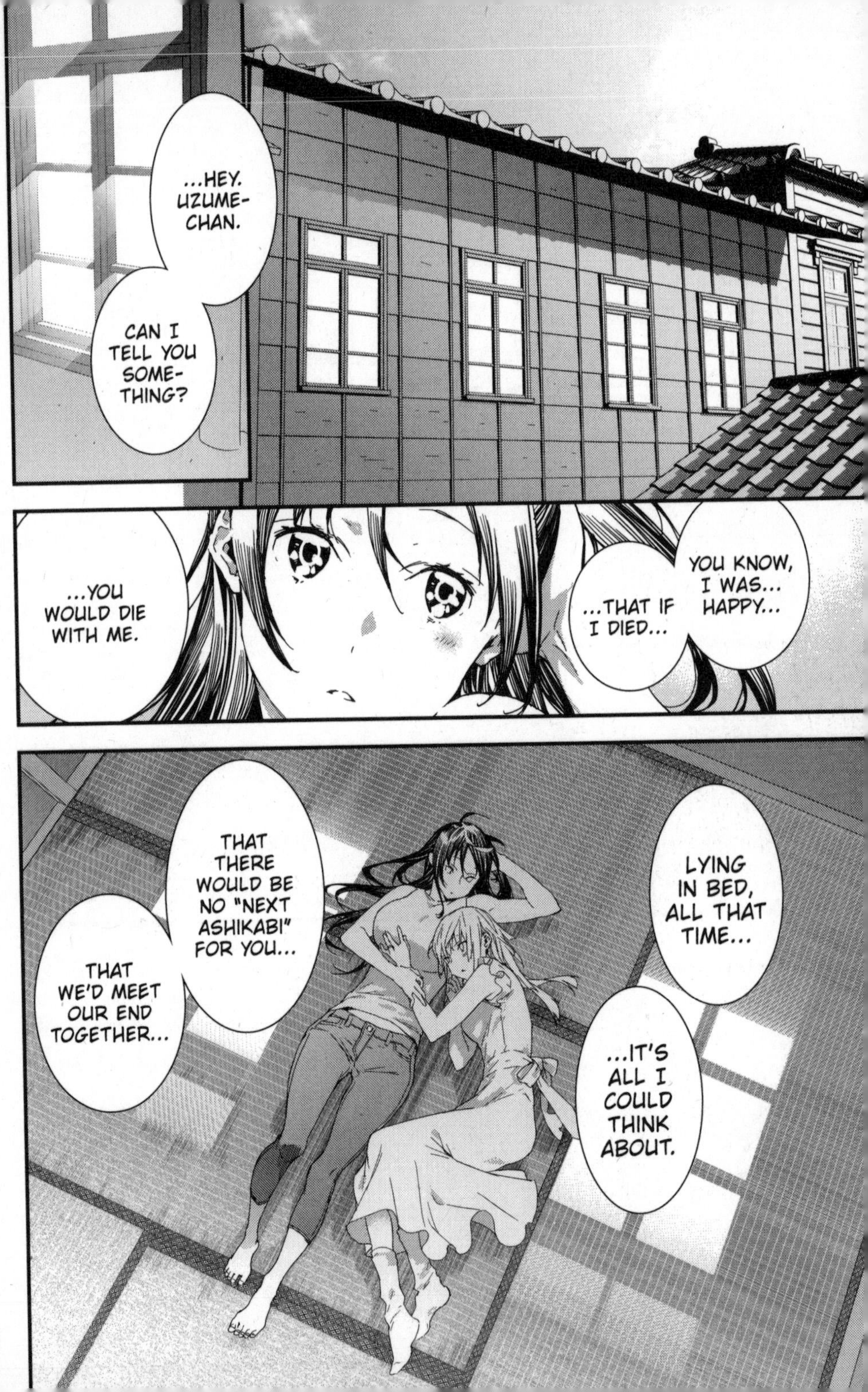
...HEY. UZUME-CHAN.
CAN I TELL YOU SOME-THING?
YOU KNOW, I WAS... HAPPY...
...THAT IF I DIED...
...YOU WOULD DIE WITH ME.
LYING IN BED, ALL THAT TIME...
...IT'S ALL I COULD THINK ABOUT.
THAT THERE WOULD BE NO "NEXT ASHIKABI" FOR YOU...
THAT WE'D MEET OUR END TOGETHER...

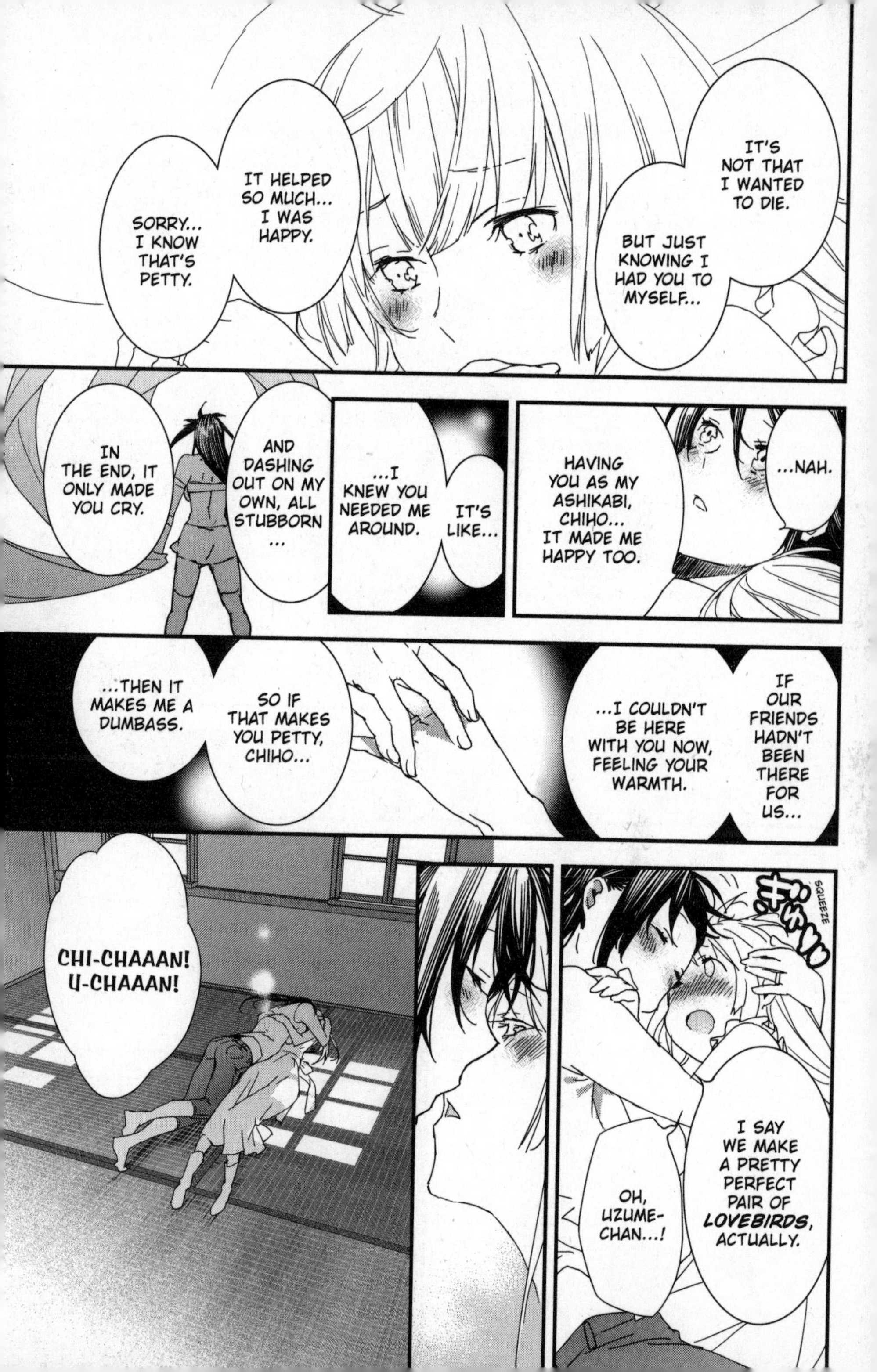
IT'S NOT THAT I WANTED TO DIE.
BUT JUST KNOWING I HAD YOU TO MYSELF...
IT HELPED SO MUCH... I WAS HAPPY.
SORRY... I KNOW THAT'S PETTY.
...NAH.
HAVING YOU AS MY ASHIKABI, CHIHO... IT MADE ME HAPPY TOO.
IT'S LIKE...
...I KNEW YOU NEEDED ME AROUND.
AND DASHING OUT ON MY OWN, ALL STUBBORN...
IN THE END, IT ONLY MADE YOU CRY.
IF OUR FRIENDS HADN'T BEEN THERE FOR US...
...I COULDN'T BE HERE WITH YOU NOW, FEELING YOUR WARMTH.
SO IF THAT MAKES YOU PETTY, CHIHO...
...THEN IT MAKES ME A DUMBASS.
SQUEEZE
I SAY WE MAKE A PRETTY PERFECT PAIR OF ***LOVEBIRDS***, ACTUALLY.
OH, UZUME-CHAN...!
CHI-CHAAAN! U-CHAAAN!

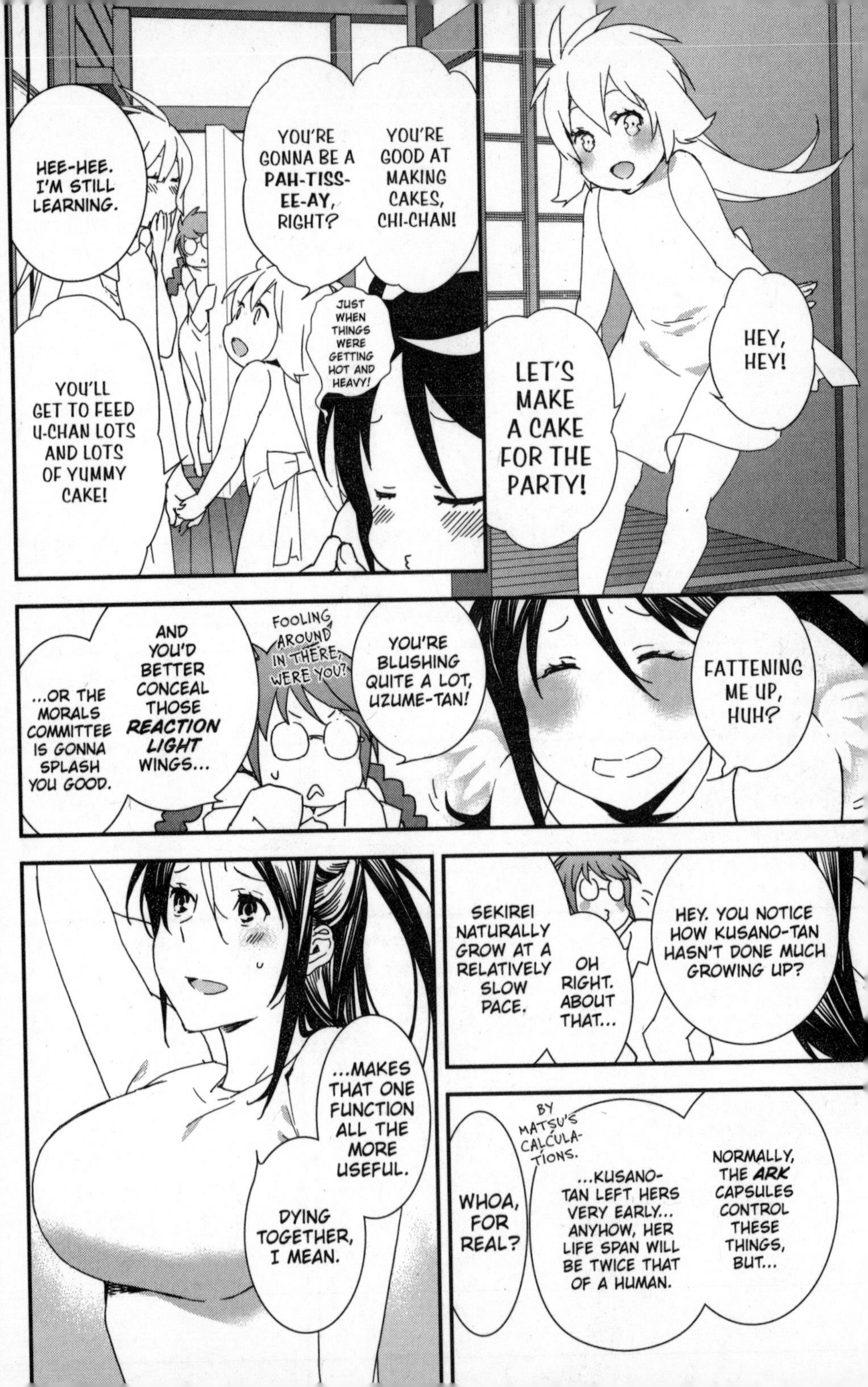
HEY, HEY!
LET'S MAKE A CAKE FOR THE PARTY!
YOU'RE GOOD AT MAKING CAKES, CHI-CHAN!
YOU'RE GONNA BE A PAH-TISS-EE-AY, RIGHT?
HEE-HEE. I'M STILL LEARNING.
JUST WHEN THINGS WERE GETTING HOT AND HEAVY!
YOU'LL GET TO FEED U-CHAN LOTS AND LOTS OF YUMMY CAKE!
FATTENING ME UP, HUH?
YOU'RE BLUSHING QUITE A LOT, UZUME-TAN!
FOOLING AROUND IN THERE, WERE YOU?
AND YOU'D BETTER CONCEAL THOSE REACTION LIGHT WINGS...
...OR THE MORALS COMMITTEE IS GONNA SPLASH YOU GOOD.
HEY. YOU NOTICE HOW KUSANO-TAN HASN'T DONE MUCH GROWING UP?
OH RIGHT. ABOUT THAT...
SEKIREI NATURALLY GROW AT A RELATIVELY SLOW PACE.
NORMALLY, THE ARK CAPSULES CONTROL THESE THINGS, BUT...
...KUSANO-TAN LEFT HERS VERY EARLY... ANYHOW, HER LIFE SPAN WILL BE TWICE THAT OF A HUMAN.
BY MATSU'S CALCULATIONS.
WHOA, FOR REAL?
...MAKES THAT ONE FUNCTION ALL THE MORE USEFUL.
DYING TOGETHER, I MEAN.

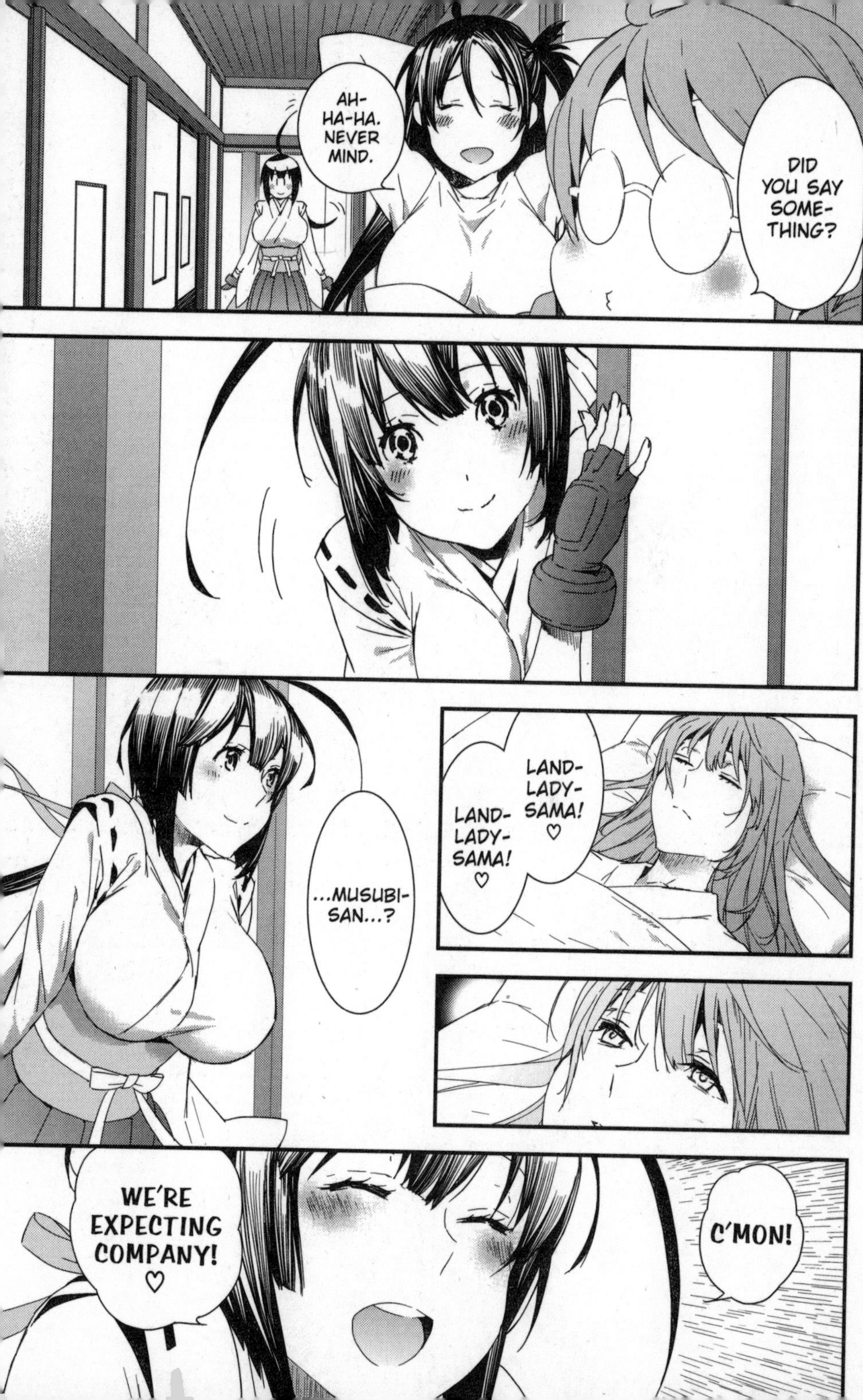
DID YOU SAY SOME-THING?
AH-HA-HA. NEVER MIND.
LAND-LADY-SAMA! ♡
LAND-LADY-SAMA! ♡
...MUSUBI-SAN...?
C'MON!
WE'RE EXPECTING COMPANY! ♡

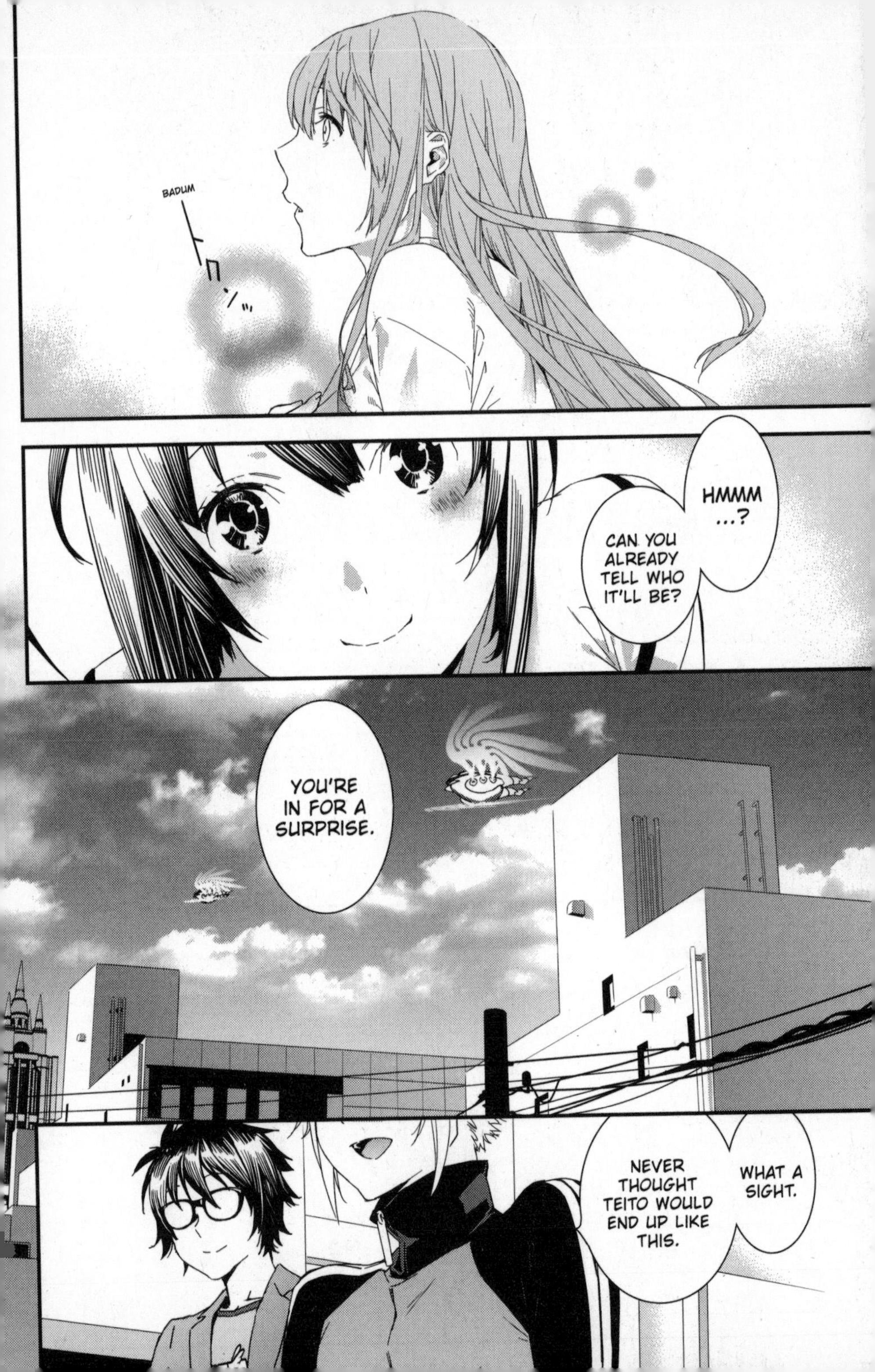
BADUM
HMMM ...?
CAN YOU ALREADY TELL WHO IT'LL BE?
YOU'RE IN FOR A SURPRISE.
WHAT A SIGHT.
NEVER THOUGHT TEITO WOULD END UP LIKE THIS.

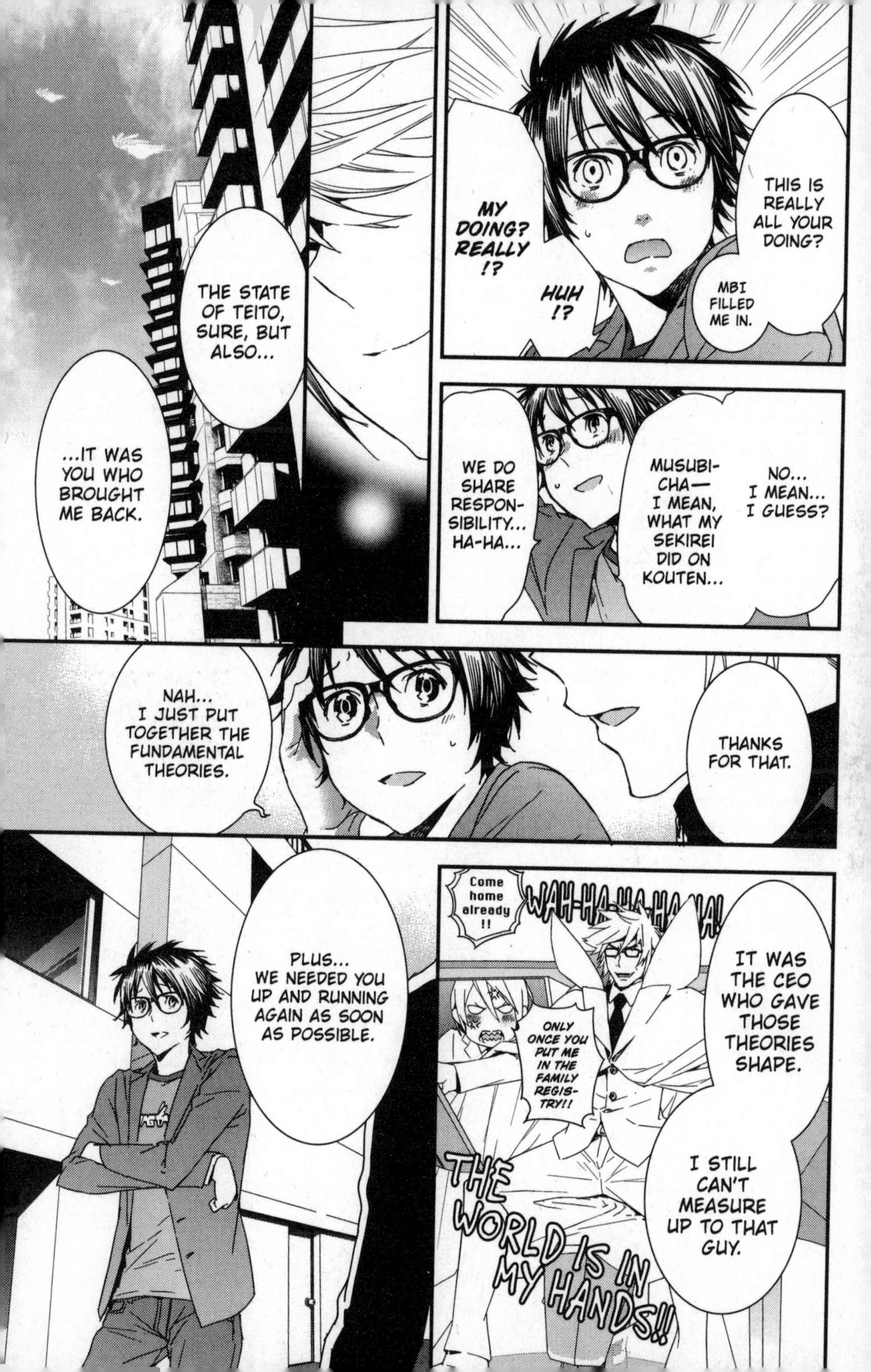
THIS IS REALLY ALL YOUR DOING?
MBI FILLED ME IN.
HUH!?
MY DOING? REALLY!?
NO... I MEAN... I GUESS?
MUSUBI-CHA— I MEAN, WHAT MY SEKIREI DID ON KOUTEN...
WE DO SHARE RESPONSIBILITY... HA-HA...
THE STATE OF TEITO, SURE, BUT ALSO...
...IT WAS YOU WHO BROUGHT ME BACK.
THANKS FOR THAT.
NAH... I JUST PUT TOGETHER THE FUNDAMENTAL THEORIES.
IT WAS THE CEO WHO GAVE THOSE THEORIES SHAPE.
WAH-HA-HA-HA-HA!
Come home already!!
ONLY ONCE YOU PUT ME IN THE FAMILY REGISTRY!!
I STILL CAN'T MEASURE UP TO THAT GUY.
THE WORLD IS IN MY HANDS!!
PLUS... WE NEEDED YOU UP AND RUNNING AGAIN AS SOON AS POSSIBLE.

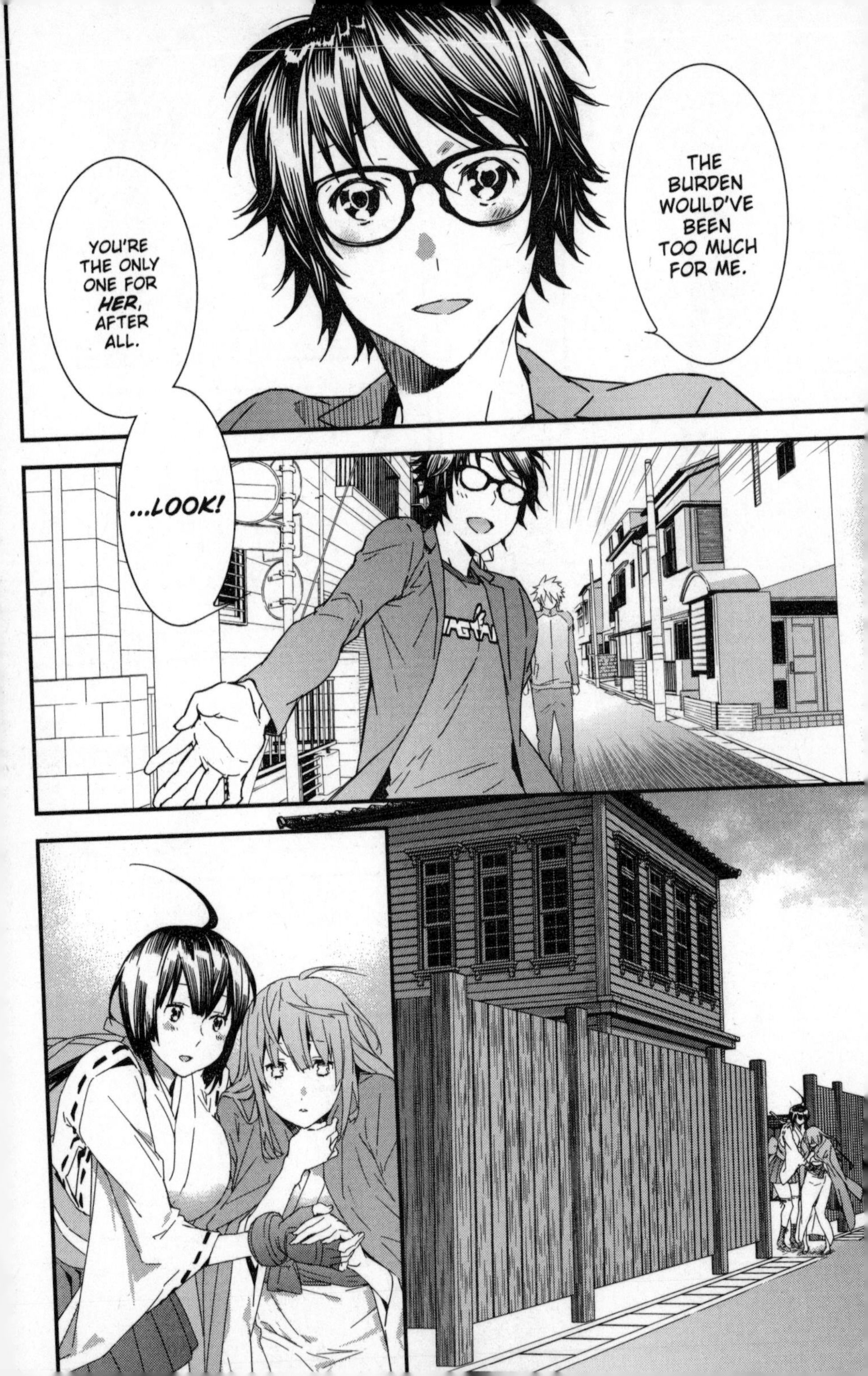
THE BURDEN WOULD'VE BEEN TOO MUCH FOR ME.
YOU'RE THE ONLY ONE FOR *HER*, AFTER ALL.
...LOOK!

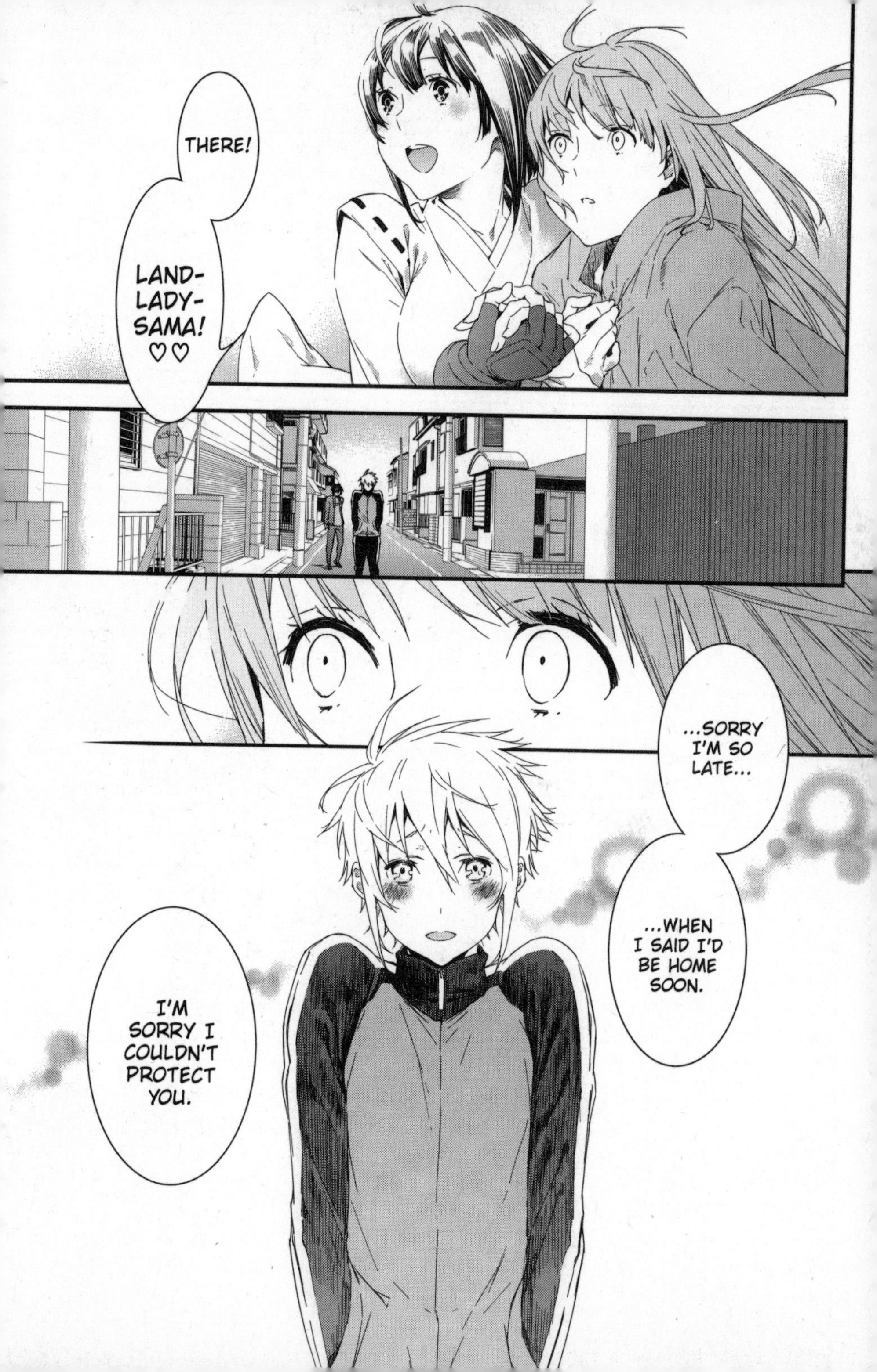
THERE!
LAND-LADY-SAMA! ♡♡
...SORRY I'M SO LATE...
...WHEN I SAID I'D BE HOME SOON.
I'M SORRY I COULDN'T PROTECT YOU.

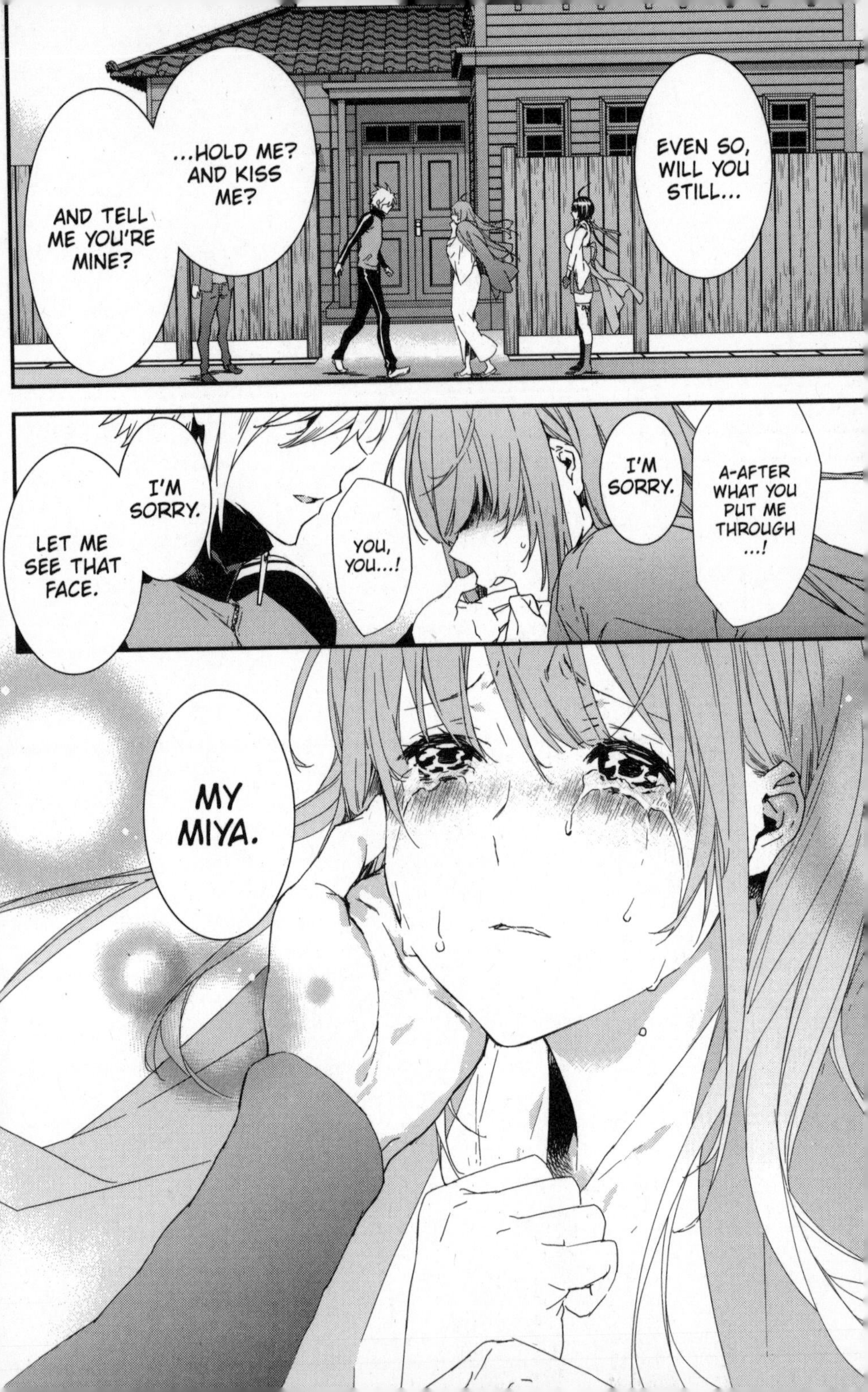
EVEN SO, WILL YOU STILL...
...HOLD ME? AND KISS ME?
AND TELL ME YOU'RE MINE?
A-AFTER WHAT YOU PUT ME THROUGH ...!
I'M SORRY.
YOU, YOU...!
I'M SORRY.
LET ME SEE THAT FACE.
MY MIYA.

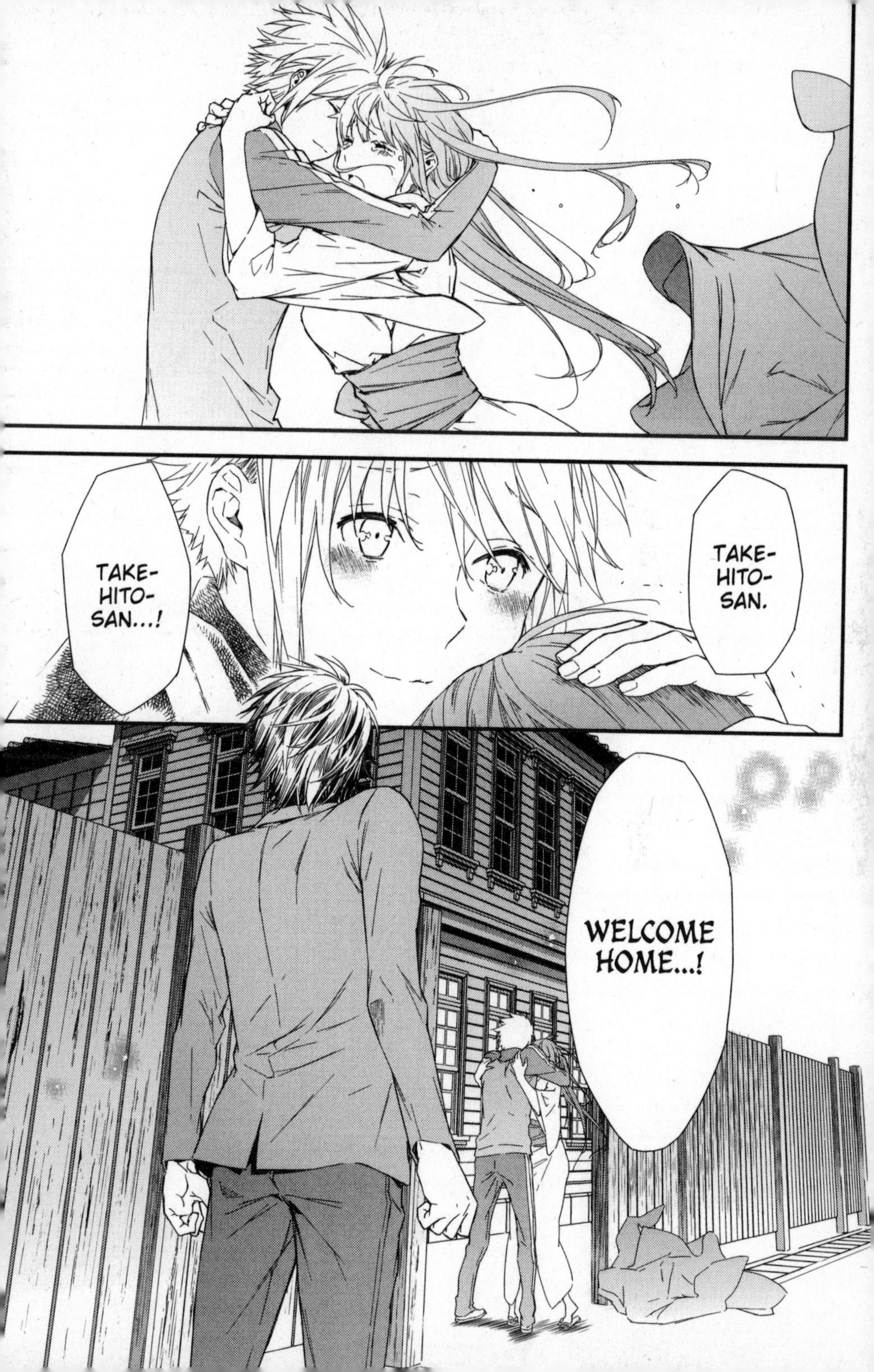
TAKE-HITO-SAN.
TAKE-HITO-SAN...!
WELCOME HOME...!

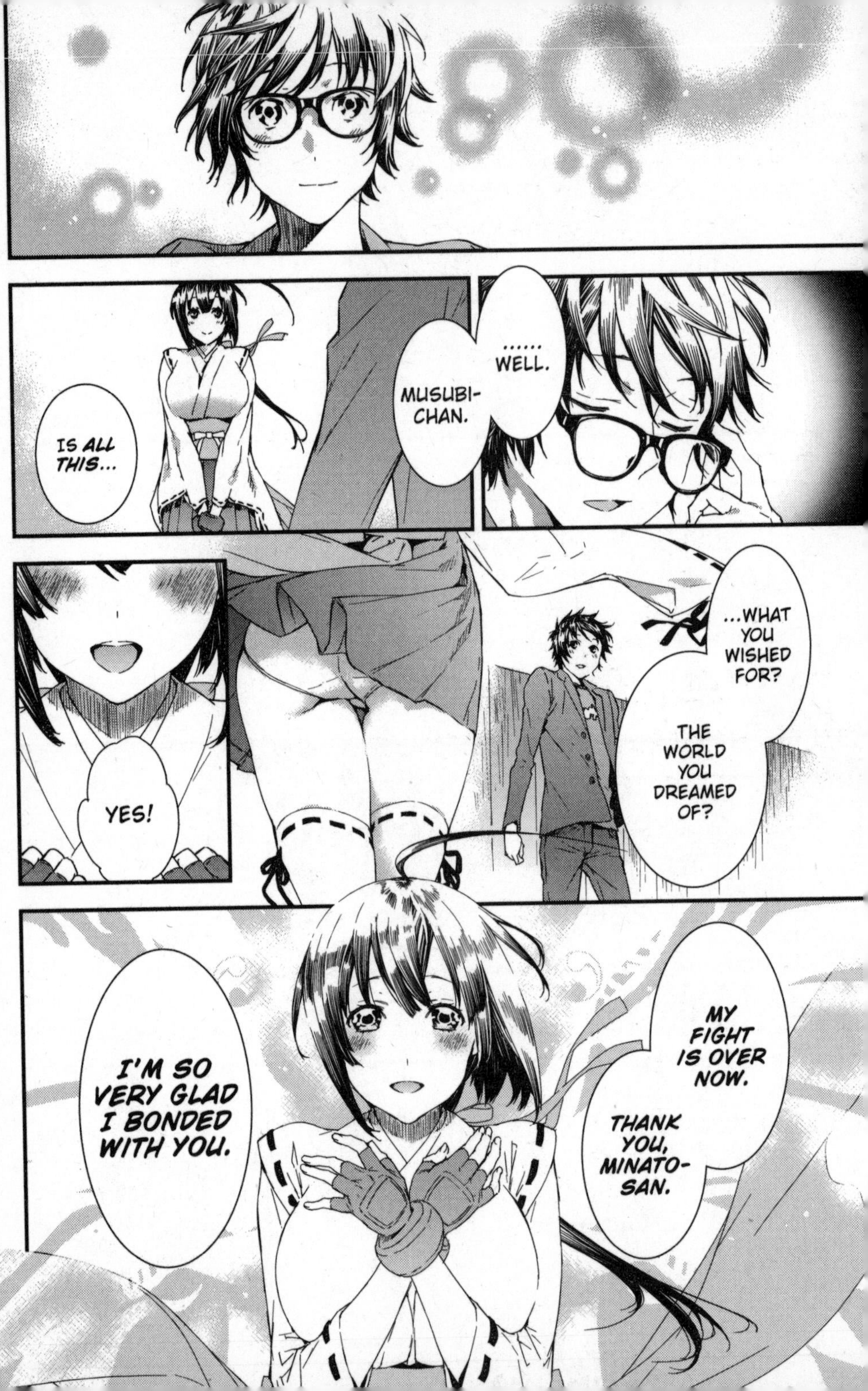
......WELL.
MUSUBI-CHAN.
IS ALL THIS...
...WHAT YOU WISHED FOR?
THE WORLD YOU DREAMED OF?
YES!
MY FIGHT IS OVER NOW.
THANK YOU, MINATO-SAN.
I'M SO VERY GLAD I BONDED WITH YOU.

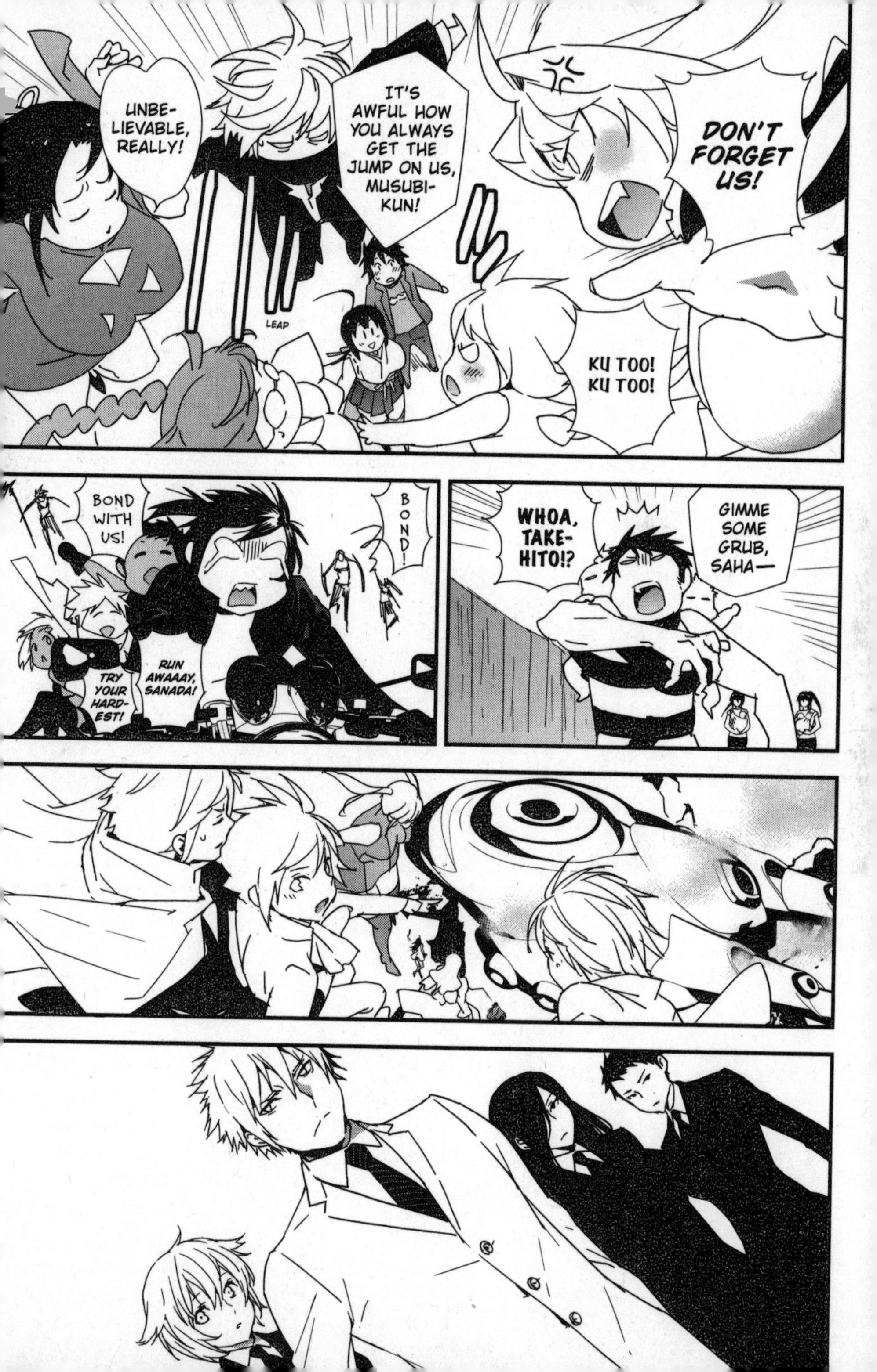
DON'T FORGET US!
IT'S AWFUL HOW YOU ALWAYS GET THE JUMP ON US, MUSUBI-KUN!
UNBE-LIEVABLE, REALLY!
KU TOO! KU TOO!
LEAP
GIMME SOME GRUB, SAHA—
WHOA, TAKE-HITO!?
BOND!
BOND WITH US!
RUN AWAAAY, SANADA!
TRY YOUR HARD-EST!

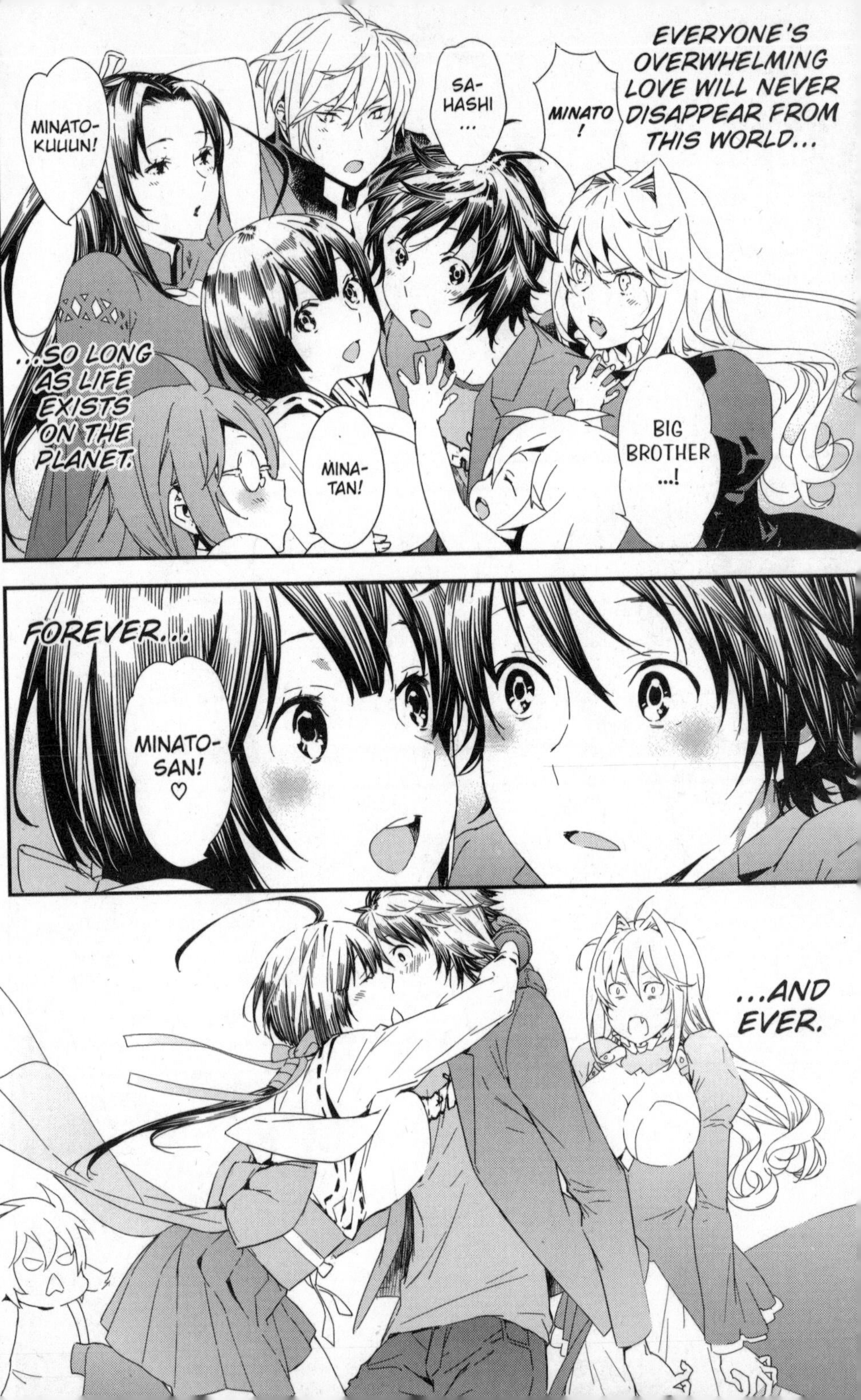
EVERYONE'S OVERWHELMING LOVE WILL NEVER DISAPPEAR FROM THIS WORLD...
MINATO!
SA-HASHI...
MINATO-KUUUN!
BIG BROTHER...!
MINA-TAN!
...SO LONG AS LIFE EXISTS ON THE PLANET.
FOREVER...
MINATO-SAN! ♡
...AND EVER.

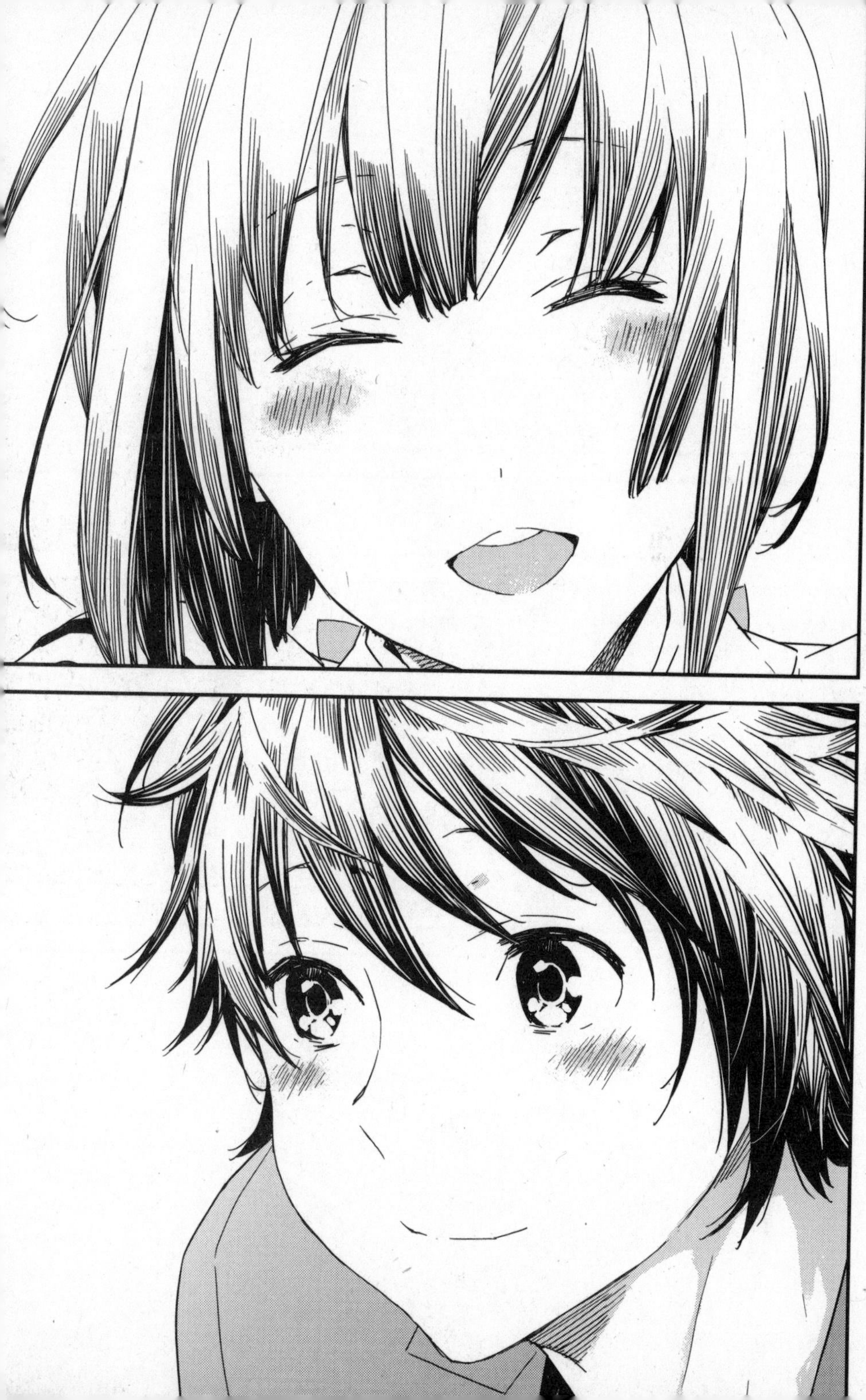

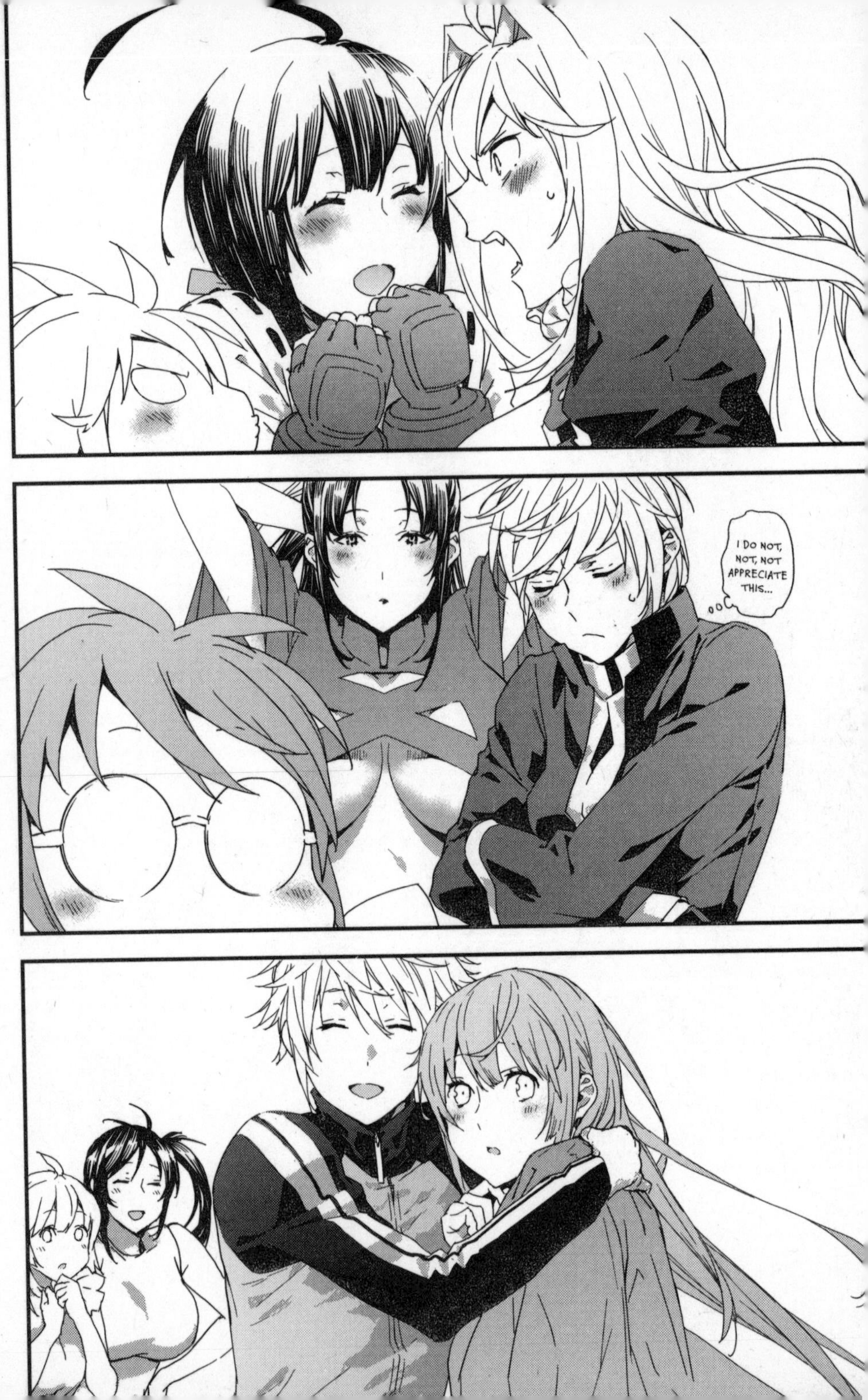
I DO NOT, NOT, NOT APPRECIATE THIS...

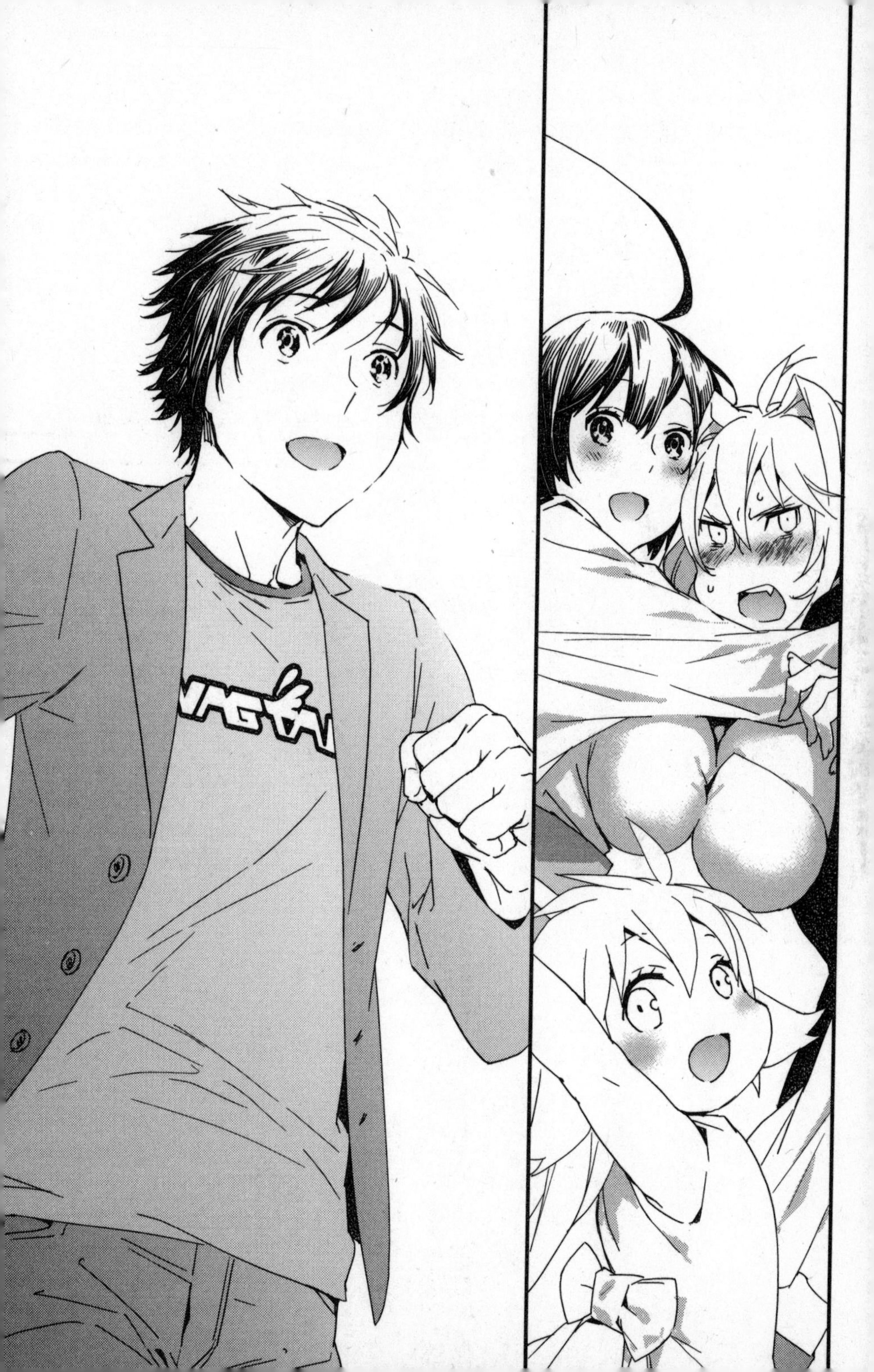

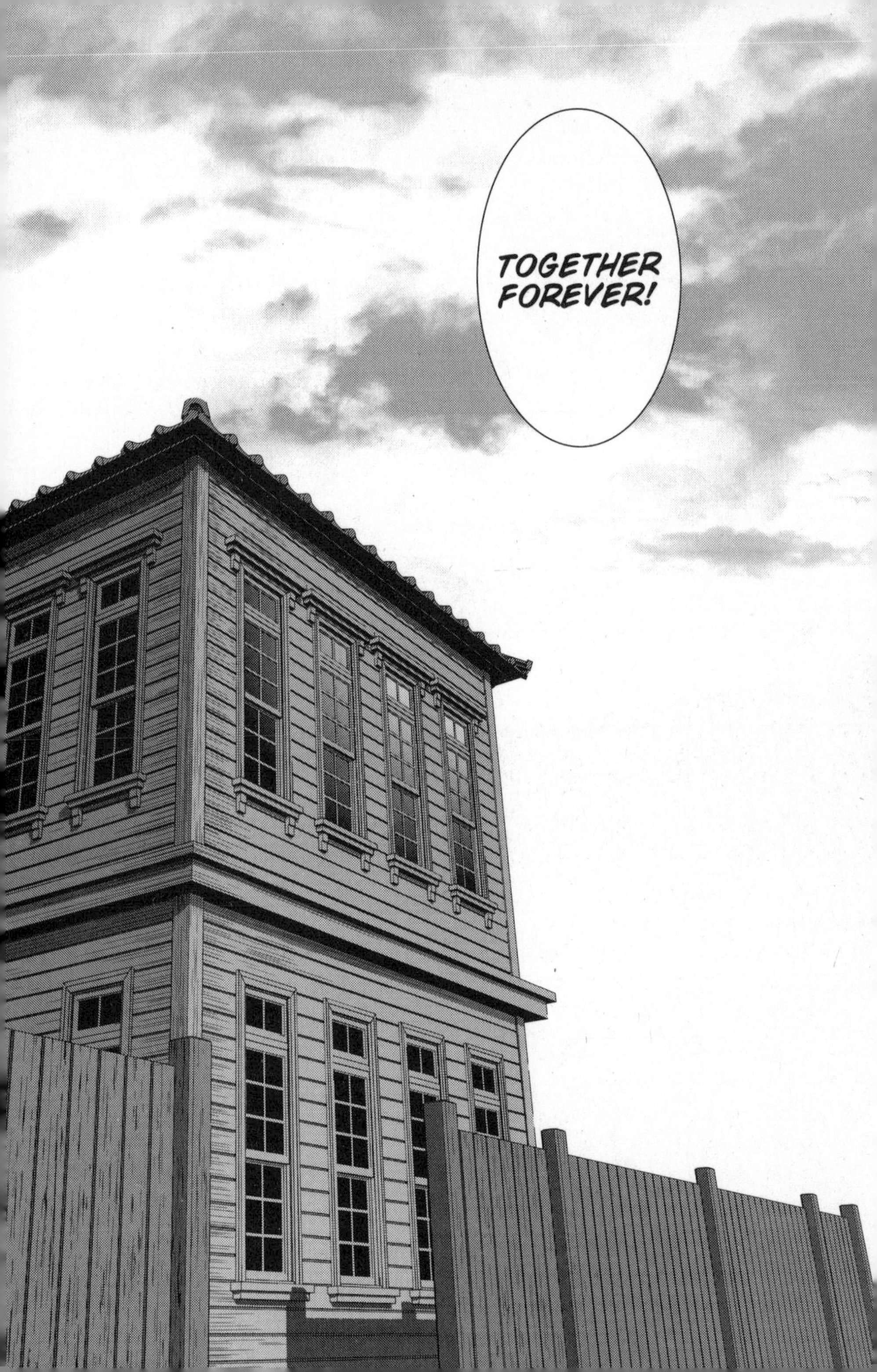
TOGETHER FOREVER!

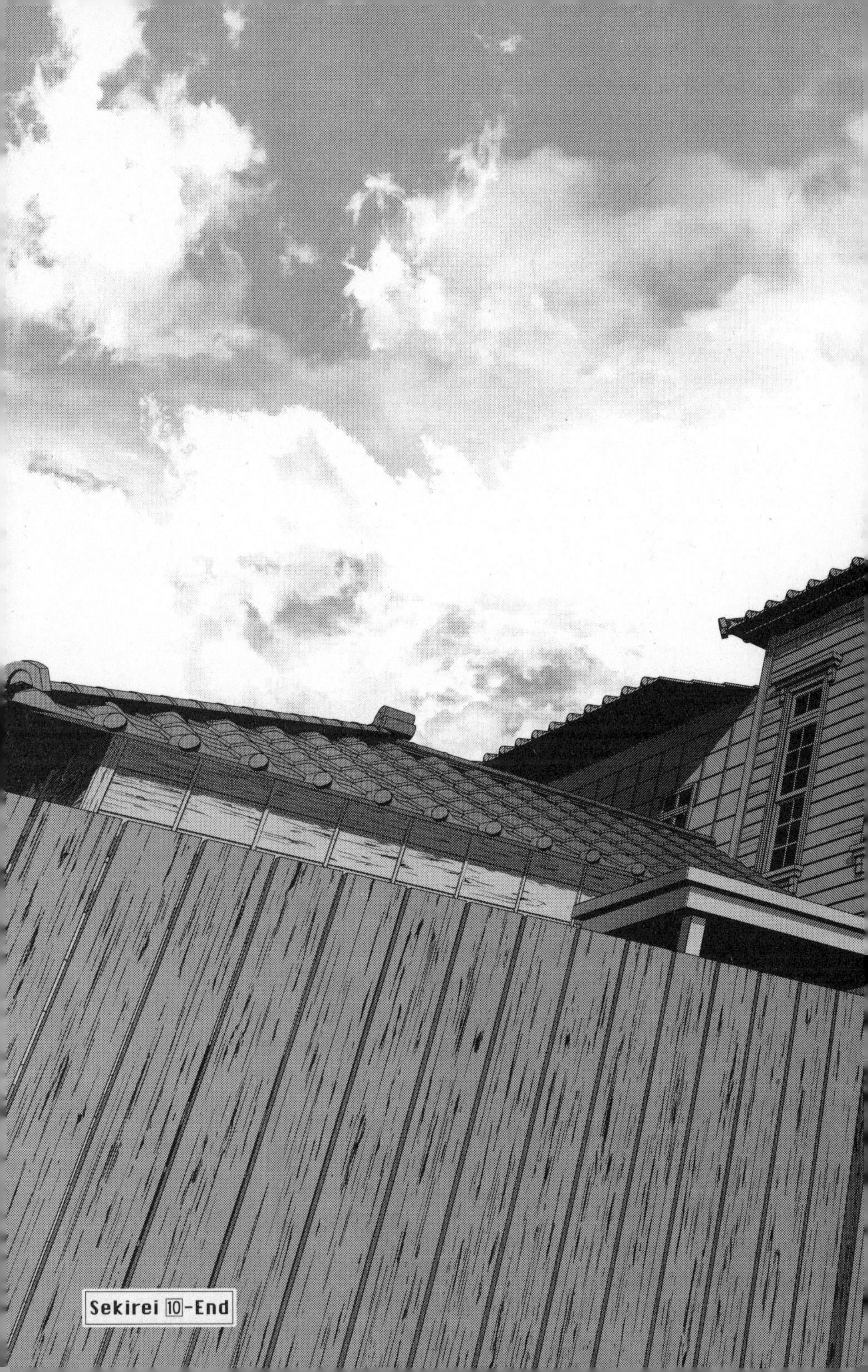
Sekirei 10-End

WARNING!!

THERE ARE SPOILERS HERE, SO READ THE VOLUME FIRST!!

THIS WAY! OPEN THE BOOK!

THE TRUE SEKIREI AFTERMATH

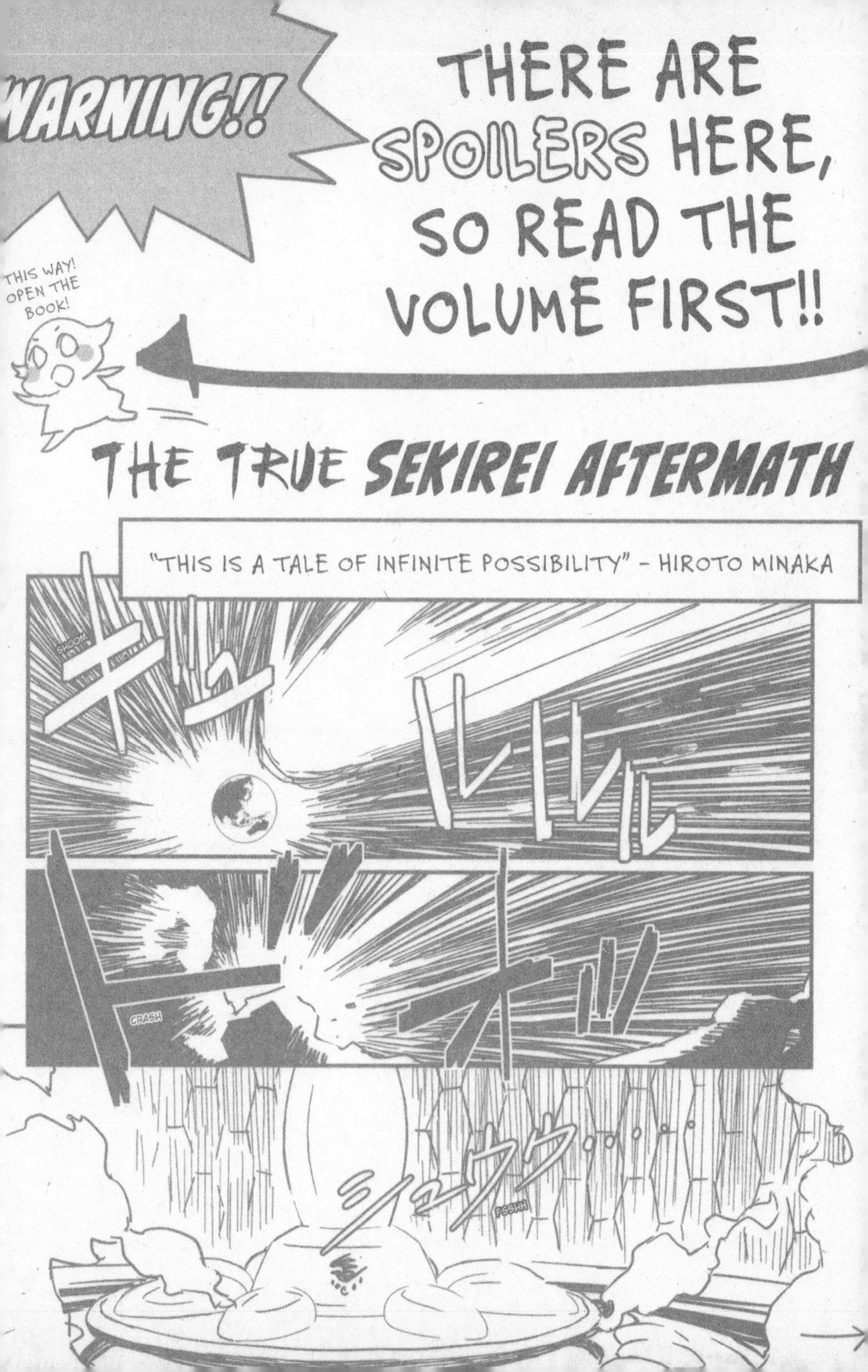
"THIS IS A TALE OF INFINITE POSSIBILITY" - HIROTO MINAKA
SHOOM
CRASH
FSSHH

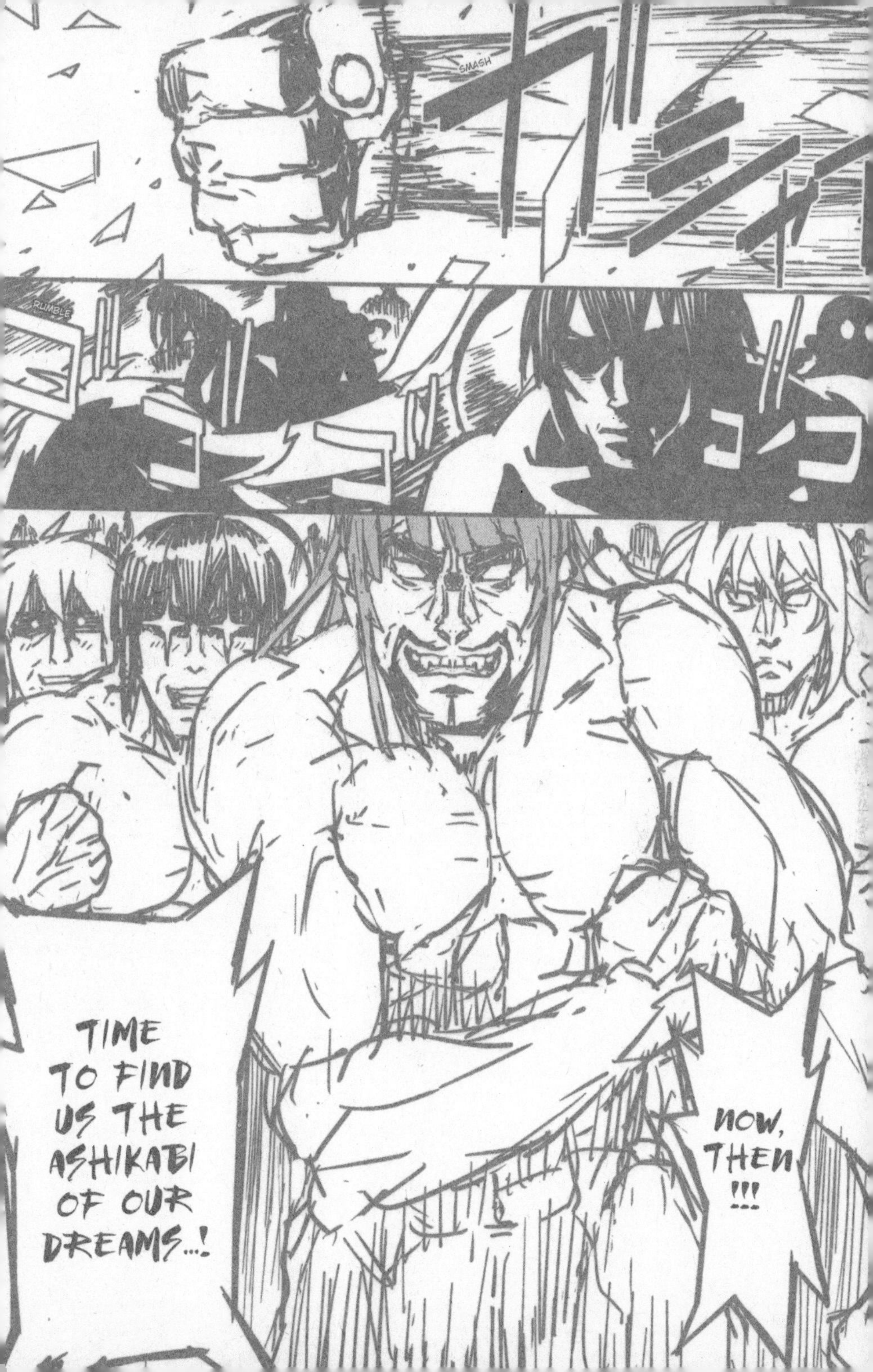
SMASH
RUMBLE
NOW, THEN!!!
TIME TO FIND US THE ASHIKABI OF OUR DREAMS...!

Translation Notes

COMMON HONORIFICS
no honorific: Indicates familiarity or closeness; if used without permission or reason, addressing someone in this manner would constitute an insult.
-san: The Japanese equivalent of Mr./Mrs./Miss. If a situation calls for politeness, this is the fail-safe honorific.
-sama: Conveys great respect; may also indicate the social status of the speaker is lower than that of the addressee.
-dono: A more archaic form of address, similar to -sama.
-kun: Used most often when referring to boys, this indicates affection or familiarity. Occasionally used by older men among their peers, but it may also be used by anyone referring to a person of lower standing.
-chan: An affectionate honorific indicating familiarity used mostly in reference to girls; also used in reference to cute persons or animals of either gender.
-tan: A cutesier version of -chan.

Page 13 - Minato's wagtail T-shirt
The Japanese wagtail is a common species of bird that prefers freshwater environments. The Japanese name for it, sekirei, also happens to be the title of the series.

Page 15 - "Obviously can't work as a host with these."
Host and hostess clubs constitute a significant part of Japanese soft-core nightlife entertainment. At host clubs, male servers cater to mostly female clientele and offer casual conversation. Since Kagari doesn't fit the mold anymore, he gets a job as a bartender instead.

Page 91 - Rounin
Though rounin once referred to masterless samurai, in modern Japanese society, it's used to denote prospective college students who've failed their entrance exams and exist in a sort of societal limbo.

Page 125 - Kuno/No-Good
Kuno's name sounds very similar to munou, which means "incompetence."

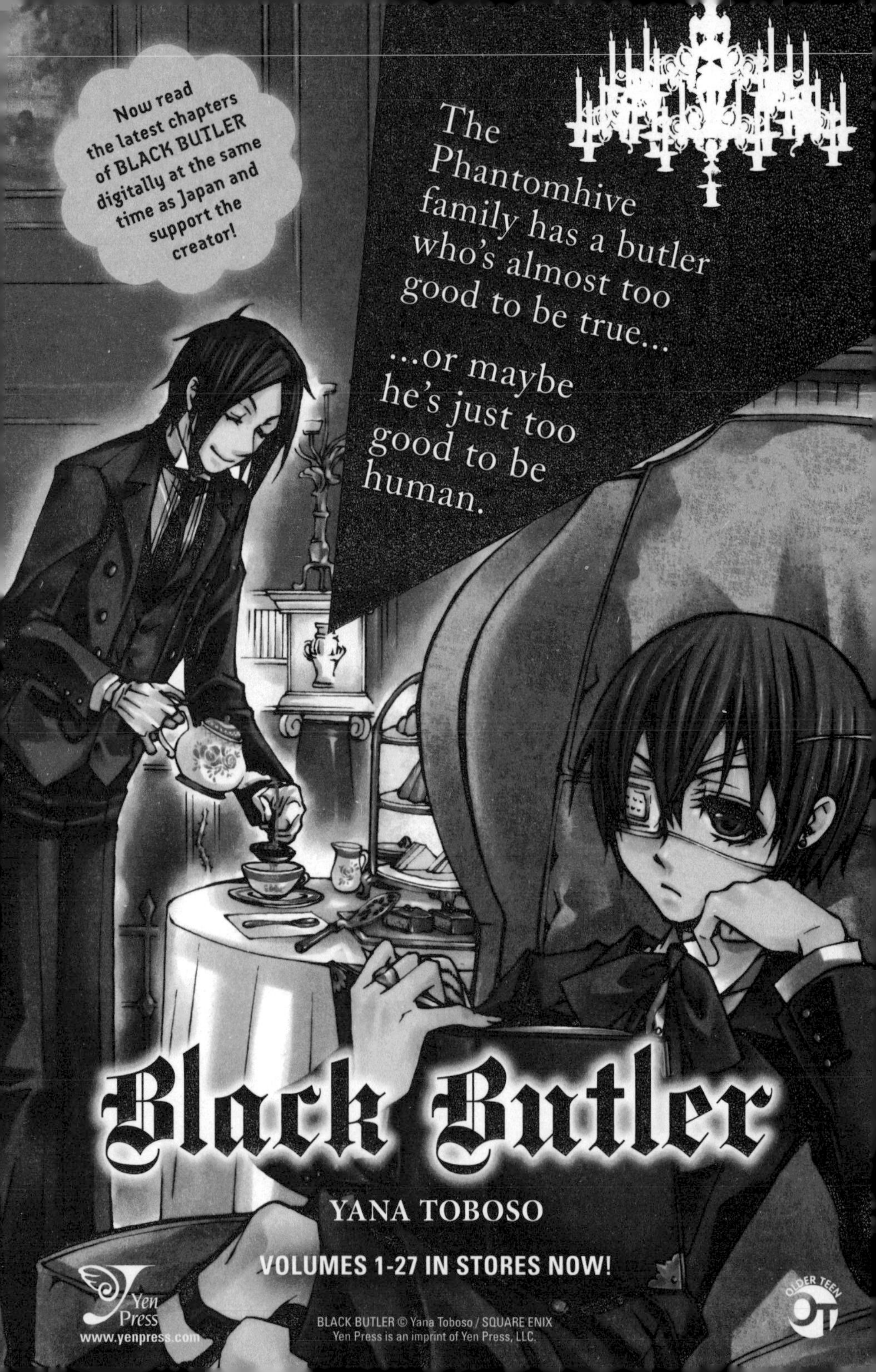
Now read the latest chapters of BLACK BUTLER digitally at the same time as Japan and support the creator!
The Phantomhive family has a butler who's almost too good to be true...
...or maybe he's just too good to be human.
Black Butler
YANA TOBOSO
VOLUMES 1-27 IN STORES NOW!
Yen Press
www.yenpress.com
BLACK BUTLER © Yana Toboso / SQUARE ENIX
Yen Press is an imprint of Yen Press, LLC.
OLDER TEEN
OT

HE DOES NOT LET ANYONE ROLL THE DICE.

A young Priestess joins her first adventuring party, but blind to the dangers, they almost immediately find themselves in trouble. It's Goblin Slayer who comes to their rescue—a man who has dedicated his life to the extermination of all goblins by any means necessary. A dangerous, dirty, and thankless job, but he does it better than anyone. And when rumors of his feats begin to circulate, there's no telling who might come calling next...

Light Novel
V. 1-6
Available
Now!

Check out the
simul-pub manga chapters
every month!

www.yenpress.com

Akame ga KILL! ZERO

VOLUMES 1-7 AVAILABLE NOW!

Yen Press

THEY BELIEVED THAT EVERY TIME THEY TOOK A LIFE, THEY BROUGHT HAPPINESS TO ANOTHER...

Before becoming Night Raid's deadliest ally, Akame was a young girl bought by the Empire and raised as an assassin whose sole purpose was to slaughter everything in her path. Because that's what makes people happy...right? Discover Akame's shocking past in *Akame ga KILL! Zero*, the prequel to the hit series *Akame ga KILL!*

For more information, visit www.yenpress.com

365
Days Without Her

SAKURAKO
GOKURAKUIN

TRANSLATION: CALEB D. COOK   LETTERING: PHIL CHRISTIE

SEKIREI KANOJO NO INAI 365NICHI NO KOTO Volume 19 ©2018 Sakurako Gokurakuin/ SQUARE ENIX CO., LTD. First published in Japan in 2018 by SQUARE ENIX CO., LTD. English translation rights arranged with SQUARE ENIX CO., LTD. and Yen Press, LLC through Tuttle-Mori Agency, Inc., Tokyo.

English translation © 2019 by SQUARE ENIX CO., LTD.

Yen Press
150 West 30th Street, 19th Floor
New York, NY 10001

Visit us at yenpress.com
facebook.com/yenpress
twitter.com/yenpress
yenpress.tumblr.com
instagram.com/yenpress

First Yen Press Print Edition: October 2019
Originally published as an ebook in November 2018 by Yen Press.

Yen Press is an imprint of Yen Press, LLC.
The Yen Press name and logo are trademarks of Yen Press, LLC.

Library of Congress Control Number: 2017939213

ISBN: 978-1-9753-3208-2 (paperback)

10 9 8 7 6 5 4 3 2 1

WOR

Printed in the United States of America